Business Governance and Society

Rajagopal • Ramesh Behl
Editors

Business Governance and Society

Analyzing Shifts, Conflicts, and Challenges

Editors
Rajagopal
EGADE Business School
Mexico City, Mexico

Ramesh Behl
International Management Institute
Bhubaneswar, India

ISBN 978-3-319-94612-2   ISBN 978-3-319-94613-9 (eBook)
https://doi.org/10.1007/978-3-319-94613-9

Library of Congress Control Number: 2018951120

© The Editor(s) (if applicable) and The Author(s), under exclusive licence to Springer International Publishing AG, part of Springer Nature 2019
This work is subject to copyright. All rights are solely and exclusively licensed by the Publisher, whether the whole or part of the material is concerned, specifically the rights of translation, reprinting, reuse of illustrations, recitation, broadcasting, reproduction on microfilms or in any other physical way, and transmission or information storage and retrieval, electronic adaptation, computer software, or by similar or dissimilar methodology now known or hereafter developed.
The use of general descriptive names, registered names, trademarks, service marks, etc. in this publication does not imply, even in the absence of a specific statement, that such names are exempt from the relevant protective laws and regulations and therefore free for general use.
The publisher, the authors and the editors are safe to assume that the advice and information in this book are believed to be true and accurate at the date of publication. Neither the publisher nor the authors or the editors give a warranty, express or implied, with respect to the material contained herein or for any errors or omissions that may have been made. The publisher remains neutral with regard to jurisdictional claims in published maps and institutional affiliations.

Cover credit: imaginima/E+/Getty

This Palgrave Macmillan imprint is published by the registered company Springer Nature Switzerland AG
The registered company address is: Gewerbestrasse 11, 6330 Cham, Switzerland

Preface

Shifts in the global economic and political order significantly affect the business patterns across the market taxonomy spread over the developed, developing, and emerging markets. Reversal of political ideologies from liberal to protectionist business frameworks are disrupting the trade flows that were rooted in the international economy since the mid-twentieth century. Organizational changes initiated by governments have a huge bearing on the governance and effectiveness of the private and public sector corporations. The recent public diplomacies about the protectionist thrust in American business and the referendum of Brexit revealed major signals of trade and economy disruption in the global marketplace. Society today is largely founded on the business environment, which determines the societal values from international to Bottom of the Pyramid (BOP) geo-demographic segments. The changes in the international business governance not only affect the societal and economic development of the region, but also wobble the mindsets and behaviors of emerging entrepreneurs, collaborators, and stakeholders.

New trends in manufacturing, financial management, marketing, and supply chain management in the twenty-first century have made a drastic drift in business practices across the global and local markets. Production sharing, reverse innovation, and blockchain technologies are being used today to grow cost-effective, transparent, and cyber secure businesses. Blockchain technology has appeared as a cost-effective tool to create efficiency improvements in supply chains, so that the market ends up with dynamic demand chains instead of rigid supply chains resulting in more efficient resource use for all. Nevertheless, challenges lie in the development and governance of the technology. Besides the emergence of these new business trends, digital business practices have increased manifold upon liberating the use of information technology among the enterprises. The use of digital applications in business has raised ethical dilemmas in reference to display of contents, advertising and communication, and digital piracy. Digital literacy plays a significant role in imparting education to people about the use of digital technology and ethical norms associated to adopt digital practices. New public policies for integrating digital literacies and digital ethics into societal sustainability are emerging in many developing countries. This involves widening of digital space for evolving sustainability in ethical awareness and digital skills in managing business and society. It also entails understanding how digital space can influence the biased, polarized thinking and unethical practices in business. Hence, the governance in business through public policies intervention has become very significant in the global marketplace today.

Business governance today is gradually shifting from market orientation to societal patronage as most companies are focusing on corporate social responsibility as a tool for outreach to consumers, society, and geo-demographic segments. The philosophy of the governance in business is more inclined towards addressing sustainability, gender, and societal causes and effects than the market competition in particular. Companies like General Electric, Nestlé, Proctor & Gamble, Pfizer, and Toyota have set examples for serving social causes. The shifts in the governance patterns are also affected by the business diplomacy across the countries and the associated public policies. However, the multinational companies are not penetrating deep into the social concerns and are engaged largely in accessing a dynamic global technology base. Though the political differences remain a steep hurdle in the way of creating a corporate strategy, they might not be able to undermine the society over the competitive leverages. The globalization has benefitted goods, and people move freely across borders and companies to compete on boundaryless business platforms. However, the power play of developed countries is bouncing back to the trade protectionist philosophy and restricting the leverage of free trade and economy in the 2020s.

In a noticeable development, more governments at federal and local levels are recognizing the strategy map to shape social and economic goals. Few efforts have been made through public- and private-sector governance in East Asia, which exhibits remarkable transformation on various social concerns like consumption of green energy, organic cultivation, managing industrial waste, and offering ecological livelihood products and services. Such shifts have been the outgrowth of public participation with government and industry in developing countries. On the capital and financial governance front, one of the major developments has emerged in defining long-term objectives and reducing risk among small and medium enterprises. Accordingly, investment in small and medium enterprises is motivated under the local public governance. Small industry owners today prefer to set a multiyear time frame for creating value, narrow down the size of sunk costs due to low performance, and then align their investments within applied capital engagement and active ownership. Big investors cultivate relationships with the regional companies to expand their scope of business by collaborating with them to optimize corporate strategy and governance. Most companies are engaged in restructuring institutional governance to support a long-term approach as well.

This collection of 23 quality chapters addressing the core topics of this book aims at bringing together the international forum for rich discussion on reviewing and learning lessons about shifts in business practices, their governance, and societal values. These contributions enrich knowledge on the global-local business imperatives, and drive trade and economy competition in the global marketplace. Various chapters in this book critically analyze the convergence of technology, business practices, public policies, political ideologies, and societal values for improving business performance at the global-local paradigm. This book enriches the knowledge and skills of contemporary business strategies against conventional wisdom of managing companies today. The book contemplates developing new visions and business perspectives to match with the changing political ideologies in emerging markets. This book also addresses competitive business management strategies in local marketplaces to generate cost-effective business models and create convergence with political and social values to drive better governance of business.

This book blends global economics and political trends with regional business prospects and presents regional research studies in reference to changing political and business trends. The peer-reviewed contributions in this volume serve as significant reference resources for future research in international business, contemporary political ideologies, and changing social values. The collection of chapters addresses recent political ideologies and corporate business strategies affecting international trade, business, and socio-economic values in developing countries in general and in particular in Asia and Latin America.

The chapters in the book cover various research areas, including agriculture, business, services, finance, international trade, and corporate social responsibilities that serve as a think tank for researchers, management students, and working managers. This is an inspiring book for entrepreneurs, market analysts, and business consultants engaged in local-global business ventures. We hope this book serves as a reference book in general, and a compendium of research studies in doctoral research programs.

Mexico City, Mexico Rajagopal
Bhubaneswar, India Ramesh Behl
April 30, 2018

Contents

1 Shifts in Business-Politics Paradigms: Exploring Lessons and Future Growth 1
Rajagopal

Part I Business Governance and Society: India 15

2 Trends in Agricultural Production and Productivity Growth in India: Challenges to Sustainability 17
Ramakrushna Panigrahi

3 Unraveling the Power of Talent Analytics: Implications for Enhancing Business Performance 29
Geeta Rana, Ravinder Sharma, and Alok Kumar Goel

4 The Impact of Customer Relationship Management (CRM) Practices on Customer Satisfaction 43
Subhasish Das and Manit Mishra

5 Customer Expectations at the Urban Bottom of Pyramid in India: A Grounded Theory Approach 55
Ritu Srivastava

6 A Qualitative Study on Work-Family Conflict, Social Support and Response Mechanisms of Individuals Working in Multi-National Corporations   75
Anjni Anand and Veena Vohra

7 Does Corporate Governance Affect the Financial Performance and Quality of Financial Reporting of Companies? A Study on Selected Indian Companies   105
Sushil Kalyani, Neeti Mathur, and Prashant Gupta

8 Factors Impacting Purchase of Private Labels in India   127
Richa Sardana, Aarti Duseja, and Pooja Misra

9 Drifts in Banking Business and Deepening Losses Amidst the Insolvency and Bankruptcy Code, 2016   143
Deepak Tandon and Neelam Tandon

10 Impact of Demographic Variables on the Attitude Towards Violence and Cooperation with Police: A Study of Extremist Affected Areas in Odisha, India   161
Bindu Chhabra

11 Emotional Intelligence in the Workplace: A Comparative Study of Male and Female Bank Employees in the Public Sector   175
Megha Sharma and Sourabh Sharma

12 Role of Leadership Style on Corporate Entrepreneurship and Firm Innovativeness: Learnings from Start-ups in Emerging Markets   189
Rajeev Verma and Jyoti Verma

13 Analysis of Factors of Advantages and Disadvantages in the Business Scenario of Northeast India: The Entrepreneur's Perspective   207
Analjyoti Basu and Kalyan Adak

Part II Business Governance and Society: Mexico 235

14 Relationship between Employee Mobility and Organizational Creativity to Improve Organizational Performance: A Strategic Analysis 237
Ananya Rajagopal

15 Persuasion and Dissuasion via Social Networking Sites: The Influence of Word-of-Mouth on Consumer Activism 251
Andree Marie López-Fernández

16 Relationship between Exports and the BRICS Countries' Gross Domestic Product: A Bayesian Vector Autoregression Approach for the Period 1978–2016 271
José Antonio Núñez Mora and Leovardo Mata Mata

17 Consumer Behavior on Social Media: A Thematic Exploration and an Agenda for Future Inquiry 281
Alberto Lopez and Raquel Castaño

18 Diffusion of Reverse Innovations across Markets: An Agent-Based Model 303
Pável Reyes-Mercado

19 Relationship Lending and Entrepreneurial Behavior: Analyzing Empirical Evidences 321
Fernando A. Moya Dávila

Part III Business Governance and Society: Nepal 349

20 The Impact of Corporate Governance on Efficiency of Nepalese Commercial Banks 351
Radhe S. Pradhan, Mukesh Kumar Shah, Nabin Bhandari, Nagendra Prasad Mahato, Namaraj Adhikari, and Nirajan Bam

21	**Impact of Corporate Governance on Dividend Policy of Nepalese Enterprises** Nar B. Bista, Nitesh Raj Bartaula, Om Shrestha, Pooja Gnawali, Poshan Lamichhane, and Pratiksha Parajuli	377
22	**Impact of Ownership Structure and Corporate Governance on Capital Structure of Nepalese Listed Companies** Raj Kumar Bajagai, Ravi Kumar Keshari, Pratikshya Bhetwal, Radhe Shyam Sah, and Rajnish Nath Jha	399
23	**Effect of Board Diversity and Corporate Governance Structure on Operating Performance: Evidence from the Nepalese Enterprises** Ritu Kumari Gupta, Rupa Chand, Sabeena Sadaula, Sangita Saud, and Sapana Ambai	421

Index   443

NOTES ON CONTRIBUTORS

EDITORS

Rajagopal is Professor of Marketing at EGADE Business School of Monterrey Institute of Technology and Higher Education (ITESM), Mexico City, and fellow of the Royal Society for Encouragement of Arts, Manufacture and Commerce, London. He is also fellow of the Chartered Management Institute, and fellow of the Institute of Operations Management, United Kingdom. He is also an adjunct professor at Boston University, Boston, Massachusetts. He has been listed with biography in various international directories. He offers courses on Competitor Analysis, Marketing Strategy, Advance Selling Systems, International Marketing, Services Marketing, New Product Development, and other subjects of contemporary interest to the students of undergraduate, graduate, and doctoral programs. Dr. Rajagopal holds post-graduate and doctoral degrees in Economics and Marketing respectively from Ravishankar University in India. His specialization is in the field of marketing management. He has to his credit 54 books on marketing management and rural development themes and more than 400 research contributions that include published research papers in national and international refereed journals. He is editor-in-chief of the *International Journal of Leisure and Tourism Marketing* and the *International Journal of Business Competition and Growth*. Dr. Rajagopal is also Regional Editor of Emerald Emerging Markets Case Studies, published by Emerald Publishers, United Kingdom. He is on the editorial board of various journals of international repute. His research contributions have been recognized by the National Council of Science and Technology (CONACyT), Government of Mexico, which awarded him the highest level of National Researcher-SNI Level-III in 2013.

Ramesh Behl is Director and Professor at the International Management Institute (IMI), Bhubaneswar, India, and a full professor at IMI Delhi. Prof. Behl is credited with building and transforming IMI Bhubaneswar to an institution of national importance. He is a United Nations fellow on Information Systems and International Operations and a SAP-Certified International Consultant. His teaching expertise includes business analytics, enterprise systems and emerging technologies. In addition to teaching, Prof. Behl is an active researcher in the area of e-business and business analytics. He has also designed and developed numerous software for various industry applications. Prof. Behl has more than 31 years of teaching, research, and consulting experience and has worked with premiere institutions like the Indian Institute of Foreign Trade (IIFT) in New Delhi, the Indian Institute of Management (IIM) in Lucknow, and *The Statesman* newspaper in New Delhi. He has done a number of research and consulting assignments for government and private organizations in the areas of information systems and international trade. He has authored 22 books, 17 case studies, and a number of research papers. Prof. Behl is an International Accredited Professor of the International Accreditation Organization in the United States. He sits on the board of leading business schools and technology companies. Prof. Behl has conducted corporate trainings and trained more than 8000 mid- and senior-level executives. He has also conducted training workshops for the faculties and students of various international universities in Singapore, Indonesia, Thailand, Hong Kong, Australia, China, Germany, and Korea. He has received accolades and significant recognition as a demonstration of his leadership qualities and innovations, such as the "Outstanding Academic Award 2010" from SAP Inc., "Best Professor in Information Technology" as part of Asia's Best B-School Awards presented by CMO Asia at Singapore in July 2011, "Best Professor in Information Technology Management" as part of the 21st Dewang Mehta Business School Awards on 23 October 2013, and "Rashtriya Jewels Award" and "Shining Achievers Award" in January 2015.

Contributors

Kalyan Adak obtained a M.Com. in Accounts from the University of Calcutta and a PhD in Entrepreneurship from Vidyasagar University, West Bengal. He has 30 years of teaching experience in Department of Commerce, Govt. Hrangbana College, Aizawl, Mizoram. He has published seven articles in national and international journals of repute, and has presented several research papers at seminars and conferences.

Namaraj Adhikari is pursuing a bachelor's degree in Management at Uniglobe College, Tribhuvan University, Kathmandu, Nepal. He is engaged in conducting market research as a part of his program.

Sapana Ambai is pursuing a bachelor's degree in Management at Uniglobe College, Tribhuvan University, Kathmandu, Nepal. She is engaged in conducting market and financial research as a part of her program.

Anjni Anand has served as an assistant professor at Delhi University since 2000. Ms. Anand has been teaching undergraduate courses in commerce. Her interest lies in subjects dealing with human behavior. She is currently pursuing a PhD in Management-Human Resources and Organizational Behavior from Narsee Monjee Institute of Management Studies, Mumbai, India. Her research area is work-family conflict. She is a published author and has presented research papers at various conferences.

Raj Kumar Bajagai is pursuing a bachelor's degree in Management at Uniglobe College, Tribhuvan University, Kathmandu, Nepal. He is engaged in conducting market and financial research as a part of his program.

Nirajan Bam is pursuing a bachelor's degree in Management at Uniglobe College, Tribhuvan University, Kathmandu, Nepal. He is engaged in conducting market research as a part of his program.

Nitesh Raj Bartaula is pursuing a bachelor's degree in Management at Uniglobe College, Tribhuvan University, Kathmandu, Nepal. He served as a lecturer at the Asian College of Information and Technology, Kathmandu. Mr. Barataula is engaged in conducting financial research as a part of his program.

Analjyoti Basu is a doctoral scholar in Tribal Entrepreneurship at the Entrepreneurship Development Institute of India, Ahmedabad, India. He has been in academics for a decade. His areas of teaching interest include operation management, development studies, and research methodology. Mr. Basu has presented papers at more than 20 national and international conferences and published his research works in various journals and books. He is currently engaged in developing a model for tribal development and entrepreneurship. Mr. Basu is actively attached to different non-governmental organizations and social organizations working for tribal and deprived children.

Nabin Bhandari is pursuing a bachelor's degree in Management at Uniglobe College, Tribhuvan University, and Kathmandu, Nepal. He is engaged in conducting market research as a part of his program.

Pratikshya Bhetwal is pursuing a bachelor's degree in Management at Uniglobe College, Tribhuvan University, Kathmandu, Nepal. She is engaged in conducting market and financial research as a part of her program. Ms. Bhetwal has interest in exploring research methodologies in the context of financial data analysis.

Nar B. Bista is Board Director of the Global College of Management, Valley View English School, Global College International, and Uniglobe Higher Secondary School. He is also the former principal of the College of Management. He also served as an assistant professor of economics at Tribhuvan University, Kathmandu, Nepal for more than a decade. He received his PhD in Economics from the University of Warsaw, Poland. In addition, he attended the Econometrics Summer School at Cambridge University, UK, as well as Management Development Program (MDP) at Indian Institute of Management (IIM), Ahmedabad, and also participated in a training on Environmental Economics by SANDEE in Bangkok. Dr. Bista has presented his research papers at international conferences. He is a renowned faculty of Economics. He has published many research articles in various international and national journals and published many books on economics.

Raquel Castaño has a PhD and is professor of Marketing at EGADE Business School, Tecnologico de Monterrey, Mexico City. She serves as co-leader of the Consumer Behavior and Value Creation strategic focus research group. Her research work has been published in top marketing journals, such as the *Journal of Marketing Research*, *Journal of Consumer Research*, and *Journal of Consumer Psychology*.

Rupa Chand is pursuing a bachelor's degree in Management at Uniglobe College, Tribhuvan University, Kathmandu, Nepal. She is engaged in conducting market and financial research as a part of her program. Ms. Chand, along with coauthors of the Banking Research Project, presented the study at the third international conference on International Business Environment held at the International Management Institute, Bhubaneswar, India in December 2017.

Bindu Chhabra is a professor at the International Management Institute, Bhubaneswar, India. She has a PhD in Psychology from Guru Nanak Dev University, India. She has more than 20 years of academic experience. Her areas of research interest include personality, work attitudes, stress management, emotional intelligence, and leadership. She has published various research papers in national and international journals. She has undertaken various management development programs with organizations such as SAIL, NTPC, BHEL, EIL, Power Grid, HPCL, Ministry of Social Defense, and various other government organizations. She is the recipient of the National Education Leadership Award for Best Teacher in Human Resource Management.

Subhasish Das is an assistant professor at Gandhi Institute of Management Studies (GIMS), Gunupur, one of the premier management institutes in the state of Odisha, India. He teaches Marketing and his area of research is customer relationship management. He has published a couple of research papers in reputed journals and in edited books. In addition, he has published a few refereed articles in the proceedings of national and international conferences.

Aarti Duseja is a research scholar and pursued her post-graduate degree in Retail Management at the Birla Institute of Management Technology, Greater Noida, India. She completed her post-graduation in 2018.

Pooja Gnawali is pursuing a bachelor's degree in Management at Uniglobe College, Tribhuvan University, Kathmandu, Nepal. He is engaged in conducting market research as a part of his program.

Alok Kumar Goel is working at CSIR-Human Resource Development Centre, Ghaziabad, India. He obtained his PhD in Knowledge Management and Human Capital Creation from IIT Roorkee. Dr. Goel is a Highly Commended Award winner of the 2013 Emerald/EFMD Outstanding Doctoral Research Awards in the Knowledge Management category. He has published nine papers in international journals and 27 papers in the proceedings of leading international conferences. He has visited Taiwan, Hong Kong, and Republic of Korea for his research endeavors. His research interests include knowledge management, innovation, and human resource management.

Prashant Gupta has a PhD in Finance and is serving as an associate professor at the International Management Institute, New Delhi, India. His research and teaching interests include financial accounting and analysis, financial management, management of financial services, tax planning, and management. Dr. Gupta has served as Branch Head at Alpic Finance Ltd. for five years and has been an active institution builder, having founded reputed management institutes in India. Dr. Gupta has presented research papers at various refereed national and international conferences, including the 2013 Webson Conference at Emlyon Business School, France, Adelphi University, NY, USA, A.I.T., Bangkok, Thailand.

Ritu Kumari Gupta is pursuing a bachelor's degree in in Management at Uniglobe College, Tribhuvan University, Kathmandu, Nepal. She is engaged in conducting market and financial research as a part of her program.

Rajnish Nath Jha is pursuing a bachelor's degree in Management at Uniglobe College, Tribhuvan University, Kathmandu, Nepal. He is engaged in conducting market and financial research as a part of his program.

Sushil Kalyani has a PhD from the University of Rajasthan, Department of Accounting and Business Statistics, a MBA in Finance, a MA in Business Economics, and an Accounting Technician Certificate (ICAI). Currently, he is associated with NIIT University, Neemrana, India as Area Director for Management and Associate Dean of Industry Linked Programs. His research interests include corporate governance, capital structure, and accounting, among others. He teaches courses in Financial Accounting and Analysis, and Cost and Management Accounting, to post-graduate students. He has also worked as a regional financial controller of a Dubai-based travel management company and was responsible for accounting at the company's 40 branches spread out over Africa.

Ravi Kumar Keshari is pursuing a bachelor's degree in Management at Uniglobe College, Tribhuvan University, Kathmandu, Nepal. He is engaged in conducting market and financial research as a part of his program.

Poshan Lamichhane is pursuing a bachelor's degree in Management at Uniglobe College, Tribhuvan University, Kathmandu, Nepal. He is engaged in conducting market and financial research as a part of his program.

Alberto Lopez is a doctoral research scholar at EGADE Business School, Tecnologico de Monterrey, Mexico City. He is part of the Consumer Behavior and Value Creation strategic focus research group. His research includes consumer-brand relationships, child consumer behavior, and the symbolic meanings of consumption. He has published scientific articles in the *Journal of Consumer Marketing*, *Advances in Consumer Research*, and *Ciencias Administrativas Teoría y Praxis*. His research work has been presented at national and international conferences.

Andree Marie López-Fernández is Professor of Business Management and a researcher at the Universidad Panamericana, Mexico City. Her research areas of interest include corporate social responsibility, marketing strategy, and consumer behavior. She has a PhD in Administrative Sciences from the EGADE Business School, Tecnologico de Monterrey, Mexico City, and is a member of the Mexican National System of Researchers by CONACYT.

Nagendra Prasad Mahato is pursuing a bachelor's degree at Uniglobe College, Tribhuvan University, Kathmandu, Nepal. He is engaged in conducting market research as a part of his program.

Leovardo Mata Mata is a professor and core researcher in Finance and Macroeconomics at EGADE Business School, Tecnologico de Monterrey, Mexico City. He has a PhD in Finance and has published more than 30 research papers on finance.

Neeti Mathur is engaged in teaching and research in the domain of accounting and finance. Her interest areas include financial reporting, quality of reporting, corporate governance, corporate finance, financial inclusion, microfinance, and risk management in banks. She has a PhD in Accounting with a specialized focus on microfinance, role of financial institutions in financial inclusion, and Self Help Group-Bank Linkage Programmes (SBLP). Currently she is an assistant professor at NIIT University.

Manit Mishra has a PhD and is serving as Associate Professor of Marketing and Quantitative Tecniques (QT) at International Management Institute, Bhubaneswar, India. He teaches Marketing Research, Business

Analytics, Consumer Behavior, and Customer Relationship Management. His research interests include behavioral modelling and methodological research. He has published research papers and articles in *Psychology & Marketing*, *Journal of Retailing and Consumer Services*, *Strategic Change: Briefings in Entrepreneurial Finance*, *Asian Case Research Journal*, and *Global Business Review*, among others. He is an associate editor for *Global Business Review* and is a member of the editorial board of *International Journal of Business Competition and Growth*. He has received funding from the Indian Council of Social Science Research (ICSSR) and the All India Council for Technical Education (AICTE).

Pooja Misra is Associate Professor at the Birla Institute of Management Technology, Greater Noida, India. She received PhD for the research on the topic Compensation Components and its Effect on Employee Engagement and Turnover Intent. Her research interests include macroeconomic dimensions of an economy, compensation, employee engagement, and current trends in business environment. She has published several research papers and articles in international and national journals and has presented papers at various national and international conferences.

Fernando A. Moya Dávila is a forward-thinking and proactive finance professional with 24 years of experience across academics and consulting. He is an industrial engineer from Tecnologico de Monterrey, and has a MBA from the State University of New York at Buffalo, and a PhD from Tecnologico de Monterrey. With studies at the University of Texas, Austin, Dr. Fernando offers a track record of expertly developing and implementing financial strategies to drive start-up funding and mutually beneficial business relationships as well as generate multimillion-dollar economic growth. Dr. Fernando is an analytical and resourceful pragmatist who excels at creating successful new business ventures by utilizing strong financial acumen. He is a former director of EGADE Business School, Mexico City, who led the strategy of the school in Latin America and towards the Executive MBA Program.

José Antonio Núñez Mora has been a professor at EGADE Business School, Tecnológico de Monterrey, Mexico City since 2015. Previously, he was director of the PhD programs in Business Administration and Financial Science at the same institution between 2006 and 2014. He obtained a PhD in Administration with a focus on finance from Tecnológico de Monterrey, Mexico City, in 2001. Concurrently, he is also a consultant to Tecnológico de Monterrey regarding the macroeconomic impact on the reforms to the retirement pensions in Mexico. His area of research and teaching is financial risk. As a researcher, he actively participates in the publication of articles in different national and international journals, books, and book chapters. In addition, the National Council of Science and Technology of Mexico has conferred on him a Level II membership in the National System of Researchers.

Ramakrushna Panigrahi is Associate Professor of Economics at International Management Institute, Bhubaneswar, India. He obtained a PhD in Environmental Economics and a M. Phil in Agricultural Economics. His primary area of research is development economics. He has published a number of research papers in journals like *Journal of International Development* and *Journal of Human Development*. He has authored business cases published by Ivey Business School that are widely used in teaching managerial economics courses. His teaching interests include economics, international business, and geopolitics.

Pratiksha Parajuli is pursuing a bachelor's degree in Management at Uniglobe College, Tribhuvan University, Kathmandu, Nepal. She is engaged in conducting market and financial research as a part of her program.

Radhe S. Pradhan is a professor at Tribhuvan University, Kathmandu, Nepal and serves as academic director at Uniglobe College, Kathmandu, Nepal. He received his master's degree in Business Administration and Commerce in the First Division from Tribhuvan University in 1975. He has done valuable research on working capital management for which he was awarded his PhD from the University of Delhi, India in 1986. He has also completed a one-year course under the Faculty Development Program at the Indian Institute of Management, Ahmedabad, India in 1979–1980. He has also served as Visiting Fulbright Faculty to the College of Business, Florida State University, Tallahassee, Florida from August 1992 to January 1993. Dr Pradhan, served in various key positions at academic institutes and in the government of Nepal.

Ananya Rajagopal is an industrial and systems engineer at Tecnologico de Monterrey, Mexico City. She has ample experience in the financial industry in Mexico City since 2006. She has published several papers in international journals of repute and contributed research works in international conferences and edited books. Currently, she is pursuing her doctoral research at the EGADE Business School, Tecnologico de Monterrey, Mexico City.

Geeta Rana is serving as Assistant Professor and Research Coordinator, Department of HSMS at Swami Rama Himalayan University, Jolly Grant, Dehradun. She earned her PhD in management from the Indian Institute of Technology, Roorkee. She is engaged in teaching, research, and consultancy assignments. She has more than 12 years of experience in teaching and in handling various administrative as well as academic positions. She has to her credit more than 33 papers published in national and international journals. Dr. Rana is a recipient of the Highly Commended Award of the BIMTECH-Stough Young Scholar Award (Gold Medal). Her research interests include knowledge management, managerial effectiveness, work values, organizational justice, and human resource management.

Pável Reyes-Mercado has a PhD from EGADE Business School, Tecnologico de Monterrey, Mexico City. He is serving as a professor at Anahuac University in Mexico City. Currently, he teaches courses in marketing at the graduate and undergraduate levels. His professional experience includes positions at Alcatel, Coca-Cola Femsa, and HSBC Bank Mexico City. His research interests include adoption of innovations, technology-enabled marketing, and entrepreneurial marketing.

Sabeena Sadaula is pursuing a bachelor's degree in Management at Uniglobe College, Tribhuvan University, Kathmandu, Nepal. She is engaged in conducting market and financial research as a part of her program. Ms. Sadaula has worked with the Banking Research Project and presented the study at the third international conference on International Business Environment held at the International Management Institute, Bhubaneswar, India in December 2017.

Radhe Shyam Sah is pursuing a bachelor's degree in Management at Uniglobe College, Tribhuvan University, Kathmandu, Nepal. He is engaged in conducting market and financial research as a part of his program. Mr. Sah has interest in exploring qualitative research methodologies in the context of financial data analysis by conducting in-depth interviews with emerging leaders.

Richa Sardana is a research scholar and pursued her post-graduate degree in Retail Management at the Birla Institute of Management Technology, Greater Noida, India. She completed her post-graduation in 2018 and subsequently joined Bata India Ltd.

Sangita Saud is pursuing a bachelor's degree in Management at Uniglobe College, Tribhuvan University, Kathmandu, Nepal. She is engaged in conducting market and financial research as a part of her program. Ms. Sangeeta is working on financial services-related research products under the supervision of the academic director of Uniglobe College.

Mukesh Kumar Shah is pursuing a bachelor's degree in Management at Uniglobe College, Tribhuvan University, Kathmandu, Nepal. He is engaged in conducting market research as a part of his program.

Megha Sharma has a PhD in Psychology from University of Rajasthan, India and is currently serving as Assistant Professor at Regional College of Management, Bhubaneswar, India. Previously, Dr. Megha was associated with the Mody Institute of Education and Research, Rajasthan as faculty in Psychology. Her teaching interests include organizational behavior, human resources management, human psychology, and industrial psychology. She has published a few research papers and working papers and has participated in national and international conferences.

Ravinder Sharma is Assistant Professor in HSMS at Swami Rama Himalayan University, Jolly Grant, Dehradun. He has more than 12 years of corporate and academic experience in various prestigious organizations all over India. He has both MBA and MCA degrees. He also qualified for UGC-NET in management. He is pursuing a PhD in Management from Uttarakhand Technical University. His areas of teaching interest include management information systems, project management, production and operations management, and e-commerce. He is also honored as a session chair in many international conferences. He has also attended various workshops, Faculty Development Program (FDPs), and MDPs. He also has several research publications and conference presentations to his credit. His research interests include employer branding, e-commerce, and digital marketing.

Sourabh Sharma has a PhD and is serving as Associate Professor for Information Systems at International Management Institute, Bhubaneswar. He is an eminent management consultant, outstanding professional practitioner, trainer, academician, and educationist counselor in management. He has been a management educator and industrial practitioner from more than 15 years. Dr. Sharma has expertise in management information systems, database management systems, digital marketing, software project management, data warehousing and mining, and many different programming languages. He has also served as a consultant to Union Bank, Ujjain to convert their pension management software from FoxPro to Visual Basic. He started his career with Reliance Communications as a database consultant and served there for four years.

Om Shrestha is pursuing a bachelor's degree in Management at Uniglobe College, Tribhuvan University, Kathmandu, Nepal. He is engaged in conducting market research as a part of his program.

Ritu Srivastava has a PhD in Marketing Management. The topic of her thesis is "Evaluation of Relationship Marketing in Financial Services in India." An academician by heart, Dr. Srivastava firmly believes that management education goes beyond the classroom and includes various components on industry interaction, social outreach, and research and development. She has nine years of experience across education and industry cutting across teaching, research, and consulting activities. Dr. Srivastava teaches post-graduate management courses on Public Policy Marketing and International Marketing.

Deepak Tandon has a PhD and is serving as Professor in Finance at the International Management Institute, New Delhi. He has 36 years of work experience spread across academics and the banking industry. He has published 124 research papers and case studies and authored six books. He received six academic awards and serves on editorial boards of various journals. He has taught at various international universities including in the United Kingdom and Thailand. He is an approved ISO Lead Auditor from Nigel Bauer & Associates (Germany), and an IRCA-certified auditor (London).

Neelam Tandon has a PhD in Finance and is a professor of Finance and Economics at Jagannath international Management School, New Delhi and has more than 18 years' experience in academics and industry. She has authored about 68 research papers published in leading international and national finance journals and periodicals with high impact factors. She authored four books in the areas of banking, statistics, and economics. She has been instrumental in conducting national seminars and international conferences in the areas of finance and economics.

Jyoti Verma has a PhD in Organizational Behavior and Human Resource Management from Institute of Management, Nirma University, Ahmedabad, Gujarat, India. She is currently working as Assistant Professor at Chandragupt Institute of Management Patna (CIMP), Bihar, India. Her research interests include exploring performance management systems, knowledge management, organizational development, and strategic human resource management. She has published many papers in journals of national and international repute and conference proceedings apart from winning Best Paper Awards at reputed institutes such as Indian Institute of Management, Calcutta, India, and Indian Institute of Science, Bangalore, India. She has conducted corporate training sessions on team building, leadership, organizational commitment, organizational ethics, motivation, and so on in various management development programs.

Rajeev Verma is a fellow of the Indian Institute of Management, Indore, India (IIM Indore) and doctoral exchange scholar at EGADE Business School, Tecnologico de Monterrey, Mexico City. He is a graduate of Forest Research Institute (FRI), Dehradun, India in the area of Forest Economics. He is currently working as Assistant Professor at Chandragupt Institute of Management Patna (CIMP), Bihar, India. Prior to this, he had experience working with the National Innovation Foundation (NIF), Ahmedabad and Indian Institute of Forest Management (IIFM), Bhopal. His research interests include marketing information systems, product management, rural development and inclusive growth, customer experience management, and marketing engineering.

Veena Vohra has a PhD and is serving as Associate Dean and Professor of Human Resources and Behavioral Sciences at the School of Business Management, Narsee Monjee Institute of Management Studies, deemed to be a university. Dr. Vohra's research interests include change management, trends in human resource management, leadership, emotional intelligence, and qualitative research paradigms. She has published a number of research papers in national and international journals. Her case studies have been published by Ivey Publishing and Emerald Emerging Markets Case Studies. She has co-authored the Indian adaptation of *Behavioral Science Interventions for Organizational Improvement* with French and Bell. She has also co-authored the Indian adaptation of the book *Human Resource Management* with Snell and Bohlander.

List of Figures

Fig. 1.1	Effects of business-politics ideological shifts on global trade and economy (Source: Author)	8
Fig. 3.1	Human resources metrics level (HR metrics levels—Adapted from Ulrich and Dulebohn 2015)	33
Fig. 3.2	Road map for talent analytics in BL (Sources: Complied by author)	37
Fig. 5.1	Steps followed for implementing the study through classical grounded theory method	65
Fig. 5.2	Integrated model of customer expectations for India (Source: Author)	70
Fig. 6.1	Work environment	84
Fig. 6.2	Managing expectations	86
Fig. 6.3	Family support	88
Fig. 6.4	Transparency effects	92
Fig. 6.5	Bi-directional communication	94
Fig. 6.6	Conflict resolution: evolutionary process	96
Fig. 6.7	Work priorities	98
Fig. 9.1	Resolution process (Source: Author's compilation)	149
Fig. 12.1	Impact of leadership style on firm outcomes	193
Fig. 12.2	Assessing impact of leadership style on corporate entrepreneurship and firm innovativeness	193
Fig. 14.1	Research model. Source: Author	244
Fig. 15.1	Persuasion and dissuasion of consumer behavior via SNSs	262
Fig. 17.1	Number of papers published by year	284
Fig. 17.2	Conceptual model of consumer behavior on social media	286
Fig. 18.1	Conceptual model for adoption of reverse innovations. Source: Adapted from Delre et al. (2010)	307

Fig. 18.2	Agent-Based Model implementation for adoption of reverse innovations. Source: Author	311
Fig. 18.3	Diffusion of a reverse innovation in a developing country exhibiting one influence at a time. Source: Author	313
Fig. 18.4	Diffusion of a reverse innovation in a developing country exhibiting one influence at a time. Source: Author	314

List of Tables

Table 2.1	Decennial trends of production of food grains in India (million tons)	22
Table 2.2	Trends of production of commercial crops in India (in million tones)	23
Table 2.3	MSP of food and commercial crops and rising inflation	26
Table 4.1	Discriminant validity	49
Table 4.2	Model fit summary for the measurement model	50
Table 4.3	Model fit summary for structural model	50
Table 4.4	(Scale for the study) questionnaire	51
Table 4.5	Regression weights: (group number 1—default model)	52
Table 4.6	Standardized regression weights: (group number 1—default model)	52
Table 7.1	Correlation matrix analysis results for all selected firms from Top 100 BSE companies	116
Table 7.2	Descriptive statistics	117
Table 7.3	Regression analysis	118
Table 7.4	Analysis of variance (ANOVA) results	118
Table 7.5	Robust analytics	118
Table 7.6	Regression coefficients	119
Table 7.7	Analysis of variance (ANOVA) results	119
Table 7.8	Robust analytics	120
Table 8.1	Pearson correlation analysis	135
Table 8.2	Regression coefficients	136
Table 8.3	Private label brands	138
Table 9.1	Insolvency bankruptcy code user details	150
Table 9.2	Particulars of operational creditors using IBC	151
Table 9.3	Admission and dismissal across different kinds of creditors	151

Table 9.4	Debt size litigated under IBC (in 10-millons)	153
Table 9.5	Average time taken for disposal of insolvency petitions at the NCLT stage	153
Table 9.6	Reasons for dismissal of insolvency petitions	153
Table 9.7	NPA and NPA ratios	156
Table 10.1	Demographic details	165
Table 10.2	Model summary of regression analysis for cooperation with police	167
Table 10.3	Result of bivariate regression model	167
Table 10.4	Model summary of regression analysis for attitude towards violence	168
Table 10.5	Result of bivariate regression model	168
Table 11.1	Composition of sample selected on availability of bank officials	181
Table 11.2	Independent sample t-test results examining differences between male and female bank employees with reference to EI dimensions	181
Table 12.1	Literature contribution in defining leadership	191
Table 12.2	Registration classification of firms (sample) under Startup India	196
Table 12.3	Sectoral classification of firms (sample)	196
Table 12.4	Profiling of the respondents	197
Table 12.5	Discriminant validity: correlations of constructs and $\sqrt{AVE}$	197
Table 12.6	Results of the least square (LS) regression	199
Table 12.7	Test results of hypothesis testing	200
Table 12.8	SEM model fit summary	200
Table 13.1	Selection of districts	219
Table 13.2	Benefits depicted by the entrepreneurs	222
Table 13.3	Disadvantages depicted by the entrepreneurs	226
Table 16.1	Unit root test	276
Table 16.2	Unit root test	276
Table 16.3	Optimal lags for VAR models	277
Table 16.4	Granger cause	277
Table 16.5	Percentage relationship between GDP and exports for the BRICS	278
Table 17.1	Number of published papers by Journal	283
Table 17.2	Number of published papers by theme and sub-themes	286
Table 17.3	Motivators to follow brands on social media: systematic summary of reviewed articles	287
Table 17.4	Demotivators to follow brands on social media: systematic summary of reviewed articles	288

Table 17.5	Consumer-brand interactions on social media: systematic summary of reviewed articles	289
Table 17.6	Effects of following brands on social media: systematic summary of reviewed articles	291
Table 17.7	Interpersonal relationships and social media: systematic summary of reviewed articles	292
Table 19.1	FirstCredit	326
Table 19.2	Currency	326
Table 19.3	Credit technology	327
Table 19.4	Type of interest rates	327
Table 19.5	Credit type	327
Table 19.6	Industry	327
Table 19.7	Descriptive statistics	328
Table 19.8	Definition of explanatory variables	329
Table 19.9	Relationship index VS premium	331
Table 19.10	Years VS premium	331
Table 19.11	Descriptive statistics of first credit	333
Table 19.12	Interest rates and relationship index, $N = 0.25$ and $w = 0.3$ (first credit, only simple credits)	335
Table 19.13	Interest rates and relationship index, $N = 0.25$ and $w = 0.3$ (first credit, fixed assets credit)	336
Table 19.14	Interest rates and relationship index, $N = 0.25$ and $w = 0.3$ (first credit, floating rate)	336
Table 19.15	Probability of default and relationship index, $N = 0.25$, and $w = 0.3$ (all credits)	339
Table 19.16	Probability of default and relationship index, $N = 0.25$ and $w = 0.3$ (simple credits)	340
Table 19.17	Probability of default and relationship index, $N = 0.25$ and $w = 0.3$ (fixed assets credits)	341
Table 19.18	Probability of asking for collateral and relationship index, $N = 0.25$, $w = 0.3$ (all first credits)	343
Table 19.19	Value of collateral and relationship index, $N = 0.25$, $w = 0.3$ (simple credits or lines of credit)	345
Table 20.1	List of sample banks selected for the study alone with the study period and number of observations	356
Table 20.2	Descriptive statistics	365
Table 20.3	Pearson correlation matrix for the selected Nepalese commercial banks	367
Table 20.4	Regression of corporate governance and dependent variable of non-performing loan	368
Table 20.5	Regression of corporate governance and dependent variable of cost efficiency	371

Table 21.1	Number of commercial banks and insurance companies selected for the study along with study period and number of observations	381
Table 21.2	Descriptive statistics	387
Table 21.3	Pearson's correlation coefficients matrix for enterprises	388
Table 21.4	Estimated regression results of FS, MO, LIQ, CEOD, GD, IO, FORTOT, ROA and LEV on dividend payout ratio	390
Table 21.5	Estimated regression results of FS, MO, LIQ, CEOD, GD, IO, FORTOT, ROA and LEV on dividend yield	392
Table 22.1	Number of enterprises selected for the study along with study period and number of observations	403
Table 22.2	Descriptive statistics	410
Table 22.3	Pearson's correlation coefficients matrix for Nepalese commercial banks	411
Table 22.4	Estimated regression of LEV on BS, BOCOM, CEO, WD, NB, INSTSH, MANGSH, SZ, ROA, and AGE	412
Table 22.5	Estimated regression of LTD_TA on BS, BOCOM, CEO, WD, NB, INSTSH, MANGSH, SZ, ROA, and AGE	414
Table 23.1	Number of enterprises selected for the study along with study period and number of observations	425
Table 23.2	Descriptive statistics	430
Table 23.3	Pearson's correlation coefficients matrix for Nepalese enterprises	431
Table 23.4	Estimated regression results of BSIZE, BMET, BDV, BHS, DUAL, LEV, and FMZ on ROE	433
Table 23.5	Estimated regression results of OUD, BSIZE, BMET, AUCOM, BDV, BHS, DUAL, LEV and FMZ on MPS of Nepalese enterprises	436

List of Exhibits

Exhibit 9.1   Corporate insolvency resolution transactions   159
Exhibit 9.2   Initiation of corporate insolvency transactions   159

CHAPTER 1

Shifts in Business-Politics Paradigms: Exploring Lessons and Future Growth

Rajagopal

INTRODUCTION

Business governance is an outgrowth of political ideology and public diplomacy. The nature of business and industry shifts in the country or a trade bloc in the context of political scenarios in the countries that dominate international business. Political power dominates in trade negotiations, and defines the contemporary trade philosophy for trade governance. The political framework of trade powers within their territorial boundaries influences key players in the economy comprising industries, governments, and non-governmental organizations exhibiting the supremacy of people in postulating the business strategy. This could help in designing domestic and international policies for major customers and suppliers, concluding acquisitions and alliances, and securing finance for business from investors and banks. Political ideology and public diplomacy drive in building industry coalitions with political bodies to influence policy makers, institutional shareholders, key opinion leaders influencing the media, and business analysts.

Rajagopal (✉)
EGADE Business School, Mexico City, Mexico
e-mail: rajagopal@itesm.mx

© The Author(s) 2019
Rajagopal, R. Behl (eds.), *Business Governance and Society*,
https://doi.org/10.1007/978-3-319-94613-9_1

Many leaders exercise their public authority drawn from the political regime to influence executive decisions. But when leaders take the governing roles in a country, the planning and implementation of business policies depend more on political influence. However, gaining the ability to shift business policies to current trends and motivate business governance in tune with international trade diplomacy is the major challenge among companies. The political roles of business icons navigate within a business-politics matrix and drive organizations to change the rules of business under the changing business diplomacy. Therefore, such government agencies lead to a critical support function for industry to shift their governance system. The shifts in the controls in human resources management, information technology, and budgetary management, and learning to practice corporate diplomacy effectively, are the rising challenges among the industries in the developing countries. The shifts in political ideologies leverage organizational alliances, business networks, and other business relationships in tune with the political ideology (Watkins 2009). The welfare marketing principle has been realized in the recent past as a global marketing practice of serving the consumers at the bottom of the pyramid to leverage their consumption patterns on par with those of elite consumers.

The Governance Trend

Globalization has become a functional dynamic of emerging firms in today's business environment. Most firms believe that globalization is a synonym for business growth, and invest perennial resources in developing strategy to go global. It has become one of the most pertinent issues for managers of growing firms around the world. A large number of companies in the developed countries are nourished by the huge domestic market, but typically lag behind their European and Japanese rivals in internationalization. Companies intending to go global exhibit two apparent objectives—to take advantage of opportunities for growth and expansion, and to survive in the business amidst growing competition. However, firms that fail to pursue global opportunities eventually lose their domestic markets, and may be pushed aside by stronger and more competitive global firms. In the middle of the twentieth century, the nature of political life changed everywhere by novel forms of political activity as new means of mass communication, an increase of popular participation in politics, and the rise of new political issues offered better understanding of international politics and popular governance in reference to global integration. Besides, the extension of the scope of governmental activity, and other innumerable social, economic, and technical developments in the developing countries, urged for stability in the government for effective implementation of international development programs. Trade policies have been one among the international priorities (Rajagopal 2016).

The majority of the world's political systems have experienced one or another form of internal warfare leading to violent collapse of the governments in power. In addition, certain crisis situations seem to increase the likelihood of breakdown in the governing politics of a region or a country. In the politico-economic scenario, the economic crisis is another common stimulus for political setbacks as may be witnessed in the recent Argentinean crisis. The Brazilian economy was also on the edge of the cliff in the late 1990s due to internal economic instability. However, most companies are attracted more by the comparative advantages in the factors of production than the political risks, and jeopardize their manufacturing and marketing operations. A sense of insecurity and uncertainty about the future, and an aggravation of the relationships among social classes, also result in the politico-economic conflicts and business chaos in a country. A severe political crisis develops distrust in the economic system of the country, triggers outbreak of revolutions in the political systems, and decreases the prospects of business growth. Political unrest due to radical ideologies in a country spurs several experimental conditions for the stability of the political system in extremely revealing ways that often induce either change in the political leadership or the restructuring of the political governance system. Since the quality of the political leadership is often decisive, those systems that provide methods of selecting able leaders and replacing them possess important advantages towards internal and global political concerns. Many studies have shown that dealing with problems in the political arena is the principal challenge facing international managers in developing pro-political strategies to run the business successfully in the host country. It is observed that each country has its own set of national goals, but most countries also share many common objectives. Nationalism and patriotism refer to citizens' feelings about their country and its interests. Such feelings exist in every country, and multinational firms, individually or collectively, may be perceived as a threat to that sovereignty. The foreign firms perceive greater threats if they are larger in size and more in number in a country. At the time of any political turmoil, the foreign firms may be targets for attack. Many countries seek "national solutions" to help troubled companies to retain what are perceived to be national champions (Rajagopal 2016).

Business in the global marketplace moved on through capitalist, socialist, democratic, and mixed political philosophies over centuries and had often changed governance patterns affecting profitability, growth, and stakeholder values. Globalization has evolved with similar burst of political ideology, public diplomacy, and industrial policies in the mid-twentieth century. After a relatively long period of success of globalization with liberal trade and economic philosophy backed by the political ideology and trade diplomacy of developed countries like the United States, Great Britain, and the European Union, the Cold War mentality, driven by the protectionist ideology and public diplomacy in geopolitics, is back in the twenty-first century. The United States, by displaying a protectionist political viewpoint (2017 onwards) and restricting the flow of international trade, investment, and movement of factors of production, has raised a violent confrontation to grow their business in isolation by setting a number of vigilante business controls and changing the existing rules of the game. Businesses across the world cannot be confident of strategic *status* quo of the political business ideology. Such ideologies are governed by the balances of power and international negotiations on foreign trade policies dominated by the super powers in the world. A corporate foreign policy has two components—geopolitical due diligence and corporate diplomacy. The former philosophy involves the assessment of local, regional, and transnational risks facing a company while the latter aims to enhance a company's ability to operate internationally (Chipman 2009).

Political intervention is a decision taken on the part of a host country's government, in its own interest, that is intended to force a change in the operations, policies, and strategies of a foreign firm. Such interventions may range from enforcing control for complete takeover to annexation of the foreign enterprise. The magnitude of intervention varies according to the company's business existing in the host country and the nature of political decisions taken thereof. In countries where foreign investment plays a significant role in the economy, the possibility of political interference in the operations of foreign firms is higher and more stringent. In addition, the political system of a country, whether it be democracy, communism, or a mix, indicates the nature of intervention. Businesses in developed countries, such as the United States and Great Britain, are ruled largely by government interventions as they are in reference to the public policies of the country. The political directions may also govern the functions related to transfer pricing, price ceiling and price floor, price contracts, price paid for local raw materials, and price paid for imported raw materials to be used in production in the host country. The activities of distribution and product retailing may also be subject to political interventions in many developing countries. Advertising and communication is another important area of a multinational firm that is affected by political interference in a country.

Major structural shifts in the global economy are creating new opportunities in transaction banking, particularly in trade finance. International trade is growing faster than global GDP, and Asia is now the center of global expansion, driving trade growth in other emerging markets and in developed economies as well. An ongoing shift in global economic activity from developed to developing economies, accompanied by growth in the number of consumers in emerging markets, is the global development that executives around the world view as most important for business and most positive for their own companies' profits over the next five years. Executives also identify two other critical positive aspects of globalization: technologies that enable a free flow of information worldwide, and increasing migrations in the global labor markets. The global economy faces significant challenges as it continues to integrate high levels of public debt in Europe and North America that are causing the fear of a negative impact on GDP growth. Emerging markets, with populations that are young and growing, will increasingly become not only the focus of rising consumption and production but also major providers of capital, talent, and innovation. Over the trend of trade liberalization as experienced in the Latin American countries in the first decade of the twenty-first century, the North American Free Trade Agreement (NAFTA) has created a single market with the United States and Canada that has helped to propel Mexico to the top ranks of manufacturing exporters (Rajagopal and Zlatev 2017).

Political ideologies have commonly been associated with particular social classes, such as liberalism with the middle class, conservatism with the landed aristocracy, socialism with the working class, and so forth. These ideas reflect the life experiences, interests, and aspirations of a social class, and help to foster a sense of belonging and solidarity. However, ideas and ideologies can also succeed in binding together divergent groups and classes within a society. A unifying set of political ideas and values can develop naturally within a society. The values of elite groups such as political and military leaders, government officials, landowners, or industrialists may diverge significantly from those of the masses. Ruling governments may use political ideas to contain opposition and restrict debate through a process of ideological manipulation. The problem today is the political aggression narrowing the business corridors on the plea of achieving political manifestos. Often leaders view politics as war, where victory is paramount, which compromises several social and business interests. Such ideologies often shift the business governance from globalization to privatization on the political manifesto of making their countries great again. However, every single policy of business gateway countries like the United States and China affects the global business systems and might either elevate or threaten to cripple the existing business dynamics. Revitalizing America's culture of democracy where the health of the nation comes first, above economy, political party, and ideology, plays a key role in international business development (Moss 2012).

Trends and Ideological Shifts

In the mid-twentieth century, with the downfall of the Soviet Union, one of the super powers driving the trade and economy in the world, American policymakers within the government and sitting at the world forums began championing neoliberal economic policies. The new doctrine focused on ensuring capitalist philosophy in business by empowering private-sector and market-led economic growth, which prompted the government to become involved only in policy-making overpowering regional trade blocs through business diplomacy and negotiations. American investment protection policy supports domestic and global investment climates and prompts structural reforms in developing countries. Such political push has monitored the General Agreement on Trade and Tariffs (GATT), which later emerged as the World Trade Organization (WTO) to work on business regulations, innovations, and patents, and as an international institution for resolving business conflicts. However, this power play has been indirectly affecting the global trade institutions as well. Over time, Russia, China, the United States, Japan, and France have emerged as power centers engaged in global surveillance and as policy-makers (e.g. Gretz 2016).

Among others, one of the basic observations that comes to the edge of trade diplomacy is the persistent divergence of income across countries over a long period of time. This effect is agitating business growth in the developing economies by typically exhibiting the possibilities to explore unexploited business opportunities. However, the efforts of industrial and business growth in developing countries often fall into the trap of power play and trade diplomacy. Most countries with emerging economies tend to catch up with the political power leaders to leverage their *trade and economy canvass*. Another observation is that a large part of economic growth can be attributed to the efficiency with which production inputs are applied, in addition to the intensity of their use. The success of a few countries, who have managed to multiply their income levels quite rapidly, has largely resulted from the booming total factor productivity.

The world markets are changing rapidly, promoting new emerging markets across the countries. In this century, China, India, South Africa, Mexico, and other Latin American economies promise new opportunities for global trade. Since 1980, the Pacific region has leapt forward in the rapid transition, in response to the global movement of trade and services. Asia may be portrayed as the fastest growing market for the top brands of Western companies, and at the same time, Asian companies began penetrating the Western markets with a low-price, high-quality strategy. While luxury and fashion goods are dominating the Asian and Far East markets, specialized products like electronics and automobiles are trying to capture considerable market share in Europe and North America. In the emerging markets, technology has homogenized with the world markets for a variety of customer and industrial needs, and the reduction in tariff barriers, duties, and the liberalization process worldwide have further stimulated international marketing across regional boundaries. The effects of shifts in political ideologies and business diplomacies of international trade and economy are shown in Fig. 1.1.

Figure 1.1 shows that due to the change in ideologies of the political superpowers towards international trade and economy, the globalization philosophy has become fragmented and has shown isolated effects on the flow of international investments, manufacturing, and services in the United States and Great Britain. The current philosophy of trade protection has made a small dent in the domestic economy of developed nations, but has given a trade boost to big emerging markets like China and India to explore new markets and grow their business agendas. By invoking Article 50 of the EU's Lisbon Treaty, the UK might not be able to gain a desired freedom in negotiating with the Commonwealth countries thus affecting trade, economy, and industry (Ghemawat 2017).

Most bilateral negotiations and Free Trade Agreements (FTAs) are on the verge of strategic renegotiations since 2016 in view of critical trade and economic analysis and changing political ideologies. Accordingly, many countries are renegotiating within their trade blocs about eliminating or reducing non-tariff and investment barriers. However, the protectionist political ideologies are recommending an increase in tariff barriers

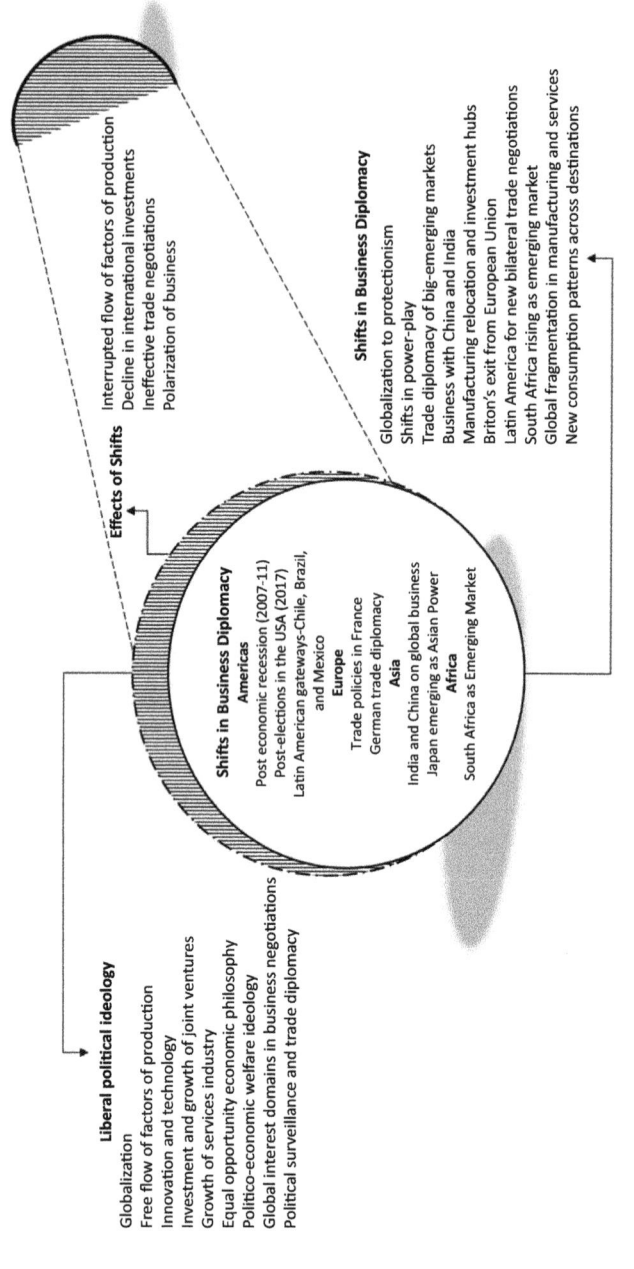

Liberal political ideology
Globalization
Free flow of factors of production
Innovation and technology
Investment and growth of joint ventures
Growth of services industry
Equal opportunity economic philosophy
Politico-economic welfare ideology
Global interest domains in business negotiations
Political surveillance and trade diplomacy

Shifts in Business Diplomacy
Americas
Post economic recession (2007-11)
Post-elections in the USA (2017)
Latin American gateways-Chile, Brazil, and Mexico
Europe
Trade policies in France
German trade diplomacy
Asia
India and China on global business
Japan emerging as Asian Power
Africa
South Africa as Emerging Market

Effects of Shifts
Interrupted flow of factors of production
Decline in international investments
Ineffective trade negotiations
Polarization of business

Shifts in Business Diplomacy
Globalization to protectionism
Shifts in power-play
Trade diplomacy of big-emerging markets
Business with China and India
Manufacturing relocation and investment hubs
Briton's exit from European Union
Latin America for new bilateral trade negotiations
South Africa rising as emerging market
Global fragmentation in manufacturing and services
New consumption patterns across destinations

Fig. 1.1 Effects of business-politics ideological shifts on global trade and economy (Source: Author)

in international trade to develop their native markets. Such steps might dichotomize global trade concerns, liberal trade, and economies of countries that were established in the mid-twentieth century and coordinated by the WTO. The trade-related negotiations among Latin American and East Asian countries should also focus on the technical norms and standards; rules of origin, anti-dumping, subsidies, countervailing measures; other liberalization and deregulation measures (privatization); sub-regional, regional, and hemispheric integration processes; and convergence and divergence between regional integration and multilateral trade regimes. The negotiations should also address simplifying rules and procedures, including non-transparent and inefficient infrastructures, differing customs, improper application of rules of origin, customs valuation, pre-shipment inspection, and import licensing. Customs problems can be especially difficult for small and medium enterprises that have less experience and fewer resources for handling these problems.

The ideological shifts in politics affecting business governance are emerging randomly across geo-demographic destinations. Ideally, political philosophy is defined by economic activity, not political borders. The major factors behind such ideological shifts are people, capital, and business, and are based on the fear of domination of foreign resources and industries. However, in emerging markets, governments give foreign companies access to domestic industries, trade, and economy. These companies confine business growth by restricting its natural flow of resources to market; they invest enormously in the developing countries and as a result destroy wealth in the long run. Although political leaders resist acknowledging the consequences of any ideology on business growth, the quality of international business relations are always questionable (Ohmae 1995). The most prominent explanations, often interrelated, for the retardation of global economic recovery include erosion of trust in institutional pillars, such as public and corporate governance, weakening consumer and investor confidence, and rising geopolitical risks. The weakness of fixed investment expenditure, particularly pronounced for non-residential investment, contributes significantly to the sluggish overall growth in industrial countries. Investment expenditures play a critical role in the business cycle. In the recent past, there were problems in sustaining the recovery once inventory levels had been re-established. Investment activity generally picks up when prospects for profitable investment opportunities increase and the utilization of existing production capacities reaches a level that calls for a further increase of these capacities (Rajagopal 2016).

Despite reverse political ideologies, business in the global marketplace is succeeding. There are debates in C-Suites about why so many global strategies fail despite powerful company–industry–government triadic negotiations and other border-crossing advantages. Because a one-size-fits-all strategy no longer stands a chance, a single political ideology might not lead the global markets. However, cross-border differences are larger than commonly assumed in a trade bloc. Most economic activities, including trade, virtual financial investment, tourism, and communication, are largely affected by political ideologies. In this pseudo-globalized political shift evidenced in US trade lobbies, Chinese business reactions, and emerging markets, global businesses have been undoubtedly affected and most business economies are under surveillance. Companies can cross home borders more profitably by basing their strategies on the geopolitical differences that matter, and identifying strategies to overcome barriers to bridge the loss in business due to geo-political shifts in ideologies. Companies need to assess the cultural, administrative, geographic, and economic differences between regions at the industry level and create value. Countries adapt to policy shifts and their consequences, and manage aggregation by overcoming differences (Ghemawat 2018).

The labor market in the changing global economic order plays a significant role in determining the production patterns across the regions in reference to the concerns of companies over cost-effectiveness and profit-making. Accordingly, the trend of production sharing, by ways of getting parts of products manufactured at different locations and assembled at another place, has become popular among the companies in developed countries, in order to take advantage of the low wages of skilled and unskilled labor. The effects of the labor market on international fragmentation of production in the United States and Europe have shown a trend of increasing relative labor wages and demand in industrial production since the 1980s. The disruptive business models indicate that with international fragmentation, a change in the relative factor intensities of the affected industries can be seen. However, the shift in the intensity of labor usage is observable in the United States and Europe, which relates to the production-sharing activity. Opening up of markets can play an important role in weakening the vested interests, and reducing economic rents associated with long-standing economic and institutional arrangements. Trade can thus spur improvement in domestic institutions that otherwise would not have been possible. In addition, international agreements can be an important external anchor and catalyst for institutional change by breaking through domestic impediments to reforms. Regional or bilateral agreements may bring faster results than the multilateral process, enable parties to conclude levels of liberalization beyond the multilateral consensus, and address specific issues that do not register on the multilateral menu. The resulting achievements in trade liberalization can be substantial complements to the WTO system, and they can be important building blocks for future multilateral liberalization. The most powerful economic arguments against regional and bilateral trade agreements are that they can cause trade diversion and trade distortions, and ultimately undermine the multilateral system because of their discriminatory nature (Rajagopal 2016).

The trade agreements have driven the Latin American countries with enormous opportunities to explore international markets and develop market competitiveness. In addition, the trade development measures to attract foreign direct investment and lower or eliminate the tariff barriers have reflected global trends in reference to the typology of these agreements. While the majority of trade agreements are bilateral, some include FTAs, which have set a very comprehensive scope for trade and economic development. Notably some FTAs signed by Peru, Colombia, and Chile with the United States and the European Union have helped in gearing up the trade and economy of these countries. However, the bilateral agreements signed with Asian countries, especially by Chile and Peru, pose a limited scope with regard to regulatory commitments, but are very ambitious with regards to their levels of opening trade and eliminating tariffs. These agreements also have a strong potential given the economic dynamism of this region. Other agreements are *pluri-lateral* involving large numbers of countries on extended geo-economic parameters, such as the Trans-Pacific Strategic Economic Partnership Agreement negotiated by Chile, New Zealand, Brunei Darussalam, and Singapore, which is now being broadened to include the United States within the framework of the negotiations for the Trans-Pacific Partnership Agreement. As manufacturers invest in local assembly facilities in emerging economies, the nature of trade is also changing, with intermediate manufactured goods, which include parts, components, and commodities, making up a greater share of cross-border flows of goods. Eventually, as large global manufacturers achieve scale in emerging markets, they may pull many of their suppliers to enter these regional markets, which could slow the growth of trade in intermediate goods. However, there are other factors too that may reshape manufacturing flows in the future.

For instance, rising labor costs in China may continue to shift more labor-intensive manufacturing to countries such as Mexico, Vietnam, and Bangladesh, which could see a resulting increase in exports.

The policy risks broadly include administrative controls on prices, investments, and transfer of funds that affect the international business in the country. Besides, the policies on nationalization and domestication of identified industry segments, and the changing macroeconomic policies of the country, carry major risk for international business. The political instability, civil unrests, bureaucracy, and corruption are also of concern to the inefficiency of the internal governance in a country that seriously affects the investments, manufacturing, and marketing operation of multinational companies attempting to do business in the destination country. International diplomacy also affects the exchange rates, investments, and international trade at the destination country. The political risks may be identified by contextually analyzing the political and social system of a country, its degree of openness to international trade, efficiency of the product markets, labor market dynamics, and its capital markets. By critically examining these contextual areas, companies can map the business contexts of any country and match their strategies to each of these contextual points; they can take advantage of strengths of destination markets. However, firms need to weigh the benefits initially against the anticipated costs (Rajagopal 2016).

The current political ideology (post-2017) of restricting globalization and bringing back the collapsed politico-economic philosophy of protectionism has not only narrowed the global flow of factors of production, but also jolted the peak of business flurry in global markets. The trends in consumer and industrial products were seized for few quarters in 2016 and 2017 due to American diplomacy and Britain exiting from the European Union. Industries and corporate houses with substantial exposure to Brexit have employed contingency plans to deal with a wide range of outcomes, including unfavorable consequences due to the business diplomacy. Hopefully, the emerging parliamentary elections in Britain will be able to reframe the political ideology to handle the upcoming Brexit negotiations (Ghemawat 2017).

Conclusions

Political influence in business is inevitable, and has greater impact on trade, economy and business negotiations. The political power play in business sets new trends of negotiation and possibilities of business expansions across destinations. The political ideology affects the manufacturing and services industries, and governs the global-local convergence of business. Like manufactured goods, global commodities are being shaped by several trends. First, the increasing participation of emerging economies is reshaping global commodities flows as both producers and consumers. Second, digitization is enabling new efficiencies in operations, which are necessary to help navigate a world that is likely to be characterized by continuing high and volatile resource prices. Finally, it is expected to see increased volatility in commodities flows because of surging demand, supply constraints, and a higher correlation between commodity prices that stems from a more tightly interconnected world alongside shifts in political ideologies, power-play lobbies, and peoples participation in prompting politics. Emerging economies are becoming larger participants in the global commodities markets, with rising levels of production, consumption, and investment.

REFERENCES

Chipman, J. (2009). Why your company needs a foreign policy. *Harvard Business Review, 94*(9), 36–43.
Ghemawat, P. (2017). *As Brexit negotiations start, companies need contingency plans*, HBR Web Article, Boston, MA: Harvard Business School Press.
Ghemawat, P. (2018). *Redefining global strategy, with a new preface: Crossing borders in a world where differences still matter*. Boston, MA: Harvard Business School Press.
Gretz, G. (2016). *Commercial diplomacy and American foreign policy, global economic governance program*. Oxford, UK: Oxford University Press.
Moss, D. A. (2012). Fixing what's wrong with U.S. politics. *Harvard Business Review, 90*(3), 134–139.
Ohmae, K. (1995). Putting global logic first. *Harvard Business Review, 67*(2), 143–154.
Rajagopal, A. (2016). *Sustainable growth in global markets: Strategic choices and managerial implications*. Basingstoke, UK: Palgrave Macmillan.
Rajagopal, A., & Zlatev, V. (2017). *Business dynamics in North America: Analysis of spatial and temporal trade patterns*. New York: Palgrave Macmillan.
Watkins, M. D. (2009). *The corporate diplomacy challenge: A leader's guide to navigating this important career transition*. Boston, MA: Harvard Business School Press.

PART I

Business Governance and Society: India

Trends in Agricultural Production and Productivity Growth in India: Challenges to Sustainability

Ramakrushna Panigrahi

Introduction

The theories of economic growth have traditionally revolved around the growth of the agricultural sector since it was believed that the production could happen only in agrarian structure and the production in the industrial sector is largely dependent on it for factor inputs. However, though the strategies of growth have been focused more on the industrial and service sectors since industrial revolution, the agricultural sector has not yet lost its dominance for the sheer reason that the requirements of basic needs can only be fulfilled from the output of the agricultural sector. In fact, in developing countries the agricultural sector continues to employ a significant proportion of the workforce. Indian agriculture, which stagnated during the first half of the twentieth century, witnessed significant growth and transformation soon after independence. The rate of growth accelerated from 0.37 per cent per annum during 1901–1944 to 2.88 per cent

---

R. Panigrahi (✉)
International Management Institute, Bhubaneswar, Odisha, India
e-mail: ramakrushna@imibh.edu.in

per annum during 1949–1950 to 2016–2017. This remarkable change was a result of vigorous policy interventions in the years of the Five-Year Plans of independent India. However, the major breakthrough in the rate of growth in Indian agriculture came with the green revolution in the late 1960s, which gave a boost to the agricultural sector and helped India become self-sufficient in food production.

There have been many theories behind the phenomenal achievement in Indian agriculture. The Boserupian argument for such stupendous turnaround in agrarian growth in India assumes prominence over all the theories considering India's higher growth in population until the 1970s. Though India is lagging far behind the developed countries in terms of productivity growth despite such a turnaround in the agricultural sector, India has traversed a long way from a hugely food-deficit country to a surplus country during the last four decades. The transition from a subsistence agrarian sector to a commercial surplus agricultural sector in India required large-scale investments and a complete transformation. However, the phenomenal growth that India has achieved especially in food-grains production and productivity is unequal across regions. There are states like Kerala and Punjab, where per hectare productivity has been more than 40 quintals, whereas states like Madhya Pradesh and Orissa have a productivity level of around 20 quintals. But the rise in prices of agricultural output is lagging behind any of the inflation indices like the Wholesale Price Index (WPI) or the Consumer Price Index (CPI). This eventually poses a serious threat to the sustainability of production in the agricultural sector as real wage increases (though quite a few other factor input prices do not rise due to subsidy) and makes farming not profitable. Though the productivity growth in the agricultural sector partly compensates for the loss due to rise in the real wage rate, rise in the prices of factor inputs and lack of a free market output price compromise the profitability aspect of the agricultural sector. As a result, required levels of private investments and entrepreneurship have been eluding the Indian agricultural sector. In the absence of a market-driven pricing system and lack of profitability in farm production, government policies like incentives will not be enough to sustain the production of agricultural output. This chapter makes an attempt to analyze productivity growth in the Indian agricultural sector and provide a policy framework to make activities of the farming sector, which employs two-thirds of India's workforce, profitable and sustainable.

An Overview of Literature on Agricultural Production and Productivity

There have been many studies on Indian agriculture analyzing the patterns of growth and productivity in the Indian context. In this section, attempt to review some of the most relevant studies that deal with agricultural growth and productivity as well as profitability in the agricultural sector in India. The study by Balkrishnan et al. (2008) analyzed the trends in production and productivity in the agricultural sector. The study observed the slow growth in the agricultural sector since 1991 and found that stagnation of public investment for almost a quarter century is one of the factors responsible for slow growth.

Dorward (2009) analyzed the role of conventional input subsidies in agricultural development in a theoretical framework by considering the effects of demand and supply inelastic ties in consumers' surplus and producers' surplus as well as the deadweight loss. He analyzed historical successes and failures of input subsidies for African economies and the role of subsidies in reducing profitability. In a neo-classical microeconomic framework, the impact of targeted subsidies on output supply was analyzed. The paper argues that stakeholders' welfare and subsidies have the greatest potential in contributing wider growth and increasing consumers' welfare via reduced food prices. Tripathi (2013) analyzed the impact of agricultural price policy on output and farm profitability in India. The paper argued that reduction in input subsidies to discourage environmentally unsustainable practices has slowed down the performance of the agricultural sector during the post-reform period. The study highlighted that agricultural price policy has ensured an increased farm income by the farmers. However, this study did not consider farm profitability in a free market equilibrium in the event of full withdrawal of subsidies on farm inputs.

Fan et al. (2007) examined the reasons behind the declining growth rate in Indian agriculture since the 1990s and empirically estimated the relative impact of various government subsidies and investments on growth and poverty reduction. This study also estimated returns in agricultural growth and poverty reduction to investments and subsidies and found that initial subsidies in credit, fertilizer, and irrigation helped farmers to adopt the new technologies. Authors found that the trade-off between agricultural growth and poverty reduction is generally small among different types of public spending and investments in agricultural research and infrastructure development have a large impact on economic growth and poverty reduction.

However, this study did not analyze the welfare loss and potential loss in farm profitability due to government provision of subsidies on farm inputs. Denning et al. (2009) analyzed the role of input subsidies in improvement of smallholder maize productivity in Malawi. The study found that pro-poor input subsidies work better for small farms and subsidies ensure that maize consumers are benefitting from lower prices though future challenges arise due to continuing surplus production. It may be noted here that subsidy-induced, lower-output prices pose a threat to the sustainability of production as the profitability for the farm is suppressed due to lesser prices of farm inputs. However, this study did not analyze the impact of input subsidies on farm profitability.

Grossman and Carlson (2011) analyzed the role of input subsidies in the agricultural policy of India. The study found that India's agricultural sector is more dependent on input subsidies than other large emerging economies like Brazil, Russia, and China. The study also found that despite inflation, the nominal prices of subsidized fertilizer in India are kept unchanged even though fertilizer prices increased all over the world due to political pressure from the farm sector, which accounts for half of India's population. There are various other studies like Balkrishnan (2000), Raghavan (2008), and Mahendra Dev (2000) that have highlighted economic reforms and their impact on Indian agricultural productivity growth in the context of changing patterns of input use. However, none of the existing studies analyzes farm profitability and the reasons for which the farming sector remains unattractive for private investments and private entrepreneurship. In this chapter, we attempt to analyze the factors influencing productivity stagnation and profitability in the Indian agricultural sector.

OBJECTIVES OF THE STUDY

The present study broadly examines the impact of subsidies on agricultural output prices and farm profitability. Specifically, the objectives of the study are:

- To analyze the trends in agricultural production and productivity growth in India since independence
- To examine the factors influencing agricultural productivity in India
- To examine the challenges faced by the agricultural sector in recent times in the context of MSP and provision of subsidies

Trends in Agricultural Production in the Post-Independence Era

Despite its continuous dwindling share in India's GDP, the agricultural sector remains the largest provider of jobs for the workforce. Even today, more than two-thirds of India's population is dependent on the agricultural sector for their sustenance. The agricultural sector has experienced phenomenal growth since the 1970s after two decades of slow growth soon after independence. Until the 1970s, due to a huge deficit of food, the primary focus of the first few Five-Year Plans was to achieve self-sufficiency in food-grains production. India had made huge investments in the agricultural sector and large-scale subsidies on inputs transformed the agricultural sector from a deficient sector to a surplus one.[1] The per capita availability of food grains increased from 348.15 grams per day in 1950–1951 to 528.09 grams per day in 2003–2004. Table 2.1 presents the trend in agricultural production (food grains) to allow for a better understanding of how India has progressed in terms of production since 1950–1951 to 2002–2003.

It is evident from Table 2.1 that production of food grains has undergone a transformation, changing the sector from a deficient to a surplus one over the years. The food-grains sector in India has moved from a deficient to sufficient, and further, to a surplus economy by registering very high rates of growth since the 1970s following the Green Revolution. However, growth in production of pulses has almost stagnated over the last two decades. Similarly, coarse cereals have not grown fast even though they have done better compared to pulses. Along with interventionist

---

[1] According to estimation of nutrition experts, the average daily requirement of cereals for an average Indian adult is 412.2 grams. For pulses, it is estimated to be 67.95 grams per day. Total requirement for cereals in the year 1950–1951(with a population of 361 million) was 54.31 million tons while production was 42.42 million tons, accounting for a deficit of 11.89 million tons, which is 28% of total production. Similarly, for pulses, the requirement was 8.95 million tons whereas production was 8.41 million tons, accounting for a marginal deficit of 0.54 million tons. For total food grains, the requirement was 63.26 million tons while production was 50.83 million tons, accounting for a deficit of 12.42 million tons. This resulted in an increase in import of food grains on a large scale, accounting for the bulk of the import bill. In addition, food security was under threat. Conversely, in the year 2015–2016, the total food-grains requirement was 232.28 million tons (with population of 1326 million) whereas production was t 251.57 million tons with a surplus of 19.29 million tons. However, India still lacks in production of pulses. In 2015–2016, production was16.35 tons against a requirement of 32.88 tons, which led to imports of pulses.

Table 2.1 Decennial trends of production of food grains in India (million tons)

Years	Rice	Wheat	Coarse cereals	Total cereals	Pulses	Total food grains
1950–1951	20.58	6.46	15.38	42.42	8.41	50.83
1960–1961	34.58	11.00	23.74	69.32	12.70	82.02
1970–1971	42.22	23.83	30.55	96.61	11.82	108.43
1980–1981	53.63	36.31	29.02	118.96	10.63	129.59
1990–1991	74.29	55.14	32.70	162.13	14.26	176.39
2000–2001	87.70	69.68	31.08	188.46	11.08	199.54
2010–2011	95.98	86.87	43.40	226.25	18.24	244.49
2015–2016	104.41	92.29	38.52	235.22	16.35	251.57

Source: *Handbook of Statistics in Indian Economy—Reserve Bank of India*, 2003 to 2016

policies at a macro level, widespread usage of HYVs, fertilizers, pesticides and irrigation and better access to credit, subsistence farmers at a micro level have started producing for the market, accounting for a large-scale marketable surplus.

If we consider commercial crops, the Indian agricultural sector has registered very high growth in cotton, sugarcane and rapeseed. In the case of sunflower, production increased from a mere 0.01 million tons in 1970–1971 to 13.79 million tons in 2016–2017, registering a more than thousand-fold increase in production. Table 2.2 presents production of major commercial crops.

It is evident from Table 2.2 that the Indian agricultural sector has registered high growth rates in major commercial crops. The following figure depicts the phenomenal rise in production of commercial crops in India. In the case of many crops, there has been acceleration in growth rates of total production. In the following section, we estimate the growth rates of all the crops for three periods: 1950–1951 to 1969–1970 before the Green Revolution; 1970–1971 to 1991–1992, the post-Green Revolution and pre-liberalization period; and 1991–1992 to 2015–2016, the post-liberalization era.

Determinants of Agricultural Productivity Growth

Indian agriculture in the late 1970s witnessed the phenomenon of the Green Revolution in which modern farm inputs were intensively used to increase productivity. However, in the initial phases, the Green Revolution was limited to only three or four states in India. Subsequently, other states caught up and productivity at all levels substantially increased. All the data

Table 2.2 Trends of production of commercial crops in India (in million tones)

Year	Ground-nut	Rapeseed & mustard	Soybean	Coffee #	Cotton (lint)	Raw jute & mesta	Sugarcane	Tea #	Tobacco
1950–1951	3.48	0.76	NA	NA	3.04	3.31	57.05	NA	0.26
1960–1961	4.81	1.35	NA	NA	5.60	5.26	110.00	NA	0.31
1970–1971	6.11	1.98	0.01	110.23	4.76	6.19	126.37	419.00	0.36
1980–1981	5.01	2.30	0.44	118.65	7.01	8.16	154.25	569.60	0.48
1990–1991	7.51	5.23	2.60	169.73	9.84	9.23	241.05	720.34	0.56
2000–2001	6.41	4.19	5.28	301.20	9.52	10.56	295.96	848.43	0.34
2010–2011	8.27	8.18	12.74	302.00	33.00	10.62	342.38	966.73	0.88
2016–2017	7.57	7.98	13.79	316.70	33.09	10.60	306.72	1250.49	NA

Tea and Coffee in millions of Kgs

Source: *Handbook of Statistics in Indian Economy—RBI*, 2003 to 2016

related to productivity, input usage, subsidies and Minimum Support Prices (MSP) are collected from secondary sources. For a couple of variables, like subsidy and MSP, continuous data are not available since 1950–1951, therefore we conducted an analysis between 1970–1971 and 2015–2016. In this section, we analyze the productivity growth in India for major crops for the period between 1970–1971 and 2015–2016.

The productivity function for all the crops can be specified as follows:

$$Y = f(F, I, S, M, T, Ut)$$

where,
Y is agricultural Output per hectare.
Fertilizer Consumption per hectare.
I is the proportion of area under Irrigation.
S is the total subsidies provided by the Union Government of India.
M is the MSP offered by the government for the surplus produce.
Ut represents all other factors affecting Yield.

For estimation of the yield function, we have specified the following double log-linear function:

$$Ln\,Y = \alpha + \beta_1 Ln\,F + \beta_2 Ln\,I + \beta_3 Ln\,S + \beta_4 Ln\,M + Ut$$

Since rice accounts for the highest share of agricultural production in India, we analyze this crop in the present study. However, with availability of data for all the crops, the study can be extended to major food and commercial crops in India. The results of the factors determining rice productivity from the regression analysis are presented below.

Estimated Regression Equation for Rice:

Ln Y = 4.248 + 0.132 Ln F + 0.566 Ln I – 0.0302 Ln S + 0.0605 Ln M
SE   (0.7602)   (0.0793)   (0.2888)   (0.0227)   (0.0454)
t-Stat (5.588)   (1.66)   (1.96)   (–1.32)   (1.33)
R^2 = 0.97, df = 41, Adj. R^2 = 0.95, F-Stat = 242.4

From the above regression result, it is evident that despite a high R^2 value, none of the explanatory variables are significant at 5 per cent level of significance. Subsequently, we have specified the model by removing the variable Gross Irrigated area and the revised model is specified as:

$$Ln\,Y = \alpha + \beta_1 Ln\,F + \beta_2 Ln\,S + \beta_3 Ln\,M + Ut$$

The estimated regression equation for the new model is:

$$\text{Ln Y} = 5.77 + 0.1811^* \text{Ln F} - 0.0116 \text{Ln S} + 0.15009^* \text{Ln M}$$
SE   (0.21799) (0.0608)   (−0.44119) (0.03822)
t-Stat (26.48)   (2.97)   (−0.441)   (3.92)
$R^2 = 0.97$, df = 42, Adj. $R^2 = 0.948$, F-Stat = 252.57

It is evident from the above regression model that both fertilizer consumption and MSP significantly influence productivity growth for the rice crop. From the log-linear model, we can conclude that a 1 per cent rise in fertilizer consumption will raise productivity by 0.18 per cent and a 1 per cent rise in MSP will increase productivity by 0.15 per cent. It may be noted that subsidies provided by the union government negatively influence productivity growth. However, the subsidy variable is not statistically significant. With a very high adjusted R^2 value of 0.948 and F-Statistic of 252.57, the overall robustness of the model explains the influence of explanatory variables to determine growth in rice productivity.

CHALLENGES FOR AGRICULTURAL SECTORS: ISSUES IN SUSTAINABILITY

The agricultural sector has come a long way since the independence era and boasts of ensuring food security for the country. However, if we compare the productivity of India's agricultural sector with that of developed nations like the United States and Japan, India is lagging far behind. The agricultural sector faces many challenges despite provision of huge subsidies and MSP and a positively interventionist policy approach by the government. Since the input market is highly regulated, the output prices do not keep pace with the rising levels of inflation and as a result, the farming sector's profitability is reduced to a significant extent. In addition, agricultural marketing infrastructure in India lacks farmer-friendly logistics and results in a huge difference in prices paid to the farmers and the prevailing market prices for agricultural products. Even though farm inputs are subsidized, agricultural labor poses a huge problem for farmers with rising wage rates and unavailability of seasonal farm laborers in rural India. Even though India's agricultural production and productivity growth has accelerated in in last four decades, sustaining the growth becomes challenging in the wake of rising wage rates and suppressed output prices for the farmers and lack of profitability in farming. Table 2.3 explains the

Table 2.3 MSP of food and commercial crops and rising inflation

Year	MSP rice	MSP coarse cereals	MSP wheat	Pulses (gram)	Sugarcane	Groundnut	Sunflower	Soyabean	CPI-AL (1960–1961 base)
1975–1976	74	74	105.00	90.00	8.5	140	150	NA	340
1980–1981	105	105	130.00	NA	13.00	206	183.00	198	395
1990–1991	205	180	225	450	22.00	580.00	600.00	400.00	803
2000–2001	510	445	610	1100	59.50	1220.00	1170.00	865.00	1744.6
2010–2011	1000	880	1170	2100	139.12	2300.00	2350.00	1440.00	2934.36
2015–2016	1410	1325	1525	3425	230.00	4030.00	3800.00	2600.00	4576

Source: *Handbook of Statistics in Indian Economy*—RBI

gap in rising wages and inflation levels and rise in agricultural output prices in India over the last four decades. The CPI has been used for agricultural laborers to represent rising wage rates and the inflation levels in the economy. The MSP of various food and commercial crops are considered since data on market prices on all crops vary and are not available from secondary sources for the time period considered.

It is evident from Table 2.3 that the output prices in the agricultural sector have not kept pace with the rising price levels and hence profitability is compromised for the farming sector. We argue that if the agricultural sector is freed from interventional policies, then equilibrium market prices will help farm profitability, which would attract private investments and entrepreneurship. This way, the Indian agricultural sector can sustain its high growth rates in production and productivity and will ensure food security of the country in the coming years.

Conclusions

This chapter attempted to analyze the trends in production and productivity of the Indian agricultural sector. The study finds that there has been acceleration in growth of agricultural production. Among food grains, cereals have registered very high growth rates since the 1970s though the growth in production of pulses has not been impressive. Among commercial crops, sunflower stands out with an impressive 118 times the production levels of 1970. Also, other commercial crops like groundnut, cotton, jute, rapeseed and mustard have been very impressive. The high levels of production could be achieved due to high productivity growth. The study finds that usage of fertilizers and provision of MSP significantly contributes to productivity growth with a 5 per cent level of statistical significance. The study also finds that though not statistically significant, subsidies negatively influence the productivity growth of the rice crop in India. The study finds that the agricultural sector faces various challenges to sustain its high levels of production and productivity growth. The regulated market prices and lack of marketing infrastructure make the farming sector unprofitable and hence unattractive to private investment and innovative entrepreneurship. The present study argues that government intervention should be aimed at providing better prices to the farmers and providing marketing infrastructure to boost the profitability of India's agricultural sector.

References

Balkrishnan, P. (2000). Agriculture and economic reforms: Growth and welfare. *Economic and Political Weekly, 35*(12), 999–1004.

Balkrishnan, P., Golait, R., & Kumar, P. (2008). *Agricultural growth in India since 1991*. Department of Economic Analyis and Policy, Reserve Bank of India, Mumbai. Retrieved from https://rbidocs.rbi.org.in/rdocs/content/pdfs/85240.pdf

Denning, G., Kabambe, P., Sanchez, P., Malik, A., Flor, R., Harawa, R., et al. (2009, January 27). Input subsidies to improve small holder maize productivity in Malawi: Towards an African Green Revolution. *PLOS Biology, 7*(1), e23. https://doi.org/10.1371/journal.pbio.1000023

Dorward, A. (2009). *Rethinking agricultural input subsidy programmes in a changing world*. Centre for Development, Environment and Policy, SOAS, University of London. Retrieved from https://papers.ssrn.com/sol3/papers.cfm?abstract_id=1808847

Fan, S., Gulati, A., & Thorat, S. (2007). *Investment, subsidies and pro-poor growth in rural India*. IFPRI Discussion Paper 00716. Retrieved from https://ageconsearch.umn.edu/bitstream/42397/2/IFPRIDP00716.pdf

Grossman, N., & Carlson, D. (2011, March). *Agriculture policy in India: The role of input subsidies*. USITC Executive Briefings on Tradem. Retrieved from https://www.usitc.gov/publications/332/EBOT_IndiaAgSubsidies.pdf

Mahendra Dev, S. (2000). Economic reforms, poverty, income distribution and employment. *Economic and Political Weekly, 35*(10), 823–835.

Raghavan, M. (2008). Changing pattern of input use and cost of cultivation. *Economic and Political Weekly, 43*(26/27), 123–129.

Tripathi, A. K. (2013). Agricultural price policy, output and farm profitability – Examining linkages during post-reform period in India. *Asian Journal of Agriculture and Development, 10*(1), 91–111.

CHAPTER 3

Unraveling the Power of Talent Analytics: Implications for Enhancing Business Performance

Geeta Rana, Ravinder Sharma, and Alok Kumar Goel

INTRODUCTION

Knowledge-intensive companies are increasingly adopting sophisticated methods of analyzing employee data to make better decisions and enhance their competitive advantage (Davenport et al. 2010). Balmer Lawrie & Co. Ltd. (BL) is beginning to understand the integral role of "talent analytics" in achieving innovative and high-quality products, processes, and services while retaining the company's top talent. BL wants better performance from their top employees—who are the company's greatest asset and have much of the responsibility for managing people. BL extended its HR approach to use valuable employee data to move the right employees in the right jobs at the right place while calculating the optimal number of employees required to deal with customers at the front desk and other service points for making the organization profitable. Talent analytics,

---

G. Rana (✉) • R. Sharma
Swami Rama Himalayan University, Dehradun, Uttarakhand, India

A. K. Goel
CSIR-Human Resource Development Centre, Ghaziabad, Uttar Pradesh, India

© The Author(s) 2019
Rajagopal, R. Behl (eds.), *Business Governance and Society*,
https://doi.org/10.1007/978-3-319-94613-9_3

which uses advanced technologies to process billions of data points to discern previously unseen patterns of potential value, shows the promise of basing decisions about hiring, training, improving productivity and retaining talent on hard numbers and even delivering insights that can make a company more competitive.

Talent analytics is known by different names: people analytics, HR analytics, workforce analytics, people research and analytics, and HR business intelligence (Marler and Boudreau 2017). Lawler et al. (2004) define talent analytics as involving "statistical techniques and experimental approaches" to show the impact of HR activities on the organization's performance metrics. Bassi (2011) reported that talent analytics "is an evidence-based approach for making better decisions on the people side of the business; it consists of an array of tools and technologies, ranging from simple reporting of HR metrics all the way up to predictive modeling." HR analytics, also called talent analytics, is the application of considerable data mining and business analytics techniques to human resources data (Carlson and Kavanagh 2012). The goal of human resources analytics is to provide an organization with insights for effectively managing employees so that business goals can be reached quickly and efficiently (Boudreau 2015). The challenge of human resources analytics is to identify what data should be captured and how to use the data to model and predict capabilities so the organization gets an optimal return on investment on its human capital (Banerjee et al. 2013). Talent analytics does not only deal with gathering data on employee efficiency. Instead, it aims to provide insight into each process by gathering data and then using it to make relevant decisions about how to improve the processes (Sen 2015).

Since analytics can be used to drive human or fully automated decisions, it can be used to support almost any business process (Davenport and Harris 2007). The proof for this can be seen in the use of analytics in finance, sales, marketing and supply chains. Compared to these functions, the HR function has been marked as a laggard and has been regarded as a rather late entrant to using analytics (George and Kamalanabhan 2016). This is rather remarkable since HR is no stranger to data. Typically, HR departments in organizations possess a treasure trove of data from both within and outside the organization. These include data related to employee benefits, compensation and performance management, incentive programs, recruitment and training as well as data from other internal departments such as consultants, suppliers, and vendors (Pemmaraju 2007). Considering the extent of data residing within HR, it is surprising that HR is not more actively involved in analytics (www.HBR_Visier_Report). An active involvement in analytics would also mean the participation of HR employees in analytical activities. This chapter explores in detail the talent analytics practices followed by BL, a Mini-Ratna Public Sector Enterprise under the Ministry of Petroleum and Natural Gas, Government of India. BL is a knowledge-intensive organization whose survival and success are highly dependent upon knowledge-based activities and processes, human skill, and talent. The talent analytics process adopted by the organization helped it improve its operational and administrative effectiveness. Thus, a case study on BL's talent analytics processes gives deep insights into how to manage and turn employee data into information in an organization so as to develop a learning culture, improve processes, and enhance efficiency.

LITERATURE REVIEW

Holsapple et al. (2014) classified talent analytics as one domain of business analytics (BA). Next to using analytics in HR, there are other domains where BA is being applied, including "marketing, business strategy, organizational behavior, operations, supply chain systems, information systems, and finance." Fitz-Enz (2010) defined talent analytics as a communication tool that combines data from different sources to describe the current situation and to predict the future. He further concluded that "analytics is a mental framework, a logical progression first and a set of statistical tools second." By this, he means that in the center of analytics is the way people see the world and try to make sense of it and the tools are a way to make this happen in practice. It begins with the understanding of the issue at hand and after that statistics are used if necessary to understand and uncover the hidden value from the masses of data.

According to Bassi (2011), talent analytics is an evidence-based and data-driven approach to better decision-making, which utilized different methods. According to Levenson (2013), talent analytics isn't used just to collect data but also to know what to do with it. In this way, the value of talent analytics comes from the knowledge of things that matter and depend on the situation, organization, and its business goals so in this way its focus is on business, not just Human Resource Metrics (HRM). In practice, the utilization of analytical tools often begins with the tools and data instead of the desirable business outcomes (Rasmussen and Ulrich 2015). Therefore, instead of just adopting new methods, it is also necessary to adopt a new kind of attitude and aspect for HRM in order to change and develop their role in organizations (Jensen and Eriksen 2016). Jensen and Eriksen (2016) stated that talent analytics is "the language of organizational management" and therefore its usage enables HR to adopt a language that is understood in the whole organization. Douthitt and Mondroe (2013) considered talent analytics as "an outgrowth of and marriage between human resource metrics and general business analysis." They emphasized that talent analytics allows the inclusion of "all BI data to both support the delivery of human resource services and influence the behavior of all levels of employees."

According to Bersin et al. (2012), talent analytics can be understood as "the application of a methodology and integrated process for improving the quality of people-related decisions for the purpose of improving individual and/or organizational performance." The process of talent analytics involves gathering of data, analysis, visualization of insights, predictive modeling, and taking actions, for example, in the form of formulating a strategy on how to deal with issues in the future (Becker et al. 2001). All in all, in the academic literature talent analytics is described as still in its infancy and is rarely utilized in HRM decisions (Pape 2016). Gale (2015) complemented this by stating that the analytics that are used are usually visualization tools, which help to organize the data instead of supporting future decision-making. According to Fitz-enz and Maddox (2014), there are typically four main reasons for gathering and analyzing data: (1) describing, (2) explaining, (3) predicting, and (4) optimizing. Measuring usually starts with the use of simple metrics and reporting, which then can be developed into complex analysis models. Metrics is an "accountability tool that enables the assessment of a function's results" (Dulebohn and Johnson 2013). It indicates how an organization or smaller unit is performing and functions as a basis for the decision-making (Carlson and Kavanagh 2015). In the mid-1990s, companies increasingly started implementing strategy maps and balanced scorecards, which connected the long-term strategic goals and the short-term operational targets of the whole organization (Douthitt and Mondroe 2013; Kaplan and Norton 1996). They included more advanced metrics from different functions and operational processes: financial, customer, internal processes as well as learning and growth. Later on, more HRM-focused "HR scorecards" were also developed (Becker et al. 2001). These scorecards typically included key HR deliverables and processes, alignment between these and the business strategy, and the indicators measuring the effectiveness of these deliverables and processes (Douthitt and Mondroe 2013).

Ulrich and Dulebohn (2015) again emphasize that it is important to understand that the metrics are just a way to measure something and the focus is on that something, not the metrics themselves. Traditionally, HRM has been preoccupied with measuring the efficiency of the HR function itself. However, instead of this limited focus on the efficiency and effectiveness of human resources as a function, measurement can be directed at how much value it generates for the overall business. Figure 3.1 illustrates this transition in HRM measuring. Measuring in HRM has usually focused on HR activities because this kind of measuring has been easy (Ulrich and Dulebohn 2015). When taking the "next step" in the measuring, organizations begin to measure the intermediate outcomes of HRM. Still, the focus is strongly on HRM itself, but the focus has already shifted to the outcomes and not the activities themselves.

The transition just discussed was illustrated with the example presented previously about the training programs. However, HRM as a strategic partner needs to show the connection between the human capital and HR initiatives and the business outcomes. In order to do this, the measuring needs to shift from HRM itself to the larger organizational setting. When adopting the outside-in approach, the starting point for HR measuring is in the business environment and on the customers' or other stakeholders' perspective. Business outcomes can be, for example, financial (i.e. shareholder value) or customer related (i.e. customer commitment or share). Still, it can be noted that it is not often easy to find a clear line of sight between the HR activities and the business outcomes and, therefore,

HR activities	Intermediate outcomes	Business outcomes
Measuring HR, people, work, performance Measuring activities	Measuring the otucomes or targets of HR	Measuring the business results

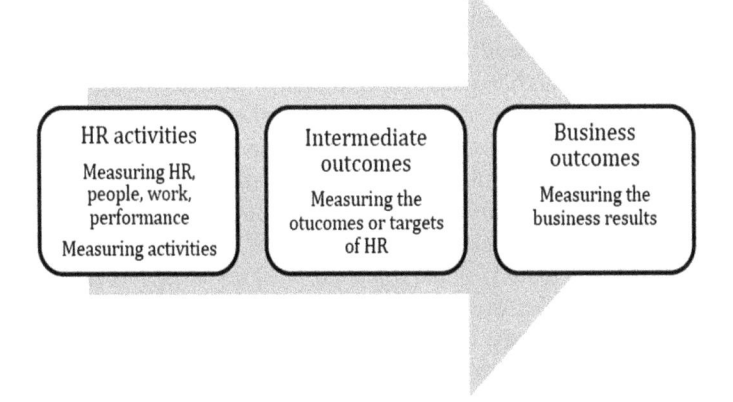

Fig. 3.1 Human resources metrics level (HR metrics levels—Adapted from Ulrich and Dulebohn 2015)

measuring the intermediate outcomes of the HR work is also important (Ulrich and Dulebohn 2015). When the correlations and causations between the HR activities, intermediate outcomes, and business outcomes can be shown, HRM work will have the possibility to deliver more strategic value. On the basis of this talent analytics literature review, it is clear that talent analytics help companies improve areas related to hiring or attrition, or pinpoint areas where labor-related savings can be found. Figure 3.1 illustrates the metric levels in human resources management.

Research Objective

On the basis of the background and research problem, the objective of this chapter is to deepen the understanding of talent analytics and its implementation. In addition, this chapter also examines the possible connections between talent analytics and decision-making of HRM. The main research question is: how does the HR profession leverage the HR analytics process at Balmer Lawrie & Co. Ltd.?

Research Methodology

The present study used a participatory research method that involved personal interaction with respondents engaged in talent analytics practices within BL. Data were collected through structured personal interviews. The participatory technique is considered to be most appropriate for in-depth learning and understanding of organizational transformation processes (Reason and Bradbury 2008). Furthermore, the participatory method allows researchers and respondents to interact in person, which allows for a certain degree of openness that otherwise would not be possible. Such personal interactions give researchers the opportunity to ask questions and exchange information and ideas that may not necessarily be a part of the structured survey instrument. As such, this process may shed light on issues that were earlier not thought of, or reveal facts that were not previously anticipated. Thus, this methodology argues in favour of the possibility, significance, and usefulness of involving research partners in the talent analytics process (Bergold 2007). Interviews were held over the duration of one week with 15 members of top management (Directors, GM and Senior Managers) and 80 employees in 2014. Respondents were randomly selected, and the researcher visited the organization to carry out the interviews. Additionally, documented information (periodical reports, financial documents, operational documents, HR records) related to the period 2014–2016 was also collected for reviewing the talent analytics process.

The Case

Balmer Lawrie & Co. Ltd. was founded by two Scotsmen, George Stephen Balmer and Alexander Lawrie, in 1867 in Kolkata, India. BL is a company engaged in a variety of businesses producing products such as steel barrels, industrial greases, specialty lubricants, corporate travel and logistic services with sites throughout India and in Bedford in the United Kingdom. It is recognized as one of the most cost-effective manufacturing plants of its kind, achieving some of the highest quality levels within the national manufacture of steel barrels in India. BL has accelerated and revitalized its leadership system since receiving a quality assurance award in the year 2016. Many changes have been made, including the introduction of talent analytics. The most significant changes have occurred under the current CEO. He was hired by the 2015 CEO prior to his retirement to lead BL to the forefront of technology and quality excellence. The current CEO is actively involved in the creation and implementation of the talent analytics system and committed to improving the business through personal HRM-driven practices. Over the past five years, BL has integrated technology into its talent analytics system. This has led to double-digit growth while improving BL's overall position in the eyes of all stakeholders.

Over the last few years, BL has struggled to get their basic reporting right. In some instances, completely unaware of their employee strength, their exact job roles and locations. In addition, BL still relies on first-generation spreadsheets to manage HR data. This problem tends to be rooted in using disparate information systems where data lie in incompatible formats or even in something as simple as having two parts of the company using different titles for the same job. This company faces a long-term challenge: to consolidate HR information systems and to develop, across units and locations, an intelligent and consistent "datamart," an archive that organizes data in ways that are relevant to specific business needs and is easily accessible to users needing information. These steps can dramatically improve a company's ability to perform meaningful talent analytics. In the meantime, a number of actions can be taken. BL designs pilot analytics projects that involve cleaning up some of the data and running limited sets of numbers. Apart from this, some challenges BL is facing in trying to revolutionize HR practices while demonstrating the business case for analytics and improve the reporting environment from an HR perspective include receiving inaccurate data, receiving a lot of useless data, data that focuses on the past, not getting data from other departments, data in different systems and forms that cannot be combined easily, collecting data that HR is accustomed to collecting, not understanding how the HR data is connected to the business data, and identifying what data is relevant.

Leveraging Analytics

BL is investing their efforts in developing talent analytics programmes. Talent analytics programmes address HR challenges and organizational development in the organization. BL finds talent analytics programmes that are dependent on authority, structure and operationalization, and responses to obstacles. The company leverages talent, shares knowledge, and uses analytics in delivering innovative solutions and insights to address business opportunities across all markets. By classifying talent analytics work into three broad categories—Data Exploration, begin with pilot projects, align with business strategy and process, take an enterprise view, develop an analytic team and involve people—BL offers a high-level roadmap for building and growing the talent analytics function (Fig. 3.2).

1. **Data Exploration:** BL is standardizing global HR systems, which is a long-term challenge, through talent analytics. It is possible to see useful results through some basic data cleanup and analysis. In-need, this approach is the only way to get better in the long term. Talent analytics is about continuous improvement over time. Basically, it consists of formal procedures for gathering quality data that can be used in a legal and ethical manner. Data collected include everything from age, education, experience, competencies, performance and potential. Employee trust and confidentiality should be maintained during the process. However, that means starting sooner rather than later.
2. **Begin with pilot projects:** HR-focused teams for talent analytics start their work with pilot projects. HR analytics teams focus on the top two or three issues of the organization as well as its critical workforce. Identify these problem areas and begin a pilot to prove the value of the longer-term talent analytics enterprise. Such initiatives

```
Intelligence  │  Involve people              │   │ Involve people through talent analytic team │
              │                              │   │                                             │
              │  Develop an analytic team    │   │ Develop deep skills                         │
Knowledge     │                              │   │                                             │
              │  Take an enterprise view     │   │ Holistic view; examine future possibilities │
              │                              │   │                                             │
              │  Align with pilot projects   │   │ Improve business performance                │
Information   │                              │   │                                             │
              │  Begin with pilot projects   │   │ Increase awareness                          │
              │                              │   │                                             │
Data          │  Data Exploration            │   │ Basic data clean up and analysis            │
```

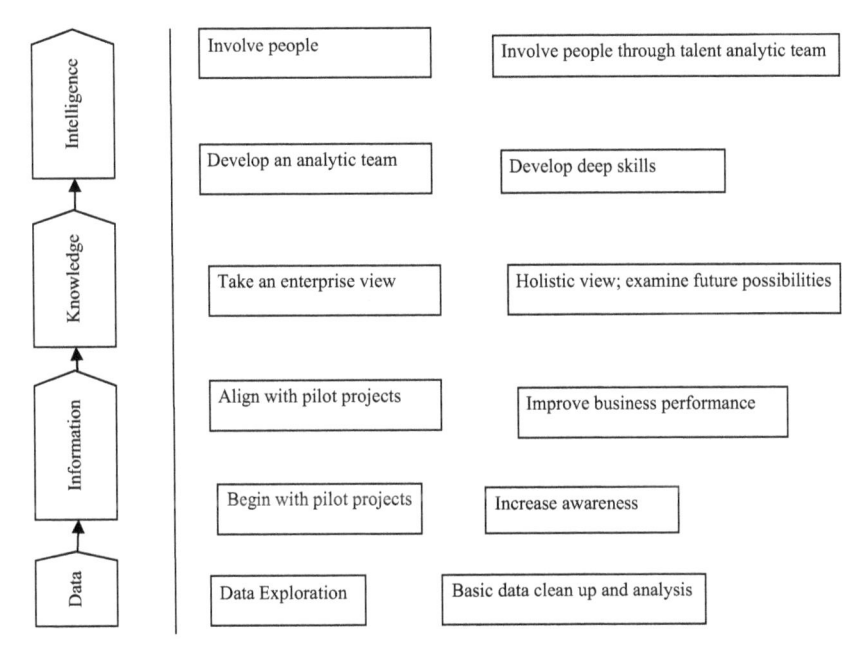

Fig. 3.2 Road map for talent analytics in BL (Sources: Complied by author)

can demonstrate value to the business and help justify investments in data infrastructure and business intelligence technology for human capital management.

3. **Align with business strategy and process**: Staying aligned with the business strategy and constantly questioning how better insights from talent data can help improve business performance. Talent analytics enables HR and talent executives to have entirely new and more important conversations with the business.

4. **Take an enterprise view:** Viewing the overall process of talent analytics from a holistic, enterprise perspective rather than as a onetime project; the lessons learned from strategic business units of the organization (e.g. steel barrels, industrial greases, corporate travel and logistic services). Also, developing customer analytics capabilities. The benefits of talent analytics can be sustainable if an organization creates an overall roadmap that identifies data, analytics and organizational capabilities required to advance in the overall analytics journey and to address the most strategic HR issues being faced across the organization.

5. **Develop an analytic team:** The company develops the analytics unit in the organization with line of structure. BL has been successful at moving HR toward better data-based decisions by having its talent analytics team report directly to the vice president of HR. Another approach for the company is to begin with a central group, sometimes called a "centre of excellence," that can help develop deep skills faster and then apportion them appropriately to parts of the organization where the potential for business impact is greatest.
6. **Involve people:** It is a paradox, but in the rush to execute in new ways based on insights from talent analytics, it is possible to overlook real people. This applies in a couple of ways. First, experienced analysts are required to interpret the data and reach sound conclusions. Second, the team needs more than just analytics and business skills. The data is, after all, about human beings, so having people who are trained in the social sciences and in change management is critical to a successful talent analytics initiative.

IMPLICATIONS: TALENT ANALYTICS SUPPORTS BUSINESS STRATEGY

Talent analytics can also take companies beyond just improving specific aspects of the employee lifecycle and organizational management to identifying, in a more open environment of potential ideas, ways that different HR strategies and initiatives can better support strategy and business performance. Where workforces tend to be large, companies look for ways to optimize their spending in terms of getting the best performance for their investment. Using analytics, companies can, for example, compare the performance of full-time and contract workers not just in terms of cost but in terms of real performance metrics, such as customer satisfaction and first call resolution. The analysis can look at the type of call, how it was handled and what category of worker handled it. This talent analytics approach can help a company deploy a new workforce segmentation strategy with the potential of delivering better customer satisfaction while also saving millions of dollars. The analytics team worked with the management to consider core channel performance issues, how to drive growth and customer satisfaction through the retail channel, and the role the workforce could have in such growth. Results like these are game changers for companies looking for insights that can improve productivity and performance of their critical workforce. From the perspective of HR practitioners, they now have unique tools in place to deliver significant business impact rather than just a few percentage points of savings or productivity improvements.

Conclusions

Another aspect shows that using analytics can also help executives with larger-scale organizational planning and performance. Workforce planning, for example, has become a challenging part of HR's responsibility, in part because of the expanding footprint of many companies and also because organizations are more likely to use a mix of internal employees, contractors or contingent workers, vendors and consultants. Preventing temporary skills gaps can be critical to a company's competitiveness, and analytics can help prevent talent shortfalls or shorten their duration. An analytics initiative enabled the company to perform a detailed assessment of the most critical goals and the business drivers of workforce demand across functions. The team then estimated future needs; analytics also enabled the team to project attrition, retirement and promotion rates. The company used the analysis to consider different approaches to resolving anticipated workforce gaps, and to determine if such gaps should be addressed by retraining existing employees or through external recruiting.

References

Banerjee, A., Bandyopadhyay, T., & Acharya, P. (2013). Data analytics: Hyped up aspirations or true potential. *Vikalpa, 38*(4), 1–11.
Bassi, L. (2011). Raging debates in HR analytics. *People & Strategy, 34*(2), 14–18.
Becker, B., Huselid, M., & Ulrich, D. (2001). *The HR scorecard: Linking people, strategy and performance*. Boston: Harward Business School Press.
Bergold, J. (2007). Participatory strategies in community psychology research—A short survey. In A. Bokszczanin (Ed.), *Poland welcomes community psychology: Proceedings from the 6th European conference on community psychology* (pp. 57–66). Opole: Opole University Press.
Bersin, J., Collins, L., Mallon, D., Moir, J., & Straub, R. (2012). People analytics. In B. Pelster & J. Schwartz (Eds.), *Global human capital trends 2016*. Retrieved from https://www2.deloitte.com/content/dam/Deloitte/global/Documents/HumanCapital/gx-dup-global-human-capital-trends-2016.pdf
Boudreau, J. W. (2015). Talent ship and HR measurement and analysis: From ROI to strategic organizational change. *People and Strategy, 29*(1), 25.

Carlson, K. D., & Kavanagh, M. J. (2012). HR metrics and workforce analytics. In M. J. Kavanagh & M. Thite (Eds.), *Human resource information systems: Basics applications and future directions* (1st ed., pp. 150–174). Thousand Oaks, CA: Sage Publishing.

Carlson, K. D., & Kavanagh, M. J. (2015). In M. J. Kavanagh, M. Thite, & R. D. Johnson (Eds.), *Human resource information systems* (3rd ed.). Thousand Oaks, CA: SAGE Publications.

Davenport, T. H., & Harris, J. (2007). *Competing on analytics: The new science of winning*. Boston, MA: Harvard Business School Press.

Davenport, T. H., Harris, J., & Shapiro, J. (2010, October). Competing on talent analytics. *Harvard Business Review*, 52–58.

Douthitt, S., & Mondroe, S. (2013). Maximizing the impact and effectiveness of HR analytics to drive business outcomes. *People and Strategy, 34*(2), 20–27.

Dulebohn, J., & Johnson, R. (2013). Human resource metrics and decision. *Human Resource Management Review, 23*, 71–83.

Fitz-enz, J. (2010). *How to measure human resources management*. New York, NY: McGraw-Hill.

Fitz-enz, J., & Mattox, J. (2014). *Wiley and SAS business series: Predictive analytics for human resources*. Hoboken, NJ: Wiley.

Gale, S. (2015, August). Predict (still in) the future. *Human Resource Management Systems, 44*–47.

George, J. H., & Kamalanabhan, J. W. (2016). An evidence-based review of talent analytics. *The International Journal of Human Resource Management, 28*(1), 3–26.

Holsapple, G., Perrewé, P., Ranft, A., Zinko, R., Stoner, J., Brouer, R., et al. (2014). Human resource reputation and effectiveness. *Human Resource Management Review, 17*(2), 117–130.

Jensen, K., & Eriksen, M. (2016). In M. Kavanagh, M. Thite, & R. Johnson (Eds.), *Human resource information systems* (3rd ed.). Thousand Oaks, CA: SAGE Publications.

Kaplan, R., & Norton, D. (1996). *The balanced scorecard: Translating strategy into action*. Cambridge, MA: Harvard College.

Lawler, E. E., Levenson, A., & Boudreau, J. W. (2004). HR metrics and analytics: Use and impact. *Human Resource Planning, 27*, 27–35.

Levenson, A. (2013). The promise of big data for HR. *People & Strategy, 36*(4), 22–26.

Marler, J. H., & Boudreau, J. W. (2017). An evidence-based review of talent analytics. *The International Journal of Human Resource Management, 28*(1), 3–26.

Pape, T. (2016). Prioritizing data items for business analytics: Framework and application to human resources. *European Journal of Operational Research, 252*, 687–698.

Pemmaraju, S. (2007). Converting HR data to business intelligence. *Employment Relations Today, 34*(3), 13–16.

Rasmussen, T., & Ulrich, D. (2015). Learning from practice: How talent analytics avoids being a management fad. *Organization Dynamics, 44*(3), 236–242.

Reason, P., & Bradbury, H. (2008). Introduction. In P. Reason & H. Bradbury (Eds.), *The Sage handbook of action research. Participative inquiry and practice* (2nd ed., pp. 1–10). London: Sage.

Sen, E. F. (2015). Data visualization. In S. Tonidandel, E. King, & J. Cortina (Eds.), *Big data at work: The data science revolution and organizational psychology* (pp. 115–157). New York, NY: Routledge.

Ulrich, D., & Dulebohn, J. (2015). Are we there yet? What's next for HR? *Human Resource Management Review, 25*, 188–204.

CHAPTER 4

The Impact of Customer Relationship Management (CRM) Practices on Customer Satisfaction

Subhasish Das and Manit Mishra

INTRODUCTION

The statement "Customers are the king of the market" seems to be true in its actual sense today. Firms can survive and sustain by creating valuable customers and keeping them forever. This requires delivering value at every customer interaction. Therefore, Customer Relationship Management (CRM) is necessary for the existence of a business. CRM can be a tool to manage the customer life cycle—acquisition, satisfaction, retention and development. Managing customer life cycle by adopting the most suitable CRM practices is the key objective of CRM. This chapter analyzes the effect of a firm's CRM practices on customer satisfaction.

S. Das (✉)
CUTM, Jatni, Odisha, India

M. Mishra
International Management Institute, Bhubaneswar, Odisha, India
e-mail: manit.mishra@imibh.edu.in

© The Author(s) 2019
Rajagopal, R. Behl (eds.), *Business Governance and Society*,
https://doi.org/10.1007/978-3-319-94613-9_4

Literature Review

CRM is an enterprise-wide business strategy designed to optimize profitability, revenue and customer satisfaction by organizing the enterprise around customer segments, fostering customer-satisfying behaviors and linking processes from customers through suppliers (Nelson & Eisenfeld 2003a). CRM is used to acquire, satisfy and retain customers; the primary goal of CRM is customer satisfaction and delight at all levels of the customer interface (Pahuja and Verma 2008).

CRM is increasingly popular and being used by both medium and large enterprises. CRM is useful only if it is implemented properly. CRM used to be practiced at the departmental level, but Nelson & Eisenfeld (2003a) suggests that CRM will not be successful unless it is implemented at the enterprise level. Gartner identifies eight building blocks of CRM that, if followed and implemented properly, will result in successful CRM. The eight building blocks are vision, strategy, valued customer experience, organizational collaboration, process, information, technology and metrics. The first four building blocks focus on best practices and the remaining four represent the areas where the practices should be applied. This study is based on Gartner's first four building blocks and their influence on customer satisfaction.

Vision

Vision includes all that is necessary to create the picture of a customer-centric enterprise. It has further been suggested that a strong vision requires development of leadership at the top that permeates the enterprise and is committed to the idea of CRM and becoming customer-centric. There should be clarity among all employees regarding the objectives of using CRM and how CRM is going to help. It has also been suggested that the enterprise must understand how unique CRM is for the enterprise (Nelson & Eisenfeld 2003a).

Strategy

It is necessary to develop a strategy to turn a customer base into assets by delivering customer value propositions. As per Nelson & Eisenfeld (2003a), this can be achieved by developing a long-term road map to fit decisions and articulating the goals and tactics to achieve them. At the same time, the enterprise must realize that CRM is a combination of technology, people, process and politics, and that all customers are not equal.

Valued Customer Experience

Nelson & Eisenfeld (2003a) suggests that customers' experience while interacting with the enterprise is highly important in shaping their perceptions about the organization. The enterprise can deliver ongoing value to customers by involving customers in the CRM process and integrating all channels seamlessly, and by getting the basics right first and managing the change and the communication with the customer.

Organizational Collaboration

CRM requires a high level of organizational collaboration. Implementation of CRM requires a change in culture from a product-centrism to a customer-centrism, a change in organization structure and behavior. Enterprises must set cross-functional teams, integrate change management and training from the start, and appoint an overall CRM leader (Nelson & Eisenfeld 2003a). The CRM best practices building blocks are applicable to CRM processes such as customer lifecycle management and knowledge management to enhance customer satisfaction and loyalty (Nelson & Eisenfeld 2003a). Satisfaction is a function of all satisfaction-oriented transactions (Johnson et al. 1995; Shin and Kim 2008).

Objective of the Study

The objective of the study is to understand the effect of Gartner's best practices for CRM on customer satisfaction. Gartner's study suggests that vision, strategy, customer experience and organizational culture will affect customer life cycle (acquisition, satisfaction, retention and development). Therefore, this study uses Gartner's framework and analyzes the influence of Gartner's CRM best practices on customer satisfaction. The hypotheses of the study are as follows:

H_{01}: Vision of the enterprise has no effect on customer satisfaction
H_{02}: Strategy of the enterprise has no effect on customer satisfaction
H_{03}: Customer experience has no effect on customer satisfaction
H_{04}: Organizational collaboration has no effect on customer satisfaction

Research Location

We conducted our research in the city of Bhubaneswar, also called the "Temple city of Odisha." It is one of the planned cities of India. With the flow of time, the city has gradually developed in both organized and unorganized retail. Today the city has around 15 organized retail giants catering to the shopping needs of the city dwellers; one of the biggest is Big Bazaar. It started its operation at Bhubaneswar in 2004, making it one of the oldest organized retailers in the city. This study focuses on the Big Bazaar retailer in Kharvel Nagar because it deals in a varied nature of products and has been able to attract different segments of the market. It is also one of the oldest retailers in the city practicing CRM.

Research Methodology

Our research is descriptive in nature and collected primary data through direct interview with the help of a questionnaire. We took care in collecting the primary and secondary sources of data as well as in its analysis. We designed the research on the basis of the objectives and the problem to be investigated. The study was conducted at Big Bazaar in Kharvel Nagar, one of the biggest shopping malls in the city. Big Bazaar attracts almost all segments of the market as it deals with a large variety of products in a wide range of prices. Therefore, it attracts all types, levels and segments of customers. Our research sample consists of 397 respondents who are employees of the retail store. The respondents are of different designations and departments. The employees belong to all the levels (top, middle, low) of the shopping mall, including store keeper, attender, sales executives, floor manager, marketing manager and so on. They also come from different departments, including sales, marketing, stock keeping, transport, maintenance and so on. The respondents were questioned with a prearranged questionnaire to bring forth the primary data.

Measures

We prepared a scale of 17 items for the study; 13 items belong to the CRM best practices suggested by Nelson & Eisenfeld (2003b) and the remaining four items are for measuring customer satisfaction (Anderson and Srinivasan 2003; Cronin and Taylor 1992; Kim et al. 2004; Oliver 1997; Shin and Kim 2008; Turel and Serenko 2006; Zeithml et al. 2011).

The scale measures constructs such as vision, strategy, valued customer experience, organizational collaboration and customer satisfaction.

Hair et al. (2007) suggests conducting a pretest before the actual survey. Therefore, we conducted a pretest with a small sample of 30 respondents who are similar to the actual respondents to check the appropriateness of the scale. We checked the scale for its appropriateness, ambiguity and ease of response, and determined it to be good. Then we finalized the scale and carried out the survey with around 450 respondents. However, some of the responses were not complete; hence our final sample consists of 397 respondents who provided complete information. First, we conducted an exploratory factor analysis to understand the underlying constructs. We followed this with a confirmatory factor analysis to check how well the specification of factors fit the data.

Data Analysis and Inferences

Structural equation modeling (SEM) is used to analyze the data and the model. SEM includes two models: a measurement model and a structural model. A measurement model tells how well the measured variables represent the constructs and a structural model describes the structural relationships among the constructs.

Measurement Model

The adequacy of the measurement model can be checked by confirmatory factor analysis (CFA) (Teo 2011). CFA helps in understanding the extent to which measured variables represent the construct (Hair et al. 2007). With the help of Amos.20 (Analysis of moment structures version 20), the measurement model is tested by taking all five constructs extracted from exploratory factor analysis done through SPSS.20. Through CFA, the parameters of the model are estimated by maximum likelihood estimation. Maximum likelihood is a better estimation method than the other estimations (Lai et al. 2007).

Before proceeding to CFA, it is necessary to check the construct validity. Construct validity ensures that the set of items actually represent the theoretical latent construct. It can be tested through convergent validity and discriminant validity. Convergent validity identifies the proportion of variance for each item. Discriminant validity examines to what extent an independent variable is truly distinct from other independent variables in measuring the dependent variable (Hair et al. 2007). Convergent validity can be tested with the help of standardized factor loadings, composite reliability (CR) and average variance extracted (AVE). Ideally, all values should be more than 0.7 (Hair et al. 2007). In this model, all values for standardized factor loadings, CR and AVE are more than 0.7, which represents a strong convergent validity (see Table 4.2). Discriminant validity can be tested with the help of AVE and maximum shared variance (MSV). AVE should be greater than MSV for the discriminant validity. In this model, AVE is greater than MSV for all constructs (see Table 4.1) indicating discriminant validity. Therefore, the measurement model shows good construct validity.

For the measurement model to have a good model fit, the root mean square of approximation (RMSEA) should be less than 0.08, and the values of goodness of fit index (GFI), adjusted goodness of fit index (AGFI), normed fit index (NFI) and comparative fit index (CFI) all should exceed a threshold value of 0.9. The ratio of chi square (χ^2) and degrees of freedom (df) should be less than 2.5 (Gerpott et al. 2001; Homburg and Baumgartner 1995; Hair et al. 2007). The summary of the measurement model is RMSEA is 0.062; GFI is 0.913 (above threshold); AGFI is 0.881 (below threshold); NFI is 0.957 (above threshold); CFI is 0.977 (above threshold); and χ^2/df is 2.074. Excluding AGFI, all other measures are more than their threshold values, indicating a good model fit (see Table 4.2). The adequacy of the measurement model indicates that the items are reliable indicators of hypothesized constructs and it allows for testing structural relationships (Teo 2011).

STRUCTURAL MODEL

Structural equation modeling is used to test the hypotheses. The summary of the structural model is as follows: RMSEA is 0.051; GFI is 0.933 (above threshold); AGFI is 0.908 (above threshold); NFI is 0.963 (above threshold); CFI is 0.981 (above threshold); and χ^2/df is 2.026. All measures are more than their threshold values, therefore the structural model indicates a good model fit (see Table 4.3).

The test of the structural model indicates that Vision ($c = 0.54$, $p < 0.01$) and Collaboration ($c = 0.238$, $p < 0.01$) are found to be significantly influencing customer satisfaction. The organizational vision is the most significant influencer of satisfaction. The second positive influencer is organizational

Table 4.1 Discriminant validity

	CR	AVE	MSV	MaxR (H)	Collaboration	Vision	Strategy	Experience	Satisfaction
Collaboration	0.898	0.696	0.213	0.944	0.834				
Vision	0.872	0.872	0.450	0.959	0.400	0.934			
Strategy	0.895	0.740	0.144	0.970	0.231		0.009		
Experience	0.931	0.772	0.000	0.982	0.013				
Satisfaction	0.965	0.875	0.450	0.989	0.461	0.671	0.379	−0.004	

Table 4.2 Model fit summary for the measurement model

CMIN					
Model	NPAR	CMIN	DF	P	CMIN/DF
Default model	46	259.299	125	0	2.074
Saturated model	171	0	0		
Independence model	18	6048.755	153	0	39.534
RMR, GFI					
Model	RMR	GFI	AGFI	PGFI	
Default model	0.053	0.913	0.881	0.667	
Saturated model	0	1			
Independence model	0.717	0.245	0.156	0.219	
Baseline comparisons					
Model	NFI	RFI	IFI	TLI	CFI
	Delta1	rho1	Delta2	rho2	
Default model	0.957	0.948	0.977	0.972	0.977
Saturated model	1		1		1
Independence model	0	0	0	0	0
RMSEA					
Model	RMSEA	LO 90	HI 90	PCLOSE	
Default model	0.062	0.051	0.072	0.037	
Independence model	0.369	0.361	0.377	0	

Model fit summary for the measurement model

Table 4.3 Model fit summary for structural model

CMIN					
Model	NPAR	CMIN	DF	P	CMIN/DF
Default model	46	253.257	125	0	2.026
Saturated model	171	0	0		
Independence model	18	6779.21	153	0	44.309
RMR, GFI					
Model	RMR	GFI	AGFI	PGFI	
Default model	0.045	0.933	0.908	0.682	
Saturated model	0	1			
Independence model	0.626	0.276	0.191	0.247	
Baseline comparisons					
Model	NFI	RFI	IFI	TLI	CFI
	Delta1	rho1	Delta2	rho2	
Default model	0.963	0.954	0.981	0.976	0.981
Saturated model	1		1		1
Independence model	0	0	0	0	0
RMSEA					
Model	RMSEA	LO 90	HI 90	PCLOSE	
Default model	0.051	0.042	0.06	0.422	
Independence model	0.331	0.324	0.337	0	

Model fit summary for the structural model

collaboration. Therefore, practices like development of leadership, employee understanding about CRM and its benefits, cross-functional teams, training and change management and appointment of a CRM leader will positively influence customer satisfaction. Strategy, valued customer experiences are not statistically significant influencers of customer satisfaction. Though strategy has an insignificant association in our study, it still has a positive influence (see Table 4.5).

Conclusion

The study finds that firm practices related to organizational vision and organizational collaboration will positively influence customer satisfaction. Therefore, companies must concentrate on the practices related to these areas, such as developing leadership, understanding the uniqueness of CRM and how it can help, establishing cross-functional teams, changing management and training from the start, and appointing a CRM leader. The responses of the respondents are based on their attitudes towards the Big Bazaar shopping mall and the study may not be generalized as it is micro in nature.

Appendix

Table 4.4 (Scale for the study) questionnaire

Sl. No	Variables	Measurement
1	V1	Development of leadership from the top.
2	V2	Understand how CRM will help
3	V3	How CRM is unique
4	S1	Development of a long term CRM roadmap
5	S2	Articulate CRM goals and tactics
6	S3	All customers are not equal
7	VCE1	Involvement of customers in CRM process
8	VCE2	Integration of all channels
9	VCE3	Manage change and communication with your customers
10	VCE4	Get the basics right first
11	OC1	Establishment of cross functional teams
12	OC2	Integrate change management and training from the start
13	OC3	Appointment of an overall CRM
14	CS1	Overall satisfaction of CRM
15	CS2	Meeting customer needs and making them happy
16	CS3	Customers feel good
17	CS4	Preferred by the customer

Table 4.5 Regression weights: (group number 1—default model)

			Estimate	S.E.	C.R.	P	Label
Satisfaction	<–	Vision	0.518	0.046	11.151	***	
Satisfaction	<–	Strategy	0.128	0.050	2.566	0.010	
Satisfaction	<–	Experiences	−0.032	0.038	−0.837	0.403	
Satisfaction	<–	Collaboration	0.238	0.047	5.106	***	
V3	<–	Vision	0.722	0.030	24.129	***	
V2	<–	Vision	0.784	0.033	24.076	***	
V1	<–	Vision	1.000				
VCE4	<–	Experiences	0.936	0.027	35.159	***	
VCE3	<–	Experiences	1.000				
VCE2	<–	Experiences	0.983	0.032	30.992	***	
VCE1	<–	Experiences	0.766	0.044	17.485	***	
S3	<–	Strategy	0.859	0.041	20.885	***	
S2	<–	Strategy	1.000				
S1	<–	Strategy	0.926	0.045	20.756	***	
OC4	<–	Collaboration	0.557	0.046	12.239	***	
OC3	<–	Collaboration	0.946	0.036	26.645	***	
OC2	<–	Collaboration	1.000				
OC1	<–	Collaboration	0.972	0.030	32.208	***	
CS1	<–	Satisfaction	1.000				
CS2	<–	Satisfaction	0.917	0.020	45.339	***	
CS3	<–	Satisfaction	0.864	0.025	33.979	***	
CS4	<–	Satisfaction	0.868	0.025	34.673		

Table 4.6 Standardized regression weights: (group number 1—default model)

			Estimate
Satisfaction	<–	Vision	0.540
Satisfaction	<–	Strategy	0.113
Satisfaction	<–	Experiences	−0.032
Satisfaction	<–	Collaboration	0.219
V3	<–	Vision	0.849
V2	<–	Vision	0.848
V1	<–	Vision	0.934
VCE4	<–	Experiences	0.960
VCE3	<–	Experiences	0.916
VCE2	<–	Experiences	0.916
VCE1	<–	Experiences	0.700
S3	<–	Strategy	0.855
S2	<–	Strategy	0.876

(continued)

Table 4.6 (continued)

			Estimate
S1	<-	Strategy	0.850
OC4	<-	Collaboration	0.548
OC3	<-	Collaboration	0.861
OC2	<-	Collaboration	0.937
OC1	<-	Collaboration	0.929
CS1	<-	Satisfaction	0.945
CS2	<-	Satisfaction	0.972
CS3	<-	Satisfaction	0.909
CS4	<-	Satisfaction	0.914

REFERENCES

Anderson, R. E., & Srinivasan, S. S. (2003). E-satisfaction and e-loyalty: A contingency framework. *Psychology and Marketing, 20*(2), 123e138.

Cronin Jr., J. J., & Taylor, S. A. (1992). Measuring service quality: A reexamination and extension. *Journal of Marketing, 56*(3), 55e68.

Gerpott, T. J., Rams, W., & Schindler, A. (2001). Customer retention, loyalty and satisfaction in the german cellular telecommunications market. *Telecommunications Policy, 25*(4), 249e269.

Hair, J. F., Jr., Anderson, R. E.,Tatham, R. L., Babin, B. J., & Black, W. C. (2007). *Multivariate data analysis* (6th International ed.). Delhi: Dorling Kindersley (India) Pvt. Ltd.

Homburg, C., & Baumgartner, H. (1995). Beurteilung von Kausalmodelen. *Marketing, 17*(3), 162e176.

Johnson, D., Anderson, E., & Fornell, C. (1995). Rational and adaptive performance expectations in a customer satisfaction framework. *Journal of Consumer Research, 21*(4), 695e707.

Kim, M., Park, M., & Jeong, D. (2004). The effects of customer satisfaction and switching Barrie on customer loalty in th ekorean telecommunication services. *Telecommunications Policy, 28*(2), 145e159.

Lai, F., Hutchison, J., Li, D., & Bai, C. (2007). An empirical assessment and application of SERVQUAL in mainland china's mobile communications industry. *International Journal of Quality and Reliability Management, 24*(3), 244e262.

Nelson, S., & Eisenfeld, B. (2003a). *CRM best practices: From strategy to collaboration*. Gartner Report COM-21-1015.

Nelson, S., & Eisenfeld, B. (2003b). *CRM best practices: From processes to metrics*. Gartner Report COM-21-1108.

Oliver, R. L. (1997). *Satisfcation: A behavioral perspective on the consumer.* New York, NY: Mc Graw Hill.

Pahuja, A., & Verma, R. (2008, January). Customer relationship management need of the hour. *Marketing Mastermind,* 26–29.

Shin, D.-H., & Kim, W.-Y. (2008). Forecasting customer switching intention in mobile services: An exploratory study of predictive factors in mobile number portability. *Technological Forecasting and Social Change, 75*(6), 854e874.

Teo, T. (2011). Factors influencing teachers' intention to use technology: Model development and test. *Computers & Education, 57*(4), 2432–2440.

Turel, O., & Serenko, A. (2006). Satisfaction with mobile services in Canada: An empirical investigation. *Telecomunication Policy, 30*(5e6), 314e331.

Zeithml, V. A., Bitner, M. J., Gremler, D. D., & Pandit, A. (2011). *Services marketing* (5th ed.). Boston: McGraw-Hill Publishing Company Limited.

CHAPTER 5

Customer Expectations at the Urban Bottom of Pyramid in India: A Grounded Theory Approach

Ritu Srivastava

INTRODUCTION: BOTTOM OF THE PYRAMID IS IMPORTANT

The marketing discipline has evolved through the context of the industrialized or developed world. However, the largest group of consumers are also the poorest. Prahalad and Hart (2002) refer to them as the Bottom of the Pyramid (BOP). They divide the world's population into four tiers. At the very top of the World Economic Pyramid are 75 to 100 million affluent Tier 1 consumers from around the world. This is a cosmopolitan group composed of middle- and upper-income people in developed countries and the few rich elite from the developing world. In the middle of the pyramid, in Tiers 2 and 3, are the poor customers in developed nations and the rising middle classes in developing countries. The remaining customers, approximately 4 billion people, are in Tier 4. This group has a per capita income of less than $2 a day, the minimum required to sustain a decent human life. Prahalad and Hart's article highlighted that the extreme inequity of wealth distribution reinforces the view that poor cannot par-

---

R. Srivastava (✉)
Management Development Institute, Gurgaon, Haryana, India
e-mail: ritu.srivastava@mdi.ac.in

© The Author(s) 2019
Rajagopal, R. Behl (eds.), *Business Governance and Society*,
https://doi.org/10.1007/978-3-319-94613-9_5

ticipate in the global market economy, even though they constitute the majority of the population. However, the bright spot was that here lies a vast opportunity that multinational corporations (MNCs) have typically ignored. Because of their familiarity with Tier 1 customers and certain assumptions about the BOP consumer group, the MNCs have ignored this population. Prahalad and Hart, however, illustrated in their article the immense potential of this consumer group to be profitable if the business models are changed. Tier 4 was not a market that allowed for traditional pursuit of high margins; instead, profits were driven by volume and capital efficiency. Margins would be low, but unit sales extremely high. The idea is that managers who focus on high margins will miss opportunity, but managers who innovate and focus on economic profits will be rewarded at the BOP. Thus, to serve these customers it is important to understand their expectations and what controls them.

Tier 4 Markets: The Context Sets the Discipline

Sheth (2011), in his article 'Impact of Emerging Markets on Marketing: Rethinking Existing Perspectives and Practices' published in the *Journal of Marketing*, makes the point that as emerging markets evolved from the periphery to the core of marketing practices, there was a need to contend with their unique characteristics and question existing practices and perspectives that have developed in a different context. The Tier 4 markets, also referred to as emerging markets, need to be looked at through the marketing perspective with the following questions: Will the emerging markets be driven by marketing as we know today, or will the emerging markets drive future marketing practice and discipline as emphasized by Sheth? The article further mentioned that as all advanced countries are aging, and aging very rapidly, their domestic markets were either stagnant or growing very slowly. Their future seemed more destined to come from emerging markets. He elaborated that the tone of extant literature in marketing was colonial in the mindsets on emerging markets. The colonial mindset was a hindrance to recognizing these markets as unique entities. Marketing as a discipline would benefit immensely if it could transcend prevailing beliefs, stereotypes and research traditions in these markets. The BOP market could be seen as a case of demand fulfillment rather than demand generation, as in these markets affordability and accessibility were more important for differential advantage than a superior but expensive product or service with limited access. These customers had no access to electricity, running water, banking or modern transportation. Most of them were illiterate and did not read newspapers, magazines or books, or watch television. The heterogeneity of emerging markets was less driven through diversity of needs, wants and aspirations of consumers and more driven by resource constraints, such as a range of haves and have-nots with respect to both income and net worth. The diversity with respect to access to products and services was enormous between rural and urban households.

Sheth emphasized that the market system needed a rethink. Because of a chronic shortage of resources, there was a need for market creation (shift to buying from making) and market development rather than market orientation. Informal, unbranded competition was abundant as products were available at cheaper prices, credit, retailer middlemen relationship and access. Companies may have to look at consumer resources before building their approach to obtaining a differential competitive advantage. If demand fulfillment and market development were the needs of this market, then the first step should be to understand the consumers and their behaviors. Kolk et al. (2014) conducted a literature review of BOP articles and identified that the majority of the articles were published in journals targeting a practitioner audience rather than an academic audience. Although subjective in view, only one third of the studies were published in pure academic journals. The authors found the asymmetry in the number of articles published in the two types of journals interesting. According to them, the large number of articles in practitioner-oriented journals may have reflected a preference of BOP scholars for high-impact articles with direct application among practitioners, but it may also have been due to the type of studies prevalent in BOP articles, including case studies or studies with limited theoretical contributions, which could be more difficult to prove in some academic journals. The authors also thought that this disparity could be due to the parochial nature of journals with editors and reviewers disfavoring new research streams. This asymmetry was also evident in the main goals of the BOP articles. Most articles focused on offering advice on strategy and marketing for companies that wanted to enter the BOP. Some articles were devoted to evaluation and critique of BOP ideas and initiatives; some were devoted to reporting on cases of BOP initiatives to describe products considered to be suitable for the BOP by the authors. A very small number of articles focused on the BOP market characteristics. The authors considered this small number surprising given the extent to which uniqueness of BOP markets is emphasized in

BOP research. A cross-sectional analysis revealed many articles in marketing, but the emphasis had been on strategy, product and promotion. However, consumers' behavior and their expectations received little attention. In the Indian context, there were a few consumer-related studies in this segment. An EBSCOhost search of BOP revealed 2096 articles; however, after filtering for 'Consumer Behavior', we found just 52 articles and only nine in the Indian BOP context, mainly from 2009 to 2017. Significantly, one author contributed to three or more articles. This result shows that BOP as a whole, and consumer behavior in particular, have not received much scholarly attention and that there is a need for India-specific studies. The unique nature of the BOP segment calls for indigenous research. To utilize the immense opportunity at the base, corporations have to start identifying and understanding customer expectations where scholarly research can bridge the gap.

The Need

There was a difference between urban BOP and rural BOP. Literature considered both as the same and had given insights mostly for rural BOP. However, the urban BOP was the next tier that MNCs could target because customers living in the cities were exposed to the same lifestyle and stimuli as other middle-income group segments and had similar aspirations.

BOP Offers Scale and Scope

Prahalad (2004), Drucker (1958), Dawar and Chattopadhyay (2000) and Mahajan et al. (2000) advocated the view that marketing to the poor in developing countries was perhaps the best way to develop emerging economies and corporate profits as BOP offers advantages in both scale and scope, but business models, products and services have to be redesigned to improve value and reduce cost.

Incrementalism Will Not Work

Firms will have to become deeply embedded with the BOP to create products and services this consumer group needs. To understand BOP customers, a qualitative approach is required before proceeding to the quantitative one as it is a new and developing area (Ireland 2008).

Defining the Urban Poor

As highlighted in the previous section, the extant literature on BOP builds on the business potential because of their advantages in scale and scope. However, success with distant, dispersed and very poor people can only be achieved if MNCs redesign their business models, products and services to drastically improve value and reduce costs (Ireland 2008). The new research attacked both sides, but there was always an important business concern related to profits. BOP will always be a profitless target because it is so impoverished that consumers in this group are unable to purchase MNC goods regardless of the financing offered or cost reductions achieved. This is the very reason that led MNCs to avoid this market that they considered terrible. Could there be a worse market in which to seek supernormal profits than one that is distant, dispersed, desperately poor, largely illiterate and heterogeneous as well as economically, politically and physically risky? Considerable evidence summarized by Karnani (2007) backs the assertion that it is difficult to make profits in rural BOP. Ireland (2008) suggested three ways to deal with the concern. First is to leave this large segment entirely; second is to appreciate that since these markets cannot become profitable they will need subsidies; and third is to make the BOP proposition work by following appropriate procedures especially in developing suitable intermediaries. Hart claimed that incrementalism was a problem and the BOP proposition could only succeed if firms became deeply embedded in BOP so that they engaged in co-creation and thus developed appropriate products and services. But Ireland, Gusselga and Marshall suggested a fourth approach: target the urban areas in emerging markets that house a growing population—the world's impoverished customers. While they belong to the BOP segment, they are not the same as rural BOP.

Many rural BOP customers have migrated to urban centers in metros or neighbouring locations in search of livelihoods and have spent considerable amount of time there. Many urban BOP residents are desperately impoverished, indeed starving, despite their relatively high incomes due to high costs of city living. Unitus seed funds have defined urban BOP as customer households with typically five to seven members and an income of Rs. 25,000 (equivalent to US $373.66 at the exchange of April 26, 2018) per month in the cities in India. This group was a layer above rural BOP whom companies tend to avoid because of low profits, also referred to as the next billion by Boston Consulting Group (BCG). Their profiles, socioeconomic characteristics and demographics are different than both rural BOP and middle- and higher-income groups, which have been the focus of corporate and marketing literature.

Many experts considered it pointless to segment the rural BOP, partly due to its market size, but also because it was naturally segmented into minute markets by language, culture and geography. Considering the urban BOP segment, which is comprised mainly of immigrants, is relatively homogeneous in macro terms such as language and culture in small pockets, with similar education and lifestyle, they could still be clubbed only as one large, price-sensitive emerging market segment. These urban residents speak the national language and move about in large cities, they are well exposed to modern advertising media, customs and fashion and tend to want the same goods as the inhabitants of formal areas of some cities. The urban BOP could be segmented on the basis of occupation, education, values, family structures, attitudes towards brands and income levels and geographic location.

There was a difference between rural and urban BOP marketing as the people in the urban group also lived in the center that surrounded planned districts and shopped at organized markets in formal areas. Since they were mostly salaried, they planned their purchases. These two traits combined to allow BOP to seek the best possible prices, subject to the constraint of convenience, by using different retailers' options on different shopping occasions. This was completely different than the rural BOP where consumers shop daily and generally in the same location. The implication would be that the successful marketing practices in rural BOP may not achieve success in the urban BOP such as on sachets, which modified the SKU size, breaking it into lower volume per piece.

Research Gap

Following the co-creation logic as proposed by Hart, the consumers in this segment must be studied in their own right. To satisfy them, it is important to understand their expectations in each emerging market context specifically, instead of adapting or generalizing research studies as has been the approach to now. This study is the start of such an initiative in the Indian context. The study aims to address a very simple research objective of trying to understand the urban BOP customers in India.

Research Approach

Scholars Gebauer and Reynoso (2013), Ray Fisk et al. (2016) and Sheth (2011) proposed that a different research approach be adopted to study BOP markets. The agenda for BOP service research of Gebauer and Reynoso (2013) included leveraging co-creation and resource integration in this context. The authors suggest that researchers and practitioners need to move from passive, traditional perspectives on the BOP to take proactive actions. This study is an attempt in this direction using a different approach detailed in subsequent sections. Practitioners should shift from just selling to the BOP to involving low-income customers as active participants in the co-creation of new services to improve their wellbeing. Researchers should shift from the survey approach to greater engagement through action research, case studies and participant observation.

Justification for the Grounded Theory Approach

In their seminal article, Prahalad and Hart (2002) suggest that the BOP offers immense potential for growth and profits, but doing business with the world's 4 billion poor people would require radical innovations in technology and business models. It would require MNCs to reevaluate the price-performance relationship for products and services. It would demand a new level of capital efficiency and new ways of measuring success. Companies would be forced to transform this understanding of scale from the ideal that bigger is to an ideal of highly distributed, small-scale operations married to world-scale capabilities. In short, the poorest populations would raise an extraordinary challenge for the world's wealthiest companies; selling to the poor and helping them improve their lives by producing and distributing products and services in culturally sensitive, environmentally sustainable and economically profitable ways. This would require breaking free from the assumptions we hold for this market and understanding them in their own right, through a new lens. Only then can innovations happen in the direction as mentioned previously. Since the start of the millennium, many scholars have highlighted the differences in otherwise neglected markets through different terms such as 'emerging markets', 'BOP markets', 'subsistence markets' and so on, but all have also emphasized following a different methodology that is more suited to the context. There have only been nine marketing studies done in India.

The present marketing literature as it has developed has taken a direction based on certain conditions. While they may be true and applicable in a given context, they may not be in certain other contexts and need to be changed. In their seminal work that launched grounded theory, Glaser and Strauss (1967) defined it as the discovery of theory from data systematically obtained and analyzed in social research. The key point was that the theory produced is grounded in data. Creswell (1998) and Dey (1999) explained the key features of the grounded theory method as listed below. It served as a good base to position this study upon.

(a) The aim of grounded theory is to generate or discover theory.
(b) The researcher has to set aside theoretical ideas in order to let the substantive ideas emerge. This is very difficult for a very fundamental topic, which this study topic is. The literature has evolved so much and most of the research scholars and practitioners, myself included, have imbibed it deeply.

Though this research approach has been less adopted in marketing, it was the most suited methodology for the present study. Marketing theory has typically followed a positivist approach whereas an interpreter's approach to the same reality can be very different in a BOP emerging market context. This reflexivity is at times desired when things are being viewed in a particular way and a new learning may arise on changing the way. It was indeed challenging to initiate the study on BOP without referring to the literature, but I chose not to dive into the literature thus avoiding any bias while letting the understanding develop from scratch given the uniqueness of the context.

Instead of choosing a quantitative approach that gets greater acceptability because of information constraints, Ireland in his research on Venezuelan BOP justified a research design based on multiple cases that were to be treated as a series of experiments to disconfirm theory (Yin 1994) and to develop new theory by contrasting data with existing theory as proposed by Glaser and Strauss (1967).

This study originated from the point of wanting to understand broadly what marketing means to BOP customers, that is, how and what are their expectations, how do they typically shop across products and what gives them satisfaction? Basically, it was important to understand how they normally made a purchase, where, when, why and how. Informal semi-structured interviews were conducted using the following questions:

1. What made them happy in their purchase?
2. How did they typically shop for different kinds of products?
3. What gave them satisfaction?
4. Who were the major influencers in their purchase decision making?
5. What was their purchase process like?

It is also important to mention studies from within the service perspective, such as those by Gronroos (2001) and Vargo and Lusch (2004). These studies explained that fundamental of any exchange is viewed as service. This service concept is now applied to all kinds of products, sectors, segments and economies. In fact, most fast-moving consumer goods (FMCG) and consumer durables industries today are competing on services. I chose the products for this study based on this philosophy so that the emerging findings do not get lost in the debate on goods versus services.

Research Philosophy

While I have already detailed the background of this research study, it is important to mention that although the field of marketing in general and services in particular has a legacy of more than 200 years, there has been no indigenous research with the aim of understanding the discipline from the Indian context only. The larger outcome has been to further the theories built in the context of industrialized nations. Although the discipline and area of this study is not a new one, changing the perspective through which you look at it may evolve a new meaning and/or theory. The subject of study and the outcome was dependent on the researcher's perception of the reality—how the world was constructed, referred to as ontology by Orlikowski and Baroudi (1991), and how knowledge was constructed, referred to as epistemology. This conceptualization phase of the research was very important as the research design was dependent on the philosophical position taken for the research. Management in general and marketing in particular had followed a positivist paradigm basically because there may have been a capitalist stance taken by the industrialized nations to development of marketing theory. It is important to mention here that we are talking of the broad marketing direction of the discipline rather than building on individual studies. Even qualitative studies have contributed to the functionalist/positivist paradigm.

This research study took a *critical realist position* that had a subjective view of reality and believed that society needs to be radically critiqued. This was the radical humanist view proposed by Burrell and Morgan (1979), which focused on why the social reality (in this case marketing) was constructed in a particular way revolving and asking whose interests were served by the construction and sublimation to the deep structure level. It revolved around four key debates about the nature of sociology and whether marketing may be seen as a social science:

1. What was the nature of reality—was it given or a product of the mind?
2. Was it necessary to experience something in order to understand it?
3. Did human beings have free will or is their behaviour determined by their environment?
4. Was understanding best gained directly or through scientific method?

Grounded Theory Methodology Adopted

To begin with the grounded theory method for the study, it was important to draw a participant profile as India is a land of heterogeneous population based on sociodemographic variables. The participants chosen belonged to an average household size of five members living in the city of Gurgaon, India with some elementary education (enough to read and write), the number of earning members in the household was approximately three and monthly household income was less than or equal to INR 300,000 per annum. This segment has typically been classified as urban BOP[1] and represents 20 percent of the Indian BOP population. The first phase of the research involved interviewing participants who fit the set parameters. The following steps were taken (Fig. 5.1);

Following this, I conducted semi-structured interviews with the participants, both men and women. Participants typically worked as domestic help, housekeeping staff, security personnel or auto-rickshaw drivers, which are classified within the unorganized sector in India. I asked them the aforementioned questions across three product categories:

- Grocery, fruits and vegetables
- Apparel

```
                    │
                    │        ⎫  Constant Comparison
                    ▼        ⎬
  Open coding of documents using GT  ⎭
                    │        ⎫
                    │        ⎬  Theoretical coding
                    ▼        ⎭
       Selective coding in GT
                    │        ⎫
                    ▼        ⎬  Theory construction
         Key emergent themes ⎭
                    │
                    ▼
  Relating key emergent themes as constructs for theory.
```

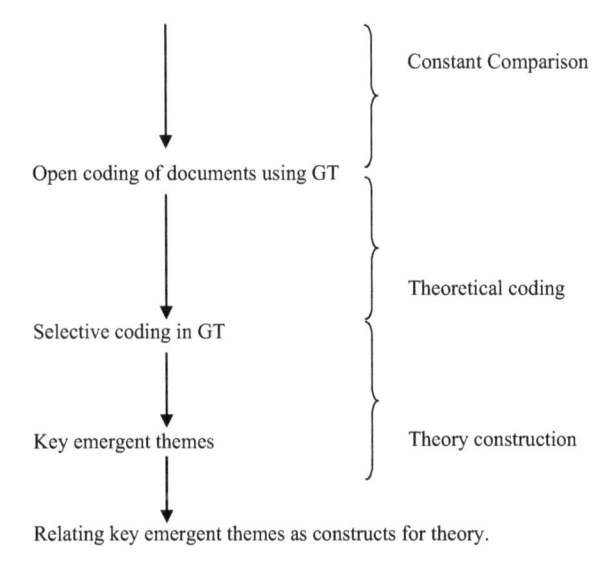

Fig. 5.1 Steps followed for implementing the study through classical grounded theory method

- Electronic gadgets and daily household use consumer durables, such as a television, refrigerator and mobile handset.

These product categories together comprised 95 percent of participants' shopping baskets or household items.

THEORETICAL SAMPLING

I conducted interviews in Hindi as the target respondents were not well versed in the English language. Memos were written through the transcripts to generate labels and draw interpretations through constant comparison and further refined in the next round of interviews. Each transcript was analyzed to prepare initial notes and highlight the emerging open codes. Accordingly, the next respondent was chosen and changes in interviewing style were made if deemed necessary. The questions, however, remained the same.

Open and Selective Coding

Open coding has been described by Glaser (1978) as coding the data in every way possible. It is the first step in coding and is deliberately open so as not to close down any directions a future theory might take. As such, along with the constant comparison method, it is a foundational technique of the grounded theory method. The act of open coding is about attaching initial labels to your data. These are subsequently grouped in larger codes as the aim is to build a theory based on them. The open code will flush out what is important and point to directions in the analysis that may not have been thought of initially. Glaser (1978) recommended coding line by line, which is what has been done for this study. This line-by-line coding helps free us from preconceptions and forces a real intimacy with the data.

The following is a list of the open codes generated manually through interview transcripts. The codes were generated at the first stage to understand customer behavior and expectations:

- Self-belief on socioeconomic status
- Money is top priority
- Informed, rational decision maker (aware)
- Customer had a price/quality equation and a specific understanding of value
- Product nature/context
- Wants growth (aspiration)
- Societal roles
- Money is a constraint in hedonic motives
- Price versus effort (value–money)
- Maximize price quality equation
- Understands brand and quality
- Credit use
- Low frequency of purchase
- Shop/place not important for all products
- Perceived risk—losing money not quality
- Behavior is not a top priority
- Trust is important
- Effort/convenience/travel—value (benefits)-money trade off
- Relationship based on price (financial bonds)
- Cooperation because of familiarity, social bonds

- Product context and buying roles
- Exploitation faced by the customer because of low incomes
- Empowered customer—only money constraint
- Utility
- Family's role in purchase decision process
- Strong sense of identity
- Buy routine-loyalty
- Fashion gives happiness/family/saving money
- Health/family important decision-making criteria
- Do not bargain if health is at stake

I followed Glaser's version of grounded theory for this study, which proceeds to the selective coding stage after open coding. Glaser (1978) defines selective coding as the stage when coding is limited to only those categories that relate to the core category. Selective coding occurs at a stage when there are no new open codes suggesting themselves or definite themes emerging; categories become saturated at this stage. The following selective codes were generated from the open codes:

- Self-belief, societal and buying roles
- Money is the top buying consideration that is constrained
- Informed and rational customer
- Strong family ties
- Family is the strongest influence in a purchase decision
- Feels exploited
- Has aspiration to grow and be fashionable
- Product nature
- Has a clear price/quality/value equation
- Efforts taken to maximize the value equation
- Buys on credit
- Behavior and place/ambience not important as a part of purchase process
- Relationship is based on financial and social bonds
- Understands brands and credibility
- Utilitarian buying behavior

Based on the selective codes, it was interpreted that the urban BOP Indian customer is an aware, informed, discretionary customer who understands things well. He is a rational decision maker and his decision basically hinges on money and family. Money was a resource and a constrained resource in this case. It is important to mention here that because of a line-by-line open coding procedure, there were multiple categories generated. Next, I grouped categories and abstracted an initial theory before beginning theoretical coding. As pointed out by Charmaz (2006), we returned many times to open codes when we were grouping the themes.

Theoretical Coding

Theoretical coding as elaborated by Glaser (1978) is the stage when emerging substantive codes are related to each other to generate theory based on relationships between the constructs. Based on the relationships, six foundational premises evolved that are interrelated and can be put into a framework to develop the theory of how the urban BOP Indian customer views value and makes a purchase decision that could lead to satisfaction. The foundational premises about the BOP Indian customer are as follows:

- **FP1**: The urban BOP customer in India is an informed discretionary customer
- **FP2**: Money is a constrained resource and top decision-making priority when it comes to making a purchase decision
- **FP3**: Value for BOP customer only constitutes hard benefits (product related), equated to the price paid for the complete offering
- **FP4**: The satisfaction is basically utilitarian in nature
- **FP5**: Family is the key influence in the purchase-related decision making
- **FP6**: There is an existing relationship already between a business and an urban BOP customer based on the cost-benefit equation between them

It emerged *that Family and Price are two anchor points* around which the purchase decision revolved and value for the customer was found in benefits versus costs.

Theoretical Integration: BOP Urban Indian Customer and Zone of Tolerance Model for His Expectations

The urban BOP customer in India, who is typically engaged in work in the unorganized sector, lacks formal professional qualification, has minimal education and earns approximately INR 300,000 annually (US $4488.34), is an informed discretionary customer. He possesses basic facilities such as a rented accommodation either with a television set or refrigerator in a city like Gurgaon, Haryana, India, and his household averages five members who each have a mobile phone. For these items and other daily necessities like groceries, fruits, vegetables and apparels, the urban BOP costumer typically spends 90 percent of his monthly household income. During the course of the study, through constant comparison, it emerged that 'family' forms the anchor point for all the customer's purchase decisions, which are basically utilitarian in nature. Money is a key constraint for the customer and he derives satisfaction or happiness on striking a deal that gives him a justification of benefits being received that are either more or equal to the price being charged. The functionality of the product weighed against the price charged constitutes value for the customer and he is willing to put forth extra physical effort and time to avail this value. He uses his judgment and discretion in deciding whether the product delivers on this functionality rather than being dependent on brand or distribution. Thus, this equation of value received versus value paid is what constitutes quality for him. His idea of value revolves around the core product and the price being paid. However, this customer does have a set of aspirations and sets his expectations along them, although presently he is satisfied with less rather than more because of monetary constraints. Thus, resource endowment, which may vary from segment to segment, forms one of the core constructs for understanding satisfaction.

If integrated with the zone of tolerance model developed by Zeithaml et al. (1993), which details how expectations are formed, this substantive theory would elaborate *the role of Family and Price* as influencers for both derived expectations and personal service philosophy in the Indian context. These stable factors work as Enduring Service Intensifiers that set the desired level of expectations in the zone of tolerance (Fig. 5.2).

Given the fact that BOP represents a sizeable market and a sizeable population in India, and with markets saturating and big market opportunity existing in the sector, it is important for firms to understand what

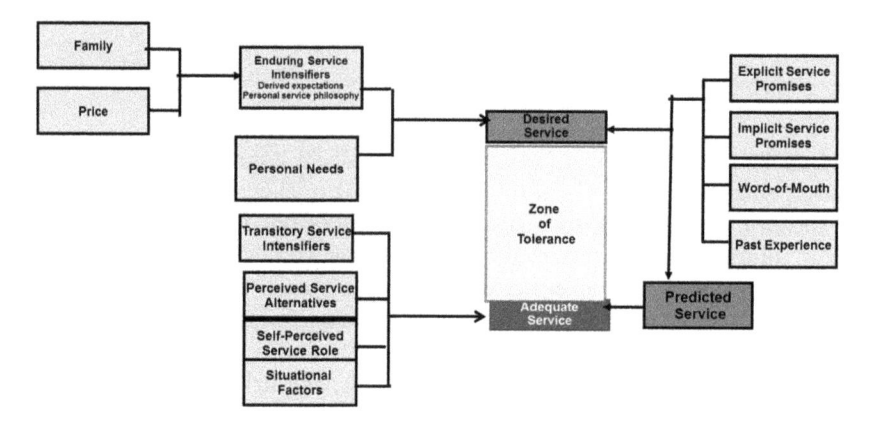

Fig. 5.2 Integrated model of customer expectations for India (Source: Author)

satisfies the urban BOP costumer, how he makes purchase decisions and what should be the focal point to differentiate. Satisfaction is the consumer's fulfilment response. It is a judgment that the product or service feature, or the product or service itself, provides a pleasurable level of consumption-related fulfilment. It means satisfaction is the customer's evaluation of a market offering in terms of whether or not it meets his needs and expectations. Failures would lead to dissatisfaction. Thus, it becomes imperative to understand what influences the customer's expectation and, accordingly, how he can be satisfied. Satisfaction is closely linked to customer loyalty and firm profitability. Service quality is a critical component of this evaluation (Zeithaml and Bitner 2001).

In such a case, if we start understanding what satisfies an urban BOP customer and what his idea of value is, we can deduce that his expectations revolve around family and price and he derives value only in technical service quality. However, given that he does not expect or understand the functional service quality and/or it does not concern him at all, this would be an erroneous assumption.

As highlighted in the previous section, through grounded theory it emerged that the urban BOP customer is an informed customer whose expectations are anchored around family and constrained by price. It is only because he comes from a collectivist culture and is constrained by money that the customer *does not see functional service quality as a differentiator for which he would pay extra money*, and many times he is exploited on this dimension as he is perceived to be powerless. But as markets mature in other regions and segments where businesses could draw a premium price for the functional quality component, because of the similarities in customers, businesses could turn to these BOP markets. *Their expectations will have to be understood differently to draw upon the zone of tolerance and service quality implications* for this segment, however. It is quite possible that *an integrated user-based, value definition of perceived service quality/value may align well for this segment.*

Conclusions

This study presents a *substantive theory that explains the purchase decisions of the BOP Indian customer.* Integration with literature provides insight that this emergent, substantive theory is the cornerstone of the BOP customer's personal beliefs in India that set the desired level of his expectation in the zone of tolerance. Additionally, given money constraints and his grounding in collectivist culture, the customer would want the complete market offering comprising both service quality and functional quality, but it is the technical quality that would be given more weight whereas the other factors would work as hygiene factors. The approach to this chapter has been on elevating the focus of coding and analysis from the descriptive to the conceptual level and trusting one's intuitive sense of conceptualization. The reason for this has been that attributing meaning is not the goal of grounded theory; rather, grounded theory aims to offer the reader a conceptual application of a latent pattern of behavior that holds significance within the social setting under study.

Future Directions

The findings emerging from the study now need to be validated. First, the influence of family and price on customer expectations and perceived value is to be established. A scale to measure integrated perceived value needs to be worked out. Subsequently, a framework for customer perceived value for the urban BOP can be proposed.

References

Burrell, G., & Morgan, G. (1979). *Sociological paradigms and organizational analysis.* Aldershot: Gower.

Charmaz, K. (2006). *Constructing grounded theory: A practical guide through qualitative analysis.* London: Sage Publications.

Creswell, J. W. (1998). *Qualitative inquiry and research design: Choosing among the five traditions*. Thousand Oaks, CA: Sage.

Dawar, N., & Chattopadhyay, A. (2000, June). *Rethinking marketing programs for emerging markets*. Working Paper Number 320, INSEAD, Fontainebleau.

Dey, I. (1999). *Grounding grounded theory: Guidelines for qualitative inquiry*. San Diego, CA: Academic Press.

Drucker, P. (1958, January). Marketing and economic development. *Journal of Marketing, 22*, 252–259.

Fisk, R. P., et al. (2016). Billions of impoverished people deserve to be better served: A call to action for the service research community. *Journal of Service Management, 27*(1), 43–55.

Gebauer, H., & Reynoso, J. (2013). An agenda for service research at the base of the pyramid. *Journal of Service Management, 24*(5), 482–502.

Glaser, B. G. (1978). *Theoretical sensitivity*. Mill Valley, CA: The Sociology Press.

Glaser, B. G., & Strauss, A. L. (1967). *The discovery of grounded theory: Strategies for qualitative research*. Chicago: Aldine Publishing Company.

Gronroos, C. (2001). The perceived service quality concept – A mistake? *Managing Service Quality, 11*(3), 150–152.

Ireland, J. (2008). Lessons for successful BOP marketing from Caracas' slums. *Journal of Consumer Marketing, 25*(7), 430–438.

Karnani, A. (2007, April). *Mirage at the bottom of the pyramid: How the private sector can help alleviate poverty*. Working Paper, The University of Michigan.

Kolk, A., Rivera-Santos, M., & Ruffin, C. (2014). Reviewing a decade of research on the 'base/bottom of the pyramid' (BOP) concept. *Business & Society, 53*(3), 338–377.

Mahajan, V., Pratini de Moraes, M. V., & Wind, J. (2000). The invisible global market. *Marketing Management*, (Winter), 31–35.

Orlikowski, W. J., & Baroudi, J. J. (1991). Studying information technology in organizations: Research approaches and assumptions. *Information Systems Research, 2*, 1–28.

Prahalad, C. K. (2004). *The fortune at the bottom of the pyramid: Eradicating poverty through profits*. Upper Saddle River, NJ: Wharton School Publishing.

Prahalad, C. K., & Hart, S. L. (2002). The fortune at the bottom of the pyramid. *Strategy + Business*, Issue 26, 1–14.

Sheth, J. N. (2011, July). Impact of emerging markets on marketing: Rethinking existing perspectives and practices. *Journal of Marketing, 75*(4), 166–182.

Vargo, S. L., & Lusch, R. F. (2004). Evolving to a new dominant logic for marketing. *Journal of Marketing, 68*(1), 1–17.

Yin, R. K. (1994). *Case study research, design and methods* (2nd ed.). Newbury Park: Sage Publications.

Zeithaml, V. A., Berry, L. L., & Parasuraman, A. (1993). The nature and determinants of customer expectations of service. *Journal of the Academy of Marketing Science, 21*(Winter), 1–12. Retrieved from https://usf.vc/resources/defining-base-of-the-economic-pyramid-in-india/

Zeithaml, V. A., & Bitner, M. J. (2001). *Services marketing: Integrating customer focus across the firm* (2nd ed.). Boston: Tata McGraw-Hill.

CHAPTER 6

A Qualitative Study on Work-Family Conflict, Social Support and Response Mechanisms of Individuals Working in Multi-National Corporations

Anjni Anand and Veena Vohra

INTRODUCTION

India, as a country, has witnessed some dynamic changes in the social and economic environment in the last two decades. The opening up of the economy as a result of economic reforms saw the coming in of multi-national corporations in a big way. This affected the lifestyle of people and more importantly, the nature of jobs changed substantially. Multi-national corporations brought with them a work culture that was highly challenging and, at the same time, highly rewarding. This opened up a plethora of opportunities for young and middle-aged job seekers. The rewards associated with working in a challenging work environment were so attractive that an increasing majority of people preferred working in such an envi-

---

A. Anand (✉)
Department of Commerce, Delhi University, New Delhi, Delhi, India

V. Vohra
Narsee Monjee Institute of Management Studies, Mumbai, Maharashtra, India
e-mail: veena.vohra@nmims.edu

ronment. Another change that was simultaneously brewing in the socio-cultural environment was an increasing number of women joining the workforce. More and more women were getting degrees in higher education and seeking jobs in these multi-national corporations. Women in India had a presence in the job market earlier too, especially in the rural sectors, but growth in employment opportunities from the mid-nineties onward saw an increase in female participation in the workforce.

So, not only was the nature of jobs becoming more challenging and more demanding of one's time and attention, but the natural distinction that existed in work roles of men being breadwinners and women taking care of the family and raising children was also becoming blurred. The social fabric of the society saw the disintegration of the joint family system, as people were moving out to newer towns and cities, either by choice, in search of better job opportunities, or compelled by the requirements of their job. These changes created a dynamic environment, which caught the attention of researchers exploring the consequences of these socio-economic changes on the general welfare level of the employees and their families.

One of the consequences of the aforementioned changes was observed as the occurrence of inter-role conflict. Kahn et al. (1964) defined role conflict as the 'simultaneous occurrence of two (or more) sets of pressures such that compliance with one would make difficult compliance with the other'. A specific form of role conflict, termed work-family conflict, arises when an individual's two most significant life domains–work and family– compete with each other for time and attention. Greenhaus and Beutell (1985) defined work-family conflict as a form of inter-role conflict in which the role pressures from the work and family domains are mutually incompatible in some respect; that is, participation in the work role is made more difficult by virtue of participation in the family role and vice versa.

This chapter is an attempt at understanding work-family conflict experienced by those working in multi-national corporations. Internationally, especially in the Western economies, there has been ample research exploring the various causes and consequences of the conflict. Comparatively, there has been lesser research in other cultures of the world and in India. Previous research has, however, established the existence of the conflict, and those working in different types of professions have admitted to experiencing work-family conflict, irrespective of gender. Taking the previous research on work-family conflict further, the present chapter attempts to understand the role of social support from the family and work domains in helping balance the multiple role demands and the coping strategies that people adopt to help them manage work and family demands. Work is increasingly being conducted in teams in organizations, which, on one hand, creates an inter-dependency to a certain extent among the members of the team and, on the other hand, facilitates co-operation amongst them. This, along with the attitude of team leaders and the overall organizational culture, constitutes the social support that an individual expects and seeks from his/her work environment. At the level of the family, the main source of social support is spousal support and secondly, parental support, which can help couples (especially dual-career couples) manage the increasing demands of their work roles. Another aspect of work-family conflict that this chapter attempts to explore is the response mechanism of the individuals when they experience this inter-role conflict. The response mechanism can range from passive acceptance to aggression in behavior; it can lead to quitting one's job and to varied mental and physical health problems. Coping strategies, adjustments and expectations from work and family are the major focus of this chapter.

Work-Family Conflict

People working in any type of profession may experience work-family conflict if the work and family domains create simultaneous pressures of time and attention on an individual, which given the time constraint and individual capacity cannot be effectively satisfied by the person. It can take the form of time-based conflict, strain-based conflict and/or behaviour-based conflict. *Time-based conflict*, as identified by Greenhaus and Beutell (1985), is consistent with the excessive work time and schedule conflict dimensions identified by Pleck et al. (1980) and role overload identified by Kahn et al. (1964). *Strain-based conflict* is consistent with fatigue and irritability, identified by Pleck et al. (1980), and exists when strain in one role affects one's performance in another role. *Behavior-based conflict* arises when the behavior expected in the performance of a particular role is inconsistent with that required for another role.

A theory that has been widely used by researchers to explain work-family conflict is the Conservation of Resources (COR) Theory (Hobfoll 1989). The COR model proposes that individuals seek to acquire and maintain resources. Stress is a reaction to an environment in which there is the threat of a loss of resources, an actual loss of resources or a lack of expected gain in resources. Resources include objects, conditions, personal characteristics and energies. Researchers have also used *identity theory* to explain how work-family conflict affects individuals and causes health-related problems in them (Burke and Greenglass 1999). Identity theory is associated with the image that an individual creates for self, in work or family domains. Frequent work-family conflict acts as an impediment to successfully meeting family or work-role requirements and undermines a person's ability to construct and maintain a positive self-image in the given field (Frone et al. 1997).

The outcomes of work-family conflict have been studied by researchers in terms of work-related outcomes, non-work-related outcomes and stress-related or domain-unspecific outcomes. In their meta-analysis, Allen et al. (2000) classified work-related outcomes as job satisfaction, organizational commitment, intention to turnover, absenteeism, job performance, career satisfaction and career success. Non-work-related outcomes were categorized as life satisfaction, marital satisfaction, family satisfaction, family performance and leisure satisfaction. Stress-related outcomes were general psychological strain, somatic symptoms, depression, substance abuse, burnout, work-related stress and family-related stress.

Carlson and Kacmar (2000) emphasized life roles as an important antecedent to work-family conflict. Life roles are the system of values an individual holds regarding the work and family domains based on what the individual believes to be important to, central to or a priority in his or her life. For example, if a single, working mother values time with her children but is forced to spend more time than she likes at work in order to support her children, work-family conflict may arise.

Researchers have found that work-family conflict experienced by individuals has increased in recent times due to a rise in the number of dual-earner couples. In the last 30–40 years, women have achieved increasingly higher educational levels and have progressively entered professional occupations in greater numbers. As a case in point, women's participation in the workforce in India has been low, but it has been is growing at a rate of 5.6% annually since 1991 (for urban females), compared to a growth rate of 2% for rural females and 3% for urban males (Report published in Business Standard on July 30, 2015). Although there are many rewards and satisfaction associated with the two-career lifestyle, members of two-career relationships are susceptible to considerable pressure and stress arising from the inter-play of their own work/family roles and those of their partners (Greenhaus et al. 1989).

There is added stress in the case of dual-earner couples as the pressures of work and family responsibilities increase, and balancing these responsibilities becomes a greater challenge for both partners. However, in the research conducted by Greenhaus et al. (1989), the impact of gender on work-family conflict was not substantial. A similar research was carried out by Kinnunen and Mauno (1998) on a sample of dual-earner couples in Finland. There were no gender differences in the experience of either work-to-family conflict or family-to-work conflict. Data was obtained from 501 employees working in four organizations and results showed that work-to-family conflict was more prevalent than family-to-work conflict for both genders. Family-to-work conflict was better explained by family-level factors and impacted family well-being. Work-to-family conflict was explained by work domain factors and affected occupational well-being.

Social Support

Hobfoll and Stokes (1988) defined social support as 'social interactions or relationships that provide individuals with actual assistance or with a feeling of attachment to a person or a group that is perceived as caring or loving'. In one of the earliest definitions of social support, Cobb (1976) described it as 'information that leads a person to believe that he or she is cared for and loved, esteemed and valued and a member of the network of mutual obligation'. Researchers have used Lazarus and Folkman's (1984) psychosocial model of stress and coping as an underlying framework to explain the role of perceived available support in assisting employees to cope with stressors such as work-family conflict. A situation that is being assessed by an individual can be categorized as irrelevant, benign-positive or stressful. Once a situation has been assessed as stressful, the individual then appraises what coping response can reduce the level of stress. Support mobilization is a part of this coping strategy, and the perception that adequate support resources are available helps in developing further coping strategies at a personal level, such as problem-focused coping.

The linkage between social support and work-family conflict can be explained through role theory and resource drain theory. *Role theory* implies that both work and family domains entail multiple roles where numerous demands are placed on the individual (Kahn et al. 1964). In an attempt to meet various work and family role expectations, many individuals succumb to role pressures. *Resource drain theory* views resources such as time, attention and energy as finite; thus role stressors in any domain take away from this finite resource available to an individual. This is akin to the COR Theory (Hobfoll 1989), which states that loss (actual or potential) of one's resources causes stress.

Workplace social support sources are mainly identified as supervisor support and co-worker support. However, Allen (2001) has cited that organizational support is very critical for the uptake of family-friendly policies offered to the employees. Non-work social support includes support from family and friends. Social support from work sources figures more importantly in the occupational stress process than does support from non-work-related sources. In organizational sciences, social support from family has received less attention than work-related sources of social support. In studies that have examined non-work social support, social support from family and friends is more strongly associated with general health and well-being and weakly associated with work-related strains (Adam et al. 1996).

Thomas and Ganster (1995) defined a family-supportive work environment as being composed of family-supportive policies and family-supportive supervisors. Family-supportive policies refer to those policies that make everyday management of family responsibilities easier (and are over and above the insurance and health-care benefits offered by the organization). These policies include child care, elder -care, flexi-time, and care for sick children, telecommuting, job sharing and family leave. A supportive supervisor is seen as one who empathizes with an employee's desire to seek balance between work and family responsibilities. In addition to supportive practices and supportive supervisors, Allen (2001) emphasized the importance of an overall supportive organizational culture and top management support for the uptake of work-life balance policies. Allen (2001) emphasized that implementation of family-friendly policies may not have the effect intended if employees do not perceive the environment of the organization as hospitable to their efforts to seek balance between their work and non-work lives. In the absence of a supportive organizational culture, employees worry that taking advantage of the family-friendly policies will jeopardize their careers (Fierman 1994; Maitland 1998; Morris 1997).

An important source of social support in the workplace is co-worker support. The interactions that an individual employee has with his/her immediate co-workers is perhaps the maximum. The importance of co-worker social support in the workplace is magnified by the trend of flatter organizational structures, team-based work and more lateral workplace interactions (Chiaburu and Harrison 2008). *Social embeddedness theory* gives the rationale and theoretical support to co-worker support. Spousal support plays a very critical role, especially in the case of dual-earner couples as it helps them prioritize their duties and plan their family responsibilities well. In collectivist nations, social support from family includes not just spousal support but also support from parents and children (Spector and Allen 2007). A job is seen as a provider to the family and professional growth is seen as a matter of pride (even if it involves more job involvement and devoting more hours to work). The family is willing to cooperate and adjust in order to provide maximum support to the breadwinner to help them grow professionally (Yang et al. 2007). An important area in which dual-earner couples look out for external support is with regard to child care. If there is a reliable childcare support available, then it provides a psychological relief to the parents, and they are able to concentrate better in their jobs.

Response Mechanism

How do people respond to situations that cause work-family conflict? The attitude of people and the response mechanism adopted by them can be guided by individual personality traits or by the general disposition of people belonging to a certain culture. Reid and Ramarajan (2016) explored the possible reactions of employees to stress arising due to working in high-intensity workplaces, under a constant pressure to live up to the image of an 'ideal worker'. The authors identified three strategies that employees relied on to respond to the stress arising at the workplace. The first strategy is of 'accepting', and 43% of the respondents belonged to this category. These respondents accepted the pressures of the work environment, prioritizing work over non-work life. If the work is highly satisfying and rewarding, then this type of strategy can give psychological satisfaction to the 'acceptors', but on the flip side, people who belong to this category set higher expectations for those who may not accept the idea of prioritizing work over non-work life.

A second strategy is of 'passing', adopted by 27% of the respondents, in which the employees indulged in non-work activities—but under the organization's radar. These employees manipulated their work time in such a way that they could indulge in non-work activities during work time and yet not make the same evident. This may include working on projects that allow one to work from home and not really travel (as others may think) or use work-related travel time to indulge in personal hobbies. The researchers found that although this may work in the short term, sustaining the same in the long run may become difficult as colleagues may get an idea of what 'passers' are indulging in.

A third strategy is 'revealing', adopted by 30% of the respondents. These are the employees who would openly talk about their personal life and would demand for structural changes in their work, like schedule flexibility or any other type of accommodation. Approximately half of the women and a little more than a quarter of men belonged to the category of 'revealers'. These employees usually suffered on the promotion front and were not the first chosen for pay raises or promotions. By making their preferences for a flexible work schedule and leave provisions known, the revealers make it clear that they do not prioritize work over family and do not typically fit into the definition of an 'ideal worker'. The present study is an attempt at exploring how much work-family conflict people working in corporations experience, the way in which this affects their non-work life, health and well-being, the role of social support in helping them achieve a better balance between work and family roles and the response mechanism or strategy adopted by them.

THE STUDY

The study design was purposively qualitative in nature as in-depth information was sought from the respondents about how much work-family conflict they experience and how do they make adjustments in their personal and professional lives to manage the conflict. Such information was not possible through a survey-based questionnaire approach. In-depth interviews with select candidates was considered as the most appropriate technique for gathering information. For the purpose of the study, employees working in multi-national corporations were contacted. Prior to this, the human resource managers of certain select organizations were contacted and informed about the aim of the study via email. After the initial exchange of emails, two organizations agreed to support the study and shared the contact details of some of their employees who were based in Delhi. There was some consideration regarding the selection of the candidates for the interview. As a lot of work is carried out in teams, we felt it was important to have team leaders/supervisors as well as team members as a part of the study sample. We also felt it important to have both male and female respondents as gender difference in response and adjustment mechanisms can then be understood better. The employees were then contacted, by email first and later on by telephone to discuss the details of the study, the aim, purpose and the information sought. Interview time and venue were fixed with each of the 12 individuals who agreed to participate in the study. Confidentiality of the interview was assured to the participants and permission was sought from them for recording the interviews (with the aim of listening to them repeatedly to draw themes and inferences). The respondents were sent a list of three questions for which responses were mainly desired, so that they could prepare for the interview and have a fair idea of the topics to be discussed during it.

In order to best understand work-family conflict experienced by those working in teams, the questions were kept simple and detailed answers to only three questions were sought:

1. How much work-family conflict do you experience?
2. How do social support factors in work and family domain reduce or improve your performance in organizations?
3. How do you normally respond to the simultaneous pressures of work and family?

In addition to these three broad questions, other relevant questions were also asked during the course of the interviews. The purpose was to further probe the interviewees and get more information that could add to the richness of the responses generated. Wherever it was felt necessary, the respondents was asked to elaborate upon any statement made by them or any instance narrated by them. Interviews were converted into transcripts, which facilitated the task of drawing codes from the responses of the candidates.

THEMES ASSOCIATED WITH EXPERIENCING WORK-FAMILY CONFLICT

Role Demands, Role Salience

Working in corporations and being a part of a team were both quoted as 'challenging' and 'demanding' and created a perception of 'too many role demands' for the respondents. The theme emerged out of various sub-themes (see Fig. 6.1) that dealt with the multiple role demands and importance of both work and family roles for an individual.

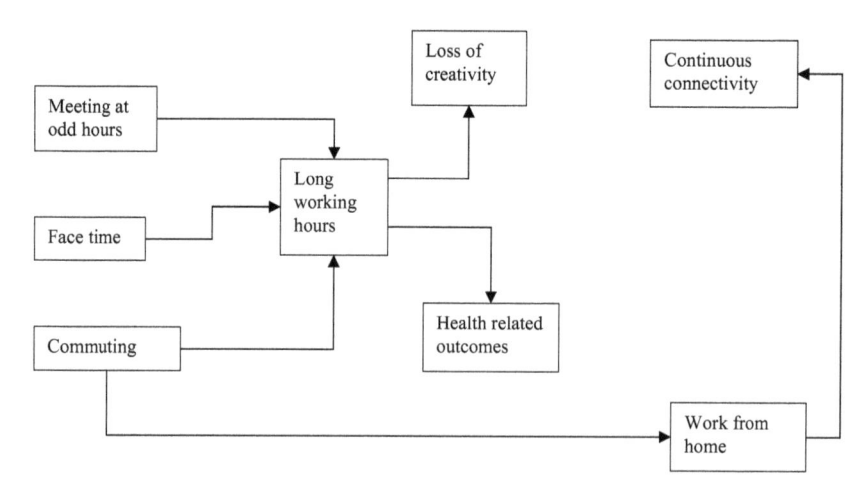

Fig. 6.1 Work environment

Sub-themes: Long working hours, commuting time = unproductive, travel out of town, meetings at odd hours, formal vs. informal style of working, work-from-home provision, child-care and adult-care responsibilities suffer, health-related outcomes (physical and mental well-being suffers), high work pressure = loss of creativity, parenthood = increased responsibility, connectivity to job, face time (Fig. 6.1).

When asked about the work-family conflict they faced, the respondents said that such conflict has become a part of their lives due to the nature of their jobs. The work environment was cited as 'highly demanding' by most. Usual daily working hours exceeded eight hours (which is the number of daily working hours on papers), and adding to it the time spent on travelling, made it a 12–13 hour work day for some of them. Travel time was regarded as 'unproductive', which only added to the total work time without enabling them to do anything constructive. These respondents felt that the organization should seriously consider a 'work-from-home option' as it will enable employees to use this unproductive travel time more constructively and reduce the stress associated with commuting long distances during rush hours.

A common problem associated with not being able to avail of work-from-home or flexi-time provisions (which were offered by some of the participating organizations) was 'holding meetings at odd hours'. This appeared to be a common problem as a majority of the respondents said that meetings were mostly conducted 'early morning' or 'late evening', making it difficult for them to either come in late or leave early. Being at work for long hours and commuting long distances to and from work is 'physically exhausting', 'leaving little time for family or personal interest and hobbies' as well as no time for any exercise or fitness program. The *boundary theory* (Ashforth et al. 2000) gives an explanation for this. According to the theory, when individuals face role overload, they engage in inter-domain transition of resources, where they behaviorally or cognitively transfer resources (time, energy) from one role (the 'accommodating role') to the other role (the 'overload' role). In the present study, the accommodating role is the 'family role', from which resources are easily shifted to the 'work' role, which is the more demanding role.

Too much to do and as cited earlier, non-clarity of expectations from bosses and management, creates an ambiguous work environment where 'everyone is in a haste to complete the task as new tasks can come up at any time', leaving little scope for being 'creative'. The employees said that 'broad goal-setting' by the superiors, followed by 'creative freedom' to the team members will help them to do the job better. It will help promoting 'out-of-the-box thinking', rather than mechanically performing the job. Formal rules and procedures also delay task completion and there is always more emphasis on formal meetings and discussions rather than an informal work environment. As one respondent said 'I end up writing mails to the person sitting on the adjacent desk, rather than walking over and talking to him about the issue'. With internet and mobile connectivity, one is within reach 24/7 and can be contacted at any time for work-related issues. Weekends are not really free, and neither is vacation time—family boundaries are more permeable. 'Face time' is important and one cannot afford to stay away from workplace for a long time. It is important to be noticed by the boss and the management, else performance evaluation suffers later on. This feeling adds to the already existing role demands.

As mentioned previously, the ideal worker syndrome and the acceptance of the same creates problems for those who may not strictly fall in the category of 'acceptors'. They may face unnecessary pressures of having to be available round-the-clock, due to unreasonable standards set by the acceptors of the definition of the ideal worker. The research found that people did not think too highly about 'acceptors' as mentors because they were all the time too occupied with their job to play the role of a mentor, coach or guide.

Family-role salience cannot be ignored—it is especially true for women professionals and somewhat true for male professionals. Male employees reported 'feeling guilty' for not being able to give adequate attention to their spouses and children. Female employees, on the other hand, reported quitting jobs due to parental responsibilities and coming back after a gap. Male respondents said that their spouses had shifted from a corporate job to a 'more accommodating job', like consultant or any other form of self-employment, which gives them more flexibility regarding working hours. This 'adjustment' was necessary in the face of rising responsibilities of children and elders in the family.

Reducing Ambiguity in Roles and Expectations

The respondents felt that the work-family conflict that they face is not just due to the actual conflict between work and family role demands but more due to the ambiguity regarding the role demands and timeline expectations that they face in work and family domains. Making conscious efforts to set expectations right with respect to those around (both at work and in the family) is seen as a way of reducing the conflict.

Sub-themes: Realistic expectation setting—with family and with colleagues and superiors, reduce last-moment surprises, temporary and continuous disturbances, clarity in role demands and timeline expectations (Fig. 6.2).

An important factor identified by the respondents that helped them achieve work-family balance and led to imbalance when it was lacking is 'setting expectations right'. This referred to their expectations from fam-

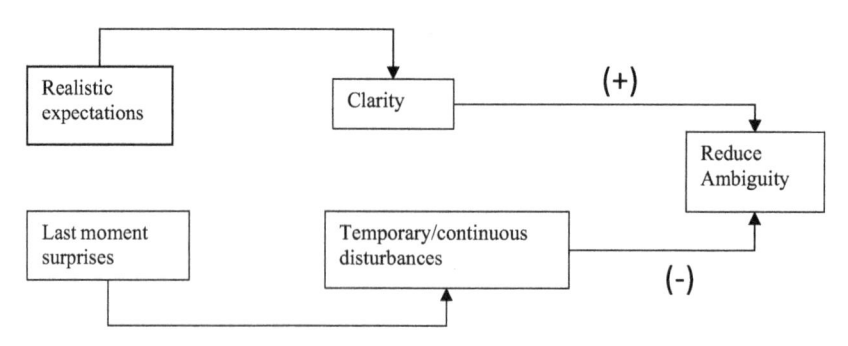

Fig. 6.2 Managing expectations

ily, the expectations of family members from them and expectations of the organization and the superiors. Clear expectations helps remove any kind of uncertainty and prevents last-moment rushes of any sort. Respondents said that clearly specifying their work schedule, travel plans and so on and having a clear knowledge of the spouse's work schedule and work demands helps in making plans in advance so that last-moment 'surprises' and 'rushes' are avoided. It helps in finding parental support, especially for child-care purposes, and results in better schedule management. Most respondents said that they learnt this the hard way.

Even with respect to the organization, getting a clear idea of what is expected from them was cited as very important by the respondents. Some of them claimed that 'lack of clear deliverables' leads to 'performance-expectation gap', which is quite stressful. Most often, they claimed that they were given tasks and targets to attain without any reality check, which disturbed them mentally. Individual Key Result Areas (KRAs) are specified at the beginning of the year only and many times the actual expectations are so different from these KRAs that it creates an environment of uncertainty for employees wherein they feel that the leader's role is most important. 'Clear communication' and a 'sense of direction' can only flow from the leader to the members in a top-down approach. With a clear idea of tasks to be performed, the relation between task performance and results and evaluation criteria will eliminate all forms of role-related ambiguity.

Some sudden expectations can always arise, both at family and at the workplace, which can upset any previous plan. But these were cited as 'temporary disturbances' by the respondents that can be accommodated. What is more troublesome is a continued atmosphere of unexpected demands wherein work-life 'balance' goes for a 'complete toss'.

THEMES ASSOCIATED WITH SOCIAL SUPPORT

Social Support from Family

An attempt was made to understand how family domain factors affect performance in the work domain and the responses showed that there are various ways in which members of immediate and extended family extend their support, which makes managing work and family roles easier.

Sub themes: Spousal support is very critical, parents—most important in child-care responsibilities, amount of support = f (work-role awareness), helps develop bond with co-workers, time spent at job = f (supportive family environment), staying away from family adds to stress, continuous work pressure = decline in support from family.

Social support from family is one of the most important reasons cited by the respondents for helping them focus on their work-role demands and perform effectively in a challenging work environment. Male respondents cited spousal support as most critical whereas female respondents cited parental support (own parents or husband's parents) as the most important source of family social support. Female respondents (with children) credited family support as the reason for being able to put in long hours at work. For dual-earner couples, parental support was considered the most 'safe' and 'reliable' option as far as child care was concerned. Some respondents even told that the family contributed towards developing better relations with co-workers by organizing/being a part of get-togethers with colleagues. This even helped develop a better understanding of each other's family background that may not otherwise be possible in a formal work environment (Fig. 6.3).

Male respondents said that they are able to give the required time and attention to temporary pressures arising at work with support from family (with spousal support as most critical). However, when work demands require one to work overtime on a regular basis and ignore family responsibilities too often, it becomes a cause of distress even for the family members. Mathews and Wayne (2014), in their longitudinal study examining the relation between role overload and work-family conflict, mention the supportive role played by family, which makes adjustments given the heavy demands and pressures associated with the job of the 'breadwinner'. The researchers call this adjustment 'episodic coping mechanisms', which help

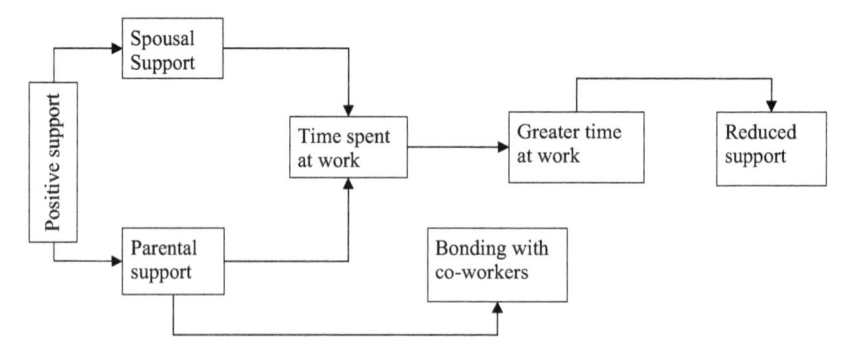

Fig. 6.3 Family support

alleviate the problem in the short run but also cause stress and strain to the providers of supportive behavior.

'Family support' and 'psychological relief 'of staying with family was something that was missed by the respondent (unmarried) who was away from the family, who reported that he had to make a lot of adjustments when staying alone. One of the male respondents who was staying away from the family said that he was 'completely relaxed mentally' when it comes to the issue of the security of wife and children, as they were staying with his parents and were able to get a protective environment. This, he called, was a 'blessing in disguise' for him as he can give undivided attention to his work.

Adams et al. (1996) conceptualized two forms of spousal support—instrumental and emotional support—and empirically tested them. Emotional support includes empathetic understanding and listening, affirmation of affection, and advice and genuine concern for the welfare of the partner. Instrumental support is the tangible help from a partner, such as with household chores and child care. Both these forms of support are associated with lower work-family conflict (Aryee et al. 1999). As mentioned in Aycan and Eskin's (2005) research on exploring the impact of child, spousal and organizational support on work-family conflict, instrumental support eases the burden of family demands and enables an individual to devote more time to work, whereas emotional spousal support enhances feelings of self-efficacy both at work and at home (Parasuraman et al. 1996). Spousal support was found to be strongly related to psychological well-being and marital satisfaction and emerged as the most significant support for women (for men, organizational support helped reduce work-family conflict more effectively). The findings of the present study associate spousal support as the most significant source of non-work support for men. Women associated family support to supportive parents and in-laws who helped in managing household chores and child-care responsibilities.

Co-Worker Support

Working in teams leads to task inter-dependency and creates bond of mutual trust and co-operation among the team members. The various facets of the relationship between team members is summed up in this theme.

Sub-themes: Inter-dependency in task completion, generally co-operative, pressure to perform and prove oneself, male colleagues less understanding (gender differences).

Most respondents said that there is an environment of co-operation among the members of the team and most often others are willing to extend help and support required by a particular member. At the same time, it is also true that there is a heavy pressure to complete one's own task and then leave, which when done by any member adds to the task burden on others. Most team jobs involve inter-dependency, which makes it difficult for any one person to be away from the job due to family considerations. Pressure to prove oneself eats into the 'co-operative behaviours of individuals'. Relationship among team members is 'mutual' and based on a 'give-and-take' relationship—the only role of the leader is to ensure that everything is clearly communicated. Even where an employee requires any special consideration, the same should be openly discussed with all so as to avoid misunderstandings. Female respondents reported that male colleagues were less understanding of their need for time-related adjustments, but among female colleagues, they got all possible help and support. Each member has a unique role to perform and is not completely replaceable, which can cause problems when one is working on tight schedules. Generation gap among members and between leader and member also causes disturbances at times.

The importance of co-worker support is magnified due to an increasing number of organizations adopting a flatter structure and preferring team-based work (Chiaburu and Harrison 2008). This leads to more lateral transactions, which makes supportive behavior from co-workers even more significant. Some studies have been able to associate perceived co-worker support to a reduction in work-family conflict, whereas others have found no relation between the two (Major et al. 2005; Frone et al. 1997).

Organizational Support

The interviewees were asked about their expectations regarding organizational support that they actually received and the changes in organizational policies that will help them attain better work-life balance. The responses were coded and grouped together in the theme of organizational support.

Sub-themes: Policies only on papers, immediate superior = culture, work-life balance = f (empathetic boss), no interaction with top management.

The respondents felt that they have no direct communication with the top management, and they do they look at the top management for any kind of support. Most of them felt that they have only little knowledge of the actual policies. They only knew as much as was communicated to them by their immediate superior. Organizational support, for them, translated into supportive line managers. A team's happiness depends on how empathetic and understanding leaders they have. For leaves or any need to work from home, the approval of immediate superior only matters. Those who were dis-satisfied with the leader/bosses reported an unfriendly and non-co-operative work environment. For the leaders, however, the situation was trickier as they looked at top management support for their individual level work-family issues. They faced greater difficulty in getting support. Policies on paper may never get translated into practice—what trickles down to individual employees are the policies that their bosses communicate to them. Research on various sources of workplace social support and work-family conflict conducted in the West has emphasized the significance of perceived organizational support, as a supportive organizational culture trickles down in the form of supportive supervisors and supportive colleagues (Allen 2001). As one of the respondents who had worked abroad for a few years said, 'policies on paper are the rule ... once they are put on paper, the employees get to know of them and can avail of them. This does not happen here. ... an employee knows only as much as is communicated to him by his line manager. ... nobody knows the written policies, nor do they bother to find it out ... they only have a vague idea of the employee benefit policies. For them, as long as their line manager listens to them and understands their problem, they are happy. If he doesn't, they accept it as their fate'.

Role of Leaders/Supervisors

Leaders/supervisors/line managers are the first point of contact for employees when they expect any kind of support from the organization in the form of flexible work schedule, leave or any other accommodation.

Sub-themes: Transparency, clearly defined performance standards, empathetic leadership, trust and cohesiveness building, understanding personal background of team members, regular performance feedbacks, clear communication.

A leader's role is very critical when it comes to team performance—this view was upheld by both leaders as well as team members. Leaders can help build a cohesive team and can create a feeling of mutual trust among the team members—which is very important as only when do co-workers have a feeling of trust are they willing to help and co-operate with each other and extend support to each other. Leaders can ensure this by, firstly, indulging in open, two-way communication with the members, secondly, by adopting common yardstick of performance for all and thirdly, by being empathetic. 'Empathetic' leadership style was the most preferred style by members and most successful as reported by the leaders. Respondents who were leaders said that they encourage their team members to speak up and communicate openly with them as well as with others so as to avoid any kind of misunderstanding. Communicating with team members also helps them understand the ethos, culture and background of the members, which sensitizes them to the needs of individual members (Fig. 6.4).

Team members showed their concern regarding performance evaluations. The targets are generally set for the team as a whole, which the team may or may not be able to attain. They expect the leader to update them regularly about performance evaluations and not give them a shock or surprise only at the end of the year. The leader is also expected to mentor and coach the team members for improving the overall performance of the team. This task is not just challenging but also creates a lot of pressure of time on leaders, as they have to take time out of their schedule for coaching

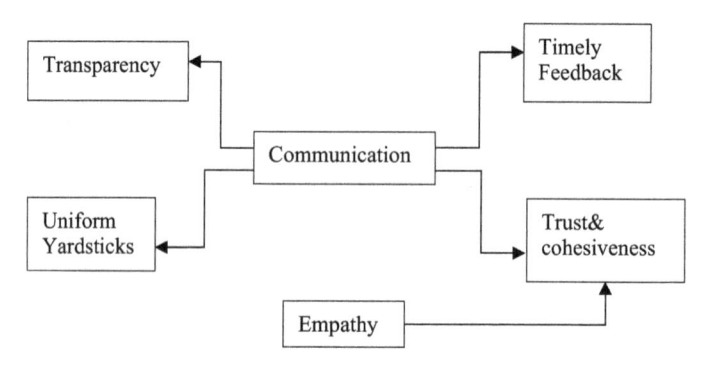

Fig. 6.4 Transparency effects

and mentoring team members. At times, it leads to a feeling of frustration for leaders, as one of the leader respondents said 'I feel I am running a training center here. ... I train them, coach them and guide them to improve performance and after learning the technique from me, they quit the job and join another organization. ... I have to start off once again with a new member'. However, the importance of mentoring as a source of workplace social support cannot be ignored and Carlson and Kacmar (2001) found that mentoring significantly helps reduce work-family conflict (especially in the direction of family to work). Kram (1985) mentions two functions that a mentor can perform that can help their subordinates. First is 'career development', which involves coaching, giving exposure and visibility, helping in accomplishing challenging tasks and protection. Second, the mentor can be a source of psychological support by offering counselling, friendship and serving as a role model. Both these behaviors of the mentor can help in improving the competence of the subordinates and in developing a feeling of belongingness towards the organization.

Leaders and members alike emphasized 'empathetic leadership style'. The team members expect the leader to be understanding of their non-work life too. From the leader's perspective, his role is extremely challenging as he is not just expected to be empathetic and understanding, but is also held responsible for the team performance and is answerable to the management. Wherever individual members are not able to perform or deliver as expected, the leader has to pitch in and take charge, else the whole team suffers. The leaders responded that they are the ones who find it most difficult to take leave and pass on their charge/responsibilities to someone else.

As far as team camaraderie is concerned, the overall work environment also has a role to play. As the respondents said, based on their previous work experience, there are organizations where the work culture is such that the teams bond together over regular dinners and get-togethers. In organizations that do not have such a work culture, the spirit of 'oneness' may vary from one team to another depending upon the role of team leader.

Communication

The theme emerged out of numerous codes that emphasized the importance of clear, two-way communication in the workplace, which creates actual as well as perceived role and expectation clarity.

Sub-themes: Two-way communication, creates awareness of work roles, spousal support = f (communication), listening to team members and co-workers, effective communication = psychological support (Fig. 6.5).

Effective communication both at work and in family has been cited by almost all respondents as an important tool in achieving balance. Communication with family members makes them aware of the work role demands and ensures a better understanding of the nature of job. It also helps develop a more co-operative attitude towards the partner in case of dual-earner couples. In addition to creating better awareness and understanding, effective two-way communication between partners provides a great source of psychological support and many times helps provide guidance too.

Similarly, effective two-way channels of communication in the workplace also help in reducing job ambiguity, clear doubts and misunderstanding and help build a more cohesive team. Communication with colleagues and co-workers helps them identify the adjustment mechanism adopted by others and how others have been successful at balancing their work and family demands. The respondents (comprising both leaders and members) said that the leader's role is critical to ensure effective communication. It helps the leader develop a clearer understanding of the personal background of the team members, their issues and concerns and expectations. By communicating with the members of his team, the leader is able to get a good idea about their culture, ethos and personal background, which helps him develop a suitable strategy to deal with them, extract their best performance and also help them with family-level issues. Respondents who were members said that a leader 'listening' to their problems was more important than the leader actually being able to do anything. It creates a

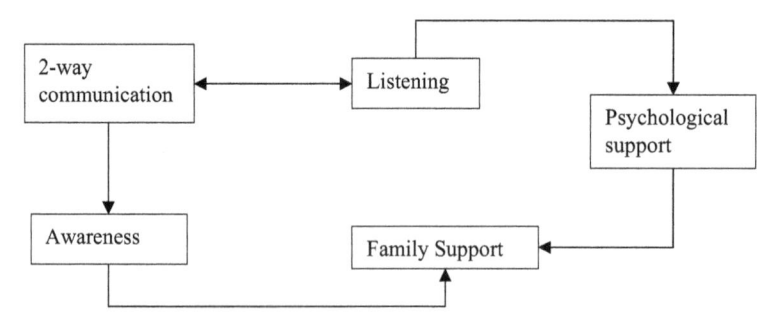

Fig. 6.5 Bi-directional communication

'perception' of supportive superiors, which provides some kind of psychological relief to team members. By encouraging two-way communication, the leaders give an opportunity to the members to come out with their concerns as well as get a platform to share their own concerns.

The importance of effective communication was emphasized by Nissen et al. (2003) in their study, which specifically focused on communication between couples as a means of reducing work-family conflict. The importance of communication has not been explored much and the researchers felt that having sufficient knowledge of each other's work-role demands and also about tasks in the family domain that require attention can help reduce role conflict and help couples plan their schedules better. Effective communication can ensure better task planning and will significantly reduce 'time-based conflict' (Greenhaus and Beutell 1985). Guterman (in Muchinsky et al. 1998, 263) mentioned a few of the demands for balancing work and family life as:

- Quality communication, spending enough time on intimate discussions about themselves as individuals and their relationships.
- Setting priorities with regard to time spent on work, managing the home, child care, leisure and other activities.
- Clarifying values, for example, work values such as challenge, growth, opportunity, security, recognition, power and prestige, and life values concerning hobbies, leisure, continued learning, religion and being part of society.
- Examining roles and their respective relative weights, such as the roles of provider, nurturer, homemaker and bill payer.
- Managing stress by identifying the sources, attempting to reduce the sources, examining one's responses to stress and taking the responsibility to manage one's own stress.

One of the most important findings of the study by Nissen et al. (2003) was that male partners experienced more conflict than their female partners if they did not have adequate information regarding the female partner's job. This is consistent with Thomas and Ganster's (1995) findings that spouses who had knowledge regarding their spouses' jobs experienced lesser conflict in their marriages. Adequate communication between partners can help resolve this problem as it will lead to both partners having good knowledge about each other's job, which can make them more understanding, supportive and empathetic.

Themes Associated with Response and Adjustment Mechanisms

Conflict Resolution

As one respondent said 'accepting the conflict is important if we want to resolve it and despite changing organizations, I have realized that no matter where you work, work-family conflict will always be there'. The theme deals with recognizing the conflict, accepting the same and trying to find ways to resolve it.

Sub-themes: Evolutionary process, ongoing process, age and experience matters, solution-oriented approach, recognizing salience of both work an family roles, identify demand patterns, standardize work procedures (Fig. 6.6).

The respondents felt that dealing with work and family-role demands and pressures and trying to develop a 'strategy' to help ensure 'balance' is a continuously evolving process. The respondents felt that as they progress with life and gain experience, they learn ways of managing their different role demands. Most of them said that it was their 'over-enthusiasm' to perform at their job in the initial stages of their career that they had to correct later on, after getting married and having children. Initial years at work witnessed performing more than the actual role responsibilities, taking over more tasks in the 'eagerness' to prove oneself. This needed correction later on, with increased family-role responsibilities. Attaining balance is a 'desirable state' and every individual 'naturally' attempts to attain balance. This starts with the 'acceptance of work-family conflict' and the 'inevitability' of it in almost all types of jobs. The 'acceptance' of the problem can only lead to a 'solution-oriented approach'. The interviewees said that they learn coping strategy from each other. Both work and family

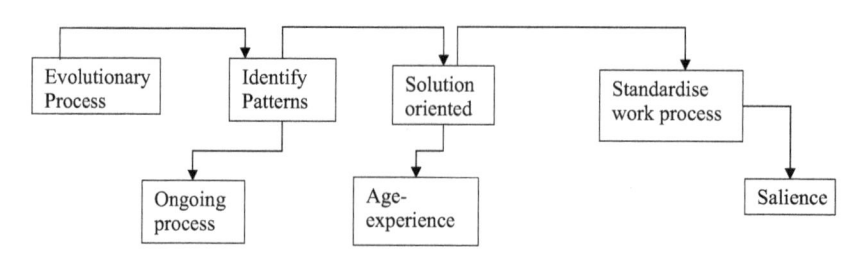

Fig. 6.6 Conflict resolution: evolutionary process

roles were cited as 'salient' by male and female respondents. Organizations were 'demanding' and nature of work in multi-national companies is such that it requires one to put in long working hours. Identifying patterns of demand and standardizing routine jobs help in reducing the time and attention that one has to give to each aspect of the job and helps the employee focus on more challenging tasks.

In the challenging corporate world, workers who prioritize work over family life and are willing to dedicate long hours to work are called 'ideal workers' (Bailyn and Harrington 2004; Rapoport and Rapoport 1969, 61). They are considered more eligible for promotions. In their research on work-like balance and career advancement potential, Lyness and Judiesch (2008) explored the higher possibility of career advancement for those managers who were able to balance their multiple role demands better, contribute more towards work-role demands and took lesser leaves and time off from work for personal (family) reasons. Their research hypothesis were based on the 'gendered culture theory', according to which, organizations give promotions to employees who focus on task accomplishment and do not let family or personal matters interfere in their work life (Acker 1990 for Gendered culture theory). In a previous research by Lyness and Judiesch (2008), the researchers found that managers who often took leaves of absence for family/personal reasons received fewer subsequent promotions than managers who did not.

In a research published in the *Harvard Business Review* (June, 2016), where several employees in the United States were interviewed to find out about the image of an 'ideal worker', how important it is to be an ideal worker and what strategies do people use to maintain the image of an ideal worker, 43% responded 'acceptance' as the strategy. As the researchers reported 'in their quest to succeed on the job, 'acceptors' prioritize their work identities and sacrifice or significantly suppress other meaningful aspects of who they are'. Such a strategy might work if one is very passionate about one's job and enjoys being occupied with it. However, when job and job demands start clouding other aspects of one's life leaving little room for developing one's interests and creativity in other areas, it poses a serious career threat, especially where the individual might find himself/herself in a situation of losing the job (which has become a part of his/her identity).

Research evidence from other cultures also show a natural tendency to attain balance between work and non-work demands as it can have consequences on the career growth pattern of an employee. The respondents in the current study also emphasized a natural movement towards attaining balance, a conscious effort towards attaining the same and reducing conflict, although this involved adjustments in the personal domain.

Cultural Differences and Collectivism

The theme covers the response mechanism of the respondents and how they make adjustments in their lives to help manage work-family conflict. It also covers the responses that deal with the relationship that respondents share with the top management and the cultural differences in these relationships in individualistic and collectivist cultures.

Sub-themes: Higher priority to job, sacrifices in non-work life, acceptance of job pressures as norm, overtime comes naturally, no direct communication with top management, family willing to adjust for the professional growth of the breadwinner, work culture of home country prevails (Fig. 6.7).

When the respondents were asked about work-family conflict affecting their work life and personal life, they accepted the presence of the conflict but did not feel very strongly about it. The general attitude was of 'acceptance'—that all jobs require time and attention, 'your job is your bread and butter' and that 'adjustments at family level are normal'. The research literature, especially that focusing on cross-cultural research (Spector and Allen 2007; Aycan 2008; Haar et al. 2014), has categorically emphasized the significant differences between attitudes of employees coming from a collectivist culture as opposed to those belonging to an individualistic cul-

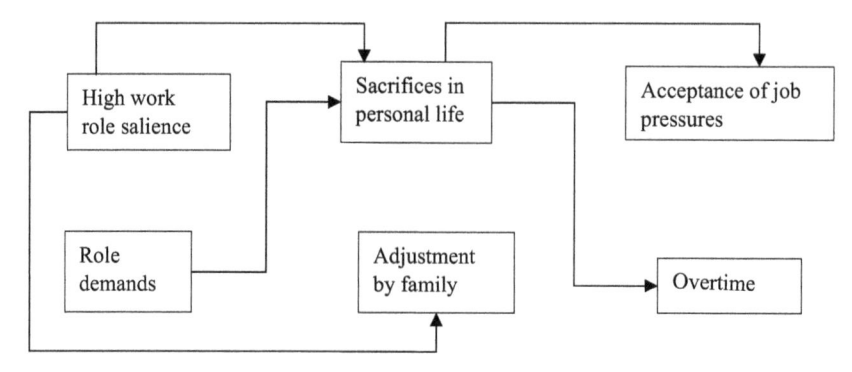

Fig. 6.7 Work priorities

ture. People in collectivist culture tend to give a lot of importance to their job and consider their job as a 'contributor to the family, rather than its competitor'. One of the respondents who has worked abroad (in the United States and Europe) reported that overtime pay is a matter of right there and even Indians working abroad claim the same. However, in India, they don't exercise this right and 'accept overtime as a part of the norm'. Work carries salience over family life. Work salience is even recognized by the family; they are willing to adjust and co-operate for the sake of growth in a job. In the cross-cultural study by Sector et al. (2004), the researchers tested for the association between working hours and work-family conflict to understand the difference between individualistic and collectivist cultures. A stronger relation between the variables was found in Anglo cultures as compared to collectivist cultures. The possible explanation for this as given by the researchers was that the Anglo economies tend to be stronger than collectivist economies and have a higher average household income. Collectivist nations are characterized by lower family incomes, huge population and vast unemployment—reasons that are enough to make a manager work longer hours to save his job. Added to this, the family support available in such cultures and the ease of availability of household help also make it possible to devote additional hours to work.

The employees have no direct contact with the top management and neither do they have a complete knowledge of all top management policies. Immediate superiors and line managers are the people who decide what policies can be availed of by the team members. There are lack of India-specific policies and most often the culture of the home country of the organization prevails.

Discussion

The study aimed at understanding how people respond to the work-family conflict that they face as a consequence of working in multi-national corporations. The objective was to understand the attitude of people towards work-family conflict and to get a general idea about role of social factors in helping people attain a better work-life balance. All the employees who were interviewed agreed to the presence of work-family conflict, although in varying degrees. Both male and female respondents reported conflict, which was mainly due to the nature of the job. Work environment, pressure of performance, stiff target setting and to some extent, role ambiguity, were cited as the work-related antecedents to work-family conflict.

Family-level factors like parenthood or presence of dependent adults were cited as factors that did increase the family-role responsibilities, but these were not reported as intervening with effective discharge of work-role responsibilities.

Researchers have categorized work-family conflict as work-to-family conflict (where work interferes in the effective discharge of family-related responsibilities) and family-to-work conflict (where family responsibilities make effective performance at job difficult). In the present study, the work-to-family conflict direction was more dominant and most respondents said that they sacrifice family time for work time and usually prioritize work over family. Social support from family was cited as very important by almost all respondents and they felt that family support was the factor that helped them devote long hours to work. While men cited spousal support as most significant, women cited parental support as most critical in helping them continue with their jobs, even post-motherhood. In cases where no parental support could be available, male respondents reported that the spouse had to either quit her job or move to a more convenient job (e.g., self-employment) that permitted more flexibility of work time.

The study aimed at understanding the general cultural environment of the country that helped in shaping the attitude of people towards work-family conflict. It emerged that as with other collectivist nations, in India too work is given a higher priority than family, especially by men (who are considered to be the main breadwinners of the family). Sacrifices made by the spouse or children or other members of the family is considered 'normal' and is looked upon as something that has to be done for a better, more secure future. Growth in a job is seen as prestigious and ensures greater economic stability for the entire family. Another attitude that emerged from the discussion was that of 'acceptance'—work-family conflict is accepted as a given and normal/natural consequence of working in a multi-national corporation, thus the thrust is on how to make adjustments in personal and work life to help manage this conflict more effectively. Due to little or negligible interaction with top management, there is little expectation of organizational support in helping employees reduce the work-family conflict that they experience. The emphasis is more on informal sources of support—from co-workers and from immediate superiors. Due to lateral interactions with co-workers, the attitude is of mutual co-operation, although some gender difference in attitude was reported by female respondents. With immediate superiors/line managers, open lines of communication with one's bosses helped in building an environment of trust and helped ensure maximum support and co-operation to everyone. The attitude of acceptance leads to lesser awareness of HR policies related to work-life balance and a lesser demanding attitude of the employees regarding the implementation of these policies.

Conclusion

Studies on work-family conflict have mainly explored the causes and consequences of the conflict occurring in work and family domains. Taking this further, the present study is an attempt to understand what shapes the response mechanism of the employees working in high-pressure work environments. This has helped shed light on the cultural factors prevalent in the economy that shape the attitude of the people. The relative importance of work and family in the life of an individual, the preference accorded to each of these domains and the stress and strain arising out of the conflict are some of the variables that are influenced by the socio-cultural environment of the country, as the socio-cultural set-up affects the behavioral response of the people.

The study has given insights into the adjustment mechanisms that happen at the level of the family to help attain work-life balance and the hierarchical and lateral relationships existing at the work front. The lack of communication and interaction with top management creates a divide between them and the employees working at middle or lower levels of management, which causes gaps in expectations and creates an ambiguous environment for the employee, where he looks for support from line managers and co-workers. The quality of interactions with co-workers and line mangers define the quality of work environment and creates a perception of support and cooperation from them.

Adjustments at the level of the family results in one of the partners giving up a high-growth career to facilitate the career advancement of the other as without a continuous parental support dual-career couples find it difficult to balance the role requirements of job and family. Organizations need to take a note of this too as it leads to them losing out on quality employees due to the lack of adequate and appropriate family-friendly policies. The employees are either not aware of what actually exists on paper or are too hesitant to demand anything as a matter of right. Both these issues can be addressed by looking into work-family conflict with a little more sensitivity and encouraging two-way communication with employees.

References

Adams, G. A., King, L. A., & King, D. W. (1996). Relationships of job and family involvement, family social support and work-family conflict with job and life satisfaction. *Journal of Applied Psychology, 81*(4), 411–420.

Allen, T. D. (2001). Family-supportive work environments: The role of organisational perceptions. *Journal of Vocational Behaviour, 58*(3), 414–435.

Allen, T. D., Herst, D., Bruck, C. S., & Sutton, M. (2000). Consequences associated with work-to-family conflict: A review and agenda for future research. *Journal of Occupational Psychology, 5*(2), 278–308.

Aryee, S., Luk, V., Leung, A., & Lo, S. (1999). Role stressors, inter-role conflict and well-being: The moderating influence of spousal support and coping behaviours among employed parents in Hong Kong. *Journal of Vocational Behaviour, 54,* 259–278.

Ashforth, B. E., Kreiner, G. E., & Fugate, M. (2000). All in a day's work: Boundaries and micro-role transitions. *The Academy of Management Review, 25*(3), 472–491.

Aycan, Z. (2008). Cross-cultural approaches to work-family conflict. In K. Korabik & D. Lero (Eds.), *Handbook of work-family conflict* (pp. 359–371). London: Cambridge University Press.

Aycan, Z., & Eskin, M. (2005). Relative contributions of child-care, spousal support and organisational support in reducing work-family conflict for men and women: The case of Turkey. *Sex Roles, 53*(7), 453–471.

Bailyn, L., & Harrington, M. (2004). Redesigning work for work-family integration. *Community, Work and Family, 7*(2), 197–208.

Burke, R. J., & Greenglass, E. R. (1999). Work-family conflict, spousal support and nursing staff well-being during organisational re-structuring. *Journal of Occupational Health Psychology, 4*(4), 327–336.

Carlson, D. S., & Kacmar, K. M. (2000). Work-family conflict in organisations: Do life roles make a difference. *Journal of Management, 26*(5), 1031–1054.

Chiaburu, D. S., & Harrison, D. A. (2008). Do peers make the place? Conceptual synthesis and meta-analysis of co-worker effects on perceptions, attitudes, OCBs and performance. *Journal of Applied Psychology, 93*(5), 1082–1103.

Cobb, S. (1976). Social support as a moderator of life stress. *Psychosomatic Medicine, 38*(5), 300–314.

Fierman, J. (1994). Are companies less family-friendly. *Fortune Journal, 129*(6), 64–67.

Frone, M. R., Yardley, J. K., & Markel, K. S. (1997). Developing and testing an integrative model of the work-family interface. *Journal of Vocational Behaviour, 50,* 145–167.

Greenhaus, J. H., & Beutell, N. J. (1985). Sources of conflict between work and family roles. *Academy of Management Review, 10*(1), 76–88.

Greenhaus, J. H., Parasuraman, S., & Granrose, C. S. (1989). Sources of work-family conflict among two-career couples. *Journal of Vocational Behaviour, 34*, 133–153.

Haar, J. M., Russo, M., Sune, A., & Ollier-Malaterre, A. (2014). Outcomes of work-life balance on job satisfaction, life satisfaction and mental health: A study across seven cultures. *Journal of Vocational Behaviour, 85*, 361–373.

Hobfoll, S. E. (1989). Conservation of resources: A new attempt at conceptualising stress. *American Psychologist, 44*, 513–524.

Hobfoll, S. E., & Stokes, J. P. (1988). The process and mechanics of social support. In S. Duck, D. F. Hay, S. E. Hobfoll, W. Ickes, & B. M. Montgomery (Eds.), *Handbook of personal relationships: Theory, research and interventions* (pp. 497–517). Oxford, England: John Wiley & Sons.

Kahn, R. L., Wolfe, D. M., Quinn, R. P., Snoek, J. D., & Rosenthal, R. A. (1964). *Organizational stress: Studies in role conflict and ambiguity*. Oxford, England: John Wiley.

Kinnunen, U., & Mauno, S. (1998). Antecedents and outcomes of work-family conflict among employed women and men in Finland. *Human Relations Journal, 51*(2), 157–177.

Kram, K. E. (1985). Improving the mentoring process. *Training and Development Journal, 39*(4), 40–43.

Lazarus, R., & Folkman, S. (1984). *Stress, appraisal, and coping*. New York: Springer.

Lyness, K. S., & Judiesch, M. K. (2008). Can managers have a life and a career? International and multi-source perspectives on work-life balance and career advancement potential. *Journal of Applied Psychology, 93*(4), 789–805.

Maitland, A. (1998, May 7). When the culture is to stay late. *The Financial Times*.

Mathews, R. A., & Wayne, J. H. (2014). A longitudinal examination of role overload and work-family conflict: The mediating role of inter-domain transitions. *Journal of Organisational Behaviour, 35*, 72–91.

Morris, B. (1997). Is your family wrecking your career? *Fortune, 135*(5), 70–76.

Muchinsky, P. M., Kriek, H. J., & Schreuder, A. M. G. (1998). *Personnel psychology*. Johannesburg: Thomson.

Nissen, B. T., Vuuren, L. V., & Visser, D. (2003). Communication of job-related information and work-family conflict in dual-career couples. *Journal of Industrial Psychology, 29*(1), 18–25.

Parasuraman, S., Purohit, Y. S., Godshalk, V. M., & Beutell, N. J. (1996). Work and family variables, entrepreneurial career success, and psychological well-being. *Journal of Vocational Behaviour, 48*, 275–300.

Pleck, J. S., Staines, G. L., & Lang, L. (1980). Conflicts between work and family life. *Monthly Labour Review, 103*(3), 29–32.

Rapoport, R., & Rapoport, R. N. (1969). The dual-career family: A variant pattern and social change. *Human Relations Journal, 22*(1), 3–30.

Reid, E., & Ramarajan, L. (2016, June). Managing high-intensity workplace. *Harvard Business Review*.

Spector, P. E., & Allen, T. D. (2007). Cross-national differences in relationships of work demands, job satisfaction and turnover intentions with work-family conflict. *Personnel Psychology, 60*(4), 805–835.

Thomas, L. T., & Ganster, D. C. (1995). Impact of family-supportive work behaviours on work-family conflict and strain: A control perspective. *Journal of Applied Psychology, 80*(1), 6–15.

Yang, N., Chen, C. C., Choi, J., & Zou, Y. (2007). Sources of work-family conflict: A Sino-US comparison of the effects of work and family demands. *Academy of Management Journal, 43*(1), 113–123.

CHAPTER 7

Does Corporate Governance Affect the Financial Performance and Quality of Financial Reporting of Companies? A Study on Selected Indian Companies

Sushil Kalyani, Neeti Mathur, and Prashant Gupta

INTRODUCTION

Suppose I have come by a fair amount of wealth, either by way of legacy or by means of trade and industry. I must know that all that wealth does not belong to me; what belongs to me is the right to an honourable livelihood, no better than that enjoyed by millions of others. The rest of my wealth belongs to the community and must be used for the welfare of the community. "*M.K. Gandhi*"

The philosophy of trusteeship states that wealth creators are trustees of society and they have responsibility to look after all components of social,

---

S. Kalyani (✉) • N. Mathur
NIIT University, Neemrana, Rajasthan, India
e-mail: sushil.kalyani@niituniversity.in; neeti.mathur@niituniversity.in

P. Gupta
Indian Institute of Management (IIM), Trichy, Tamilnadu, India
e-mail: prashant@iimtrichy.ac.in

economic and natural environments. The concept of trusteeship promulgated by Mahatma Gandhi implies stewardship without ownership and the stewardship is not for private profit but for the welfare of all. The Gandhian philosophy of trusteeship is a moral foundation of corporate governance. Those firms that have a broader aim than profit maximization focus on ethical practices in business, accountability towards stakeholders and the environment in which these operate.

The Organisation for Economic Co-operation and Development (OECD) Principles of Corporate Governance state: "Corporate governance involves a set of relationships between a company's management, its board, its shareholders and other stakeholders. Corporate governance also provides the structure through which the objectives of the company are set, and the means of attaining those objectives and monitoring performance are determined." The Principles explain the system as: "Corporate governance involves a set of relationships between a company's management, its board, its shareholders and other stakeholders. Corporate governance also provides the structure through which the objectives of the company are set, and the means of attaining those objectives and monitoring performance are determined."

SCOPE OF CORPORATE GOVERNANCE

Primarily, transparency, accountability, responsibility and fairness are core guiding principles of corporate governance. Corporate governance is significant for the organizations whose motives are long-term sustainability, growth and good corporate image. Corporate governance has a broad scope of ensuring economic growth, long-term sustainability and wealth maximization of stakeholders. It ensures investors', employees', management's, customers' and government's interest as a whole and the result is holistic growth and development of the organization. Good corporate governance provides operational and financial efficiency in organization and control measures to reduce operational, financial and credit risk. It helps in quality control, waste minimization and shrinks probability of frauds, bribery and misrepresentation. It helps in developing good brand and corporate image. Klein et al. (2005) analyse the relationship between firm value, as measured by Tobin's q, and newly released indices of effective corporate governance for a sample of 263 Canadian firms. The results indicate that corporate governance does matter in Canada. However, not all elements of measured governance are important, and the effects of governance do differ by ownership category. For the entire sample of firms we find no evidence that a total governance index affects firm performance. This is mainly because we find no evidence that board independence, the most heavily-weighted sub-index, has any positive effect on firm performance. Indeed, for family-owned firms we find that the effect is negative. In general, sub-indices measuring effective compensation, disclosure and shareholder rights practices enhance performance, and this is true for most ownership types. It is a right path towards the strategic goal of the owners. Financial companies, domestic and international, are required to have appropriate levels of corporate governance standards owing to their sensitive role in the economy to maintain credibility in the marketplace (Karamanou and Vafeas 2005). There is a need to improve the quality of financial reporting and strengthen the control of managers by setting up good governance structures in order to prevent failure in financial disclosure. Lawrence Imeokparia (2013) discusses the corporate governance and financial reporting in the banking institutions in Nigeria. This study was embarked upon to explore the intricacies of corporate governance and financial reporting issues in the banking industry. The recommendations highlighted by this study may be summarized into a singular action plan, which entails the unification of ethical regulations and introduction of legal enforcement to ensure compliance in governance and its consequent reporting.

Obona and Ebimobowei (2012) opined that financial reporting forms the basis for economic decision making by various stakeholders and that the financial reports produced by the accountant should be based on certain fundamental qualities for various stakeholders to understand the content of the report. Corporations with better corporate governance have better operating performance than those companies with poor corporate governance (Bhagat and Black 2002). The research evidence shows that board composition changes and the board's degree of independence does not produce any influence on the quality of the accounting information in Portugal. Corporate governance is needed to create a corporate culture of transparency, accountability and disclosure. It refers to compliance with all the moral and ethical values, the legal framework and voluntarily adopted practices. As per Narendra Sharma (2014), corporate governance disclosure has seen renewed interest by researchers, policy makers, and regulating bodies internationally, but has remained only an emerging construct in Nepal.

Literature Review on Corporate Governance

Das and Ghosh (2004) claimed that the role and the need of good corporate governance in India have been reiterated in several forums. The major challenge in progressing to good corporate governance, according to them, is to build essential knowledge on relevant laws, duties and responsibilities, financial analysis, strategy, business ethics and effective decision-making. Eduardo (2004) states that the challenge for corporate governance reform in Asia is to channel the energies and operations of relationship-based businesses into structures that are more transparent and consequently more clearly equitable for non-family investors. Nwokoma (2005) states that "corporate governance has to be perceived and understood in a much broader spectrum, encompassing all players involved in the business, instead of restricting it only to board and executive management." Mishra et al. (2001) say that, however, the impact of founding family directors on firm value is not affected by corporate governance conditions such as firm age, board independence, and number of share classes. Sharma (2004) highlights that due to the high incidence of fraud in Australia, regulatory reports suggest strengthening the monitoring role of the board of directors (BOD). These reports recommend greater independence and no duality (chairperson of the BOD should not be the CEO) on the BOD. Sanusi (2003) opines that along with corporate responsibility, corporate governance provides the foundation of market integrity and thus imposes a lot of responsibility on the board of directors, thus requiring them to strike a delicate balance between the interests of the various stakeholders and Management. La Porta et al. (1999) used data on ownership structures of large corporations in 27 wealthy economies to identify the ultimate controlling shareholders of these firms. They found that, except in economies with very good shareholder protection, relatively few of these firms are widely held, in contrast to Berle and Means's image of ownership of the modern corporation. Rather, these firms are typically controlled by families or the State. Equity control by financial institutions is far less common. The controlling shareholders typically have power over firms significantly in excess of their cash flow rights, primarily through the use of pyramids and participation in management.

Bhattacharya et al. (2011) talk about how companies can use corporate responsibility towards stakeholders as a channel for nurturing company goals. Ultimately, stakeholders prefer companies that produce tangible and psychological benefits; that favor good corporate governance. Better governance reforms reduce uncertainty and are engines of stability and continued progress. Qaiser Rafique Yasser (2011) analyzed the link between the corporate governance quality and performance of firms in Pakistan. Performance effects of corporate governance quality with reference to both valuation and operating performance is the primary focus of this analysis. The author compared the Corporate Governance Scoring Index with operating performance and valuation and found positive results between them. Kansal et al. (2014) observed this in a comprehensive study that makes a value-adding contribution to the existing CSR literature by investigating various financial and non-financial determinants of CSRD in India. The study found that overall disclosures are low; these results are similar to those reported by earlier studies in developing countries. The results highlight that a firm's industry affiliation and profitability significantly influence its CSRD.

Mohammed Darweesh (2015) reveals that corporate governance has a significant role in improving a firm's performance. The results indicate that leaders should consider good and robust governance in the areas of mechanisms of larger board size, excessive executive compensation, and minimal number of board committees to improve corporate financial performance. Haniffa and Hudaib (2006) found that board size and substantial shareholdings to be significantly associated with both market and accounting performance measures. In addition, they found a significant relationship between multiple directorships and market performance while role duality and managerial shareholdings are significantly associated with accounting performance. The result is robust with respect to controls for gearing, company size, industry membership and growth opportunities. Akeju and Babatunde (2017), in their paper on corporate governance and financial reporting quality in Nigeria, established the relationship between corporate governance mechanisms (board characteristics, audit committees, board independence, board size and growth) and financial reporting quality. The findings of the study revealed that corporate governance improves the financial reporting quality in Nigeria. Adegbie and Fofah (2016) found that Nigerian banking sector has witnessed financial distress which has led to the liquidation of some financial institutions from pre-independence to date. It was discovered that non-compliance with relevant ethical codes and poor corporate governance affected the preparation of quality and faithful financial reports. The study therefore purposed to evaluate ethics and corporate governance in financial reporting and looked at the role of International Financial Reporting Standards (IFRS) in the harmonized global reporting system. The study adopted survey research design with the use of structured questionnaire in obtaining opinion from the operators and regulators. Ujunwa (2012) discovered by using a panel data regression model drive that board size and CEO/chairman duality are negatively related with firm performance, whereas board independence has a positive impact on firm performance. Corporate governance and board research have mainly been influenced by agency theory, stewardship theory and resource dependency theory. Ponnu (2008) concluded that the impact of CEO duality and proportion of independent directors on company performance has received close attention by researchers in corporate governance in recent years.

Wu et al. (2005) found that board composition is positively and significantly related to firm performance while similar results have been concluded by Javid and Iqbal (2008) who concluded in their study that board composition has a positive and significant impact on firm performance. Yasser et al. (2011) found there is no significant relationship between Return on Assets (ROA) and CEO/chairman duality. Latif et al. (2013), in their paper "Impact of Corporate Governance on Firm Performance: Evidence from Sugar Mills of Pakistan," state that corporate governance and board size have significant impact on firm performance, while board composition has an insignificant impact on ROA and CEO/chairman duality has a significant impact on ROA. Collectively, all independent variables have significant impact on corporate governance. Lam and Lee (2012) determined that board composition is positively (negatively) related to firm performance. Such positive or negative relationship depends on the independence or non-independence of the composition of the board. Asyiqin et al. (2014) examine the relationships between corporate governance structure and the likelihood of fraudulent financial reporting. They conclude that effective corporate governance structure is paramount in enhancing the credibility of financial reporting. Agrawal and Chadha (2005) studied about Corporate governance and accounting scandals. They empirically examined whether certain corporate governance mechanisms are related to the probability of a company restating its earnings. They examined a sample of 159 U.S. public companies that restated earnings and an industry-size matched sample of control firms. They assembled a novel, hand-collected data set that measured the corporate governance characteristics of these 318 firms. Norwani et al. (2011) state that Corporate governance became important when most of the big companies collapsed. The failure in corporate governance forced rules and regulation to be enacted. Countries around the world find the best solution to battle the corporate governance issues.

Research Methodology

To answer the research questions, we collected data from the Top 100 BSE companies. We used a convenient sampling technique to select samples from the population from financial years 2015 and 2016.

This study was conducted based on the secondary data of the selected companies using the Prowess database. Apart from this, information was also obtained from the databases of CMIE Prowess Package and Capitaline, and annual financial statements were downloaded from the websites of respective companies. For this study, we analyzed data from twenty companies selected from the Top 100 BSE companies. Judgement sampling, which is a non-random sampling technique, is chosen for sample selection. Desecrate statistics, correlation and multiple regression analysis were used to study the influence of independent variables, such as financial disclosure, board size, board independence, board ownership, independence of audit committee, and whistleblower policies on dependent variables for the financial performance represented by ROA, chosen amongst other ratios such as return on equity (ROE), return on capital employed (ROCE) and net profit ratio.

Limitations and Scope for Further Study

Analysis of the study is based on finance data collected from the CMIE Prowess Package and Capitaline Database. The quality of the study depends purely upon the accuracy, reliability and quality of secondary data. A detailed trend covering a lengthy period could not be done due to lack of time. Due to the influence of some extraneous variables, the intercept is very high in a few regression model analysis. Hence, for future studies, it is better to include those independent variables to find the true impact of those variables on the financial decision in respect of capital structure and profitability.

Hypothesis Framed

The following null hypotheses were framed and tested.

H01: There is no significant relation between Financial Disclosure and Financial Performance.

H02: There is no significant relation between Board Size and Financial Performance.

H03: There is no significant relation between Board Independence and Financial Performance.

H04: There is no significant relation between Board Ownership and Financial Performance.

H05: There is no significant relation between Independence of Audit Committee and Financial Performance.

H06: There is no significant relation between Whistleblower Policies and Financial Performance.

Tools Used for Analysis

We used Pearson's correlation coefficient and a regression analysis model as well as descriptive statistics such as mean, mode, standard deviation and so on to analyze the unique impact of corporate governance disclosure on financial performance of firms.

Dependent Variables

The following paragraphs describe the dependent variable used in the study as well as other variables which represent the financial performance.

Corporate financial performance, or ROA, is measured as the ratio between earnings before interest and tax (EBIT) and total assets. Profitability is a very vital variable for a firm. A firm with high profitability and sales turnover would not rely on debt capital, but if it goes for external financing, it would face no difficulty in bearing the fixed charges associated with it.

Corporate Financial Performance (Profitability) =
Avg. EBIT / Avg. Total Assets

Net profit ratio expresses the relationship between net profit after taxes and sales. This ratio is a measure of overall profitability. Net profit is arrived at after taking into account both the operating and non-operating items of incomes and expenses. The ratio indicates what portion of the net sales is left for the owners after all expenses have been met. The higher the net profit ratio, the higher the profitability of the business.

Net Profit Ratio = (Net Profit after Tax / Net Sales) × 100

Return on capital employed (ROCE) is a financial ratio that measures a company's profitability and the efficiency with which its capital is employed. Capital employed is the sum of shareholders' equity and debt liabilities; it can be simplified as: Total Assets − Current Liabilities

ROCE = Earnings before Interest and Tax (EBIT) / Capital Employed

Return on equity (ROE) is the amount of net income returned as a percentage of shareholders' equity. Return on equity measures a corporation's profitability by revealing how much profit a company generates with the money shareholders have invested.

ROE = Net Income / Shareholder's Equity

Reporting quality pertains to the quality of information in financial reports, including disclosures in notes. High-quality reporting provides decision-useful information that is relevant and faithfully represents the economic reality of the company's activities during the reporting period as well as the company's financial condition at the end of the period.

Independent Variables

The following paragraphs describe the independent variables used in the study.

Financial disclosure is required of public officials and employees because it enables the public to evaluate potential conflicts of interest, deters corruption, and increases public confidence in a corporate.

Board size is the total number of directors on a board. An optimal board size should include both executive and non-executive directors. The effectiveness in structuring the board is important for governing company quality.

Board independence refers to percentage of the total number of independent non-executive directors to the total number of directors (Prabowo and Simpson 2011). The Companies Act 2013 defines an "Independent Director" as a director other than a managing director or a whole-time director or a nominee director.

CEO duality is a situation in which the CEO of a firm is also the chairman of the board. Several studies report that CEO duality is negatively and significantly related to firm performance.

The **independence of the audit committee** refers to having an auditor who is independent throughout the audit engagement as well as the period covered by the financial statements to be audited. When considering the independence of a potential or returning auditor, the audit committee should take a broad view to capture any relationships or services that could be viewed as impairing independence.

Whistleblowing policy refers to an internal process for addressing complaints. Whistleblowing is the reporting by employees of suspected misconduct, illegal acts or failure to act within the organization.

A whistleblower is an employee who reports an activity that is considered to be illegal or dishonest to one or more of the parties specified in the company's policy. The whistleblower is not responsible for investigating the activity or for determining fault or corrective measures; appropriate management officials are charged with these responsibilities.

Multiple Regression Model
The following multiple regression model has been used to test the theoretical relation between financial performance and other independent variables for corporate governance.

$$Y = a + b_1 X_1 + b_2 X_2 + b_3 X_3 + b_4 X_4 + b_5 X_5 + b_6 X_6 + e$$

where Y is the financial performance of the firm, a is the constant, b is the coefficient, X1 is financial disclosure, X2 is board size, X3 is board independence, X4 is CEO duality, X5 is independence of audit committee, X6 is whistleblower policy, and e is error rate.

Data Analysis and Results

Pearson correlation analysis establishes the linear correlation between two variables. Correlation analyses of the variables in our study provide an early sign that there is positive correlation between financial disclosure, which is an independent variable, and ROCE, which is a dependent variable (corr. = 0.454). Correlations for all other variables are shown in Table 7.1. Significant correlation between several independent variables such as financial disclosure and board size (corr. = 0.543), independence of audit committee and board size (corr. = 0.543), and independence of audit committee and board ownership (corr. = 0.987) indicate a possible multicollinearity problem. Correlation is considered significant when the probability value is less than 0.05.

Table 7.2 presents the descriptive statistics of the dependent and independent variables. The mean value of ROA of the Top 100 BSE companies during the research period equals 0.18. The mean net profit ratio is 0.34, the mean ROE is 1.47 and the mean ROCE is 0.50 during the same period. Standard deviation for ROA is 0.23, 0.43 for net profit ratio, 2.76 for ROE and 0.01 for ROCE. It is observed from table that the minimum and maximum range for ROE is significant.

A multiple regression model is used to find the impact of corporate governance on financial performance of the BSE-listed companies.

Table 7.3 shows a coefficient of determination ($R2$) of 0.74 and an adjusted $R2$ of 0.367, which explains the relationship between corporate governance and financial performance. The $R2$ of 0.74 indicates that 74% variation in financial performance is explained by corporate governance. This shows that the result is a good fit with the model. When we analyze Table 7.4, we observe an F statistic of 9.080, which is highly significant at 0.501. Hence, because the p-value is less than 0.05, there can be a linear regression relationship between the dependent (represented by net profit ratio) and independent variables. We also observe from the regression analysis in Table 7.5 that financial disclosure has a p-value of 0.021 and a corresponding t-value of 0.324; board size has a p-value of 0.345 and a corresponding t-value of −0.542; and board independence has a p-value of 0.0453 and a corresponding t-value of −2.946. This signifies that these particular variables are not important in the model. In contrast, independence of audit committee has a p-value of 0.730 and a corresponding t-value of −0.348, board ownership has a p-value of −0.589 and a corresponding t-value of −2.545, and whistleblower policy has a p-value of 0.471 and a corresponding t-value of −0.729, signifying that these variables are important enough in the model.

Table 7.1 Correlation matrix analysis results for all selected firms from Top 100 BSE companies

	ROA	Net profit ratio	ROE	ROCE	Financial disclosure	Board size	Board independence	Independence of audit committee	CEO duality	Whistle blower policies
ROA	1									
Net profit ratio	0.3	1								
ROE	−0.169	0.293	1							
ROCE	−0.113	−0.208	−0.280	1						
Financial disclosure	0.457	0.346	0.654	0.454	1					
Board size	−0.434	0.314	0.209	−0.285	0.543	1				
Board independence	−0.434	0.317	0.299	−0.245	0.433	0.345	1			
Independence of audit committee	−0.485	0.286	0.161	−0.283	0.235	0.578	0.965	1		
CEO duality	−0.489	0.318	0.189	−0.267	0.433	0.471	0.786	0.987	1	
Whistleblower policies	−0.431	0.328	0.234	−0.342	0.544	0.756	0.698	0.768	1	1

Table 7.2 Descriptive statistics

	ROA	Net profit ratio	ROE	ROCE	Financial disclosure	Board size	Board independence	Independence of audit committee	CEO duality	Whistle blower policies
Mean	0.18	0.34	1.47	0.5	0.34	6.52	6.52	6.43	6.38	6.38
Standard error	0.05	0.37	0.6	0.03	0.45	0.21	0.21	0.2	0.2	0.2
Standard deviation	0.23	0.43	2.76	0.01	0.36	0.97	0.97	0.94	0.92	0.92
Minimum	−0.16	−1.76	−0.63	0.02	0.56	3	0.34	0.45	0.35	0.65
Maximum	1.01	0.4	8.41	0	0.47	13	0.56	0.54	0.56	0.46
Count	40	40	40	40	40	40	40	40	40	40

Table 7.3 Regression analysis

Multiple R	0.307
R square	0.740
Adjusted R square	0.367
Standard error	2.801
Observations	40.000

Table 7.4 Analysis of variance (ANOVA) results

	df	SS	MS	F	Significance F
Regression	6.000	28.487	4.748	9.080	0.501
Residual	35.000	274.521	7.843		
Total	41.000	303.008			

Table 7.5 Robust analytics

	Coefficients	Standard error	t Stat	P-value	Lower 95%	Upper 95%	Lower 95.0%	Upper 95.0%
Intercept	−1.311	3.560	−0.368	0.715	−8.539	5.917	−8.539	5.917
Financial disclosure	0.000	0.000	0.324	0.021	0.012	2.118	0.001	0.166
Board size	0.000	0.000	0.542	0.345	0.236	3.176	0.010	3.123
Board independence	2.261	2.290	0.987	0.045	−2.388	6.910	−2.388	6.910
Independence of audit committee	−1.122	3.224	−0.348	0.730	−7.667	5.424	−7.667	5.424
CEO duality	1.824	3.347	−2.545	0.589	−4.971	8.619	−4.971	8.619
Whistleblower policies	−2.560	3.512	−0.729	0.471	−9.689	4.569	−9.689	4.569

Corporate Governance and Financila Reporting Quality: Further we used two models to analyze the relationship between corporate governance and financial reporting quality of the BSE-listed firms. **The first model** expresses this relationship as:

$$Y = \beta 0 + \beta 1 X 1 + \beta 2 X 2 + \beta 3 X 3 + \beta 4 X 4 + \beta 5 X 5 + \mu t$$

where Y is reporting quality, β is the regression coefficient, X1 is financial disclosure, X2 is independence of audit committee, X3 is board independence, X4 is board size, X5 is CEO duality, X6 is whistleblowing/Vigil Mechanism, and μt is the stochastic error term.

We conducted regression analysis of the dependent variable of financial reporting quality and six independent variables: financial disclosure, board size, board independence, independence of audit committee, board ownership and whistleblower policies. We observe from Table 7.6 that R2 is 0.640, meaning that 64% of the dependent variable is explained by independent variables. When we analyze Table 7.7, we observe that the F statistic is 15.556, which is highly significant at 0.000. Hence, because the p-value is less than 0.05, there can be a linear regression relationship between the dependent (represented by reporting quality) and independent variables.

We also observe from the regression analysis in Table 7.8 that financial disclosure has a p-value of 0.012 and a corresponding t-value of 0.234, and board size has a p-value of 0.032 and a corresponding t-value of −0.342, signifying that these variables are not important in the model. In contrast, board independence has a p-value of 0.013 and a corresponding t-value of −2.946, independence of audit committee has a p-value of 0.017 and a corresponding t-value of 0.515, board ownership has a p-value

Table 7.6 Regression coefficients

Multiple R	0.800
R square	0.640
Adjusted R square	0.542
Standard error	1.095
Observations	40.000

Table 7.7 Analysis of variance (ANOVA) results

ANOVA	df	SS	MS	F	Significance F
Regression	6.000	74.625	12.437	15.556	0.000
Residual	35.000	41.975	1.199		
Total	41.000	116.600			

Table 7.8 Robust analytics

	Coefficients	Standard error	t Stat	P-value	Lower 95%	Upper 95%	Lower 95.0%	Upper 95.0%
Intercept	-0.971	1.392	-0.698	0.49	-3.798	1.855	-3.798	1.855
Financial disclosure	0	0	0.234	0.021	0.012	2.015	0	0.154
Board size	0	0	0.342	0.032	0.015	3.016	0.014	0.127
Board independence	-2.638	0.895	-2.946	0.013	-4.456	-0.820	-4.456	-0.820
Independence of audit committee	3.171	1.261	2.515	0.017	0.611	5.73	0.611	5.73
CEO duality	0.488	1.309	-3.073	0.711	-2.169	3.145	-2.169	3.145
Whistle blower policies	0.255	1.373	-0.186	0.854	-2.533	3.043	-2.533	3.043

of 0.711 and a corresponding *t*-value of −3.073, and whistleblower policy has a *p*-value of 0.854 and a corresponding *t*-value of −0.186, signifying that these variables are important enough in the model.

The second model we used to judge the relationship between financial reporting quality and corporate governance is Altman's multivariate analysis model (Altman 1986). It was created by Edward I. Altman and is used to predict the likelihood of bankruptcy in a company. In his study, Altman took into consideration 22 accounting and non-accounting ratios that had been deemed to be predictors of corporate distress and grouped those into 5 groups, namely liquidity, profitability, leverage, solvency, and activity. After his study, only 5 were selected from 22 variables which he considered as the best combination to predict bankruptcy. The purposes of these five selected ratios are as follows:

1. To measure liquidity position of the firms
2. To measure reinvestment of earnings of the firms
3. To measure profitability of the firms
4. To measure financial leverage condition of the firms
5. To measure sales-generating ability of firms' assets

Altman developed the following discriminant function for public manufacturing companies:

$$Z = 1.2X1 + 1.4X2 + 3.3X3 + 0.6X4 + 1.0X5$$

He also developed a revised Z-score model for privately held firms:

$$Z = 0.717(X1) + 0.847(X2) + 3.107(X3) + 0.420(X4) + 0.998(X5)$$

where Z is the overall index, X1 = current liabilities/total assets, X2 = retained earnings/total assets, X3 = EBIT/total assets, X4 = book value of equity/total liabilities, and X5 = sales/total assets. A change in the weight factor is also calculated.

The Z-Score calculated for a firm as an example for this study is as follows:

$$Z = 0.717(0.231) + 0.847(0.686) + 3.107(0.224)$$
$$+ 420(1.852) + 0.998(0.659)$$
$$Z = 2.986$$

There are three zones decided by the model as follows:
Z > 2.9—"Safe" Zone
1.23 < Z < 2.9—"Grey" Zone
Z < 1.23—"Distress" Zone

The Z value we calculated for our purposes is more than 2.9, which shows that the quality of reporting is good as the firms are in the Safe Zone. Similary a detailed analysis was done for all the companies and we found the results to be in sync with our observations of their financial performances.

Result of Hypothesis Testing

The null hypotheses framed earlier have been accepted or rejected as follows.

H01 :There is no significant relation between Financial Disclosure and Financial Performance. (H01 is not accepted as there is significant relation between Financial Disclosure and Financial Performance.)

H02 :There is no significant relation between Board Size and Financial Performance. (H02 is not accepted as there is significant relation between Financial Performance and Board Size.)

H03 :There is no significant relation between Board Independence and Financial Performance. (H02 is not accepted as there is significant relation between Financial Performance and Board Independence.)

H04 :There is no significant relation between Board Ownership and Financial Performance. (H02 is not accepted as there is significant relation between Financial Performance and CEO Duality.)

H05 :There is no significant relation between Independence of Audit Committee and Financial Performance. (H02 is not accepted as there is significant relation between Financial Performance and Independence of Audit Committee.)

H06 : There is no significant relation between Whistleblower Policies and Financial Performance. (H02 is not accepted as there is significant relation between Financial Performance and Whistle Blower Mechanism.)

Conclusion

This chapter examines corporate governance disclosure and its influence on financial performance and quality of financial reporting of selected BSE-listed companies. Governance mechanisms are represented by board characteristics, audit committees, board independence, board size and whistleblower mechanism. The findings of the study revealed that there is a significant positive relationship between corporate governance disclosure and financial performance of listed companies on the basis of Pearson correlation and multiple regression analysis. Findings on financial reporting quality show that the higher the level of board characteristics, audit committees, board independence, board size and whistleblower mechanism, the higher the financial reporting quality in BSE-listed companies based on regression modeling and Altman's multivariate analysis model.

References

Adegbie, F. J., & Fofah, E. T. (2016). Ethics, corporate governance and financial reporting in the Nigerian banking industry. *Global Role of International Reporting Standards, 5*(1), 1–14.

Agrawal, A., & Chadha, S. (2005). Corporate governance and accounting scandals. *Journal of Law and Economics, 48*(2), 371–406.

Akeju, J. B., & Babatunde, A. A. (2017, February). Corporate governance and financial reporting quality in Nigeria. *International Journal of Information Research and Review, 4*(2), 3749–3753.

Altman, E. I. (1986). *Handbook of corporate finance, 15*. New York: John Wiley and Sons Inc.

Altman, E. I. (2000). Predicting financial distress of companies: Revisiting the Z-score and zeta® models. Handbook of Research Methods and Applications in Empirical Finance, 2013, 428–456.

Asyiqin, W. A., Razali, W. M., & Arshad, R. (2014). Disclosure of corporate governance structure and the likelihood of fraudulent financial reporting. *Procedia – Social and Behavioral Sciences Science Direct, 243*–253.

Bhagat, S., & Black, B. S. (2002). The non-correlation between board independence and long-term performance. *Journal of Corporation Law, 27*, 231–273.

Bhattacharya, C. B., Korschun, D., & Sen, S. (2011). *What really drives value in corporate responsibility?* McKinsey Report.

Das, A., & Ghosh, S. (2004). Corporate regulations and quality of financial reporting: A proposed study, corporate governance in banking system. *Economic and Political Weekly*, 1263–1266.

Eduardo, T. G. (2004). Impact of corporate governance on productivity: Asian experience. *European Journal of Business and Management*, Asian Productivity Organization: Tokyo, 47–57.

Haniffa, R. M., & Hudaib, M. (2006). Corporate governance structure and performance of Malaysian listed companies. *Journal of Business Finance and Accounting*, 33(7), 1034–1062.

Kansal, M., Joshi, M., & Batra, G. S. (2014). Determinants of corporate social responsibility disclosures: Evidence from India. *Advances in Accounting*, 30, 217–229, online April 2014.

Karamanou, I., & Vafeas, N. (2005). The association between corporate boards, audit committees, and management earnings forecasts: An empirical analysis. *Journal of Accounting Research*, 43(3), 453–486.

Klein, P., Shapiro, D., & Young, J. (2005). Corporate governance, family ownership and firm value: The Canadian evidence. *Corporate Governance*, 13(6), 769–784.

La Porta, R., Lopez-de-Silanes, F., & Shleifer, A. (1999). Corporate ownership around the world. *Journal of Finance*, 54, 471–518.

Lam, T. Y., & Lee, S. K. (2012). Family ownership, board committees and firm performance: Evidence from Hong Kong. *Corporate Governance*, 12(3), 6–10.

Latif, B., Shahid, M. N., Haq, M. Z. U., Waqas, H. M., & Arshad, A. (2013). Impact of corporate governance on firm performance: Evidence from sugar mills of Pakistan. *European Journal of Business and Management*, 5(1), 51–59.

Lawrence Imeokparia. (2013). Corporate governance and financial reporting in the Nigerian banking sector. *An Emperical Study – Asian Economic and Financial Review*, 3(8), 1083–1095.

Mishra, C. S., Randoy, T., & Jenssen, J. I. (2001). The effect of family influence on firm value and corporate governance. *Journal of International Financial Management and Accounting*, 12(3), 235–259.

Mohammed, S. Darweesh. (2015). *Correlations between corporate governance, financial performance, and market value*. Walden Dissertations and Doctoral Studies Collection, Walden University.

Narendra, S. (2014). Extent of corporate governance disclosure by banks and finance companies listed on Nepal stock exchange. *Advances in Accounting*, 30, 425–439.

Norwani, N., Mohamad, Z. Z., & Chek, I. A. (2011, November). Corporate governance failure and its impact on financialreporting within selected companies. *International Journal of Business and Social Science*, 2(Special Issue), 205–213.

Nwokoma, N. I. (2005). Issues and challenges in banking sector consolidation and economic development in Nigeria. *The Nigerian Stockbroker*, 6(3), 3–12.

Obona, G. N., & Ebimobowei, A. (2012). Effects of ethical accounting standards on the quality of financial reporting of banks in Nigeria. *Current Research Journal of Social Science, 4*(1), 69–78.

Ponnu, C. H. (2008, March). Corporate governance structures and the performance of Malaysian public listed companies. *International Review of Business Research Papers, 4*(2), 217–230.

Prabowo, M., & Simpson, J. (2011). Independent directors and firm performance in family controlled firms: evidence from Indonesia. *Asian-Pacific Economic Literature, 25*(1), 121–132.

Sanusi, J. O. (2003). Embracing good corporate practices in Nigeria. Paper presented at the 2003 directors' seminar organised by Financial Institute Training Center, Nigeria on 17–19 June, 2003.

Sharma, V. D. (2004). Board of director characteristics, institutional ownership, and fraud: Evidence from Australia. *AUDITING: A Journal of Practice & Theory, 23*(2), 105–117.

Ujunwa, A. (2012). Board characteristics and the financial performance of Nigerian quoted firms. *Corporate Governance, 12*(5), 5–5. Vol. 04, Issue, 02, 2017, pp. 3749–3753.

Wu, M. C., Lin, H. C., Lin, I., & Lai, C. F. (2005). *The effects of corporate governance on firm performance. Companies Act 2013*. Retrieved October 26, 2017, from www.sebi.gov.in

Yasser, Q. R. (2011, June). Corporate governance and performance (a case study for Pakistani communication sector). *International Journal of Trade Economics and Finance, 2*(3), 204–214.

Yasser, Q. R. (2013). Corporate governance and performance: An analysis of Pakistani listed firms. *International Research, Journal of Library, Information and Archival Studies, 5*(1).

Yasser, Q. R., Entebang, H., & Mansor, S. A. (2011). Corporate governance and firm performance in Pakistan: The case of Karachi stock exchange (KSE)-30. *Journal of Economics and International Finance, 3*(8), 482–492.

CHAPTER 8

Factors Impacting Purchase of Private Labels in India

Richa Sardana, Aarti Duseja, and Pooja Misra

INTRODUCTION

With a valuation of USD 672 billion and contributing to about 10% of GDP, the Indian retail industry has seen significant growth with some strong players entering the market. India, as the fifth largest destination in the global retail space, is growing at 12% per annum. The retail industry can be categorized as organized and unorganized. Unorganized retail constitutes 91% of the sector whereas organized retail constitutes 9% of the total. Although India has a low retail penetration compared to other countries like the United States, where it is 85%, the Indian economy is expected to grow 7.2% and 7.7% in FY18 and FY19, respectively, according to the International Monetary Fund (IMF). The retail industry is expected to grow at a compounded annual growth rate of 17% over the next four years, which would lead it to achieve USD 1300 billion by the end of 2020 according to India Brand Equity Foundation (IBEF). With many factors such as growing income levels, changing lifestyles and

---

R. Sardana (✉) • A. Duseja • P. Misra
Birla Institute of Management Technology, Greater Noida,
Uttar Pradesh, India
e-mail: richa.sardana18@bimtech.ac.in; aarti.duseja18@bimtech.ac.in; pooja.misra@bimtech.ac.in

© The Author(s) 2019
Rajagopal, R. Behl (eds.), *Business Governance and Society*,
https://doi.org/10.1007/978-3-319-94613-9_8

preferences, organized retail is growing at a fast pace. One of the emerging factors that has given a push to organized retail is the concept of private labels (Ratings 2017).

Private labels are those products or services that are provided by a company under another company's brand. Although this concept of private labels is at an early stage with an estimated share of less than 7–8% of the retail sales of the organized sector, it is growing quickly. The growth is primarily due to the increased preference to value loyalty over brand loyalty, increased variety in private label products, emergence of newer ones in areas where strength of brand is lower and an ever-increasing modern trade (Kumar et al. 2015). Also, according to industry experts, these private brands are expected to capture 50% of the market in the near future with the opening up of more and more retail space. Anything greater than 50%, which is the saturation point for retailers, leaves the customers with the view of not having enough choices. Countries like the United Kingdom and Switzerland have reached this saturation point and India is expected to reach it soon (Subha et al. 2014a, 2014b).

As far as the market for private labels is concerned, the category of food alone contributes 76% of the total sales. In this food category, packaged grocery holds the dominant position accounting for 53% of the total sales. As far as the non-food segment is concerned, household cleaners are at the top contributing about 48% of total private label sales. Other non-food categories that contribute significantly include fabric care, personal care and the general category. This growth in the segment has been due to the changing characteristics of the modern shopper who now has more disposable income to spend and experiment with. This particularly applies to the grocery shopping habits of the customer where he is looking at shopping as a sensorial experience rather than taking it as a chore, and this shift has made consumers less dependent on the fixed list of brands. Also the increasing preference of private labels has been due to the assurance to the consumer of having a direct interaction with the retailer while shopping. This change in the buying behavior of people has been primarily due to the access to more knowledge by buyers through the emergence of more and more marketing tools (Dhaktod and Chib 2016). When we compare private brands with national brands, a Market Track survey found that 78% of shoppers purchase store brands. The survey also found that the purchasers include older demographics rather than younger ones (Market Track 2017).

With the changing times, private labels are no longer considered as low-cost alternatives to the national brands due to which many national brands now consider these brands as their competitors. This change in mindset happened when retailers tried to develop private labels at attractive prices using their expertise. One more reason for the increasing sales of private labels is the demographics of the majority purchasing group; individuals younger than 30 years old comprise 60% of buyers. Having more risk-taking abilities, this generation is more attracted to these new products. Also this chunk of the population is in favor of maximum value derived from their income. Retailers are also working to change the perception of consumers towards the quality of the private labels. The products once considered low-cost alternatives are now being developed with regards to better packaging and labelling in order to make them more attractive. Additionally, sampling is being used in stores to make the customers aware of the quality of the products. Along with sampling, researchers use many other methods for promoting products, including heavy discounts. Many of these retailers have been sharing manufacturing capacity with national players to create an ecosystem of a better competitive environment. With the increasing market share of private labels, retailers can look for more channels to increase their penetration. According to Nielson's 2010 global online survey in which 27,000 respondents were taken from 53 countries, the private label is a phenomenon that is going to stay (Nielson 2011).

Literature Review

Private labels have gained momentum in recent years. On one hand, national brands are growing at a rate of 2–3% per annum, and on the other hand, the private label market is growing at a rate of 6% worldwide. There are retailers like Tesco and Walmart who have been able to achieve tremendous success through private labels with sales of these private label products contributing more than 40% of total sales (Kumar and Gurunathan 2016). According to the experiences of European countries, it has been observed that the growth of a private label accelerates when market share is in the 5–8% range (Patra and Jena 2016). In the Indian context, private labels are still in their nascent stage, contributing less than 7–8% of organized retail sales. Retailers like Future Group, Aditya Birla Retail Ltd., and Tata have been increasingly focusing on their private labels, which are leading to an increase in their market share. This growth is driven by the preference of high 'value loyalty' over brand loyalty by Indian consumers and the rapidly increasing modern trade. The major concern pertaining to private labels was the perception that the consumer had regarding them. Private labels were perceived as products available for a low price. However, this perception is quickly changing as consumers are now evaluating private label products as quality products (Patra and Jena 2016). In addition, interestingly, there is a status symbol attached to owning these products. Hariprakash (2011) stated that there is a need for developing private label products that are of good quality and offer more value. Sainsbury's, a UK-based supermarket is an example. According to Hariprakash, even if private labels are doing well in the market, there is a need for the retailer to focus on national brands if it wants a greater retention of customers. Also, he states that private labels will only occupy 50% of Indian retail space if the government opens up retail. Again, 50% is the saturation point; anything higher and consumers feel that they lack choices.

Innovation is yet another requirement for a private label to grow. Increase in private label sales is directly proportional to the increase in their promotions by strong retailers. Thus, for the overall success of private labels, a duplicate or copied product would not work. Instead, retailers need to work on customer loyalty, store image and competitive edge (Dhaktod and Chib 2016). When consumers get more convenience and value for money, they are more likely to be attracted to private label brands (Paswan and Vahie 2006).

Price

Gone are the days when private labels were looked upon as only low-cost alternatives to national brands. According to a 2014 Nielson report, 70% of people who purchase private labels do so to save money, 67% were of the view that these brands provide good value for the cost, and 62% felt that their purchases make them feel like smart shoppers (Nielson 2014). These changes have occurred as retailers are shifting their focus from the price game to developing a structured portfolio of store brands along with positioning them distinctly. Also, there is less scope of private labels doing well by just keeping their price levels cheap. Good quality and value also hold equal importance in the minds of the consumers.

Store Loyalty

With regards to consumer loyalty, the reserach states that they are not loyal. Almost three fourths of shoppers would prefer switching to another brand if that brand is on sale. However, according to the Nielson report (2014), shoppers in Asia are strongly brand loyal. Also, it is a risky proposition for a shopper from a low-income group to spend his money on a brand he does not trust. In Indonesia, 59% of consumers believe that whenever they buy new brands, they are risking wasting their money. In Thailand, 58% of consumers believe this. This is the reason why people prefer buying brands advertised on television every week (Nielson 2014). Thus, store loyalty is one of the very important factors a consumer uses in determining whether to purchase a private label product.

Store Image

Consumers' perception of private labels is made by the image of the store to which they belong. There is definitely a great need for retailers to create a favorable image of their stores. A strong store image can be created by improving on various factors, such as adopting suitable pricing strategy, offering quality products, offering a variety of products, and focusing on improving in-store atmosphere. Store image positively influences people's perception of quality and store loyalty, which play a major role in consumers' decision-making process when it comes to private labels. Additionally, customers assume that there is more variety of private labels in a grocery store, which has a positive store image, compared to a store that has not managed to build a strong image in the eyes of the consumer (Ji 2011). Also, consumers may be rational in perceiving that the store that is unattractive stocks poor-quality products. Alternatively, a store can have a positive image irrespective of whether or not it is a part of a chain of stores, which would help to curb the negatives of poor store attractiveness (Richardson et al. 1996).

Visibility

For a retailer, the shelf space allocated to the products plays a very important role. Since a retailer has to place both the national and store brands, this task becomes very critical. It has been said that there is a negative relation between shelf space allocated and bargaining power of the customers.

Also, more shelf space is allocated by the retailer to the private brands as compared to national brands. According to the results, 20% more shelf space is allocated to private brands. The private labels are often placed near national brands to develop a perception of high quality (Zameer et al. 2012). When it comes to the promotion of private labels, in-store promotions are done heavily. Direct media and mass media are also channels for marketing (Accenture 2012). Thus, in-store promotions are major contributors in promotions and help to drive sales of a product.

Packaging

Packaging of a private label product plays an important role in building a perception of its quality. In his research, Nair (2011) states that people have negative perceptions regarding the packaging of private label products. Almost 63% were of the view that the packaging of private label products is unattractive. Also, the packaging of a private label is crucial to persuading the customers of the similarity of the core content of private labels to that of the other manufacturer brands. To attract customers to the packaging, it has been said that foil stamping provides the real advantage. Elimination of over-packaging of products also works positively for the image of the retailers, especially in the context of sustainable development since consumers do not have to deal with unnecessary packaging. Monnot et al. (2014) state that as far as communication strategies of private labels are concerned, more emphasis should be placed on the price, convenience, and so on, and these strategies should focus on the fact that elimination of over-packaging does not affect the product quality.

Product Type

The penetration of private labels is different from that of national products. For products that have low penetration, retailers need to come up with technological improvements to sustain them in the market. In the case of increasing penetration of private labels, there is a need to change the packaging in such a manner that adds value to it. In a market with well-established penetration, there is a need to cut the costs in the supply chain so that the money saved can be reinvested in the business (Quelch and Harding 1996). The products that have low penetration are generally feminine hygiene or baby products. The products with higher penetration include dried pasta or ready-to-eat meals. Globally, chilled ready meals have a 47% share of the market. Also, it is seen that share of the market is highest where there are commodity-based products and inexpensive technical innovation. The variety offered by private labels in a certain category requires the attention of the retailer because if the assortment is small, a customer will not be able to find the product and this in turn would affect the private label share (Wagner 2014). Thus, it is a difficult proposition for a retailer to decide the product mix.

Although the market of private labels is in its nascent stage, its growth prospects are huge. Thus, it becomes necessary to understand the factors that can accelerate its growth. This chapter highlights all those growth-related factors. In our research work, we have analyzed factors such as price, store loyalty, store image, packaging, visibility and the kind of product, which influence the purchase of private labels in the Indian market.

Research Objectives and Focus Issues

Interestingly, research in India has not yet fully investigated the impact of the aforementioned factors on the purchase of private labels. The scope of this study is the retail industry in India with specific reference to Delhi and the National Capital Region (NCR). The research objectives are as follows:

- To analyze the impact of price, store loyalty, store image, packaging, visibility and the kind of product on purchase of private label products in the market.
- To investigate the strength of relationship, if any, between price, store loyalty, store image, packaging, visibility and the kind of product and purchase of private label products.

Analysis and Interpretation

Research Methodology

Given the exploratory nature of the research, it was ex post facto in nature. The design of the investigative approach included self-completed questionnaires and possible secondary sources (statistical handbooks, books, reports, journals, internet information). Primary data was collected through administered questionnaires to assess the impact of price, kind of product, packaging, store loyalty, visibility and store image on purchase of private label products. We collected data from 129 consumers in Delhi and the NCR region. The respondents were approached personally for their responses and interviews.

Reliability

We used Cronbach's alpha to analyze the reliability of our questions. Cronbach's alpha for the purchase of private label, price, kind of product, packaging, store loyalty, visibility and store image are 0.56, 0.57, 0.59, 0.75, 0.60, 0.78 and 0.82, respectively, which indicates medium to strong internal consistency amongst the questions asked.

Table 8.1 shows that there is a moderate to strong correlation between purchase of private label and factors such as store loyalty, visibility and store image. The correlation in the case of purchase of private label shows that independent factors such as price, packaging and type of product have a moderate impact.

REGRESSION ANALYSIS

Regression analysis helps us understand how the typical value of the dependent variable changes when any one of the independent variables is varied while the other independent variables are held fixed. On taking the independent parameters as price, kind of product, packaging, store loyalty, visibility and store image and the dependent variable as purchase of private label, we observed that the value of R^2 derived was 53.4%, which shows that 53.4% of the variation in purchase of private label can be explained by price, kind of product, packaging, store loyalty, visibility and store image (Table 8.2).

The equation derived from regression analysis is as exhibited below:

$$\text{Purchase of Private Label} = 2.58 + 0.133\,\text{Price} + 0.138\,\text{Kind of Product} \\ + 0.156\,\text{Store Loyalty} + 0.111\,\text{Visibility} \\ + 0.189\,\text{Store Image}$$

This shows that purchase of private label is expected to increase by 0.133 due to price change, 0.139 due to the product kind, 0.138 due to store loyalty on the part of the consumer, 0.111 due to the visibility or the private label merchandise being stocked in such a way that it is visible to the consumer and 0.189 because of the store image.

Table 8.1 Pearson correlation analysis

	Price	Kind of product	Packaging	Store loyalty	Visibility	Store image	Purchase of private label
Price	1						
Kind of product	0.026969	1					
Packaging	0.428629	0.356118	1				
Store loyalty	0.420243	0.236674	0.405853	1			
Visibility	0.341223	0.223483	0.477032	0.564089	1		
Store image	0.383169	0.297279	0.511344	0.59137	0.684022	1	
Purchase of private label	0.420198	0.464813	0.486896	0.564045	0.586867	0.637016	1

Correlation is significant at the 0.01 level (2-tailed)
Correlation is significant at the 0.05 level (2-tailed)

Table 8.2 Regression coefficients

Regression statistics

Multiple R	0.730867
R square	0.534167
Adjusted R square	0.511257
Standard error	1.395427
Observations	129

ANOVA

	Df	SS	MS	F	Significance F
Regression	6	272.4084	45.4014	23.31604	3.31E-18
Residual	122	237.5606	1.947218		
Total	128	509.969			

	Coefficients	Standard error	t stat	P-value	Lower 95%	Upper 95%	Lower 95.0%	Upper 95.0%
Intercept	2.575775	0.81835	3.147523	0.00207	0.95577	4.19578	0.95577	4.19578
Price	0.133254	0.065004	2.049916	0.042516	0.004571	0.261936	0.004571	0.261936
Kind of product	0.138483	0.053583	2.584452	0.010931	0.03241	0.244555	0.03241	0.244555
Packaging	0.037254	0.045223	0.823779	0.411672	−0.05227	0.126777	−0.05227	0.126777
Store loyalty	0.155676	0.075422	2.064051	0.041133	0.00637	0.304982	0.00637	0.304982
Visibility	0.10985	0.052158	2.106087	0.037247	0.006597	0.213103	0.006597	0.213103
Store image	0.189168	0.067263	2.812377	0.005733	0.056015	0.322321	0.056015	0.322321

Confirmatory Factor Analysis

The confirmatory factor analysis (CFA) was done using Amos 18.0. The CFA helped to identify the manifest variable that in the minds of the employees is of utmost importance. CFA helped establish the 'measurement model', which had a good fit for purchase of private labels in NCR. The CFA, with all the manifest variables and latent variables taken into consideration, produced a low Goodness of fit index (GFI). Thus, we checked values of squared multiple correlations, which explain the total amount of variance a measured variable has in common with the construct upon which it loads or the variance explained in a measured variable by the construct, and those manifest variables that had a value less than 0.5 on average were dropped. The result for the final model was $X^2/df = 1.64$; GFI = 0.823; Adjusted goodness of fit index (AGFI) = 0.766; and Root mean square error of approximation (RMSEA) = 0.071.

From the CFA or the measurement model, we observed that the manifest variables listed in Table 8.3 are the most important. These, measured variables must be duly considered by senior management of the retail industry for strategizing to increase sales.

Structural Equation Model

On obtaining the solution through the measurement model, that is, CFA for the purpose of testing and estimating causal relations and the hypothesis, we proceeded to work on the structural model. This helped us develop a hybrid model with multiple indicators or manifest variables for each latent variable or construct and paths specifying the beta coefficient connecting the latent variables. This model would be of help to senior management in the retail industry for understanding the mindset and perspective of consumers who could be engaged in purchase of private labels. The fit indices of the structural model were: $X^2/df = 2.85$; GFI = 0.817; AGFI = 0.738; and RMSEA = 0.082.

Thus, from the structural model, we arrived at the p value and standardized regression weight or beta value connecting the latent variables, helping in accepting or rejecting of the developed hypothesis.

			P value (0.001 level)	Standardized regression weight (β)
PP	<–	SI	***	0.295
PP	<–	PA	0.043	0.394
PP	<–	SL	0.001	0.832
PP	<–	V	0.006	0.553

Table 8.3 Private label brands

Manifest variable	Factor loading
P1 High price means high quality	0.538
P2 The price of a national brand affects the purchase of private label brands (national brands include Sunfeast, Nestlé, etc.)	0.604
P3 I would buy a premium-priced private label if it is offered at a better quality	0.327
KP1 I would give a private label a try if it is a consumer durable (e.g., electronics)	0.413
KP2 I would give a private label a try if it is apparel/clothing	0.667
KP3 I would give a private label a try if it is footwear	0.633
PA1 The packaging of a private label adds to the decision-making process of my purchase	0.731
PA2 The packaging in smaller packets is a feasible option for the initial purchase	0.651
PA3 I compare the packaging of a private label with that of a national brand	0.713
PA4 A better packaging means better quality	0.581
SL1 My purchase decision for private label would also be affected by the kind of customer experience	0.606
SL2 If I am frequent buyer of a private label, I would consider switching to some other brand in case of non-availability of private label at some point in time	0.496
SL3 I would prefer buying private label products from a store that I am loyal to	0.679
V1 In-store promotions (leaflets, banners, etc.) affect my purchase decision	0.686
V2 Sampling in store, especially on weekends, affects my purchase decision	0.635
V3 The location or allocated shelf space to private label products affects my purchase decision	0.672
V4 For me, private labels include impulse buying (buying of goods without planning in advance)	0.775
SI1 I would trust a private label based on the perception of the store created by others in my mind	0.775
SI2 The promotions by a renowned store through digital media affects my purchase decision	0.823
SI3 The location or allocated shelf space to private label products affects my purchase decision	0.732
PP1 I would give a private label a try if from a store I am loyal to	0.614
PP2 I can recall a private label if asked to do so	0.531
PP3 Acceptance of prices would be different for different categories (skincare products, apparel, electronics, etc.) in the case of private labels	0.276

Thus when store image increases by 1, the positive impact on purchase of private labels is 0.295; when packaging increases by 1, purchase of private labels is increased by 0.394; when store loyalty increases by 1, purchase of private labels is increased by 0.832; and when visibility increases by 1, the purchase of private labels increases by 0.553.

Managerial Implications and Conclusion

The growth of private label sales in the Indian retail industry is primarily due to the increased preference of value loyalty over brand loyalty, increased variety in private label products, emergence of newer ones in areas where strength of brand is lower, and an ever-increasing modern trade (Kumar et al. 2015). The research study shows that in the case of private labels, consumers see a moderate to strong correlation between purchase of private label products and factors such as store loyalty, visibility and store image while there is only a moderate impact for factors such as price, packaging and kind of product. As per the analysis, 53.4% of the variation in purchase of private label products can be explained by price, kind of product, packaging, store loyalty, visibility and store image. There can be other factors, such as word of mouth and promotion strategies that can additionally impact purchase of private label products. As per the study, the purchase of private label products is expected to increase by 0.133 due to price change, 0.139 due to the product kind, 0.138 due to store loyalty on the part of the consumer, 0.111 due to the visibility or the private label merchandise being stocked in such a way that it is visible to the consumer, and 0.189 because of the store image.

The measurement model or CFA gives insight into the manifest variables that are of utmost relevance for retail industry senior management to understand and build on the factors that impact purchase of private labels. Keeping the high margins that private labels help retailers make, the factors that have a high impact on purchase of these products are of extreme importance to retailers. It is interesting to note that price factors, such as the price of a national brand, affect the purchase of private label brands, and high price means high quality leading consumers to purchase premium-priced private label products over less expensive national brand products. The analysis shows that consumers are more willing to buy private label apparel and footwear products in comparison to electronic items. In the case of electronic items, consumers still prefer national brands. Packaging subfactors are also important to consumers; better packaging means better quality. Consumers tend to compare the packaging of a private label with that of a national brand, the form of private label packaging affects their decision-making process, and packaging in smaller packets is a more feasible purchase. This corroborates the research done by Nair (2011), which states that the packaging of a private label is crucial to persuade the customers of the similarity of the core content of private labels to that of the other manufacturer brands.

In the case of store loyalty, research shows that the factors that influence consumers' purchasing decisions include customer experience and whether the private label is from a store they are loyal to. In the case of visibility, factors such as in-store promotions (leaflets, banners, etc.), impulse buying (buying of goods without planning in advance), the location or allocated shelf space to private label products, and sampling in store, especially on weekends, positively impact sales of private labels. In the case of store image factors, such as perception of the store created by others in the consumer's mind, promotions by a renowned store through digital media, and the location or allocated shelf space to private label products are very strong influencers on purchase decisions. This corroborates a study that states that store image would later positively influence perception of people towards the quality and store loyalty which play a major role in the decision making process of private labels.

The structural model helps represent, estimate and test a network of relationships between manifest variables and latent constructs. Based on data collected from consumers, the established model shows that when store image increases by 1, the positive impact on purchase of private labels is 0.295; when packaging increases by 1, purchase of private labels is increased by 0.394; when store loyalty increases by 1, purchase of private labels is increased by 0.832; and when visibility increases by 1, the purchase of private labels increases by 0.553. This model would be of help to senior management in the retail industry for understanding the mindset and perspective of consumers who could be engaged in purchase of private labels.

In the present study, the sample was largely drawn from Delhi and the NCR region. Therefore, the generalizability of these results for regions across India may have to be done with caution. A larger sample size can also be studied.

REFERENCES

Accenture. (2012). *Harnessing the power of private label in retail.* Accenture.
Care Ratings. (2017). *Indian retail industry – Structure & prospects.* India: Care Ratings.
Dhaktod, M., & Chib, D. (October 2015–March 2016). Private labels: A changing perspective in Indian retailing. *International Journal of Management and Commerce Innovations, 3*(2), 282–288. Retrieved from www.researchpublish.com
Hariprakash. (2011). Private labels in INDIAN retail industry. *ZENITH International Journal of Multidisciplinary Research, 1*(8), 335–340.
Ji, J. (2011). *Consumer's attitude towards store image and private label brand image.* A dissertation submitted to Auckland University of Technology.
Kumar, D., Gurunathan, D. K., & VenkatKistaReddy, G. (2015, April–June). The growth and prospects of private label brands in Indian retail industry. *Journal of Contemporary Research in Management, 10*(2), 4–7.
Kumar, R. S., & Gurunathan, K. B. (2016, January–June). Growth and prospects of private label brands in Indian retail industry. *Vidwat*.
Market Track. (2017). *Shopper-driven transformation trends in private label promotions.* Market Track.
Monnot, E., Reniou, F., & Beatrice, P. (2014). Consumer responses to elimination of overpackaging on private label products. *International Journal of Retail and Distribution Management,* Emerald, *43*(4/5), 329–349.
Nair, P. (2011, January). Private labels brands in food & grocery: The changing perceptions of consumers & retailers in India – A study in the Pune region. *Researchers World – Journal of Arts Science & Commerce, II*(1).
Nielson. (2011). *The rise of the value-conscious shopper.* Nielson.
Nielson. (2014). *The state of private label around the world.* Nielson.
Paswan, A., & Vahie, A. (2006). Private label brand image: Its relationship with store image and national brand. *International Journal of Retail and Distribution Management, 34*(1), 67–84. https://doi.org/10.1108/09590550610642828
Patra, R. K., & Jena, D. (2016, June). An exploratory study on the growth of private label brands in India. *Abhinav National Monthly Refereed Journal of Research in Commerce & Management, 5*(6), 65–68.
Quelch, J., & Harding, D. (1996, January–February). Brands versus private labels: Fighting to win. *Harvard Business Review.*
Richardson, P., Jain, A. K., & Dick, A. (1996). The influence of store aesthetics on evaluation of private label brands. *Journal of Product & Brand Management, 5*(1), 19–28. https://doi.org/10.1108/10610429610113384

Subha, T., Kirthika, R., & Narayanasamy, P. S. (2014a). Private label brands in Indian retail industry. *International Journal of Research and Development – A Management Review (IJRDMR)*, 37–39.

Subha, T., Kirthika, R., & Narayanasamy, P. S. (2014b). *Private label brands in Indian retail industry.* IRD India.

Wagner, F. H. (2014). *Is there an 'optimal share' of private label brands for a grocery retailer?* Master thesis.

Zameer, H., Waheed, A., & Mahasin, S. S. (2012). Factors involved in retailer's decision to allocate shelf space to private and national brand and its impact on sales. *International Journal of Academic Research in Business and Social Sciences*, *2*(8), 356–366.

CHAPTER 9

Drifts in Banking Business and Deepening Losses Amidst the Insolvency and Bankruptcy Code, 2016

Deepak Tandon and Neelam Tandon

INTRODUCTION

When the Insolvency and Bankruptcy Code, 2016 (IBC) was passed in May 2016, the legal framework for insolvency resolution in India underwent a structural change. IBC proposes a paradigm shift from the existing "Debtor in possession" to a "Creditor in control" regime. It aims at consolidating all existing insolvency-related laws as well as amending multiple legislation, including the Companies Act, 2013, and has an overriding effect on all other laws relating to insolvency and bankruptcy. The code aims to resolve insolvencies in a strict time-bound manner.

D. Tandon (✉)
International Management Institute (IMI), New Delhi, Delhi, India
e-mail: deepaktandon@imi.edu

N. Tandon
Jagannath International Management School (JIMS),
New Delhi, Delhi, India
e-mail: neelam.tandon@jagannath.org

The first cases of insolvency started being admitted in the National Company Law Tribunal (NCLT), the quasi-judicial tribunal vested with adjudication powers under the IBC to take over the management of a company, once the provisions relating to corporate insolvency were notified (November 2016). In the World Bank's index on the ease of resolving insolvency, India currently ranks 136 out of the 186 countries. India's weak insolvency regime and delay in carrying out timely proceedings are a couple of the reasons for the distressed state of credit markets and Indian's global ranking on the World Bank's index. According to the World Bank data, 1.5 years is the average time taken in the United States to complete insolvency proceedings compared to 4.3 years in India. As the IBC is gaining stature, it is legitimate to take steps to ensure that the resolution process is carried out in a time-bound manner and ensure the value of assets of the insolvent firms through early identification of the financial failure.

Moreover, strict timelines for resolution may have a negative effect on banks as they may force some companies into liquidation. The strict timelines to resolve a case under IBC have a maximum period of 270 days (180 days initially with a 90-day extension—one time). After this timeframe, a company will be automatically liquidated. With the current burgeoning nonperforming asset (NPA) levels, banks have limited capacity to absorb losses from a write-off that may need to be taken for a resolution. A bank's profitability over the next year would be greatly affected if it needed to take large write-offs for those assets. This would also accent the capital needs of weaker government banks, which may require a larger capital infusion from the Indian government. Despite these challenges, the IBC is a welcome overhaul of the existing framework dealing with insolvency of corporations, individuals, partnerships and other entities. The unified regime envisages a structured and time-bound process for insolvency resolution and liquidation, which should significantly improve debt recovery rates and revitalize the ailing Indian banking sector and the insolvency of corporations.

Overview of the Insolvency and Bankruptcy Code (IBC)

The IBC, set to strengthen India's insolvency framework, has overriding effect on all other laws or any other instrument enacted earlier.

(A) Important changes in the IBC:

- Under a consolidated institutional framework, the IBC runs as a summary trial with a resolution professional (RP) having unlimited liability, who oversees the resolution process. Proceedings can be initiated by financial/operational creditors as well as corporations. Earlier, the institutional framework was fragmented.
- For an insolvency proceeding to be initiated, the minimum defaults must be Rs 0.1mn. In earlier frameworks, criteria were linked to net worth erosion or inability to repay 50% or more debt of secured creditors.
- The power to declare transactions void and reverse recent transactions undertaken to diverge funds out of the corporate has been mandated to IBC.

(B) Key reasons for failure/low recoveries under earlier mechanisms:

- Under SICA and the Board for Industrial and Financial Reconstruction (BIFR) established under SICA, actions were initiated on erosion of net worth, leaving limited scope for revival thereby leading to liquidation after a lengthy proceeding.
- To provide temporary relief to borrowers rather than making a comprehensive effort to revive businesses, Corporate Debt Restructuring (CDR) was intended and ended up being used as a mechanism for postponing stressed assets recognized as NPAs.
- Challenges, under Strategic Debt Restructuring (SDR), included lack of unified laws to stop parallel proceedings, multiple headwinds like incomprehensive documentation, banks being in charge of preparing a resolution plan without having any sweeping powers and unfavourable macroeconomic environment and valuation disputes.
- The Scheme for Sustainable Structuring of Stressed Assets (S4A) has been found to have limited eligibility for the set of stressed cases as it prescribes a short-term cash-flow visibility and does not allow change in repayment terms.

(C) Benefits expected out of IBC:

- The average time taken for recovery processes in India stands at 4.3 years with a 26% recovery rate. With IBC, speedy and time-bound proceedings are expected to lead to higher recoveries.

- Under IBC, the strict timelines to resolve a case set a maximum period of 270 days (180 days initially with a 90-day extension—one time). After this, a company is automatically liquidated.
- The IBC is now aligned with international benchmarking standards, which stipulate that for countries with high recovery rates, duration of the resolution process be contained at 12–18 months. The focus is to ensure that the entity remains an ongoing concern by quickly ensuring change in management or otherwise. Non-lending entities are typically involved in preparing the resolution plan.
- Efforts among banks towards decision making and willingness to take higher haircuts as failure to come up with a resolution plan would lead to liquidation of corporations.
- As even operational creditors can initiate insolvency proceedings under the new framework, financial discipline across corporations is likely to improve. Decisions of the NCLT can be challenged at the National Company Law Appellate Tribunal (NCLAT), followed by the Supreme Court of India, wherein we expect the judgements to be delivered in a reasonable timeframe.

(D) Challenges in smooth implementation of IBC:

- Getting shareholder approval is an issue for actions like changes in capital structure for corporations, selling assets and reclassifying promoters as public shareholders.
- There may be delays in proceedings vis-à-vis stipulated timelines due to inadequate NCLT benches/trained RPs to handle the large number of cases that are referred under IBC.
- There are clarity issues on various aspects of the code, such as how to arrive at liquidation value, priority in claims of homebuyers, and so on.

(E) Expected impact for banks:

- Expected accelerated provisioning on NPA accounts owing to the haircuts that banks may have to take post resolutions are approved.
- The majority of NPA accounts will require higher provisioning compared with current levels, based on the residual economic value of the assets.

Review of Literature

Kohli (2017), in his book *Practical Guide to NPA Resolution*, has deliberated that it is a very healthy sign that the banking industry will be at a more advantageous position to wipe out their bad debts by implementing new amendments like the IBC, and he believes that it will help clean their balance sheets to a large extent in times to come. He says that the IBC has created a line of action for quick winding up of ailing companies and fostering faster recovery of banks' stressed assets.

Kaveri (2017), in her article "Ordinance on New NPA Resolution Policy—an Overview," underlines and evaluates the effectiveness of the various mechanisms that deal with NPA, like Corporate Debt Restructuring (CDR), framework for monitoring of Special Mention Accounts (SMAs), and the 5/25 Flexible Restructuring of Long-Term Project Loan scheme.

Special Debt Restructuring

Despite SDR schemes like IBC and S4A and many other measures, the level of NPAs is now unprecedented and is shaking the confidence of bankers in taking decisions on huge write-offs as part of resolving of mega problematic projects.

In his article "Indian banks decentivised by insolvency code," Brian Yap (2017) deliberated that public lenders have been wary of taking action under the IBC due to the absence of provisioning benefits in proceedings filed under the insolvency code. Banks may be reluctant to approach the NCLT under the new bankruptcy regime and opt to continue to enjoy the benefits of the Joint Lender's Forum (JLF) where banks have an option of having a new or existing creditor provide additional finance for restructuring stressed accounts. Dissenting lenders refusing to participate in a joint corrective action plan can also sell their NPA exposure to a new or existing creditor. The Reserve Bank of India (RBI) needs to incentivize the banks to use the code by extending the provisioning benefits, which are available under JLF, to proceedings under the new insolvency regime.

Chatterjee et al. (2017), in their article "Watching India's Insolvency Reforms," have analysed the IBC in terms of its effectiveness in actually facilitating the debt resolution mechanism and they are of the view that IBC is still in a nascent stage and there are many obstacles still to address. Arundhati Bhattacharya, in her Livemint article "Ecosystem not ready for insolvency law," deliberates that under the IBC the "ecosystem" for rapid dispute resolution is not ready yet. She said that the sector has gotten the law it wanted, but implementation of the new code will take time.

OBJECTIVE OF THE STUDY

This research study aims to analyse the IBC in terms of its effectiveness and implementation and evaluates its performance after its implementation. Information was collected from the final orders published by the NCLT in the first six months of operationalization of the IBC and subsequent data released until recently by NCLT and RBI. In this chapter, we also apply the data illustratively to answer questions about the economic impact of the IBC and the functioning of the judiciary under it. Thereafter, we present the summary statistics on the IBC and our preliminary findings relating to the working of the IBC, keeping in view economic analysis of the law. Parameters include: who are the initial users of the insolvency process under the IBC, the average time taken by the NCLT to dispose of cases, what kind of evidence are the users using to support their claims before the NCLT, reason for dismissal of a case, the variation in admission and dismissal across the nine benches of the NCLT and the outcome of the proceedings. We apply the data to answer six questions relating to the economic impact and analysis of the law:

1. Does the law improve the balance between rights of the creditors and the firm debtor during insolvency?
2. Does the law empower various types of creditors when the firm defaults?
3. Does the law empower only large-sized debt holders?
4. Does the NCLT function within the timelines set in the law?
5. What is the role played by the NCLT as visualized within the IBC?
6. What is the situation in terms of the NPA of Indian banks and how has IBC fared?

RESEARCH METHODOLOGY

Information collected from the final orders published by the NCLT in the first six months (December 1, 2016 until May 15, 2017) of operationalization of the IBC and the subsequent orders and data published by NCLT and RBI on NPA is used in arriving at answers to the research questions.

This includes parameters such as who are the initial users of the insolvency process under the IBC, the average time taken by the NCLT to dispose of cases, what kind of evidence are the users using to support their claims before the NCLT, reason for dismissal of a case, the variation in admission and dismissal across the nine benches of the NCLT and the outcome of the proceedings. Also, RBI data and CRISIL's (2017) analysis on NPA of banks were used to judge the situation of the NPA in banks and the trends that have then been used to draw inferences to our research questions.

Findings and Inferences

We apply the data to answer six questions relating to the economic impact of the law:

Does the IBC law improve the balance between rights of the creditors and the firm debtor during insolvency?

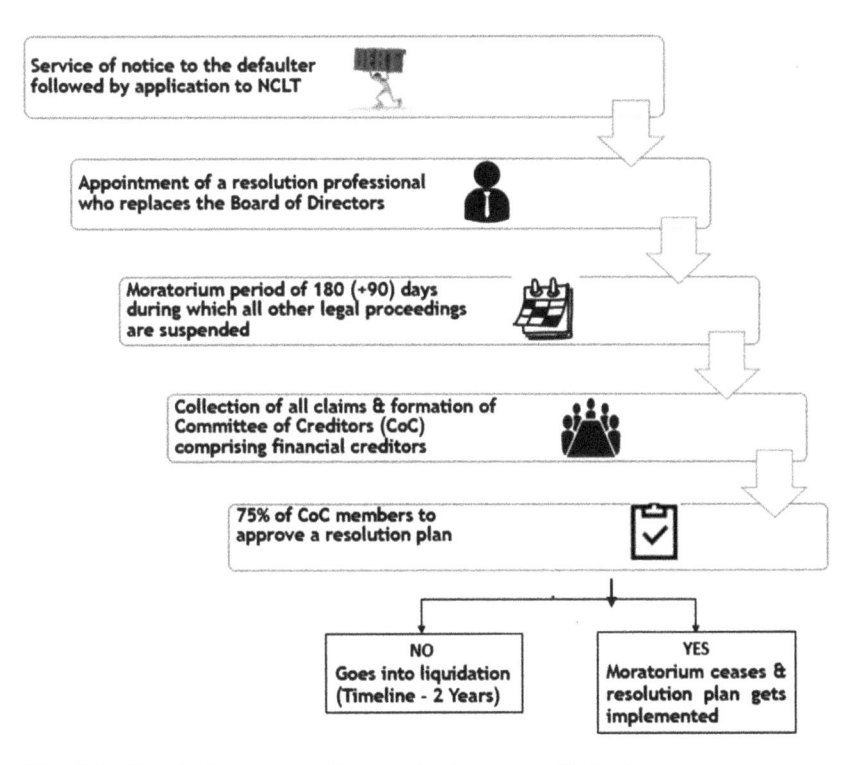

Fig. 9.1 Resolution process (Source: Author's compilation)

Preceding the IBC, the Indian legal regime conferred weak rights on creditors, especially unsecured creditors. There was scope for the judiciary to intervene in the commercial matters of debt re-structuring. The law, and the courts and tribunals enforcing it, also exhibited a rehabilitation and pro-debtor bias. The early data after operationalization of IBC indicates that there has been a shift in the enforcement of creditors' rights under the IBC. Table 9.1 shows who used the IBC during the first six months of its operationalization.

Out of the 110 cases that were disposed of during the period, creditors were the triggers for 75 percent of the cases. Of these, unsecured operational creditors filed 75 percent of cases. This is a clear indication that operational creditors, who had weak enforcement rights, have taken recourse to the IBC to enforce their claims. For the relatively low number of financial creditors taking recourse to the IBC during the first six months, there may be multiple reasons. Evidence suggests that firm debtors default to financial creditors the last. Financial creditors may choose to enforce their claim by realizing their security. The reason for the divergence in creditor behavior in triggering the IBC is unclear. In the absence of data on default or the enforcement of security by financial creditors in India, however, the behavior of the debtor is another interesting feature to look at. In general, the debtor will avoid resorting to insolvency because the IBC moves away from the debtor-in-possession model to a framework model. Here, the debtor's board is suspended and the affairs of the debtor are run by an independent insolvency professional. However, contrary to this belief, around 24 percent of the petitions in this early six-month period have been filed by debtors.

Of the 110 cases that were filed, 50 percent have been admitted by the NCLT and are now undergoing a mutually negotiated debt-restructuring process. Thus, unlike the previous regime where the judicial bodies exhibited a pro-debtor bias, there is no explicit admission or dismissal bias for

Table 9.1 Insolvency bankruptcy code user details

Particulars of petitions filed via IBC	Number
Petitions filed by operational creditors (OC)	62
Petitions filed by financial creditors (FC)	21
Petitions filed by creditors (operational + financial) (O + D)	83
Petitions filed by debtors (D)	26
Unknown applicants (UA)	1
Total	110

insolvency cases under the IBC. Also, creditors are using the new insolvency and bankruptcy regime with increasing confidence compared to the earlier system.

Does the law empower various types of creditors when the firm defaults?

Table 9.2 shows the kind of various operational creditors who resorted to the IBC during the period. We find that even holders of decrees are taking recourse to the IBC, while the majority of the operational creditors are suppliers to the debtor.

The outcomes of the insolvency cases filed by different kinds of creditors are shown in Table 9.3. The percentage of dismissal for operational creditors is slightly higher at 58 percent compared to 43 percent of the cases filed by the financial creditors.

We find from the reading of Tables 9.2 and 9.3 that that even during the earliest days of its operationalization, a wide variety of creditors have shown the ability to trigger insolvency proceedings under the IBC. Earlier, only a certain number of creditors were able to trigger insolvency proceedings against firm debtors, and other creditors had to file cases in civil courts. Thus IBC has truly helped empower the creditors.

Table 9.2 Particulars of operational creditors using IBC

Particulars of operational creditors	Number
Employees	5
Vendors	43
Others	6
Not known	8
Total	62

Table 9.3 Admission and dismissal across different kinds of creditors

Particulars	No of Petitions filed	Admitted	Dismissed
Operational creditors	62	26	36
Financial creditors	21	12	9
Debtors	26	23	3
Unknown	1	0	1
Total	110	61	49

Does the law empower only large-sized debt holders?

The size of debt claims that have been used to trigger the IBC is shown in Table 9.4. The Minimum and Maximum figures in Crore for different types of stakeholders, namely corporate debtors, operational creditors and financial creditors, are shown in the table.

The smallest claim to trigger the IBC was filed by an operational creditor with a claim of debt default of Rs 1.09 lakh[1] while the smallest debt against which a financial creditor triggered the IBC was Rs 30.69 lakh, which was 30 times larger. Debt default maximum was claimed by an operational creditor and was Rs 131.9 crore while the largest default to a financial creditor was Rs 856.5 crore, which was only eight times larger. Thus, it can be observed that operational creditors, who had considerably weaker rights under the previous regime, had considerably large debt repayments due from firm debtors. Thus, we see most of the cases tend to be triggered using debt defaults that are almost 10 to 100 times larger than the threshold of Rs 100,000 set in the law.

Does the NCLT function within the timelines set in the law?

The IBC mandates NCLT to dispose of an insolvency petition within 14 calendar days from the date on which it is filed. Based on the data, we have divided the life cycle of an insolvency petition as follows: The date on which the case is filed (D1), date on which it first comes up for hearing (D2) and the date on which it is disposed of (D3). The time that elapses between D1 and D2 could be attributed to the internal processes in scheduling hearings for a case by the NCLT. Analysis of data shows that the NCLT exceeds the timeline of 14 days mandated by statute. Table 9.5 shows the detailed time taken.

Thus, the average time taken from the date of filing the insolvency petition (D1) to the date on which it first comes up for hearing (D2) is 18 days. The average time taken between the date on which it first came up for hearing (D2) and the date on which it is finally disposed of (D3) is

---

[1] In this paper the currency quotations in INR to be converted in international standards according to following pattern:

Indian quotation	Amount	International quotation
1 lakh	100,000.00	100 thousands
10 lakhs	1,000,000.00	1 million
1 crore	10,000,000.00	10 million
10 crores	100,000,000.00	100 million

16 days. Finally, the average time taken for disposal is 24 days (D1 to D3). This is way more than the stipulated timeline of 14 days prescribed under the IBC.

What is the role played by the NCLT as visualized within the IBC?

While IBC law allows an insolvency to be triggered if the debtor has committed a default in repayment of an undisputed debt and enumerates specific grounds for dismissing an insolvency case, the NCLT has dismissed petitions on considerations beyond specific grounds as well. Table 9.6 shows the various grounds for dismissal of the insolvency petitions.

In an insolvency petition filed in the Mumbai bench, the NCLT extended the inquiry scope to the balance sheet of the debtor. It said that since the debtor had sufficient assets on its balance sheet, it would not be

Table 9.4 Debt size litigated under IBC (in 10-millions)

Size of debt reported	Corporate debtors	Operational creditors	Financial creditors
Minimum	0.92	0.01	0.3
Maximum	2580.07	131.9	856.52

Table 9.5 Average time taken for disposal of insolvency petitions at the NCLT stage

NCLT stage	No. of cases for which data is available	Average time (in days)
D1 to D2	12	18
D2 to D3	52	16
D1 to D3	24	24

Table 9.6 Reasons for dismissal of insolvency petitions

Grounds for dismissal	No. of insolvency petitions dismissed
Existing dispute	8
Applicant was not a creditor as defined in IBC	7
Settled out of court	5
Debt recovery barred by limitation	3
Incomplete application	2
Operational creditor failed to issue statutory demand notice prior to filing the case	2
Others	22
Total	49

fair for the debtor if the petition were admitted, thus it ignored the creditor's argument that the provisions of the IBC did not include balance sheet analysis. This indicates that the NCLT seems to be viewing the admission of an insolvency case against a debtor as a harsh step. The data, thus, shows that the working of the NCLT is not always in accordance to the letter and spirit of the IBC.

As a corollary, we found that the non-availability of basic information about the case hindered the ability of the NCLT to monitor the efficiency of its own benches and the ability to identify systemic lapses in the functioning of tribunals and in designing appropriate interventions. Efficiency of the adjudicator of the law strengthens the legal framework and is especially so for a procedural law like bankruptcy law. Lapses in the NCLT are likely to hinder the working of the legal framework, reduce the efficiency of resolution and leave the bankruptcy reforms process undone. As these are still the early days, there is wide scope for correction. As the insolvency cases increase and as more data gets published, relevant fields, such as recovery rates and expenses associated with the recovery process, can potentially be integrated for analysis.

Relevant Judgments by NCLT, Under IBC

(A) Jaypee Infratech Ltd.—Case showing swift adaptations by institutions under IBC

Case background: Insolvency application of IDBI Bank against Jaypee Infratech was admitted by NCLT, Allahabad Bench for defaulting on an outstanding loan of Rs 5.3 billion because it had not completed its residential projects.

Issues:

- Neither a financial nor an operational creditor, as per IBC, flat owners being consumers expressed fears that their flats, for which 80–90% of payments had been made, would be treated as assets of the company and be sold off during liquidation.
- There was a contention because as per section 36 of IBC, the properties held by the insolvent entity in trust should get protection from liquidation by creditors, while section 18 suggests that Interim Resolution Professional (IRP) cannot take control and custody of these assets.

Actions:

- A third category of creditors for home buyers was introduced who can neither be financial nor operational creditors and cannot trigger the Corporate Insolvency Resolution process.
- The Supreme Court of India later instructed the resolution professional to keep the interests of home buyers in mind and come up with a resolution plan within 45 days vs. 180+90 days allowed under IBC. It refused to lift the stay on Real Estate Regulation Act (RERA), indicating priority of proceedings under IBC over other laws.

(B) Innoventive Industries Ltd. vs. ICICI Bank

Case background: Under NCLT, ICICI Bank had filed a case to initiate a Corporate Insolvency Resolution process on Innoventive Industries. The company filed an appeal and claimed relief under a state law under which no action for recovery of loans or dues can be taken against the company.

Issues and Implications:

- For a financial debt that is disputed, non-payment, even when due, would constitute a default under the IBC and it does not matter if the same is disputed.
- NCLT ruled that provisions of individual states will not prevail over IBC. Financial creditors don't require any consent from JLF in filing an application under IBC code.

What is the situation in terms of the NPA of Indian banks and how has IBC fared?

With the IBC formalized in December 2016, bankers were of the view that they could finally show some tough face to the borrowers misusing the system. Earlier, the general perception, among bankers and RBI, was that because of the absence of a strong bankruptcy code NPAs have periled the banking system. In less than a year, banks seemed to have lost interest in the new framework. Bankers now don't want to invoke the IBC to all companies. The first case brought under the IBC that clearly spooked the banks was that of Synergies Dooray Automotive Ltd. Here the NCLT ruled in favor of a 94 percent haircut. This came as a great blow to banks, and bankers now say haircuts could be as large as 75 percent in many cases. Even CRISIL says potential write-offs could be in the 25 percent to 75 percent range. To make matters worse, RBI has mandated banks to provide 50 percent provision if a case is referred to the NCLT and 100 percent if a liquidation order is set. CRISIL estimated that banks had to set aside close to Rs 3.3 lakh crore in 2017, or 50 percent more than the Rs 2.2 lakh crore they had provided in 2016.

Significant progress has been made in recognition of NPAs. The asset quality review of RBI has shown that the gross NPA ratio of both public and private sector banks is higher than was earlier thought, but in the public sector undertaking (PSU) banks it is highly alarming. Table 9.7 shows the NPA and NPA ratio figures of Scheduled Commercial Banks (SCBs) in India. It shows a clear uptrend even when the IBC became fully functional in December 2016. Also, this is an underestimate because it does not include assets that are "stressed" but not yet NPAs.

Faced with shortage of capital and a huge burden to set aside money for bad loans, commercial banks now want the RBI to relax provisioning norms. For the first batch of 12 cases referred for insolvency in June 2016, banks have been making provision for these for many quarters. However, there is severe pressure on balance sheets when they have to decide on cases from the second batch and beyond. Also, there is a concern about locating money when interest income is already weak. Even invoking of personal guarantees of companies by banks is not possible until a resolution of cases is concluded. In many cases, banks have a clear disincentive to head for insolvency proceedings where promoters have given personal guarantees for loans.

With auditors running steel companies, another concern is falling production. And with banks refusing to lend more funds, production at the NCLT-referred companies is falling, compared to a rise in production just before these companies were referred by the RBI to the NCLT. Their suppliers and customers have also withdrawn support, thus impacting their flows and lowering the valuation of their assets.

Table 9.7 NPA and NPA ratios

	NPA (in CR)	NPA ratio
Mar-16	571,841	7.69
Jun-16	618,109	8.42
Sep-16	651,792	8.81
Dec-16	677,443	9.18
Mar-17	711,312	9.06
Jun-17	829,338	10.21
Sep-17	971,104	11.62

Over the next 12 months or so, the IBC process is expected to clean up the books of the banks, but it will also lead to depletion of capital and corresponding acceptance of large losses. The Synergies Dooray Automotive Ltd. case under NCLT ended up with a haircut of 94 percent! The lenders (banks) want an amendment to the IBC to remove certain inconsistencies so that promoters of defaulting companies can be completely kept out of the resolution process. When some of the large companies are involved, any resolution plan won't end at the NCLT but will ultimately end up at the Supreme Court of India. And resolution plans are likely to be challenged and ultimately, the Court will have to come in and lay down the ground rules, which will further complicate things and lengthen proceedings and final resolution and recovery. On September 1, 2017, the Supreme Court of India ruled in favour of ICICI Bank after Innoventive Industries appealed an NCLT verdict and said that if dues are not paid, the management cannot continue and a central law should prevail over state law whenever the two are contradictory.

If a resolution is not found, about 30 companies with loans amounting to 1.25 lakh crore which was set has been refereed to bankruptcy Courts by December 31, 2017 as resolution did not materialise. Bankers are expected not to try the defaulters under the IBC since that would lead to potential acquirers putting in low bids and there are instances that portray that the value of the assets drops dramatically once an account reaches the bankruptcy courts.

Conclusion

This chapter illuminates aspects relating to the economic impacts of the IBC. The research questions that the chapter analyses provide holistic coverage of the law substantiated by data from the IBBI. One common analysis that emerged was that the IBC is still in its early stage of implementation and a lot more changes, incorporations and additions need to be done for the law to emerge as a successful one with emphasis on recovery of bad debts.

With banks' NPAs at an all-time high and continuous pressure from the RBI, bankruptcy proceedings keep away potential bidders, which leads to very low bids. This ultimately erodes banks' loan values, leaving the promoter in a position to keep the asset. Banks are in a serious dilemma to use IBC for recovery of their loans, which can be very well seen from the past data presented in the chapter. It is difficult to get investors due to the slowdown, even in cases that are outside bankruptcy court, thus making things tougher for the bankss after cases are taken to NCLT.

There are grey areas in interpreting the IBC and new situations and arguments will continue to test IBC's application. At present, the system lends itself to those with the fastest march on their counterparties. On the one hand, creditors who commence the insolvency process sooner rather than later limit the potential of defences by debtors. On the other hand, debtors may seek to side-step the insolvency process by preemptively raising disputes or commencing legal actions on frivolous grounds to frustrate creditors. With the stakes so high, there is a real likelihood of multiple legal proceedings with more showdowns expected at the NCLT.

The new IBC has been lauded as a game changer for the bad debt problem in India. When triggered, a company is funneled at breakneck speed into an insolvency resolution process with only two possible outcomes—restructure or liquidate. The ultimate objective—to get bad debt off banks' books and jumpstart the credit environment—is an appealing one. But with the stakes of losing control of a company, creditors and debtors have wrestled with each other to avoid application of the IBC. Creditors have turned to the IBC as a means of gaining leverage in the hope of securing quicker repayment while savvy debtors have been quick to preemptively dispute debts owed by triggering other court or arbitration proceedings to halt and lengthen the insolvency process.

Impact and Future Suggestions

The role of the corporate debtors has to be clarified more. The amendments to the Insolvency & Bankruptcy Act will stop willful defaulters from buying stressed assets that they previously owned. The proposed amendment in IBC will support the financial creditors who form part of the Committee of Creditors to take a calculated decision to hand over stressed assets/accounts to promoters/directors who are not willful defaulters."

The absence of bids can increase the losses in banks' balance sheets and hamper the recovery processes in the long run. Honest promoters will be roped in by gullible defaulters. The bids have to be tempered and promoters must be allowed to bid for their assets, which is not addressed in the IBC provisions. Most of the initial dozen resolutions carried out under the IBC involve companies who have defaulted for more than a year and hence it is "highly unlikely" that promoters in any of these companies can bid for their assets.

Of the 12 companies that collectively owe Rs 2.5 trillion, or a quarter of total of bad loans of Rs 10 trillion, are under bankruptcy resolutions. If the IBC is accepted in totality, the companies with their investments in factories, furnaces, trucks, textile looms, heavy equipment and land will be placed under supervision of the creditors within six months, failing which they will be liquidated. This is an alarming scenario.

Acknowledgements The authors are grateful to anonymous referees of the journal for their extremely useful suggestions for improving the quality of the paper. The usual disclaimers apply.

APPENDIX

Exhibit 9.1 Corporate insolvency resolution transactions

Quarter	Number of corporations undergoing resolution at the beginning of quarter	Admitted	Closure			Number of corporations undergoing resolution at the end of quarter
			Appeal/review	Approval of resolution plan	Commencement of liquidation	
Jan–Mar 17	0	37	1	–	–	36
April–June 17	36	125	10	–	–	151
July–Sep 2017	151	214	3	2	7	353
Oct–Tilldate	NA	376	14	2	7	353

Source: The Insolvency and Bankruptcy Board of India

Exhibit 9.2 Initiation of corporate insolvency transactions

Quarter	Number of corporate resolutions			Total
	Financial creditors	Operational creditors	Corporate debtor	
Jan–Mar 17	9	7	21	37
April–June 17	31	59	35	125
July–Sep 2017	182	101	31	314
Oct–December 2017	22	167	87	276

Source: The Insolvency and Bankruptcy Board of India

References

Bhinder, B. (2017, September). India overhauls insolvency framework. *International Financial Law Review*.

Brian, Y. (2017, September). Indian banks decentivised by insolvency code. *International Financial Law Review*.

Care Ratings. (2017, June). *NPA in banks*. Retrieved from http://www.care-ratings.com

Chatterjee, S., Shaikh, G., & Zaveri, B. (2017). Watching India's insolvency reforms. *Quint*.

CRISIL. (2017, October). *Operating profits of banks to stabilise by year end*. Press Release.

EY. (2017, August). *Insolvency and bankruptcy code – 2016, Experiencing the code*.

Insolvency and Bankruptcy Board of India. Newsletter. Retrieved from http://www.ibbi.gov.in/IBBI_Newsletter_Web.pdf

Insolvency and Bankruptcy Board of India. Orders. Retrieved from http://www.ibbi.gov.in/webfront/allorder_tab.php

Insolvency and Bankruptcy Board of India. Press Release. Retrieved from http://www.ibbi.gov.in/webfront/press.php

Kaveri, V. S. (2017). Ordinance on new NPA resolution policy – An overview. *Journal of Commerce and Management Thought, 8*(4).

Kohli, R. C. (2017). *Practical guide to NPA resolution*. New Delhi: Taxmann Publications.

Mondol, D. (2016). The last mile. *Business Today, 25*(11).

Reserve Bank of India. Retrieved from https://www.rbi.org.in

Stern, N. (2016, May). Proposed India bankruptcy update would establish needed improvements. *Business Credit, 118*(5).

CHAPTER 10

Impact of Demographic Variables on the Attitude Towards Violence and Cooperation with Police: A Study of Extremist Affected Areas in Odisha, India

Bindu Chhabra

INTRODUCTION

We seem to be living in increasingly violent times and extremism is prevalent in many parts of the world. India has been at the receiving end of extremist violence especially in the last few decades. Whether it is international terror groups or insurgencies in Northeast India, extremism is posing a serious threat to national security. However, the gravest challenge to the Indian state comes from Left Wing Extremism (LWE), also popularly known as Naxalism or Maoism, which affects large parts of Central and Eastern India. The so-called Red Corridor runs mainly through the provinces of Andhra Pradesh, Telangana, Chhattisgarh, Odisha, Jharkhand, and Bihar apart from affecting some areas of Maharashtra, Bengal, Madhya Pradesh, and Utter Pradesh. In all, 106 districts across nine states are

---

B. Chhabra (✉)
International Management Institute, Bhubaneswar, Odisha, India
e-mail: bindu@imibh.edu.in

affected by Maoist violence in India. As per the Ministry of Home Affairs (MHA), between 2010 and 2017 (up to May 15, 2017) as many as 2457 civilians and 930 security force personnel have been killed due to LWE violence in India.[1] In Odisha, where the present study was conducted, 19 districts are considered affected by LWE violence. Approximately 250 civilians, 211 security force personnel, and 180 LWE cadres have been killed in the state since 2000. The level of violence and number of police casualties are much higher than in other terror attacks or insurgencies. Malkangiri, which is flanked by Chhattisgarh on one side and Andhra Pradesh on the other, is the worst affected district in Odisha.

One of the important features of the LWE movement is its significant presence in tribal areas, which are largely poor and underdeveloped. Due to large-scale poverty, underdevelopment, and failure of governance, the Maoist narrative of "exploitative state" and need for a "Proletariat Revolution" have found some support amongst the disenfranchised classes. The ideology exhorts the people to rise against the state. Police, which are the primary enforcement agency of the state and are charged with the responsibility to maintain public order, are specifically targeted by the Maoists because of both ideological and tactical reasons. They want to challenge the writ of the state by eroding the very legitimacy of state institution and police are their primary target.

In India, the police system devised by the British colonial rulers in 1861 is still largely in force even after Independence in 1947. A strong need for revamping the police has been felt because they are widely felt to be brutal, inefficient and corrupt. The legitimacy of the system has consequently been corroded to some extent. Indian Police, already suffering from poor public image and a trust deficit due to their colonial legacy, cannot fight this existential battle without the support of the larger society and public. They need to isolate the extremists from the general population in order to minimize collateral damage that leads to further alienation and erosion of legitimacy. It is therefore imperative to bolster the legitimacy of the police to secure necessary cooperation from the public and to wean youth away from indulging in violence against the state. For this, it is important to understand the factors that lead to formation of attitudes condoning or supporting violence among the population, especially the youth, as they are the primary target groups for enrolment by the extremists.

---

[1] https://mha.gov.in/naxal_new?&contrast=high, accessed on 12 December 2017.

It is now generally accepted that police cannot provide safety and security without the active involvement of the community. Past research suggests that people support and cooperate with the police force willingly if they feel that they are a legitimate authority that needs to be obeyed (Tyler and Fagan 2008). Apart from the sanction of law, there is also a moral dimension in play, that is, it is our obligation to cooperate with legitimate authority. Another important aspect is the level of trust that the community has in the police. Studies show that trust is a function of the manner in which police work, that is, whether they are just and fair in their dealing with people, how decisions are made, and how these are implemented (Sunshine and Tyler 2003). Recent research (Jackson et al. 2013) also shows that people's attitudes towards acceptance of violence as justifiable are related to their perceptions about the legitimacy of the institutions of the state.

When authorities want cooperation from the public, it helps if they are perceived to be legitimate. Previous research suggests that coercion and incentives have only a limited impact. In democratic societies, willing public cooperation is crucial for any institution, let alone police, to perform its function effectively. It is a desirable social value quite in contrast with self-interest (Tyler 2003). The realization that legitimacy is a driver of willing public cooperation provides the law enforcement agencies with an important instrument with which to ensure and enhance public support for their efforts. Such support can be forthcoming in various forms, from free reporting of crimes to coming forward as witnesses and helping in investigations. Even efforts of police to secure communities are likely to be more successful if people participate in neighborhood watch systems. Such cooperation is also qualitatively different as it is intrinsic and therefore more sustainable.

Effect of Demographic Variables on Attitude Towards Violence and Cooperation with Police

Different strata of society react to encounters with police in different ways. Studies have found that certain demographic variables are significant predictors of satisfaction with police (Correia et al. 1996; Reisig and Correia 1997; Rosenbaum 1994; Skogan 1978; Wu and Sun 2010). Factors like age, race, gender, education, and place of residence have been frequently studied as factors in citizens' perceptions of police in much of the developed world. Age has been used consistently as a factor to predict citizen satisfaction with police. It is commonly reported in the literature that older citizens tend to have more favorable attitudes toward police than younger citizens (Cao et al. 1996; Wu and Sun 2010). Gender is found to be an inconsistent or insignificant factor (Benedict et al. 2000; Thurman and Reisig 1996) in predicting citizen satisfaction with police, with a few studies finding that females held positive attitudes (Cheurprakobkit 2000; Huebner et al. 2004) and few reported it otherwise (Hurst and Frank 2000; Reisig and Correia 1997).

Similarly, education attainment is sometimes negatively associated with citizens' attitudes toward the police (Sunshine and Tyler 2003; Tankebe 2010). Hwang et al. (2005) found education as negatively related to citizen satisfaction with the police, a view also reported in a previous study (Brown and Benedict 2002). Also, a positive correlation between higher education and higher income is frequently cited, implying that the citizens with a higher socioeconomic status (SES) and with higher educational attainments are likely to view police less positively. On the contrary, Brandl et al. (1994) and Reisig and Parks (2000) found a positive linear relationship between education and global satisfaction with police. While previous studies have focused on establishing a relationship between level of education and perceptions, which has been inconclusive, Wu and Sun (2010) found support for Brown and Benedict's (2002) speculation that students majoring in liberal arts (e.g. English, philosophy, or sociology) held more critical views of police than those majoring in science, technology, or business fields (e.g. hospitality management, business management, or nursing).

Current literature is seemingly inconclusive in establishing a clear relationship between SES and satisfaction with police (Larsen and Blair 2009). While some studies reported a negative relationship (Brown and Coulter 1983; Sampson and Bartusch 1998), another study reported the opposite (Hagan and Albonetti 1982). Hwang et al. (2005) measured SES by looking at education, income, and occupation and found that lower SES citizens were more satisfied with police than high SES groups, but similar research in the United States yielded contrary results (Decker 1981; Reisig and Parks 2000). Research also indicates that small-town residents tend to view police more favorably than residents in cities (Zamble and Annesley 1987). When compared to rural areas, there was a significant drop in satisfaction levels with police in the large and mid-sized cities (Hwang et al. 2005). Additionally, suburbanites are more likely to view police performance more satisfactory than urbanites (Kusow et al. 1997).

As discussed, public support and cooperation is imperative for the police to perform their core function of providing safety and security to the public at large. Public cooperation is in turn a function of the perceptions of police efficacy and legitimacy as these are the most visible symbol of the state authority. In the context of LWE violence, which primarily impacts youth, police need to wean youth away from violence and ensure greater public cooperation to succeed. There is also the need to understand why some people are more prone to committing violence than others. The present study aims to understand the perceptions of youth about police in a heavily LWE affected area and how the demographic variables impact their attitudes towards cooperation with the police and acceptability of violence against the state.

Study Design

The data was collected from the youth of nine Community Governance Organizations (locally known as gram panchayats, which refers to village administration) of Malkangiri district of Odisha, covering the entire geographical spread of the district except the inaccessible, cut-off area. This is the most severely Maoist-affected area and has the highest incidents of Naxal violence in Odisha. In all, about 500 respondents were contacted, but only 405 completed questionnaires were collected (response rate of 81%). The demographic detail of the respondents is depicted in Table 10.1.

Table 10.1 Demographic details

Gender	Males 357	Females 48		
Age	Minimum 18	Maximum 29	Mean 22.45	Standard deviation 4.23
Caste	General 38	SC 51	ST 312	OBC 4
Educational qualification	Class 5 & below 217	Between class 6 and 12 87	Above class 12 74	Graduate & above 27
Family income	Below Rs. 10,000 296	Between Rs. 10,000 & Rs. 25,000 73	Above Rs. 25,000 36	

The youth were contacted and asked to fill out the questionnaire. They were apprised regarding the academic purpose of the study and confidentiality of responses was ensured. The questionnaire was divided into two sections; the first section required the participants to fill in their demographic details and the second section focused on the questions related to cooperation with police and attitude towards violence.

The factor on Cooperation with Police was measured with seven items from the scale by Sunshine and Tyler (2003). These items were measured on a five-point scale where 1 is strongly disagree and 5 is strongly agree. Attitude towards Violence was assessed by four items from the scale by Jackson et al. (2013). These items were measured on a five-point scale where 1 is strongly disagree and 5 is strongly agree.

Since the ambit of study was regionally confined, and the vernacular language was Oriya, the items were translated in this language. Back translation of items was also done to see that the meaning and purpose of items does not change. The procedure was followed strictly to avoid linguistic effect. The questionnaire was edited and printed for data collection and further analysis.

Results and Analysis

Dummy variable regression was used to study the impact of various demographic variables on two dependent variables: attitudes towards violence and cooperation with police. Demographic variables used for study were gender, age, caste, educational qualification, and family income. Age was measured in years. With respect to gender, male was kept as a reference. Caste had four categories: general, scheduled caste (SC), scheduled tribe (ST), and other backward castes (OBC). For caste, a General category was kept as reference. Educational qualification also had four categories: Class 5 and below (AEQ), Between Class 6 and 12 (BEQ), Above Class 12 (CEQ), and Graduate and above (DEQ). Class 5 and below was kept as a reference in this case. Family income had three categories: Below Rs. 10,000 (AFI), Between Rs. 10,000 and Rs. 25,000 (BFI), and Above Rs. 25,000 (CFI). In this case, the category of Below Rs. 10,000 was kept as a reference. The demographic details of the sample are given in Table 10.1.

Tables 10.2 and 10.3 show the results of the dummy variable regression with cooperation with police as a dependent variable.

As can be seen from Table 10.2, the results of the regression indicated that the demographic variables explained 9.5% of the variance ($R^2 = 0.095$,

F (10,394) = 5.26, $p < 0.01$). As is evident from Table 10.3, age, financial income, and gender does not impact cooperation with police significantly. However, the impact of caste and educational qualification on the dependent variable is significant. With respect to the caste, the analysis shows that the respondents belonging to SC ($\beta = -3.68$, $p < 0.01$), ST ($\beta = -3.40$, $p < 0.01$) and OBC ($\beta = -11.92$, $p < 0.01$) categories show less cooperation with police compared to the respondents from the general category. With respect to educational qualification, the analysis shows that the respondents whose educational qualification is between class 6 and 12 ($\beta = -2.63$, $p < 0.01$), above class 12 ($\beta = -2.91$, $p < 0.01$), and graduate and above ($\beta = -5.86$, $p < 0.01$) show less cooperation with police compared to the respondents who are less educated (i.e. below class 5).

Tables 10.4 and 10.5 show the results of the dummy variable regression with attitude towards violence as a dependent variable.

As can be seen from Table 10.4, the results of the regression indicated that the demographic variables explained 14.2% of the variance ($R^2 = 0.142$, F (10,394) = 7.69, $p < 0.01$). As is evident from Table 10.5, age, financial income, and gender does not impact attitude towards violence significantly. However, the impact of caste and educational qualification on the dependent variable is significant. With respect to the caste, the analysis shows

Table 10.2 Model summary of regression analysis for cooperation with police

R	R square	Adjusted R square	F	Sig.
0.343	0.118	0.095	5.264	0.000

Table 10.3 Result of bivariate regression model

Model	β-value	t-value	Sig.
Age	0.066	1.082	0.280
SC vs. general	−3.683	−2.731	0.007
ST vs. general	−3.401	−2.934	0.004
OBC vs. general	−11.924	−3.828	0.000
BEQ vs. AEQ	−2.627	−3.295	0.001
CEQ vs. AEQ	−2.909	−2.908	0.004
DEQ vs. AEQ	−5.857	−4.255	0.000
BFI vs. AFI	−0.503	−0.572	0.567
CFI vs. AFI	0.923	0.739	0.460
Female vs. male	0.354	0.354	0.723

Table 10.4 Model summary of regression analysis for attitude towards violence

R	R square	Adjusted R square	F	Sig.
0.404	0.163	0.142	7.687	0.000

Table 10.5 Result of bivariate regression model

Model	β-value	t-value	Sig.
Age	0.041	1.416	0.157
SC vs. general	2.979	4.688	0.000
ST vs. general	2.666	4.882	0.000
OBC vs. general	4.686	3.193	0.002
BEQ vs. AEQ	1.729	4.603	0.000
CEQ vs. AEQ	1.777	3.769	0.000
DEQ vs. AEQ	1.727	2.662	0.008
BFI vs. AFI	0.462	1.116	0.265
CFI vs. AFI	0.288	0.489	0.625
Female vs. male	−0.754	−1.600	0.110

that the respondents belonging to SC ($\beta = 2.98$, $p < 0.01$), ST ($\beta = 2.67$, $p < 0.01$), and OBC ($\beta = 4.69$, $p < 0.01$) categories show significantly more attitude towards violence compared to the respondents from general category. With respect to educational qualification, the analysis shows that the respondents whose educational qualification is between class 6 and 12 ($\beta = 1.73$, $p < 0.01$), above class 12 ($\beta = 1.78$, $p < 0.01$), and graduate and above ($\beta = 1.73$, $p < 0.01$) show more attitude towards violence compared to the respondents who are less educated (i.e. below class 5).

Discussion

The present study was conducted to see the effect of demographic variables on attitudes towards violence and cooperation with police. The variables taken for the study were Age, Caste, Educational Qualification, Family Income, and Gender. The findings based on a sample from the LWE affected district of Malkangiri in Odisha, India suggest that age, family income, and gender do not significantly impact the cooperation with police and attitude towards violence. Prevailing literature indicates that age is a significant factor in predicting citizens' perception towards police with older people having more favorable attitudes towards police than younger people (Cao et al. 1996; Wu and Sun 2010). It may be because maturity leads people to temper their attitudes and expectations whereas youth have more energy and impatience with the system. However, it needs to be seen that the present study was conducted only on youth wherein the age range of the participants varied from 18 to 29 years. There is no contrasting cohort of older population here to be compared with and therefore no definitive conclusions can be drawn regarding difference in attitudes between different age groups, which are not within the scope of this study. The study does, however, confirm the fact that the youth as a cohort hold similar perceptions regarding their attitude towards police and age does not have an impact on this perception within that specific cohort.

With respect to gender, the earlier studies have shown inconsistent results as some studies (Huebner et al. 2004) show that women hold positive attitudes towards police; whereas others find no difference between men and women regarding their attitude towards police (Hurst and Frank 2000). The present study confirms the fact that men and women do not differ significantly with respect to their attitude towards violence and cooperation with police. What it may indicate at best is that age is a more important factor than gender in determining attitudes and that in one cohort, views held by men and women may not differ in a significant manner.

The study also shows that the family income of the respondents does not impact their attitude towards violence and cooperation with police. Previous studies have also found inconclusive results with respect to the relationship between SES and satisfaction with police (Larsen and Blair 2009). It needs to be seen here that the district of Malkangiri, where the study was conducted, is generally a poor area and the income level of people is less. Furthermore, there is not a marked difference in the income categories taken for the purpose of study and hence the results regarding the impact of income level on the attitude towards police cannot be generalized.

As far as caste is concerned, the present study shows that people from general caste exhibit higher attitude towards cooperation with police and lower inclination towards acceptance of violence compared to the respondents from scheduled castes, scheduled tribes, and other backwards classes. This difference may be attributable to the complexities of the Indian caste system where the higher castes have traditionally controlled the institutions and there is a perception that social, economic, and political systems have a built-in bias against the poor and downtrodden. People from backward castes as well as tribal people generally belong to lower SES and there is a lot of cynicism about how various institutions and even the whole system operate. Viewed in this context, it is no surprise that police are often seen as an institution favoring the rich and powerful, which is reflected in their response with respect to the lack of cooperation with police.

Educational qualification is another demographic variable that has shown to have an impact on the youths' attitude towards violence and cooperation with police. The study shows that the respondents who are less educated have lesser attitude towards violence and are in general more cooperative towards police compared to the respondents who are more educated. These results are in line with the previous research that shows that education attainment is negatively associated with citizens' attitude towards police (Sunshine and Tyler 2003; Tankebe 2010). Specifically, higher education leads to more critical views of the police because education attainment leads to a better understanding of the normative obligations of public institutions towards citizens and thus greater awareness of social injustice by these institutions.

Implications for Research and Practice

The research can have implications from theoretical as well as policy perspectives. How police perform in any society has been a much researched subject and what factors determine the public perceptions about police is an important area for researchers. While there have been many studies exploring how different demographics respond to police practices, especially in the context of cooperation and willingness to empower the police, very few studies have explored the similar link with attitudes towards violence. Further, most of this research has taken place in the western context (i.e. in the United States or Europe) and there is hardly any study exploring the effect of demographics in the Indian context and that too in a setting of a conflict zone in a heavily LWE affected area in India. It is therefore a useful addition in the sparse body of literature in this domain. This study opens a new field for future researchers to determine the impact of demographics on various policies and practices of police. Attitudes towards cooperation and violence are complex constructs depending on many other variables like police effectiveness, experience of procedural justice, and so on, which can be a profitable area for future research.

From a policy perspective too, there are benefits that can accrue. It will be quite useful to know how different demographics relate to police. Attitudes are likely to be reflected in behavior patterns and an accurate assessment of such attitudes can provide policy makers a useful tool to target specific demographics for desired results. This study can help the policy makers to accurately identify the most vulnerable sections of population and devise appropriate policies, especially to prevent and for deradicalization of youth. It can also help police to identify areas to enhance public cooperation and empowerment of police. This can help the police to improve their image and performance.

LIMITATIONS OF THE STUDY

Every research has limitations and this one has many. It is an exploratory study that needs to be followed up by both intensive and extensive research. The limitations are both in scope and methodology. The study is limited to a specific locale and targets only the youth. The findings cannot therefore be generalized without further research. There are many other factors apart from demographics that will influence the public perceptions and decisions to cooperate with police or to show inclination for violence, for example, the cultural context, political beliefs, instrumental considerations, and so on, which are not in the scope of the present research. Further study is therefore indicated to explore these areas. The research only studies the attitudes towards violence and cooperation with police, which may not finally reflect in actual behavior of cooperation or violence. However, it does have some predictive value.

REFERENCES

Benedict, W. R., Brown, B., & Bower, D. J. (2000). Perceptions of the police and fear of crime in a rural setting: Utility of a geographically focused survey of police services, planning, and assessment. *Criminal Justice Policy Review, 11*(4), 275–298.

Brandl, S. G., Frank, J., Worden, R. E., & Bynum, T. S. (1994). Global and specific attitudes toward the police: Disentangling the relationship. *Justice Quarterly, 11*, 119–134.

Brown, B., & Benedict, W. (2002). Perceptions of the police. *Policing, 25*(3), 543–580.

Brown, K., & Coulter, P. B. (1983). Subjective and objective measures of police service delivery. *Public Administration Review, 43*, 50–58.

Cao, L., Frank, J., & Cullen, F. T. (1996). Race, community context, and confidence in police. *American Journal of Police, 15*, 3–22.

Cheurprakobkit, S. (2000). Police-citizen contact and police performance: Attitudinal differences between Hispanics and non-Hispanics. *Journal of Criminal Justice, 28*, 325–336.

Correia, M. E., Reisig, M. D., & Lovrich, N. P. (1996). Public perceptions of state police: An analysis of individual-level and contextual variables. *Journal of Criminal Justice, 24*, 17–28.

Decker, S. H. (1981). Citizen attitudes toward the police: A review of past findings and suggestions for future policy. *Journal of Police Science and Administration, 9*, 80–87.

Hagan, J., & Albonetti, C. (1982). Race, class, and the perception of criminal justice in America. *American Journal of Sociology, 88*, 329–355.

Huebner, E. S., Suldo, S. M., Smith, L. C., & McKnight, C. G. (2004). Life satisfaction in children and youth: Empirical foundations and implications for school psychologists. *Psychology in Schools, 41*, 81–93.

Hurst, Y. G., & Frank, J. (2000). How kids view cops: The nature of juvenile attitudes toward the police. *Journal of Criminal Justice, 28*, 189–202.

Hwang, E., McGarell, E. F., & Benson, B. L. (2005). Public satisfaction with the south Korean police: The effect of residential location in a rapidly industrializing nation. *Journal of Criminal Justice, 33*(6), 585–599.

Jackson, J., Huq, A. Z., Bradford, B., & Tyler, T. R. (2013). Monopolizing force? Police legitimacy and public attitudes toward the acceptability of violence. *Psychology, Public Policy, and Law, 19*(4), 479–497.

Kusow, A. M., Wilson, L. C., & Martin, D. E. (1997). Determinants of citizen satisfaction with the police: The effects of residential location. *Policing: An International Journal of Police Strategy & Management, 20*, 655–664.

Larsen, J. E., & Blair, J. P. (2009). The importance of police performance as a determinant of satisfaction with police. *American Journal of Economics and Business Administration, 1*, 1–10.

Reisig, M. D., & Correia, M. E. (1997). Public evaluations of police performance: An analysis across three levels of policing. *Policing: An International Journal of Police Strategies & Management, 20*, 311–325.

Reisig, M. D., & Parks, R. B. (2000). Experience, quality of life, and neighborhood context: A hierarchical analysis of satisfaction with the police. *Justice Quarterly, 17*, 607–629.

Rosenbaum, D. P. (1994). *The challenge of community policing: Testing the promises*. Thousand Oaks, CA: Sage.

Sampson, R. J., & Bartusch, D. J. (1998). Legal cynicism and (subcultural?) tolerance of deviance: The neighborhood context of racial differences. *Law and Society Review, 32*, 777–804.

Skogan, W. G. (1978). Citizen satisfaction with police services: Individual and contextual effects. *Police Studies, 7,* 469–479.

Sunshine, J., & Tyler, T. R. (2003). The role of procedural justice and legitimacy in shaping public support for policing. *Law & Society Review, 37*(3), 513–548.

Tankebe, J. (2010). Legitimation and resistance: Police reform in the (un)making. In L. K. Cheliotis (Ed.), *Roots, rites and sites of resistance: The banality of good.* Basingstoke: Palgrave Macmillan.

Thurman, Q. C., & Reisig, M. D. (1996). Community-oriented research in an era of community-oriented policing. *American Behavioral Scientist, 39*(5), 570–586.

Tyler, T. R. (2003). Procedural justice, legitimacy, and the effective rule of law. *Crime and Justice, 30,* 283–357.

Tyler, T. R., & Fagan, J. (2008). Legitimacy and cooperation: Why do people help the police fight crime in their communities? *Ohio State Journal of Criminal Law, 6,* 231–275.

Wu, Y., & Sun, I. Y. (2010). Perceptions of police: An empirical study of Chinese college students. *Policing: An International Journal of Police Strategies & Management, 33*(1), 93–113.

Zamble, E., & Annesley, P. (1987). Some determinants of public attitudes toward the police. *Journal of Police Science and Administration, 15,* 285–290.

CHAPTER 11

Emotional Intelligence in the Workplace: A Comparative Study of Male and Female Bank Employees in the Public Sector

Megha Sharma and Sourabh Sharma

Introduction

Emotional intelligence (EI) is the ability to identify, use, understand, and manage your emotions in positive and constructive ways. It's about recognizing your own emotional state and the emotional states of others. EI is also about engaging with others in ways that draw people to you. It is defined as a set of competencies demonstrating the ability one has to recognize his or her behavior, moods, and impulses, and to manage them best according to the situation. It is the ability to see one's own emotions, understand what they are telling you and realize how your emotions affect people around you. It is also your perception of others, understanding how they feel, and gives you the power to manage relationships more effectively.

M. Sharma (✉)
NIIS, Bhubaneswar, Odisha, India

S. Sharma
International Management Institute, Bhubaneswar, Odisha, India
e-mail: sourabh@imibh.edu.in

There have been three largely popular approaches to EI: Bar-On, Goleman, and Mayer and Salovey:

1. The Mayer–Salovey model defines this construct as the ability to perceive, understand, manage, and use emotions to facilitate thinking;
2. The Goleman model views it as an assortment of emotional and social competencies that contribute to managerial performance and leadership; and
3. The Bar-On model describes EI as an array of interrelated emotional and social competencies, skills, and behaviors that impact intelligent behavior.

Each theory has been put forward in an attempt to better understand and explain the skills, traits and abilities associated with social and emotional intelligence (Emmerling and Goleman 2003). While these three approaches have somewhat different measures, all of them seek to understand how emotions are used and, if used appropriately, increase success when dealing with others. Organizations constantly accrue the cost of training new employees because of retention problems. EI is not defined or understood in many human resources departments. Many managers are not aware of how to assess EI of their staff members or the job applicants (Fleming 1999). Countless people are unfamiliar with the different traits that make up the term emotional intelligence. According to Miller (1999), "the components of EI—self-awareness, self-regulation, motivation, empathy and social skills—are the qualities of a well-rounded person." Thus, if recruiting professionals measured the EI of job applicants, doing so could help in finding people who would fit well in their work environment.

EI is a skill that can be learned and improved. Goleman (1998) stated that simply being high in EI does not guarantee that a person will have learned the emotional competencies that matter for work; it means only that they have excellent potential to learn them. Thus, training and development of EI in an organization must be taken seriously for it to be effective. EI is your ability to recognize the impact of your own emotions upon your behavior and to be aware of the emotions of others around you. When you have an employees with great qualifications and experiences who just cannot work with others or guide others towards a goal, that employee is lacking EI. Having poorly developed EI may not necessarily have held you back in the past; today, in a workplace where people are more self-aware and less tolerant of arrogance and ignorance, low levels of EI will poison the workplace quickly to your demise. Many a seemingly competent person has been passed over for promotion or even moved on without being able to pinpoint the reason why. After all, they were very efficient and effective; regrettably, they also managed to get everyone offside, did not consider the human cost of their conquests and lacked the ability to manage their own emotions and impulses.

Being emotionally aware is not easy. You do need to work at it constantly. Our brains tend to move into "fight or flight" mode very easily, causing us to react before we have time to think. As your parents were fond of saying, think before you act! The way to combat this instinctive reaction is to hone your awareness of your own emotional states. For example, certain events will trigger a negative emotional response in each of us. Just by being aware of your own emotional states will help you be more aware of the emotional state of others. In being so, your empathy levels will be much higher. By being aware of those trigger points that point to a possible negative reaction, you are becoming more aware, you are managing your responses and you are moving from being reactive to being proactive.

Literature Review

The popularity of EI during the past decade has led researchers to examine its potency in various areas of human functioning. In recent years, there has been an increasing interest in how emotional reactions and experiences affect both physical as well as psychological health. For example, it has been claimed that negative emotional states are associated with unhealthy patterns of physiological functioning, whereas positive emotional states are associated with healthier patterns of responding in both cardiovascular activity and immune system (Herbert and Cohen 1993).

In another study, Mayer et al. (1999) reported that individuals who can regulate their emotional states are healthier because they accurately perceive and appraise their emotional states, know how and when to express their feelings and can effectively regulate their moods states. This set of characteristics, dealing with the perception, expression and regulation of moods and emotions, suggests that there must be a direct link between EI and physical as well as psychological health. Indeed, Taylor (2001) argues that if you are emotionally intelligent then you can cope better with life's challenges and control your emotions more effectively, both of which contribute to good psychological and physical health.

Moreover, Bar-On (1997) includes stress management and adaptability as two major components of EI, while Matthews and Zeidner (2000) stated that adaptive coping might be conceptualized as EI in action, supporting mastery emotions, emotional growth and both cognitive and emotional differentiation.

EI is now being considered to be important in organizational factors such as organizational change (Ferres and Connell 2004; Singh 2003); leadership (Ashkanasy 2002; Dearborn 2002; Gardner and Stough 2002; Weymes 2002); management performance (Slaski and Cartwright 2002); perceiving occupational stress (Nikolaou and Tsaousis 2002; Oginska-Bulik 2005); and life satisfaction. To meet organizational ends (Lord et al. 2002), it is not uncommon to use emotions and emotion-related thoughts and behavior as the ingredients in an institutionalized recipe of emotional culture.

Many scholars have theorized that high IE contributes to success in various aspects of life including work and relationships (e.g. Goleman 1995; Salovey and Mayer 1990). Because EI theoretically includes the ability to understand and regulate others' as well as one's own emotions, it may be related to both characteristics that build relationships and the quality of those relationships (Schutte et al. 2001) Furthermore, scholars have theorized that high EI would lead to greater feelings of emotional well-being (Goleman 1995; Saarni 1999; Salovey and Mayer 1990; Salovey et al. 1995; Schutte et al. 2001). Some empirical evidence that EI is associated with emotional well-being comes from research indicating that higher EI is associated with less depression, greater optimism (Schutte et al. 1998) and greater self-esteem (Schutte et al. 2001). Moreover, research found that individuals with higher EI were better able to maintain a positive mood and self-esteem when faced with a negative state induction (Schutte et al. 2001).

In a study by Nelis et al. (2009), participants were divided into two groups. One group received EI training consisting of four group sessions of two and a half hours each. The other group did not receive any training. After the treatment was completed, the training group showed a significant increase in emotion identification and emotion management compared to the control group. Six months later, the training group still had the same improvement on emotion identification and emotion management. The control group showed no change. Song et al. (2010) studied the impact of general mental ability (GMA) and EI on college students' academic and social performance. While GMA and EI both had an influence on academic performance, EI was found to be a stronger predictor of academic performance and also related to the quality of social interaction with peers.

There are many tests of EI and most seem to show that females tend to have an edge over males when it comes to these basic skills for a happy and successful life. That edge may matter more than ever in the workplace, as more companies are starting to recognize the advantages of higher EI when it comes to positions like sales and leadership. However, it's not that simple, for instance, some measures suggest females are on average better than males at some forms of empathy, and males do better than females when it comes to managing distressing emotions. Whenever we talk about gender differences in behavior, we get two different bell curves, one for males and one for females, that largely overlap. What this means is that any given male might be as good as or better than any female at empathy, and a female might be as good as or better than a specific male at handling upsets.

Objective of the Study

The primary objective of the research is to find the dimensions to assess EI. Based on the dimensions of EI, the main objective of the investigation is to compare the EI among male and female bank officials and to emphasize the significance of EI in the workplace.

Methodology

The qualitative research methodology has been used in this study. It provides insights into the problem or helps to develop ideas or hypotheses for potential quantitative research. Qualitative research is also used to uncover trends in thoughts and opinions, and dive deeper into the problem. Qualitative data collection methods vary using unstructured or semi-structured techniques.

Measure

The EI test used in this research has been developed by Singh (2006) and Chadha and Singh (2001). According to the test, EI constitutes three psychological dimensions—emotional competency, emotional maturity and emotional sensitivity—that motivate an individual to recognize truthfully, interpret honestly and handle tactfully the dynamics of human behavior.

I. **Emotional Competency:** This competency is about tackling emotional upsets, frustrations, conflicts, inferiority complexes and so on. It also means avoiding emotional exhaustion such as stress, burnout and negativity of emotion.
II. **Emotional Maturity:** Some of the important aspects of emotional maturity are self-awareness, developing others, delaying gratification, adaptability and flexibility.
III. **Emotional Sensitivity:** In the psychological sense, sensitivity means the characteristic of being peculiarly sensitive and judges the threshold for various types of stimulations, evoking sensations, feelings and emotions.

Sampling Technique

The sample of the present investigation was drawn from 10 nationalized banks in Bhubaneswar and Cuttack. For this purpose, a list of the nationalized banks and their different branches was collected. Initially, approximately 268 banks officials constituted the sample, out of which 133 were female and 135 were male, but later on only 212 bank officials were selected, 99 female and 113 male. Banks covered during this research were the branches of the State Bank of India, Punjab National Bank, Canara Bank, Central Bank of India, Union Bank, Allahabad Bank, Oriental Bank of Commerce, UCO Bank, Karnataka Bank and Andhra Bank (Table 11.1).

DATA ANALYSIS AND FINDINGS

To address the objective, we employed an independent sample t-test. Two independent samples are male and female bank employees. Number of male and female bank employees are 113 and 99, respectively. Table 11.2 shows the dimension-wise result of the independent sample t-test:

The result of the t-test reveals statistically significant differences between the mean of male and female bank employees with reference to the three dimensions of EI. As per Table 11.2, for dimension one, "emotional sensitivity," it states that there is a significant difference among male and female bank employees. The mean score of male employees (M = 14.628) is signifi-

Table 11.1 Composition of sample selected on availability of bank officials

S. No.	Female	Total no. of officials
1	State Bank of India	13
2	Punjab National Bank	12
3	Canara Bank	9
4	Central Bank of India	10
5	Union Bank of India	5
6	Allahabad Bank	11
7	UCO Bank	11
8	Oriental Bank of Commerce	10
9	Karnataka Bank	7
10	Andhra Bank	11
Total		99

S. No.	Male	Total no. of officials
1	State Bank of India	19
2	Punjab National Bank	13
3	Canara Bank	11
4	Central Bank of India	9
5	Union Bank of India	12
6	Allahabad Bank	10
7	UCO Bank	9
8	Oriental Bank of Commerce	11
9	Karnataka Bank	8
10	Andhra Bank	11
Total		113

Table 11.2 Independent sample t-test results examining differences between male and female bank employees with reference to EI dimensions

Dimensions	Group	N	Mean	SD	Std. error mean	t-test	Sig (2-tailed)
1. Emotional sensitivity	Male	113	14.628	2.38	0.2242	10.887	0
	Female	99	11.283	2.05	0.2056		
2. Emotional maturity	Male	113	12.788	1.59	0.1497	−5.804	0
	Female	99	14.062	1.60	0.1607		
3. Emotional competence	Male	113	11.885	1.69	0.1586	−10.221	0
	Female	99	14.061	1.37	0.1376		

cantly greater than female bank employees (M = 11.283) at 5% significance level [(t = 10.887), $p < 0.05$]. The mean difference in male and female bank employees shows that males are more emotionally sensitive compared to females. The studies by Spoor and Kelly (2004) state that males are more emotionally sensitive compared to females. Males remember more emotional information. Males react more to provocation and physiological response to conflict and competitions in a more intense manner and males are more likely to ruminate and dwell on feelings. Males are better at reading emotional cues of others. Females smile, gesticulate, touch, are touched and discuss their emotions more than males. Females express their vulnerability more openly than males. There are two types of coping in different situations: emotion-focused coping—where one expresses emotions in response to stress—and problem-focused coping—where one distracts their emotions in response to stress (such as by focusing on other works, or thinking of a solution to the problem). Males tend to use emotion-focused coping and use less problem-focused coping. Males are efficient in interpreting human expressions and respond to them with sensitivity. Males are good at maintaining rapport, harmony and comfort while dealing with groups. Males can understand how others would evaluate them and then release it. Males more or less empathize and help people in distress.

Findings related to the second dimension, "emotional maturity," reveal that the mean score for female bank employees (M = 14.062) is significantly greater than male bank employees (M = 12.788) at 5% significance level ($t = -5.804$, $p < 0.05$). The difference between the means of the emotional maturity shows that females are more emotionally mature compared to males. Research done by Salovey and Mayer (1990) states that emotional maturity seems to be a prerequisite for happiness and is associated with fun, and also with entanglements, transference, parental alienation, burnout and shallow relationships. Keys to emotional maturity include self-esteem, clarity and a stable sense of integrity, and dissolve mentor damage and help us find inspirational mentors for living life we want. Females are more emotionally mature compared to males; they have better self-control, accept and control passions, emotions, desires and wishes, choosing what is right. In females, biological maturity, psychological maturity and social maturity may correspond to Erikson's stages of adult development.

Emotionally mature females generally have increased self-control, settle conflicts peacefully, take personal responsibilities, delay gratification of long-term goals, preserve, complete projects, are dependable and resourceful and make decisions and keep them to solve problems. Many studies support the result that females are smarter in knowing one's emotions, managing emotions, motivating oneself, recognizing emotions in others and handling relationships.

Another study reveals that females change themselves for the best to make their lives better. It's clear that estrogen is closely linked with female's emotional well-being. Depression and anxiety affect females in their estrogen-producing years. Researchers have found that males always tend to take decisions from the mind rather than the heart, while it's the other way around for females. This is the reason why females mature at a younger age than males. Older males tend to be wiser, but still they can never compete with females. A female at any time and at any place is much wiser and better at making decisions with their brains as well as their hearts when compared to males. That's why in today's world females are advancing in the workplace and leaving males behind in almost every field. A number of examples of Indian females who have attained the highest positions in the organizational sector include, Chanda Kochhar (CEO of ICICI Bank), Kaku Nakhate (President and Country Head India at Bank of America Merrill Lynch India), Shikha Sharma (CEO of Axis Bank), Indra Krisknamurthy Nooyi (CEO of PepsiCo) and Mallika Srinivasan (CEO of TAFE Motors and Tractors Limited [TMTL]). They are competent and show emotionally mature behavior. What females lack in strength they compensate with wisdom. It is scientifically true that females tend to have a better developed sixth sense than males.

Perhaps due to nurturing instincts that teach responsibility earlier in life, females become enlightened more quickly than males. Females are found to be more emotionally mature; they are taught from childhood to adapt to all situations. They tend to appreciate others' point of view. They do not react to a situation instantaneously; rather, they try to delay their reactions.

The findings related to the third dimension, "emotional competence," reveals that mean score for female bank employees ($M = 14.061$) is significantly greater than male bank employees ($M = 11.885$) at 5% significance level ($t = -10.221$, $p < 0.05$). The difference in emotions may be attributed to the fact that females are more emotionally competent compared to males. Females scored higher in adaptability and service orientation. Their peers rated females high on emotional self-awareness, conscientiousness, developing others and service orientation and communication.

Many researchers have proved that females are more emotionally competent; they may be better at reading the signals. Females are more polite and generous and apologetic. Females can communicate their attitudes, moods and feelings through non-verbal communication and can also understand the same because they are taught from a young age to run the emotional life of the family; they are better attuned to what's not being said. Generally, females are more expressive and males are suppressive. Females tend to avoid ego problems and have healthy interpersonal relations. In angry situations, they tend to express emotional self-control and this helps to cool down their tempers. They express optimism in terms of emotional competence. They communicate effectively with others. Socialization practice helps them to learn to avoid negativity of emotions. They are excellent in tackling ego problems in interpersonal life, they are efficient in handling inferiority complexes and they respond in an emotionally intelligent manner when they are frustrated.

Managerial Implications

- Understanding EI can further help in determining the tremendous potential for improving the human conditions, especially in an organizational structure.
- The study can enable management of an organization to design training methods and modules to improve the performance of their employees in an efficient and relatively inexpensive manner by enhancing employees' optimism level and self-efficacy beliefs by understanding and handling emotional behavior.
- It is perhaps the right time to emphasize the role of EI in improving the positive elements in employees in order to improve the quality of work life as well as personal life. The present study is an honest attempt to explore the relevance of EI in organizations.
- By managing EI, an employee can better adapt to new technology, marketing and challenges. Adaptability and responsiveness are essential to survive and thrive.

Limitations

- The locale of the present study was confined to Bhubaneswar and Cuttack. Subsequently, the investigation may be extended to other cities of Orissa and to other states of the country to obtain comparative studies.

- To substantiate the findings further, data from a large sample, from rural and urban areas, can be separately studied.
- Other professionals groups, such as sales, customer service, IT, and so on, can be studied further.
- Other aspects such as happiness, resilience and subjective well-being could be studied along with EI.

Conclusion

In a modern organization, leadership is not confined only to those with management titles. Everyone has a capacity to provide leadership. A key aspect of providing leadership is being able to build relationships, foster collaboration, communicate and influence others. This requires that you be balanced, that positive aspects are enhanced and negative aspects are recognized and anticipated. It requires you to be open to the ideas of others, not to feel threatened by the opinion of others. It requires you feeling sufficiently confident in your own abilities so as to know when to lead and when to step back and allow others to lead. These are the things we do as we build long-term, sustainable relationships that, in turn, provide the resources to achieve outcomes.

EI is a set of competencies that direct and control one's feelings towards work and performance at work. The set of competencies is the ability of the individual to control and manage his or her moods and impulses, which contribute to best situational outcomes. Understanding one's own moods and the impulses of others or any situation helps one to respond and behave in accordance with expectations. In a work situation, workers' effective use of skill and knowledge in time depends on the effective regulation of emotions at work and employees' readiness to contribute their best in their target accomplishment. Knowing one's emotions and feelings as they occur, and tuning one's self to the charged situation, requires the emotional competency, emotional maturity and emotional sensitivity that determine the success of adaptability and adjustment with the change scenario. In a work situation, since it involves groups of people with different ideas, suggestion and opinions, effective conglomeration of all these determine the best outcome. Thus, EI plays a significant role at work.

The mean differences indicate that females are more emotionally intelligent compared to males. There are many tests of EI and most seem to show that females tend to have an edge over males when it comes to these basic skills for a happy and successful life.

The edge may matter more than ever in the workplace as more companies are starting to recognize the advantage of high EI when it comes to positions like sales and leadership. Females tend to be better at emotional empathy than males, in general. This kind of empathy fosters rapport and chemistry. People who excel in emotional empathy make good counselors, teachers and group leaders because of this ability to sense in the moment how others are reacting. Neuroscientists tell us one key to empathy is a brain region called the insula, which senses signals from our whole body. When we're empathizing with someone, our brain mimics what that person feels and the insula reads that pattern and tells us what that feeling is and the female tendency to stay tuned in helps enormously to nurture and support others in emotionally tiring circumstance; it's part of the "tend-and-befriend" responses to stress. The difference in the nerve mass and balance in the brain of females makes them able to multitask and manage work well compared to males.

Females are able to discuss their feelings as well as emotions with others while males are far away from this particular task. This happens because males take their problems and worries lightly. This is the reason females are supposed to be best at verbal skills whereas males are supposed to be sensitive.

Another great thing that proves that females are more emotionally intelligent compared to males is their intellectual development during pregnancy. During that time, females' intelligence improves and they develop impressive caregiving skills along with acutely accurate judgment capabilities. Females generally manage human relationships better than males. The female brain is expert at reading faces, interpreting tone of voice and assessing emotional nuance. This research confirms the common view that females can handle relationships and manage them better than males.

References

Ashkanasy, N. M. (2002). Studies of cognition and emotion in organisations: Attribution, affective events, emotional intelligence and perception of emotion. *Australian Journal of Management, 27*(Special Issue), 11–20.

Bar-On, R. (1997). *The emotional quotient inventory (EQ-i): Technical manual.* Toronto, Canada: Multi-Health Systems.

Chadha, N. K., & Singh, D. (2001). How to measure your EQ. In D. Singh (Ed.), *Emotional intelligence at work: A professional guide.* New Delhi: Response Books.

Dearborn, K. (2002). Studies in emotional intelligence redefine our approach to leadership development. *Public Personnel Management, 31*(4), 523–530.
Ferres, N., & Connell, J. (2004). Emotional intelligence in leaders: An antidote for cynicism towards change? *Strategic Change, 13*(2), 61–71.
Gardner, L., & Stough, C. (2002). Examining the relationship between leadership and emotional intelligence in senior level managers. *Leadership & Organisation Development Journal, 23*(1/2), 68–78.
Herbert, T. B., & Cohen, S. (1993). Stress and immunity in humans: A meta-analytic review. *Psychosomatic Medicine, 55*, 364–379.
Lord, G. R., Klimoski, R. J., & Kanfer, R. (2002). *Emotions in the workplace: Understanding emotions in organisational behavior.* San Francisco, CA: Jossey-Bass.
Matthews, G., & Zeidner, M. (2000). Emotional intelligence, adaptation to stressful encounters, and health outcomes. In R. Bar-On & J. D. A. Parker (Eds.), *The handbook of emotional intelligence.* San Francisco, CA: Jossey-Bass.
Mayer, J. D., & Salovey, P. (1993). The intelligence of emotional intelligence. *Intelligence, 17*, 433–442.
Mayer, J. D., & Salovey, P. (1995). Emotional intelligence and the construction and regulation of feelings. *Applied and Preventive Psychology, 4*, 197–208.
Mayer, J. D., & Salovey, P. (1997). What is emotional intelligence? In P. Salovey & D. Sluyter (Eds.), *Emotional development and emotional intelligence: Implications for educators* (pp. 3–31). New York, NY: Basic Books.
Mayer, J. D., Caruso, D., & Salovey, P. (1999). Emotional intelligence meets traditional standards for an intelligence. *Intelligence, 27*, 267–298.
Mayer, J. D., Salovey, P., & Caruso, D. (1997). *Emotional IQ test (CD ROM).* Needham, MA: Virtual Knowledge.
Mayer, J. D., Salovey, P., & Caruso, D. R. (2000). Models of emotional intelligence. In R. J. Sternberg (Ed.), *Handbook of intelligence* (pp. 396–420). New York, NY: Cambridge University Press.
Mayer, J. D., Salovey, P., & Caruso, D. R. (2004). Emotional intelligence: Theory, findings, and implications. *Psychological Inquiry, 60*, 197–215.
Mayer, J. D., Salovey, P., & Caruso, D. R. (2008). Emotional intelligence: New ability or eclectic traits? *American Psychologist, 63*, 503–517.
Nelis, D., Quoidbach, J., Mikolajczak, M., & Hansenne, M. (2009). In-creasing emotional intelligence: (How) is it possible? *Personality and Individual Differences, 47*, 36–41.
Nikolaou, I., & Tsaousis, I. (2002). Emotional intelligence in the workplace: Exploring its effects on occupational stress and organisational commitment. *International Journal of Organisational Analysis, 10*(4), 327–342.
Oginska-Bulik, N. (2005). Emotional intelligence in the workplace: Exploring its effects on occupational stress and health outcomes in human service workers. *International Journal Occupational Medicine and Environmental Health, 18*(2), 167–175.

Goleman, D. (1995). *Emotional intelligence*. New York, NY: Bantam Books.
Goleman, D. (1998). *Working with emotional intelligence*. New York, NY: Bantam Books.
Goleman, D. (2005). *Emotional intelligence* (10th anniversary ed.). New York, NY: Bantam Books.
Emmerling, R. J., & Goleman, D. (2003). Emotional intelligence: Issues and common misunderstandings. *Issues in Emotional Intelligence*, [On-line serial], *1*(1).
Fleming, C. (1999). Creating a higher EQ workplace. *Credit Union Executive Journal, 39*(3), 26–27.
Miller, M. (1999). Emotional intelligence helps managers succeed. *Credit Union Executive Journal, 65*(7), 25–26.
Saarni, C. (1999). *The development of emotional competence*. New York: Guilford.
Schutte, N. S., Malouff, J. M., Hall, L. E., Haggerty, D. J., Cooper, J. T., Golden, C. J., et al. (1998). Development and validation of a measure of emotional intelligence. *Personality and Individual Differences, 25*, 167–177.
Schutte, N. S., Malouff, J. M., Bobik, C., Coston, T. D., Greeson, C., Jedlicka, C., et al. (2001). Emotional intelligence and interpersonal relations. *Journal of Social Psychology, 141*, 523–536.
Singh, D. (2003). *Emotional intelligence at work* (2nd ed.). New Delhi: Sage Publications.
Slaski, M., & Cartwright, S. (2002). Health, performance and emotional intelligence: An exploratory study of retail managers. *Stress and Health, 18*, 63–68.
Salovey, P., & Mayer, J. D. (1990). Emotional intelligence. *Imagination, Cognition, and Personality, 9*, 185–211.
Salovey, P., Mayer, J. D., Goldman, S., Turvey, C., & Palfai, T. (1995). Emotional attention, clarity and repair: Exploring emotional intelligence using the trait meta-mood scale. In J. D. Pennebaker (Ed.), *Emotion, disclosure, and health* (pp. 125–154). Washington, DC: American Psychological Association.
Singh, D. (2006). *Emotional quotient test, emotional intelligence at work: A professional guide* (3rd ed.). New Delhi: Sage Publication.
Song, L. J., Huang, G-H., Peng, K. Z., Law, K. S., Wong, C-S., & Chen, Z. (2010, January–February). The differential effects of general mental ability and emotional intelligence on academic performance and social interactions. *Intelligence, 38*(1), 137–143.
Spoor, R. J. & Kelly, R. J. (2004). The evolutionary significance of affect in groups: Communication and group bonding. *Group Processes and Intergroup Relations, 7*, 398–412.
Taylor, G. J. (2001). Low emotional intelligence and mental illness. In J. Ciarrochi & J. P. Forgas (Eds.), *Emotional intelligence in everyday life: A scientific enquiry* (pp. 67–81). Philadelphia, PA: Taylor & Francis.
Weymes, E. (2002). Relationships not leadership sustain successful organisations. *Journal of Change Management, 3*(4), 319–331.

CHAPTER 12

Role of Leadership Style on Corporate Entrepreneurship and Firm Innovativeness: Learnings from Start-ups in Emerging Markets

Rajeev Verma and Jyoti Verma

Introduction

A start-up is defined as a young company that could be an entrepreneurial venture or a new business, a partnership or temporary business organization designed to search for a repeatable and scalable business model (Bluedorn and Martin 2008). India is amongst the top five countries in the world in terms of start-ups. India, one of the fastest growing emerging markets is a thriving under-penetrated consumer-driven market with a scope for exponential growth (Barkema et al. 2002). Internet penetration and its increasing importance will drive most of the businesses (NASSCOM 2017). The larger problems plaguing the businesses include, an unorganized and fragmented Indian market, lack of clear and transparent policy initiatives, lack of infrastructure, lack of knowledge and exposure, complications in doing

R. Verma (✉) • J. Verma
Chandragupt Institute of Management, Patna, Bihar, India
e-mail: rajeev.verma@cimp.ac.in; jyoti@cimp.ac.in

business, and so on (DIPP 2017). However, the framework and course of regulations need to be updated and adopted as per the times. Currently, only 18 Indian states have their own start-up policy.

As these companies are young, so is the work force. The reported average age of work force in the start-up ecosystem is between 29 and 36 years depending upon the sector, and the average age for top management is 38 years (DIPP 2017). As the management is young, so are their leadership styles. It has been widely studied that leadership and the different associated styles have an immense impact on how employees perform in an organization. This becomes more relevant when we investigate the impact of leadership styles on firm innovativeness, as a predictor of corporate entrepreneurship in the context of start-up firms in emerging markets. For ages, leadership has been a subject of much debate and deliberation and how the different styles of leadership evoke different responses in longitudinal studies (House and Aditya 1997).

Various researchers, notably Bass and Avolio (1997), Nel et al. (2004) and Cole (2005), defined leadership as the process whereby one individual influences others to willingly and enthusiastically direct their efforts and abilities towards attaining defined group or organizational goals. Apart from various financial and non-financial outcome performance parameters, corporate entrepreneurship as a concept has recently emerged as an important output-based parameter that gets incorporated into the start-up philosophy by top management (Barringer and Bluedorn 1999). It involves defining the direction of a team and communicating it to people, motivating, inspiring and empowering them to contribute to achieving organizational success.

Our research model is based on the trait theory of leadership, which suggests people inherit certain qualities and traits that direct them toward specific types of leadership behaviours and related actions (Hogan and Kaiser 2005; Judge and Piccolo 2004; Ling et al. 2008). These traits may explain certain corresponding leadership behaviours and related outcomes, although traits alone may not completely explain the effectiveness of these behaviours (Chen and Nadkarni 2017; Kirkpatrick and Locke 1991) and hence there is scope of in-depth analysis of these trait-related outcomes. Leaders with the desired traits have high potential for specific leadership behaviours, hence they need certain skills and must take certain actions to actualize this potential and to be successful (Chen and Nadkarni 2017; Yukl 2006; Zaccaro 2007). These may include longevity of decision making, risk-taking capacity or decentralization of power.

We integrated leadership theories and temporal research from psychology to examine the strategic implications of top management's leadership in corporate entrepreneurship. The objective of this study is twofold. The first is to explicate leadership behaviour of top management by examining conceptually rigorous and methodologically valid dispositional constructs such as corporate entrepreneurship. The second objective is to understand the mediating role of decentralization and risk-taking ability on key strategic behavioural outcomes.

Theoretical Background

According to Bass and Avolio (1993), a single specific definition of leadership is a very complex task as literature and studies on this topic are varied and there is no definition that is widely and universally accepted. We build our research model on the basis of the trait theory of leadership, which suggests people inherit certain qualities and traits that predispose them toward specific types of leadership behaviour (Bass and Avolio 1990; Hogan and Kaiser 2005; Judge and Piccolo 2004). Although traits may explain certain corresponding leadership behaviour, traits alone may not completely explain the effectiveness of this behaviour (Chen and Nadkarni 2017; Judge and Piccolo 2004; Kirkpatrick and Locke 1991). Although leaders with the requisite traits have great potential for specific leadership behaviours, they need certain skill sets that must get converted into desired actions to actualize this potential and to be successful (Simsek et al. 2007; Yukl 2006; Zaccaro 2007). Following is the summary table of reviewed literature describing leadership using trait theory of leadership (Table 12.1):

Table 12.1 Literature contribution in defining leadership

Author	Literature contribution (leadership defined)
Hersey et al. (2001)	The process of influencing the activities of an individual or a group in efforts toward goal accomplishment
Senge (1990)	Leadership is associated with stimulants and incentives that motivate people to reach common objectives
Stogdill (1948)	The process of influencing people so that they make an effort by their own will and enthusiasm towards obtaining the group's goals
Kotter and Heskett (1992)	Means of reducing the probability of mistakes occurring
Nel et al. (2004)	Process whereby one individual influences others to willingly and enthusiastically direct their efforts and abilities towards attaining defined group or organizational goals
Cole (2005)	Dynamic process whereby one influences others to contribute voluntarily for the realization and attainment of the goals objectives

Background Studies and Theory on Leadership Style

Vroom and Yetton (1973) developed a model that was designed to guide a leader through a rational process to choose an appropriate leadership style that fits with a given situation. The basic premise of this model is the degree to which the leader should share decision-making power with subordinates depends on the situation. It also depends upon the risk-taking capability of the team members. In this model, Vroom and Yetton (1973) argued that the ultimate effectiveness of decisions could be judged on the following factors:

1. The quality or rationality of the decision,
2. Risk-taking capability,
3. Decentralisation of power, and
4. Strategic decision-making approach

The work by Vroom and Yetton (1973) has been supported by contemporary researchers and is considered as one of the benchmark approaches for leadership style classification (Burns 1978; Landy 1989; Schermerhorn et al. 1982). Many researchers studied the rationale of this model in light of Maslow's hierarchy of needs (Judge and Bono 2000). Following the Vroom and Yetton model, transactional and transformational leadership styles were first introduced by Burns (1978). A few years later, Bass (1985) expanded the theory and came up with the Multifactor Leadership Questionnaire (MLQ). The full range of leadership models that was introduced by Avolio and Bass (1991) advanced the theory further. This theoretical model included three styles of leadership: transactional, transformational and laissez-faire.

Proposed Model and Hypothesis Development

Based on the reviewed literature, we narrowed down two prominent leadership styles in our research framework: transformational and transactional. Transformational leaders encourage subordinates to put in extra effort and to go beyond what they expected before (Burns 1978). The subordinates of transformational leaders feel motivated, trustworthiness, admiration, loyalty and respect toward leaders and are motivated to perform extra-role behaviours (Bass 1985; Burns 1978; Katz and Kahn 1978). Transformational leaders are able to inspire their subordinates to raise their capabilities for organisational success and develop subordinates' innovative capabilities and corporate entrepreneurship (Bass 1985). Hence, our study broadly proposed the following (Fig. 12.1).

Transactional leaders focus mainly on the physical and the security needs of subordinates. The relationship that evolves between the leader and the follower is based on exchange or reward systems (Bass 1985; Bass and Avolio 1993). In our current study, the leadership factors used to measure transformational and transactional leadership style in this study are from the MLQ developed by Bass and Avolio (2004) based on the theory of transformational leadership. Thus, the measure of firm innovativeness in the current study represented the degree to which a company achieved its business objectives. The research model is illustrated in Fig. 12.2.

Previous research suggest that by providing organizational team members with greater motivation and sense of responsibility, transformational leaders fully empower team members and this may help in building corporate entrepreneurship (Dvir et al. 2002). Hence, fellow team members

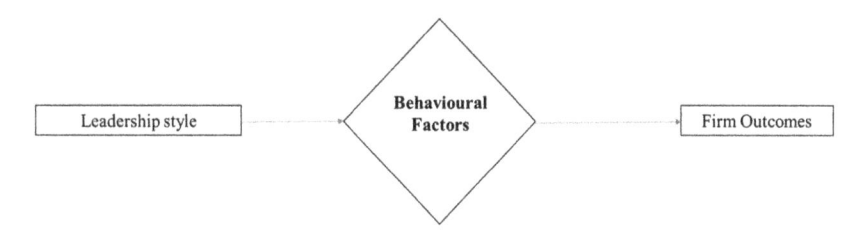

Fig. 12.1 Impact of leadership style on firm outcomes

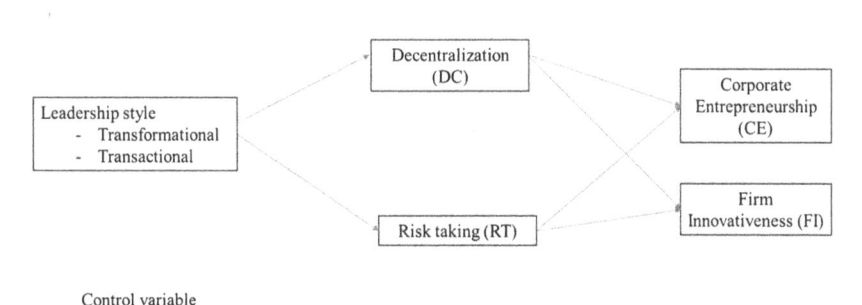

Fig. 12.2 Assessing impact of leadership style on corporate entrepreneurship and firm innovativeness

contribute more to firm innovativeness. Research has shown that highly agreeable leaders follow a transformational leadership style (Judge and Bono 2000; Rubin et al. 2005) and they tend to promote decentralization of power within their teams (Peterson et al. 2003). Research has shown that transformational leaders not only empower team members by giving them higher autonomy (Smith et al. 2004) but also increases their risk taking-capabilities. Therefore, we propose the following:

Hypothesis 1a Transformational leadership is positively associated with top management team decentralization of responsibilities.

Hypothesis 1b Transactional leadership is positively associated with top management team decentralization of responsibilities.

A preference for risky growth opportunities is likely to be enhanced by transformational leaders because such leaders possess both vision and a measured degree of optimism about change (Bass 1985; Chen and Nadkarni 2017). Research suggest that when a transformational leader stimulates team members' efforts to be innovative and creative by questioning the team's assumptions, and encouraging new ways to approach existing situations, the leader helps to alleviate some of their concerns associated with such undertakings (Amabile et al. 2004; Chen and Nadkarni 2017), thereby enhancing the team's propensity to take greater risks than they would with a transactional leader. Therefore, we propose the following:

Hypothesis 2a Transformational leadership is positively associated with top management risk propensity in decision making.

Hypothesis 2b Transactional leadership is positively associated with top management risk propensity in decision making.

Corporate entrepreneurship is a broad, multi-dimensional concept that lies at the intersection of entrepreneurship and strategic management (Dess et al. 2003; Hitt et al. 2001; Ling et al. 2008; Simsek et al. 2007; Zahra 1996). It has been defined as a set of firm activities encompassing innovation, corporate venturing and strategic renewal (Zahra 1996) that helps increasing firm overall productivity. Innovation reflects a firm's commitment to create and introduce new products, processes and organizational systems (Zahra and Covin 1995). Caruana et al. (1998) found that centralization limits firms' entrepreneurial behaviour and hence their innovativeness. Damanpour (1991) found a negative relationship between centralization and organizational innovativeness. Atuahene-Gima (2003) reported that decentralization is positively related to new product development in fast-changing environments. Thus, we propose the following:

Hypothesis 3 Top management team decentralization of responsibilities is positively associated with (a) corporate entrepreneurship and (b) firm innovativeness.

Entrepreneurial activities like innovation, start-ups and strategic renewal entail considerable risk because time, effort and resources must be invested before the distribution of their returns is known, but they also entail the potential for considerable return (Chen and Nadkarni 2017). Consequently, it would follow that the more a team prefers risky growth opportunities, more eager the firm is to engage in corporate entrepreneurship and firm innovativeness (Finkelstein and Hambrick 1996), it would follow that the more a team prefers risky growth opportunities, the more apt the firm is to engage in corporate entrepreneurship and firm innovativeness. Supporting this prediction, Knight et al. (2001) found a positive relationship between managerial risk taking and innovative task performance. Thus, we hypothesize the following:

Hypothesis 4 Top management team risk propensity is positively associated with (a) corporate entrepreneurship and (b) firm innovativeness.

Research Methodology

Research Setting

The proposed research methodology includes empirical testing of the research framework with an aim to study the impact of leadership style on firm innovativeness and corporate entrepreneurship. The proposed model has been tested collecting data from the firms registered under the Startup India programme. To be registered as start-ups firms must experience turnover of less than 25 million/annum and have a team size of no more than 50 full-time employees. Firms in our sample are geographically located in Bihar in East India and have been around for less than five years, meaning all the firms were registered during or after 2013. Their registration classification is based on ownership pattern and shown in Table 12.2.

Table 12.2 Registration classification of firms (sample) under Startup India

Firm type	No of firms	Percentage of firms
Proprietorship	14	12.84%
Partnership	22	20.18%
LLP	57	52.29%
Private Ltd.	16	14.67%

Table 12.3 Sectoral classification of firms (sample)

Sectoral classification	Number of firms
E-commerce companies	65
Transportation companies	8
Manufacturing firms	11
Business Process Outsourcing (BPO)/ Knowledge Process Outsourcing (KPO)	22
Others	3

Respondents are senior executives working in these start-ups at the managerial levels; it means they are either heading an important department or heading the organization itself. Attention has been given to identify respondents working in independent work teams that have significant impact on firm performance. Similarly, in the manufacturing industry, respondents are from the product-innovation departments. This was done purposefully to explore the firm resource allocation under different projects and their contributions. The sectoral classification of these firms are shown in Table 12.3.

Sampling and Data Collection

In order to measure the role of leadership on corporate entrepreneurship and firm innovativeness, we approached start-up promoters and top management (men and women). We selected our sample of firms from Startup India's database. We collected data on the independent and dependent variables through a five-point Likert Response Format (LRF)-type questionnaire. Out of a total of 500 distributed questionnaires, we collected data from 109 respondents from 109 organizations over 75 days, giving us a response rate of 21.8 percent. Questionnaires were initially drafted in English and later translated in Hindi because it is the vernacular language of the Bihar region where the start-ups are located. Professional translators carried out the translations of questionnaires both ways (framing questions and responses). All precaution was taken to retain the original sense of responses made in Hindi. A pilot test showed that respondents understood the statements correctly (Table 12.4).

Operationalization and Measures

Two aspects of validity were examined: convergent validity and discriminant validity. For all constructs, convergent validity, assessed by the average variance extracted (AVE), met the criterion of 0.50 set by Fornell and Larcker (1981). Discriminant validity is confirmed for all latent constructs since the square root of each construct's AVE is greater than the bivariate correlation with the other constructs in the model (Table 12.5).

Model Description, Results and Discussion

The hypothesized relationship as depicted in Fig. 12.2 was tested using the two-step, linear step-wise regression technique. In included testing of the direct relationship between independent and dependent variables apart from testing the mediating roles of decentralization and risk taking. The main effect model was also explained using the path analysis under a structural

Table 12.4 Profiling of the respondents

Demographic		Proportion of sample
Gender	Male	89%
	Female	11%
Age	18–24	4
	25–34	86
	35–44	19

Table 12.5 Discriminant validity: correlations of constructs and $\sqrt{AVE}$

	Variables	1	2	3	4	5
1	LS	**0.79**				
2	DC	0.33	**0.78**			
3	RT	0.23	0.29	**0.86**		
4	CE	0.44	0.12	0.29	**0.81**	
5	FI	0.26	0.18	0.11	0.03	**0.78**

Bold main diagonal are square root of corresponding AVE

equation model (SEM). The regression model was tested separately for the two leadership styles mentioned earlier: transformational and transactional. Hypotheses were tested using the following system of equations simultaneously used for both the leadership styles as,

$$FI = \alpha_1 + \beta_{11}DC + \beta_{12}RT + \beta_{13}LS \qquad (12.1)$$

$$CE = \alpha_2 + \beta_{21}DC + \beta_{22}RT + \beta_{23}LS \qquad (12.2)$$

wherein,
LS = Leadership Style
DC = Decentralization
RT = Risk Taking
FI = Firm Innovativeness
CE = Corporate Entrepreneurship

Based on the data received from the MLQ, we segregated the data into two datasets, defining transactional and transactional datasets separately. We tested each set as Model 1 and Model 2 using the two-step, simultaneous linear regression technique. The test results for hypotheses 1 through 4 show the relationship between leadership styles, decentralization, risk taking, firm innovativeness and corporate entrepreneurship using multistage regression analysis. All the relations were found to be significant (Table 12.6). Results show that transformational leaders support decentralization of work ($\beta = 0.541, p < 0.001$) more than transactional leaders ($\beta = 0.341, p < 0.005$). Results for hypothesis 2 suggest that transformational leaders are risk takers, however, the relation was found to be insignificant for transactional leadership. Under Models 1 and 2, decentralization was found to be significant for firm innovativeness and corporate entrepreneurship (Hypothesis 4b). However, the direct effect of risk-taking ability is greater on firm innovativeness under Model 2 ($\beta = 0.799, p < 0.001$) and was found to be insignificant under Model 1 (Hypothesis 4a) (Table 12.7).

Testing the Structural Model

The main effect model was explored with an SEM. An SEM takes a confirmatory approach to testing the dependence relationships and accounting for measurement errors in the process of testing the model. The assessment of model fit was done using the various fit indices as shown in Table 12.8.

Table 12.6 Results of the least square (LS) regression

Hypo. no	Variable	Model 1 (a)			Model 2 (b)		
		Parameter estimate	Standard error	P-value	Parameter estimate	Standard error	P-value
1	Dependent: DC						
	Intercept	0.527	0.628	0.001	0.421	0.248	0.001
	LS	0.341	0.057	0.005	0.641	0.154	0.001
2	Dependent: RT						
	Intercept	1.577	0.533	0.001	1.348	0.442	0.001
	LS	0.032	0.328	0.034	0.544	0.113	0.001
3a	Dependent: FI						
	Intercept	1.31	0.065	0.001	0.034	0.651	0.001
	DC	0.151	0.041	0.001	0.992	0.033	0.001
3b	Dependent: CE						
	Intercept	4.111	0.443	0.001	3.154	0.221	0.001
	DC	0.542	0.004	0.001	0.122	0.051	0.001
4a	Dependent: FI						
	Intercept	0.223	0.041	0.004	3.423	0.041	0.001
	RT	0.099	0.056	0.085	0.799	0.077	0.001
4b	Dependent: CE						
	Intercept	1.128	0.335	0.001	0.578	0.345	0.001
	RT	0.181	0.911	0.001	0.191	0.131	0.001

Model 1: for the promotors classified as Transactional Leaders
Model 2: for the promotors classified as Transformational Leaders

The chi-square/df ratio of 2 to 3 is taken as good or acceptable fit. The various incremental fit indices include the Normal Fit Index (NFI), Comparative Fit Index (CFI) or the Tucker-Lewis Index (TLI), with suggestions for a cut of 0.90 for a good fitting model (Hu and Bentler 1999). Further, the absolute fit index of Adjusted Goodness of Fit Index (AGFI) is greater than the minimum 0.75 cutoff. The multiple R square for the model is 0.51.

Table 12.7 Test results of hypothesis testing

Hypo. no.	Model 1	Model 2
	Hypothesis test results	Hypothesis test results
1	Significant	Significant
2	Non-significant	Significant
3a	Significant	Significant
3b	Significant	Significant
4a	Non-significant	Significant
4b	Significant	Significant

Table 12.8 SEM model fit summary

$\chi2/df$	AGFI	PGFI	NFI	TLI	CFI	PNFI	RMSEA	RMR
2.81	0.771	0.693	0.891	0.91	0.95	0.825	0.043	0.051

CONCLUSION AND FUTURE RESEARCH DIRECTIONS

The identification of appropriate leadership style as a major enabler of corporate entrepreneurship and firm innovativeness with reference to the researched model provides a unified CE and FI framework with which more focused and synergistic research can be conducted. While much of the previous research has been made with a disaggregated approach taking leadership as a unified construct, the proposed model studies the impact of transformational and transactional styles on identified constructs and hence can help in achieving significant insights into the topic. We understand that the relationship between academic and strategic implementation of corporate entrepreneurship and firm innovation strategy can be improved using the current framework.

We had identified the integrated CE and FI framework as a potential unified paradigm that allows for a fully informed understanding of the nature of exchange between innovation and entrepreneurship enablers. From the fundamental nature of the economic exchange of service, or application of one resource for the benefit of another (composite or interconnected resources), we redesigned leadership style architecture using strategic innovation (Rajagopal 2012) and corporate entrepreneurship literature to converge them into a unified system for enhancing firm performance, customer value and social wellbeing. Further, at the firm level it provokes a need for an improved environment conducive to innovation and knowledge management.

The framework presented in this chapter emphasizes the strategic importance of utilizing a shared understanding of corporate entrepreneurship innovation enablers to guide organizational resource investment towards value creation activity and a need to adopt the cross-functional perspective in marketing. This framework presents a pathway for marketing researchers to explore the connection between leadership style and firm resources to plan what is necessary for implementing and executing a strategic approach for improving a firm's competitive advantage.

Our findings show a strong and direct link between transformational leadership and corporate entrepreneurship. Future research might address finer-grained conceptualizations of the relationships between the variables specified in our model. For example, although we did not find conclusive evidence to support a direct link between leadership style and firm innovativeness, in our post hoc analysis we did find that the transformational leadership style positively and more strongly influences firm innovativeness. Although this finding is exploratory, it does raise the broader issue for future research as to the more precise nature of the relationships between leadership-style characteristics and firm-level outcomes. Our findings also suggest that decentralization of responsibilities and risk-taking propensity are significantly linked to corporate entrepreneurship when keeping product portfolio as a control variable. It will be interesting to further research the existing model keeping economic conditions as the control to compare this model against different emerging economies.

LIMITATIONS AND DIRECTIONS FOR FUTURE RESEARCH

This study has several limitations, which provide fruitful avenues for future research. First, the use of firms located in Bihar limits the generalizability of the findings for emerging markets, especially BRICs (Brazil, Russia, India, China and South Africa) countries. Future researchers may want to replicate this study with start-ups across India in diverse industries (e.g., micro, small and medium enterprises [MSMEs]).

Second, although leadership style captures important individual differences, researchers could examine the effects on corporate entrepreneurship activities of other enablers that are important sources of corporate entrepreneurship and firm innovativeness, such as temporal dispositions. As adopting a long-term time horizon gives executives insights necessary for innovation, creativity and promoting entrepreneurial actions (Bluedorn and Martin 2008), a short-term time horizon facilitates transactional success.

Finally, future studies could build on the results of this study by going beyond the mediating roles of decentralization and risk-taking ability and consider additional factors, such as problem-solving, decision-making, planning and time-management skills, in predicting the effectiveness of leadership styles. We believe that emotional intelligence can be an important intellectual tool for creating new research opportunities to address a variety of temporal issues in the strategic and behavioral research.

References

Amabile, T. M., Schatzel, E. A., Moneta, G. B., & Kramer, S. J. (2004). Leader behaviours and the work environment for creativity: Perceived leader support. *Leadership Quarterly, 15*, 5–32.

Atuahene-Gima, K. (2003). The effects of centrifugal and centripetal forces on product development speed and quality: How does problem solving matter? *Academy of Management Journal, 46*, 359–373.

Avolio, B. J., & Bass, B. M. (1991). *The full range of leadership development.* Binghamton, NY: Bass, Avolio & Associates.

Barkema, H. G., Baum, J. A. C., & Mannix, E. A. (2002). Management challenges in a new time. *Academy of Management Journal, 45*, 916–930.

Barringer, C. R., & Bluedorn, A. C. (1999). The relationship between corporate entrepreneurship and strategic management. *Strategic Management Journal, 20*, 421–444.

Bass, B. M. (1985). *Leadership and performance beyond expectations.* New York: Free Press.

Bass, B. M., & Avolio, B. J. (1990). Developing transformational leadership: 1992 and beyond. *Journal of European Industrial Training, 14*, 21–27.

Bass, B. M., & Avolio, B. J. (1993). Transformational leadership and organizational culture. *Public Administration Quarterly, 12*, 113–121.

Bass, B. M., & Avolio, B. J. (1997). *Full range leadership development: Manual for the multifactor leadership questionnaire.* Palo Alto, CA: Mindgarden.

Bass, B. M., & Avolio, B. J. (2004). *Multifactor leadership questionnaire: Manual and sampler set* (3rd ed.). CA: Mind Garden, Inc..

Bluedorn, A. C., & Martin, G. (2008). The time frames of entrepreneurs. *Journal of Business Venturing, 23*, 1–20.

Burns, J. M. (1978). *Leadership.* New York: Harper & Row.

Caruana, A., Morris, M. H., & Vella, J. (1998). The effect of centralization and formalization on entrepreneurship in export firms. *Journal of Small Business Management, 36*, 16–29.

Chen, J., & Nadkarni, S. (2017). It's about time! CEOs' temporal dispositions, temporal leadership, and corporate entrepreneurship. *Administrative Science Quarterly, 62*(1), 31–66.

Cole, G. A. (2005). *Personnel and human resource management.* London: ELST Publishers.

Damanpour, F. (1991). Organizational innovation: A meta-analysis of effects of determinants and moderators. *Academy of Management Journal, 34,* 555–590.

Dess, G. G., Ireland, R. D., Zahra, S. A., Floyd, S. W., Janney, J. J., & Lane, P. J. (2003). Emerging issues in corporate entrepreneurship. *Journal of Management, 29,* 351–378.

Department of Industrial Policy and Promotion (DIPP), Government of India. (2017). *Report on industry update.*

Dvir, T., Eden, D., Avolio, B. J., & Shamir, B. (2002). Impact of transformational leadership on follower development and performance: A field experiment. *Academy of Management Journal, 45,* 735–744.

Finkelstein, S., & Hambrick, D. C. (1996). *Strategic leadership: Top executives and their effects on organizations.* St. Paul: West.

Fornell, C., & Larcker, D. F. (1981). Evaluating structural equation models with unobservable variables and measurement error. *Journal of Marketing Research, 18*(1), 39–50.

Hersey, P., Blanchard, K., & Johnson, D. E. (2001). *Management of organizational behavior* (8th ed.). Englewood Cliffs, NJ: Prentice Hall.

Hitt, M. A., Ireland, R. D., Camp, S. M., & Sexton, D. L. (2001). Strategic entrepreneurship: Entrepreneurial strategies for wealth creation. *Strategic Management Journal, 22,* 479–491.

Hogan, R., & Kaiser, R. B. (2005). What we know about leadership. *Review of General Psychology, 9,* 169–180.

House, R. J., & Aditya, R. M. (1997). The social scientific study of leadership: Quo vadis? *Journal of Management, 23,* 409–473.

Hu, L., & Bentler, P. M. (1999). Cut-off criteria for fit indexes in covariance structure analysis: Conventional criteria versus new alternatives. *Structural Equation Modelling, 6*(1), 1–55.

Judge, T. A., & Bono, J. E. (2000). Five-factor model of personality and transformational leadership. *Journal of Applied Psychology, 85,* 751–765.

Judge, T. A., & Piccolo, R. F. (2004). Transformational and transactional leadership: A meta-analytic test of their relative validity. *Journal of Applied Psychology, 89,* 755.

Katz, D., & Kahn, R. L. (1978). *The social psychology of organizations.* New York: Wiley.

Kirkpatrick, S. A., & Locke, E. A. (1991). Leadership: Do traits matter? *Academy of Management Executive, 5,* 48–60.

Knight, D., Durham, C. C., & Locke, E. A. (2001). The relationship of team goals, incentives, and efficacy to strategic risk, tactical implementation, and performance. *Academy of Management Journal, 44,* 326–338.

Kotter, J. P., & Heskett, J. L. (1992). *Corporate culture and performance.* New York: The Free Press.

Landy, F. J. (1989). *Psychology of work behavior.* Pacific Grove, CA: Thomson Brooks/Cole Publishing Co.

Ling, Y. A. N., Simsek, Z., Lubatkin, M. H., & Veiga, J. F. (2008). Transformational Leadership's role in promoting corporate entrepreneurship: Examining the CEO-TMT interface. *Academy of Management Journal, 51*(3), 557–576.

The National Association of Software and Services Companies (NASSCOM). (2017). *Internet and Indian economy.* India.

Nel, P. S., Van Dyk, P. S., Haasbroek, G. D., Schultz, H. B., Sono, T. J., & Werner, A. (2004). *Human resources management* (6th ed.). New York: Oxford University Press.

Peterson, R. S., Smith, D. B., Martorana, P. V., & Owens, P. D. (2003). The impact of chief executive officer personality on top management team dynamics: One mechanism by which leadership affects organizational performance. *Journal of Applied Psychology, 88,* 795–808.

Rajagopal, A. (2012). Role of systems thinking in developing marketing strategy: Some conceptual insights. *Journal of Transnational Management, 17*(4), 258–276.

Rubin, R. S., Munz, D. C., & Bommer, W. H. (2005). Leading from within: The effects of emotion recognition and personality on transformational leadership behaviour. *Academy of Management Journal, 48,* 845–858.

Schermerhorn Jr., J. R., Hunt, J. G., & Osborn, R. N. (1982). *Managing organizational behaviour.* New York: John Wiley & Sons.

Senge, P. (1990). *The fifth discipline: The art and practice of the learning organization.* New York, NY: Doubleday Currency.

Simsek, Z., Veiga, J. F., & Lubatkin, M. H. (2007). The impact of managerial environmental perceptions on corporate entrepreneurship: Towards understanding discretionary slack's pivotal role. *Journal of Management Studies, 44,* 1398–1424.

Smith, B., Montagno, R. V., & Kuzmenko, T. N. (2004). Transformational and servant leadership: Content and contextual comparisons. *Journal of Leadership and Organizational Studies, 10,* 80–91.

Stogdill, R. M. (1948). Personal factors associated with leadership. *Journal of Psychology, 25,* 35–71.

Vroom, V. H., & Yetton, P. (1973). *Leadership and decision making.* Pittsburgh: University of Pittsburgh Press.

Yukl, G. A. (2006). *Leadership in organizations* (6th ed.). Upper Saddle River, NJ: Pearson Prentice Hall.

Zaccaro, S. J. (2007). Trait-based perspectives of leadership. *American Psychologist, 62*, 6–16.

Zahra, S. A. (1996). Governance, ownership, and corporate entrepreneurship: The moderating impact of industry technological opportunities. *Academy of Management Journal, 39*, 1713–1735.

Zahra, S. A., & Covin, J. G. (1995). Contextual influences on the corporate entrepreneurship performance relationship—A longitudinal analysis. *Journal of Business Venturing, 10*, 43–58.

CHAPTER 13

Analysis of Factors of Advantages and Disadvantages in the Business Scenario of Northeast India: The Entrepreneur's Perspective

Analjyoti Basu and Kalyan Adak

INTRODUCTION

A country's development depends upon the synchronous development of its each and every region and part. Various authors and researchers in their studies and research advocated for the same (Datt and Ravallion 1996; Lucas 1988; Mazumdar 1996; Preston 1979). However, for India, the concept of equal growth and development falls short with imbalanced growth and development in certain regions and parts. The northeastern region of India, comprising eight states (Sikkim, Assam, Manipur, Meghalaya, Mizoram, Tripura, Nagaland and Arunachal Pradesh), is experiencing imbalanced

A. Basu (✉)
Entrepreneurship Development Institute of India, Gandhinagar, Gujarat, India
e-mail: analjyoti01@ediindia.org

K. Adak
Commerce Department, Government Hrangbana College, Mizoram University, Aizawl, Mizoram, India

regional growth. The region is considered the economic laggard of the country due to an inefficiently managed economy, lack of political vision and inefficiency in exploring the abundant natural resources of the region (Singh 2016).

Northeast India comprises eight states that cover a geographical area of 0.26 million km², accounting for 7 % of the country's total area (Das and Ali 2003). The region is a gateway to Southeast Asia as it is bordered by Bangladesh, Bhutan, Myanmar, Nepal and China. The Northeast Region (NER) of India is one of the vibrant and complex areas to administer. Of the 600 odd ethnic communities that inhabit India, more than 200 groups are found in this region.[1] According to the 2011 census, the population of the region is approximately 4.5 crores, which is just 3.8% of the total Indian population of 121 crores.[2]

After India's independence, the partition that created East Pakistan from Bengal separated the NER from the rest of the country. Only a small strand, known as the 'Chicken's Neck' (also known as the Siliguri Corridor), in the state of West Bengal, which is approximately 33 km wide on the eastern side and 21 km on the western side, joined NER with the rest of India (Singh 2016). The partition at the time of independence further blocked the natural sea route through the port city of Chittagong (Bangladesh). Thus, the partition of the country handicapped the NER by land blocking the natural transportation facilities to a great extent (Das 2010; Singh 2016).

Therefore, the geographic disadvantage due to partition along with administrative, political and economic laggardness has pushed the region behind in terms of development. However, the situation is changing and there are some signs of unified growth and development. The GSDP growth of all eight states (2004–2005 prices) has surpassed India's average GSDP growth of 4.74 (Updated 19 August 2015 by the Ministry of Statistics and Programme Implementation, Govt. of India).[3] The GSDP of the states includes the agricultural allied sector, industry, manufacturing and services (along with agriculture, mining and quarrying) (Planning

---

[1] www.nirth.res.in/thrf/thb_special_issue2014.pdf
[2] www.northeastindiastat.com/table/demographics/7/population/582603/582607/data.aspx
[3] http://statisticstimes.com/economy/gdp-growth-of-indian-states.php

Commission Data 2014).[4] Hence growth in GSDP indicates the growth in the mentioned sectors of the NER. A big portion of the mentioned sectors, like the agricultural allied sector, manufacturing and services, intersect with the Micro, Small and Medium Enterprises (MSMEs).

One important demographic aspect of Northeast India is its tribal population. In the NER, the tribal population is almost 30% (27.27%, according to the 2011 census),[5] that is, approximately one-third of the population in the NER is tribal. If further elaborated in terms of individual states, the percentage of tribal population in each state is as follows: Mizoram = 94.4%, Nagaland = 86.5%, Meghalaya = 86.1%, Arunachal Pradesh = 68.8%, Manipur = 35.1%, Sikkim = 33.8%, Tripura = 31.8%, and Assam = 12.4%. Excluding Assam, the other seven states in the region have at least one-third tribal population. Obviously, the argument arises that the growth and development of this region, especially the growth scenario discussed previously, to great extent depends upon the tribal population. The growth of MSMEs, with respect to those run by tribal entrepreneurs, is evidence of this point.

The Fourth All India Census of MSME (2006–2007) found that, for all the northeastern states, the percentage of enterprises owned by tribals is higher than the national average percentage of 3 %.[6] The percentage of enterprises owned by tribal entrepreneurs in the individual states breaks down as follows: Mizoram (94.4%), Meghalaya (93.4%), Nagaland (86.5%), Arunachal Pradesh (73.8%), Sikkim (25%), Assam (25%), Manipur (24.5%) and Tripura (3%).

The same census, considering state-wise percentage distribution of entrepreneurship in the rural areas that are owned by tribals, reports the following: Mizoram (96.86%), Meghalaya (94.66%), Nagaland (86.39%), Arunachal Pradesh (64.55%) and Sikkim (26.67%). The remaining two states, although at lower percentages, have also surpassed the national average of 4.02%: Assam (8.56%) and Tripura (4.75%). There is a similar scenario when the same criterion are taken for the urban area enterprises of the northeastern states. Mizoram takes the top spot with 93.94%, followed by Meghalaya (88.82%), Nagaland (85.88%), Arunachal Pradesh (82.74%) and Sikkim (15%). However, of the remaining two states, only

---

[4] http://planningcommission.nic.in/hindi/data/datatable/index.php?data=b_misdch.htm
[5] http://www.nirth.res.in/thrf/thb_special_issue2014.pdf
[6] http://www.dcmsme.gov.in/publications/FinalReport010711.pdf

Assam (4.60%) was able to surpass the national average of 1.92% (Fourth All India Census of MSME: Registered Sector) (see Note 6).

Based on this information, the present study tries to find the reason for growth and development, and the obstacles to growth and development, of enterprises in the NER over the last five years. For this purpose, we selected and interviewed the tribal entrepreneurs of densely populated tribal districts of Northeast India. The districts selected were East Khasi Hills and Ri-Bhoi in Meghalaya, Churachandpur in Manipur, and Aizawl in Mizoram where tribal population is more than two lakhs and tribal population density with respect to the total population of the district is more than 80% (2011 census) (see Note 5).

In the following section, we discuss the literature on entrepreneurship with respect to the NER. Then, we follow up with a discussion on research methodology. Next, we discuss the scholastic views on benefits and disadvantages of the business scenario in the region. The scholars' view will be followed by the views of the entrepreneurs regarding the benefits and disadvantages faced by them in the business scenario. Finally, we present a conclusion of our findings, pointing out benefits and problems.

ENTREPRENEURSHIP IN LITERATURE IN NORTHEAST INDIA

This study is mainly based on the views of the tribal entrepreneurs of Northeast India. The present section discusses the literature on different aspects of entrepreneurship in this particular region. The overview of the present literature generally focuses on topics of rural entrepreneurship development (Bhattacharjee and Das 2013; Dadina and Dey 2015; Deb 2013; Paul 2015; Sharma 2015), female entrepreneurship development (Aye 2013; Barua and Devi 2004; Chakravarty 2013; Chanu and Chanu 2014; Devi 2014, 2015, 2016; Guha and Adak 2014; Kurbah 2013; Lalhunthara 2015; Ram et al. 2013; Sharma 2017; Sharma and Bora 2015; Singh and Punitha 2012; Singh and Singh 2012; Upadhyay and Barman 2013), tribal entrepreneurship development (Aye 2013; Deb 2013; Kurbah 2013; Paul 2015; Upadhyay and Barman 2013), tourism development for entrepreneurship growth (Barman et al. 2015; Baruah 2013; Bhattacharjee and Das 2013; Kalita and Barman 2013; Paul 2015), support of micro-finance for the growth of entrepreneurship (Devi 2014; Goswami et al. 2017; Sharma 2017; Sharma and Bora 2015), entrepreneurship endeavors by the youth population (Kalita and Bora 2015; Thakur 2017), growth of entrepreneurship in the hands of different indigenous groups (Saikia 2015) and the factors of business performance (Das and Goswami 2017).

Some research is applicable to two and even three topics at the same time. For example, the study by Bhattacharjee and Das (2013) is relevant for both rural entrepreneurship and tourism development in the NER. Going in-depth, the sub-topics of the study focused on problems, strategy formulation, including marketing (depending upon cases), opportunities, entrepreneurial behavior (mainly in case of tribal entrepreneurship and women's entrepreneurship) and performance factors of entrepreneurship.

Rural Entrepreneurship

The Fourth All India Census of MSME, for both registered and unregistered sectors, indicates that more than 90% of enterprises in the MSME category are micro-enterprises (Source—Fourth All India Census of Micro, Small & Medium Enterprises, 2006–2007, Unregistered Sector; Fourth All India Census of Micro, Small & Medium Enterprises, 2006–2007, Registered Sector) (see Note 6).[7] According to the definition given by the Micro, Small and Medium Enterprise Development (MSMED) Act, 2006,[8] micro-enterprises in the manufacturing and service sector have a maximum investment of 25 lakhs in plants and 10 lakhs in machinery. Naturally, with respect to entrepreneurship development in the NER, a large volume of literary works are dedicated to rural enterprises. In this connection, with reference to Arunachal Pradesh, Deb (2013) felt that the state has good potential for the growth of rural enterprises, which will benefit the rural youths to grow their entrepreneurship. However, obstruction is coming in the form of the existing political system (e.g. Inner Line System), local-level corruption (e.g. taking undue benefits of subsidy linked Scheme, license issuing system, lure to become a political leader), lack of work culture (e.g. lack of entrepreneurial orientation, loss of the dignity of labor among contemporary youths, tendency to earn easy money and live an easy life), and lack of infrastructure for business growth (e.g. power, road and rail transport, a weak banking network, and stringent loan-granting practices). However, Deb is not completely pessimistic

---

[7] http://dcmsme.gov.in/publications/Final%20Report%20of%20Fourth%20All%20India%20Census%20of%20MSME%20Unregistered%20Sector%202006-07.pdf
[8] https://dcmsme.gov.in/ssiindia/definition_msme.htm

about the situation. Banking on the concept of the economic power of entrepreneurship emphasize to create an atmosphere for entrepreneurship based development. The author expressed the need for providing essential facilities for rural areas, boosting up industries based on local raw materials and ensuring the market for local products. In line with Deb (2013), Dadina and Dey (2015) captured the problem of rural enterprises in the context of Manipur. They analyzed the problems of entrepreneurs in fish farming in Manipur. The result of their study revealed that the barriers to fish farming are positively correlated to knowledge of the fish farming process and negatively correlated to the size of the family, the longevity of fish farming and productivity of fish. They further suggested the way out for successful fish farming by emphasizing more training to farmers, a participatory approach among stakeholders for sustainability, focusing on "fisheries for development" rather than a "development of fisheries" approach and establishing policy for fish farmers for taking liberalization benefits. Opportunities linked with rural entrepreneurship came up in the works of Bhattacharjee and Das (2013), Paul (2015) and Sharma (2015). Works by Bhattacharjee and Das (2013) and Sharma (2015) focused on the rural tourism of Assam while Paul (2015) studied the same in Sikkim. These authors realized the potentiality of rural entrepreneurship development in Assam. Bhattacharjee and Das (2013) stressed "understanding the rural environment, demography, socio-cultural, economic and political background of that place" backed by the government endeavor while Sharma (2015) emphasized traditional activities of women like weaving, knitting, embroidery, and food processing works for growth of more entrepreneurs from the present eco-system. Building and further nurturing the enterprise of home-stay came in the work of Paul (2015). Paul took up the case of Hee Gaon, a village of western Sikkim, and described how by the help of NGOs the locals of the village developed the business of home-stay, which afforded the area opportunity for generation of more employment.

Role of Micro-Finance

Micro-finance has good linkage with MSME growth (Kumar et al. 2010; Sievers and Vandenberg 2007; Singh 2009) where micro-finance is used to provide financial assistance to the MSMEs. Further, the Fourth All India Census of MSME, for both registered and unregistered sectors, indicated that most of the enterprises coming under the segment of MSMEs are micro-enterprises considering the rural enterprises of the northeastern part of India (Source—Fourth All India Census of Micro, Small & Medium Enterprises, 2006–2007, Unregistered Sector; Fourth All India Census of Micro, Small & Medium Enterprises, 2006–2007, Registered Sector) (see Notes 6 and 7). Naturally, a lot of authors have chosen micro-finance and the matters related to micro-finance in their research related to Northeast India. Opportunities attached in using micro-finance for the development of entrepreneurship came in the works of Devi (2014), Sharma and Bora (2015), and Sharma (2017). Exploring the role of micro-finance in developing the financial position of women entrepreneurs of Self-Help Groups (SHG), Devi (2014), in the context of Manipur, found that micro-finance resolves the needs of women entrepreneurs as they get easy financial support for their businesses during times of emergency. The work of Sharma and Bora (2015) second the findings of Devi (2014) in the context of Sonitpur in Assam, where they found that the main advantage of micro-finance is to provide entrepreneurship opportunities to the poor who can't get bank loans. The entrepreneurship opportunity helped the poor to increase their standard of living. The research of Sharma (2017) further supported the findings of Sharma and Bora (2015).

Women's Entrepreneurship

In various parts of the NER, the norms and culture of the matrilineal form of society are followed (Khongsdier 2005; Mitra 2008). Matrilineal culture is having an impact on the business and economic environment of the region. Women entrepreneurs largely contribute to the economy of the NER (Sorokhaibam 2006). The data regarding existing enterprises clearly spells the bigger role of women for the growth and development of enterprises in this region. The Fourth All India Census of MSME for registered MSMEs spells in favor of this fact (see Notes 6 and 7). With respect to the percentage of registered rural women enterprises, Meghalaya (39.31%), Mizoram (35.91%) and Manipur (30.49%) take the first three positions within the Indian states. For registered urban enterprises run by women, Meghalaya (39.58%), Mizoram (34.49%) and Arunachal Pradesh (27.27%) occupy the first three positions. This story also prevails in the unregistered section of MSMEs. Meghalaya (33.76%) and Nagaland (29.68%) take the top two spots for un-registered rural MSMEs run by women (see Note 7). For un-registered urban MSMEs run by women, Mizoram (33.8%) and Meghalaya (31.77%) take the top two spots (Source—Fourth All India

Census of Micro, Small & Medium Enterprises, 2006–2007, Unregistered Sector; Fourth All India Census of Micro, Small & Medium Enterprises, 2006–2007, Registered Sector) (see Notes 6 and 7). With this said, it is not surprising that topics related to women's entrepreneurship have their priority in the literature related to the business of the NER. Studies by Barua and Devi (2004), Singh and Singh (2012), Aye (2013), Devi (2016), Chakravarty (2013) and Lalhunthara (2015) mainly focus on the problems and possible ways out of women's entrepreneurship. Barua and Devi (2004) and Devi (2016) studied the struggle of women entrepreneurs in Manipur. Barua and Devi (2004) focused on women entrepreneurs of the Ima Market in Imphal while Devi (2016) concentrated on the molasses entrepreneurs of Kakching. The Ima Market in Imphal is totally run by women, but has faced incidents of threats from different forces. However, despite all threats, the market is running successfully, combating all the odds. The women entrepreneurs of Kakching have developed efficient production processes for molasses and have avoided extinction.

Threats to sustainability of women-run enterprises (specifically the rural ones) also come from the marketing practices and business outlook that are not on par with the present trends and that are dominated by lower self-esteem, lower access to resources, and technical and financial constraints (Chakravarty 2013; Singh and Singh 2012). The outcome is that the number of women entrepreneurs is less with respect to their male counterparts (Lalhunthara 2015). The authors felt that entrepreneurial restructuring and developing existing ventures is needed to bridge the gap and to make these enterprises successful. Further, it's very important to impart proper training for skill and marketing talent growth in women entrepreneurs. Lalhunthara (2015), on the topic of decreasing the numbers gap, felt that a profound initiative should be taken from the government's side. According to the author, special schemes of assistance and incentives should be introduced for women entrepreneurs, especially for small and medium enterprises. These could include financial support, marketing support, infrastructure support, training support and waivers for collateral security. Upadhyay and Barman (2013) and Prabha (2006) support this view. Upadhyay and Barman (2013) placed their view in perspective of women entrepreneurs' engagement in the sericulture industry of Meghalaya, which is considered an important agro-based cottage industry of Mizoram. Prabha (2006) highlighted the need of training in the context of women entrepreneurs of the Kamrup district in Assam and the Imphal district in Manipur. Aye (2013) addressed the obstacles faced by women entrepreneurs in the shape of societal obstruction. Aye (2013) tried to establish this fact in the context of Nagaland where the society has high respect for women, but the conservative set-up of the society stops women from taking entrepreneurship as a career option. However, the author feel that there is a wind of change coming with the educational advancement of Naga women. More and more women are embracing fashion-based business, transport-based business and restaurant-based business to move forward in the career of entrepreneurship.

For sustainability, there is a high need for spreading the stories of successful women entrepreneurs to the next generation. The research on entrepreneurship opportunities for women was further carried out by Singh and Punitha (2012), Upadhyay and Barman (2013), Ram et al. (Ram et al. 2013), Guha and Adak (2014), Devi (2014), Sharma and Bora (2015), Devi (2015), Chanu and Chanu (2014) and Sharma (2017). The studies suggest that there is a growth in the MSME industries. It floors the question of preference of entrepreneurship as a career and following it the status of women entrepreneurship in the region. Studies by Devi (2015), Ram et al. (2013) and Chanu and Chanu (2014) shed light on the issue. Devi's (2015) research finds that becoming financially independent, combating unemployment, earning a livelihood for oneself, supporting the family, utilizing one's skills and education, and social recognition are some of the reasons women choose to become entrepreneurs. Ram et al. (2013) also support this view. They researched the status of women entrepreneurs in Manipur and found that factors like education, family size, annual income and socio-economic status play an important role in growing entrepreneurial behavior among women in the region. Research by Chanu and Chanu (2014) also found this to be the case as they also selected Manipur as their study area. Following Chanu and Chanu (2014), it could be said that women's entrepreneurship in Manipur mostly belongs to the MSME sector and a majority of the enterprises are joined with the manufacturing sector. Women in Manipur are mainly engaged in embroidery, weaving, tailoring, cattle rearing, fittings, jewelry works, computer jobs, videography and jobs at beauty parlors.

Apart from building an enterprise, the success of an enterprise rests on its ability to withstand in the changing business environment. In this matter, branding and labelling are two essential parts of marketing products and remaining competitive in the market. However, the practice of marketing is very rare among the women entrepreneurs of Manipur though the findings by Chanu and Chanu (2015) advocate that educational qualification of the women entrepreneurs has no impact on the nature of marketing practices carried out by them. In this point, Chanu and Chanu (2014) emphasized having more innovative practice to compete globally. In connection with competing outside the state's market, Singh and Punitha (2012) and Upadhyay and Barman (2013) presented a bright future for the anthurium business and sericulture industry, both run by the women entrepreneurs in Mizoram. It can be inferred from this scholarship that the anthurium business is a good example of a public-private partnership where the Mizoram government played a significant role and that sericulture is an important agro-based industry employing a large population of women in Mizoram. The sericulture and weaving industries are important as they have helped the state of Mizoram alleviate the problem of unemployment. On the role of society in promoting entrepreneurship among women, Kurbah (2013) and Guha and Adak (2014) presented strong evidence from the Khasi society in Meghalaya and the Mizo society in Mizoram, respectively. Though Guha and Adak (2014) slightly differed from Kurbah (2013), the authors have equal views in terms of high participation of women in enterprise building. According to Kurbah (2013), the society not only thrashes the concept of gender inequality, but gives women the right to enjoy the property and participate in different "social, cultural, religious, political or economic activities," which promotes entrepreneurial traits in the women for building a good economic base. However, based on work by Guha and Adak (2014), there are gender biases in ownership of entrepreneurship. According to them, the license or ownership is in the hands of the male members, but total management of entrepreneurship development rests on the female counterpart. Devi (2014), Sharma and Bora (2015) and Sharma (2017) have explored the linkages of micro-finance with women entrepreneurship and vice versa.

Tourism Industry

The beauty of nature always attracted nature-loving explorers, nature-loving vacationers and change seekers. The NER is a potential hub for tourism because of the region's natural beauty (Dey and Sarma 2010). Data show growth in the tourism industry of the NER. According to the Union Tourism Ministry and the different tourism departments of the northeastern states, tourism increased 11.63 percent from 2014 to 2015 (from 128 crores in 2014 to 143 crores in 2015). In this period, Manipur (26.55%) registered the highest growth in domestic tourism followed by

Assam (13.78%). Tripura (30.72%) and Manipur (17.73%) had the highest growth in foreign tourism (Source—24t July, 2016, *The Telegraph*).[9] This tourism growth is reflected in the works of Barman et al. (2015), Baruah (2013), Bhattacharjee and Das (2013), Kalita and Barman (2013), and Paul (2015). In the context of Assam, Kalita and Barman (2013), Bhattacharjee and Das (2013), and (Barman et al. 2015) advocated for the overall growth of the tourism industry by exploring the state's natural beauty. In their view, tourism growth in the area will help entrepreneurs to come up with their enterprises and alleviate the problem of unemployment. Kalita and Barman (2013) felt that tourism in Assam has every opportunity to excel because it has a rich mixture of natural beauty, wildlife sanctuaries, eco-tourism spots, hill stations, lakes and places of religious and historical interest. However, simply having these things is not enough for any state.

A proper marketing for the available resources (Barman et al. 2015) and understanding the overall environment of the concerned place (Bhattacharjee and Das 2013) is the need of the hour. Understanding this need, Barman et al. (2015) suggested a servuction model that includes all the stakeholders of the tourism business. Baruah (2013) gave new insight into the study of the tourism industry and the consequent growth in entrepreneurship. The author placed the idea of entrepreneurship growth in the context of tea-based tourism. The logic placed by him is related to the downfall of the tea industry in recent times, which is one of the main revenue-earning industries of Assam (Hazarika and Subramanian 1999), and the subsequent rise of the tourism industry in Assam. The authors mixed both the events and proposed tea tourism in Assam riding on the natural beauty of the tea gardens. Paul (2015) worked on the growth of the tourism industry in Sikkim.

Tribal Entrepreneurship

A lot of the literature on entrepreneurship development in the NER is invested in depicting the position of tribal entrepreneurship in the same region. The works of Aye (2013); Kurbah (2013); Upadhyay and Barman (2013); Deb (2013); and Paul (2015) could be considered significant contributions in this area, as previously discussed. Research by Aye (2013), Kurbah (2013) and Upadhyay and Barman (2013) focused on women's

---

[9] www.telegraphindia.com/1160724/jsp/northeast/story_98424.jsp

entrepreneurship with a connection to tribal entrepreneurship. In the same way, research by Deb (2013) and Paul (2015) were based on rural entrepreneurship as well as on tribal entrepreneurship. Aye discussed the plight of Naga tribal women entrepreneurs and a possible solution to the problem. On the flip side of Aye's work is Kurbah's (2013) work on the societal opportunity provided by the Khasi tribal community to its women entrepreneurs. Upadhyay and Barman (2013) pulled up both bright and dull pictures for women entrepreneurs in the sericulture industry of Mizoram. Deb (2013) discussed the overall problems faced by the tribal entrepreneurs of rural Arunachal Pradesh while, in the context of Hee Gaon, a village in western Sikkim, Paul (2015) discussed the growth factors of the rural enterprises with the help of a case study.

Youth Entrepreneurship

A survey conducted by the National Youth Research Survey (NYRS) in collaboration with the National Council of Applied Economic Research in 2009, revealed a huge pool of youth population in the NER.[10] In terms of numbers, it could be said that all the states (except Manipur) have more than 50 percent population in the age group of 13 to 35 years. Six out of eight states (except Manipur and Mizoram) have crossed the national average of 56.5 percent. Considering the high percentage of youth population of the NER, some of the authors have contributed their scholastic work on the matters of youth entrepreneurship (Thakur 2017; Kalita and Bora 2015) in the northeastern states. In this matter, Thakur (2017) pointed towards the endeavors of the youths of Mizoram in building successful business models in their state. According to the author's observation, most of the youths of the state educate themselves outside the state and come back to the state packed with modern knowledge of entrepreneurship. Further, they blend their modern knowledge from outside with the traditional knowledge of business prevailing in the state. Finally, they build up a successful and sustainable business model. Pressing on the essentiality of bringing more and more youths to the entrepreneurship career, Kalita and Bora (2015) expressed the need to start entrepreneurship education at the college level in Assam. They felt the education will provide the youths with necessary knowledge and skill sets. Apart the main

[10] www.ncaer.org/free-download.php?pID=110

issues, issues like the need for an entrepreneurial network for the growth of small firms in Northeast India (Das and Goswami 2017) and growth of entrepreneurship in the hands of different indigenous groups (Saikia 2015) also came up in the scholarly works.

Research Methodology

We present the benefits and disadvantages of entrepreneurship in two steps. First, in section "Entrepreneurship in Literature in Northeast India", we analyzed the scholastic views on benefits and disadvantages of the business scenario in the NER. Second, on the base of these scholarly findings, we carried out interviews with entrepreneurs regarding their views of the benefits and disadvantages they face in business. Next, we discuss sample selection and our primary data collection process.

Sample

We selected the tribal entrepreneurs from the district of Northeast India, where the total tribal population is more than two lakhs and the percentage of the tribal population with respect to the district population is more than 80% (Tribal Health Bulletin 2014). Under the chosen criteria, came East Khasi Hills and Ri-Bhoi in Meghalaya, Churachandpur in Manipur, and Aizawl in Mizoram (see Table 13.1). Further, we took care to include tribal entrepreneurs that have a minimum of three years of experience in their business and have at least three members (mainly, the criteria of the GEM study was taken into consideration) working in their organization. Their sales turnover also ranged between 1 lakh to 10 lakhs a month. In all, we interviewed 40 tribal entrepreneurs from each of the aforementioned four districts for a total of 160 tribal entrepreneurs.

Table 13.1 Selection of districts

State	Districts	Population	Tribal population	Total percentage of population (w.r.t district)
Mizoram	Aizawl	4,00,309	3,73,542	93.31
Manipur	Churachandpur	2,74,143	2,54,787	92.94
Meghalaya	Ri-Bhoi	2,58,840	2,30,081	88.89
Meghalaya	East Khasi Hills	8,25,922	6,61,158	80.05

Source: Census (2011)

Data Collection

A broader research was carried out in which the entrepreneurial intensity of the tribal entrepreneurs of the densely populated tribal districts of the NER was studied. The present research paper is a part of the aforesaid study. So, for the broader study, we collected data by following two steps:

Step A: In this step, we constructed a questionnaire regarding entrepreneurial intensity. In the questionnaire, along with other questions, we included questions about the benefits and disadvantages faced by the entrepreneurs.

Step B: In this step, we conducted interviews with the tribal entrepreneurs based on the questionnaire. Along with questions on entrepreneurial intensity, we included questions about the benefits and disadvantages faced by the entrepreneurs.

THE BENEFITS AND DISADVANTAGES: A LITERATURE REVIEW

The earlier literature review focused mainly on the issues of rural entrepreneurship development, women's entrepreneurship development, tribal entrepreneurship development, tourism development for entrepreneurship growth, support of micro-finance for the growth of entrepreneurship, entrepreneurship endeavors by the youth population and the factors of business performance with respect to Northeast India. These are the issues that are highly attached to the overall business development of the region. However, in all the sections of study, the factors of problems and benefits were also focused on by the authors and researchers.

Focusing on the problems pointed out in the scholarly research, it appears that the political system, local-level corruption, lack of work culture and lack of infrastructure for business growth (Deb 2013) are some of the problems obstructing business growth in the NER. In doing business, proper marketing of the products, processes, and services also matter a lot. Proper marketing and placing the products is another problem in this region (Prabha 2006). Lack of proper marketing highlights another disadvantage—the lack and mismatch of business outlooks that ignore the present trends of the market (Chakravarty 2013; Singh and Singh 2012). The lack of business outlook further could be attributed to the constraints of lower self-esteem, lower access to resources and technical and financial constraints (Chakravarty 2013; Singh and Singh 2012). Kabra (2008) presented an overall view of the problems that are hindering the overall development of the region. According to the author, poor connectivity within the region and with the rest of India, poor roads, poor water supply, land lockedness, high price of different commodities produced in this region, diversion of financial resources to fight insurgency, and oversized administrative machinery eating up the financial resources of the region are the overall problems faced by the people as well as the entrepreneurs of this region. Laskar (2010) and Singh (2016) supported most of the points put forward by Kabra.

The point of prospects was also showcased in the works of the researchers and scholars. Research carried out by Devi (2014), Sharma and Bora (2015) and Sharma (2017) focused on the contribution of micro-finance in the growth of enterprises in this part of India. According to them, micro-finance played an important role in growing business among the poor. The silver spark of the NER is also traced by Thakur (2017). Thakur's findings are encouraging for the youths of the region who are considered the future of the region. According to the author, the youths (mostly educated outside their states) are making a good blend of traditional knowledge and modern knowledge to revamp their business that as a whole is adding to the betterment of the business environment of the region. As problems, prospects are also reflected in the work of Kabra (2008). In the author's view, relief in the matter of land, tax and center funding, high budgetary support from the central government is an important support system in this part of India. If the internal situation is analyzed then, following Mohan (2003, as cited in Singh 2016), it could be inferred that high literacy rate, high skill levels in certain areas, abundant and unexplored natural resources, good potential for tourism industry development and potential of high export business in this region spells out the positive points in favor of this region.

The Benefits and Disadvantages: The Entrepreneurs' View

This section is mainly built on the literary works presented by scholars and researchers on the benefits and disadvantages faced by the entrepreneurs of the region. Our interviews with more than 150 entrepreneurs provide further insight into the problems and benefits of entrepreneurship in the NER. The main purpose of adding the views of the entrepreneurs after the scholars' is to compile all the problems and advantages about doing business in the region by all concerned parties.

Benefits and Short Description

Based on our interviews with 160 entrepreneurs from the aforementioned four districts of three states, it was determined that infrastructure development and better governance in the last five years are the major reasons for development. These reasons helped in growth in tourism, small business development, agricultural development and overall business development. These benefits are elaborated upon and presented in Table 13.2.

Market Location Near Main Cities

All four districts considered for the present study are either near the capital city or the capital city of the city. Churachandpur lies near Imphal, the capital town of Manipur while Ri-Bhoi lies between Shillong and Guwahati. Shillong is the capital of Meghalaya and Guwahati is the capital of Assam. The other two districts, East Khasi Hills and Aizawl, house the capital cities of the states. East Khasi Hills houses Shillong while Aizawl itself is the capital of Mizoram. So, in all cases, the market of the main cities is near the districts under study. The proximity of the markets gives benefit to the entrepreneurs.

Table 13.2 Benefits depicted by the entrepreneurs

Benefits	Main region (that supported the response)	Total percentage (%)
Market location near main cities	East Khasi Hills, Ri-Bhoi and Aizawl	82
Population increase	East Khasi Hills, Aizawl	68
Border trade	Churachandpur, Aizawl and east Khasi Hills	59
Native preference	East Khasi Hills and Aizawl	67
Building eco-system of business	East Khasi Hills and Aizawl	69
Tourism opportunities	East Khasi Hills and Aizawl	54
Women's empowerment.	East Khasi Hills, Ri-Bhoi and Churachandpur	86
Easy information flow	East Khasi Hills and Aizawl	51
Supportive government	East Khasi Hills and Aizawl	77
Friendly environment for business	East Khasi Hills	76

Source: Based on primary survey

Population Increase

This point received support from the entrepreneurs of the district headquarters' towns in the study area. Specifically, the entrepreneurs of Shillong (district headquarters of East Khasi Hills) and Aizawl (capital of Mizoram) advocated for this point. According to them, Shillong and Aizawl are the places of tourist interest and business. Therefore more and more people from different parts of the state accumulate in these towns for their livelihood. The result is also visible in terms of high urbanization in these two states of Meghalaya and Mizoram.

Border Trade

We already discussed at the start of the chapter that the NER is a gateway to Southeast Asia and is bordered by Bangladesh, Bhutan, Myanmar, Nepal and China, hence the region has a good prospect for border trade. This is also reflected in our interviews with the entrepreneurs of the region. Mostly, the owners of the enterprises in Churachandpur of Manipur and East Khasi Hills advocated for this point. Churachandpur and Aizawl are very near the Myanmar border and East Khasi Hills is close to the Bangladesh border. From the interviews with the entrepreneurs of Meghalaya (East Khasi Hills and Ri-Bhoi), it came up that under the state's industrial policy a lot of government subsidy and incentives are provided to the business people of the border areas.

Native Preference

In business issues, preference is given to the natives. This point is supported by the fact that the tribal people of the study area, which is dominated by the tribal population, don't have to pay income tax. However, people from outside the states have to pay taxes if they come from outside the area to do business. Also, the tribal groups are all homogeneous and closely knitted and, so united, they try to solve all the business problems coming their way (this point is mainly applicable for Aizawl).

Building Eco-System of Business

This point came up while interviewing the entrepreneurs of East Khasi Hills and Aizawl. A youth brigade that has studied outside the state and worked in different business organizations, or even practiced business outside, after garnering experience and knowledge in their respective fields, are returning to the state and investing for the growth of business in their homeland. This breed, is building up a favorable business ecosystem in this region.

Tourism Opportunities

We already discussed the divine beauty of Northeast India. The present study area includes many different places of tourist interest, such as Loktak (Manipur), Imphal (Manipur), Shillong (Meghalaya), Umiam (Meghalaya), and Aizawl (Mizoram). Tourists crowd these places throughout the year creating good employment opportunities for the local entrepreneurs.

Women's Empowerment

In Northeast India, most of the states are under the influence of the matrilineal society. The result is high participation of women in business and related activities in this region (already discussed in section "Entrepreneurship in Literature in Northeast India"). This specific characteristic of the NER is almost absent in other parts of tribal-dominated regions. This matrilineal culture has created an ecosystem in which the whole society, both men and women, participate in business.

Easy Information Flow

This feedback mainly came from the entrepreneurs of Aizawl and the East Khasi Hills district. The districts house the capitals of Mizoram and Meghalaya, respectively. The entrepreneurs of these districts, mainly the second-generation ones, are close to the government officials and government corridors that help them to get easy information regarding the pros and cons of running their respective businesses. Shillong, an old city that houses the district headquarters of East Khasi Hills, has grown its own heritage in community-based economy mainly since the time of British rule.

Supportive Government

The states of the NER are small in geographic size and have small populations compared to most states outside the region. Only the population of Assam is counted in crores while the rest of the states count their populations in lakhs. The small population makes it possible for local governments to be close to the people and support them. This is quite true for the entrepreneurs, too. As the entrepreneurial community is very small, the problem of developing effective schemes becomes easier for the respective governments. The entrepreneurs from Aizawl, East Khasi Hills and Ri-Bhoi said that their local governments have arranged training while the entrepreneurs from Aizawl, specifically, said that the government arranged different raw materials needed for their businesses during shortage periods. In many cases, the District Industry Center (DIC) works with the local entrepreneurs to implement all the government schemes for business development in the area. For example, in Mizoram, which comes under the ambit of the present study, the local government has imposed an Inner Line System to benefit the local entrepreneurial fraternity. Under this law, outsiders of the state can reside there, but only the permanent residents are eligible to do business. If the outsiders are doing business, they have to do so in the name of the local tribes.

Friendly Environment for Business

As already mentioned, the districts are quite small in geography and so apart from getting good support from the local government and the DIC, the entrepreneurs also get the advantage of small places. In small places, people are known to each other. Therefore, they always prefer a specific business for specific goods. The entrepreneurs try to help each other out during times of need. There is also a tendency to buy things from people of the native community. Also, due to income tax exemption for the people belonging to the local tribal community, the purchasing propensity of the people (mainly in Aizawl and East Khasi Hills) has increased. This affords entrepreneurs a good opportunity to expand their business ventures. Moreover, in the present study area, the strikes and blockades have almost disappeared generating a conducive environment for business growth. There are unions in Aizawl though, but whenever a strike-like situations arises, the government, the union and the religious group come together to settle the matter of dispute. The media nowadays plays an important role in business growth in this region. Often, they place the information that is important for the business entity.

Disadvantages and Short Description

The main points of disadvantages that came up during our interviews of 160 entrepreneurs from four districts in three states include transportation problems, growth in competition and unavailability of skilled workers, among others. The full list of disadvantages is given in Table 13.3.

Growth in Competition

In the last few years, business activities in the NER have increased. This is a positive sign for the economy of the region. However, it is resulting in steep competition in the local business community. Now, business owners have to face competition from businesses in different parts of India who have directly or indirectly invested their money in local business. Apart from this issue, foreign goods from China, Bangladesh and Myanmar are flooding the local markets also increasing competition.

Table 13.3 Disadvantages depicted by the entrepreneurs

Disadvantages	Main region (that supported the response)	Total percentage
Growth in competition	East Khasi Hills and Aizawl	76
Unpredictable weather	Aizawl, east Khasi Hills and Ri-Bhoi	83
Water scarcity	East Khasi Hills, Aizawl, Churachandpur and Ri-Bhoi	82
Presence of pressure groups	Ri-Bhoi and Churachandpur	53
Transportation problems	East Khasi Hills, Aizawl, Churachandpur and Ri-Bhoi	93
Space unavailability	East Khasi Hills and Aizawl	52
Unavailability of skilled workers	East Khasi Hills, Aizawl, Churachandpur and Ri-Bhoi	89
Rise in commodity prices	East Khasi Hills, Aizawl, Churachandpur and Ri-Bhoi	87
Marketing-related problems	East Khasi Hills, Churachandpur and Ri-Bhoi	64
People's mindset	Churachandpur and Ri-Bhoi	53
Finance-related problems	Churachandpur and Ri-Bhoi	56
Religious influence	East Khasi Hills, Aizawl, Churachandpur and Ri-Bhoi	92
Geographical constraints	Aizawl and Churachandpur	58

Source: Based on primary survey

Unpredictable Weather

The northeastern states come under heavy to excessive rainfall.[11] This causes damage to the roads, landslides, blocked roads, and damage to goods that are transported in and out of this region.

Water Scarcity

Even though the region experiences excessive rainfall, there is still a lack of infrastructure to store the water and as a result, there is a scarcity of water in the winter and summer seasons. This adversely affects enterprises based on manufacturing, livestock and perishable goods.

Presence of Pressure Groups

The target entrepreneurs, mainly in the districts of Churachandpur and Ri-Bhoi, discussed the problem of pressure groups, but only very hazily. According to them, there is a group (who may be ex-ultras or the members of some dormant ultra-outfits) who often asks for their share from the business. Often, these groups are backed by the NGOs and political leaders. There are also cases where the surrendered ultras, who have a lot of money, pump money into different businesses. They ultimately become threats to the businesses with small capital. Various cases came up, which indicates that government officials are not always "clean" in all cases. Allegedly, there are cases where officials pressure entrepreneurs for bribes.

Transportation Problems

The point of transportation problems received overwhelming support from the entrepreneurs of all four districts. According to them, the road infrastructure is quite inadequate. The roads are filthy and potted roads increase the risk of accidents. Further, the problem adds to increased travelling time and transportation costs. The increased cost of transportation in turn increases the cost of doing business. The position of the roads becomes worse at the time of monsoon when landslides often block the roads.

---

[11] www.impottantindia.com/8667/rainfall-distribution-of-india/

Space Unavailability

In this case, it came out that some positive development led to disadvantages in business in this region, especially for the capital towns of Shillong and Aizawl (the cities are considered within the present study). Over the last few years, the number of business establishments has increased and existing establishments have expanded; marketplaces expanded where the rural business community got the opportunity to sell their products. No doubt that these are all positive points with respect to development. However, the existing infrastructure is not ready or it was not made ready to take on the extra burden of expansion. The result is traffic jams are more commonplace, upcoming businesses are not getting adequate space for expansion, land prices are skyrocketing, and there is an increase in the tendency to cut hills and make space, which places further pressure on the environment.

Unavailability of Skilled Workers

The entrepreneurs also pointed out the unavailability of laborers and skilled workers. According to them, most skilled workers take jobs in different metros of India. In the NER, to deal with the shortage, the entrepreneurs have to pay high wages for unskilled or semi-skilled laborers.

Rise in Commodity Prices

The prices of commodities in the NER are quite high. This point is also reflected in the voices of the entrepreneurs. According to them, the rise in prices of commodities increases the production costs leading them to face tough competition in the market. There are times when paying wages to employees is difficult.

Marketing-Related Problems

Regarding marketing-related problems, the entrepreneurs brought up the problem of inadequate packaging facilities. According to them, due to the lack of adequate packaging, a good portion of their goods get damaged at the time of transportation, which increases manifold during monsoon season. Apart from this, there is also a population problem; the NER population is low compared to the rest of India. Lower population implies a smaller consumer market, so whenever anything is produced on a large scale, the local enterprise owners have to check about exporting the goods outside of the state. Also, a big chunk of the present population under study is coming under the grip of online shopping. As a result, local products are often neglected by the native people and traditional businesses are faltering. The fashion world is highly affected by this trend. People prefer the fashion trends of the United States, Korea and China. The multinationals of these countries are taking the concepts of their local fashions, developing them, and finally selling them to the native population. The prospect of selling local products online was addressed, however, the point did not garner much support because of the lower education level of the local entrepreneurs.

People's Mindset

In Churachandpur and Ri-Bhoi, people seem to have a problem accepting new goods and new techniques for business development. The logic given by the entrepreneurs was that placing new goods or adding some new features to existing goods is not acceptable to the people of the region. Thus, it is not always a good idea to introduce new goods; the process is not without problems. Another important aspect that came up was the entrepreneurs' tendency to gain profit in a short period. This inclination often forces them to compromise the quality of their goods and further damages their long-term reputations.

Finance-Related Problems

Another problem that came at the time of interviews is the weak linkage of the tribal entrepreneurs with the existing financial system. The local governments have introduced different schemes for the betterment of the tribal entrepreneurs. However, the schemes are unable to reach the target section and they are unable to access it at need. Getting bank loans and expanding business gets harder at times. So, planning and execution-related gaps came up during our interviews. The problem is more prominent in the Churachandpur district where, according to the entrepreneurs, NGOs are not that active in letting them know about schemes. In the words of the entrepreneurs of Aizawl, it is this inadequacy of knowledge from the side of government officials that is causing the problem.

Religious Influence

Religion has great influence on the present study region. Religion is the reason that businesses are closed on Sundays. Also due to the influence of religion, businesses generally close between 5:00 and 7:00 p.m. (mainly in Aizawl, Churachandpur and Ri-Bhoi). Late business hours are almost absent in the present study area.

Geographical Constraints

The entrepreneurs expressed problems due to being landlocked. Being landlocked is a highly relevant problem in Aizawl and Churachandpur. Aizawl's economic lifeline goes through Silchar of Assam, and Manipur's goes through Nagaland. If there is a road blockade due to strike or inclement weather, it has an adverse effect on the businesses of this region.

DISCUSSION AND CONCLUSION

The benefits and disadvantages of entrepreneurship in the NER are very similar to those of in the rest of the country. The points discussed by different researchers and scholars, to a great extent, matched the views of the entrepreneurs regarding the problems and benefits faced by the business fraternity in this part of India. However, the entrepreneurs did not focus on low work culture, low self-esteem, lower access to resources and oversized administrative machinery, which the scholars did address. The entrepreneurs also did not raise the points of the role of micro-finance, unexplored abundant natural resources and a big population having knowledge of English, which are all highly relevant factors for business growth.

The interviewed entrepreneurs mentioned several issues that are very important to the growth of business in the NER. Population increase providing market enlargement for entrepreneurs, close-knit community of the tribals, and support from religious and community leaders are some of the points in this respect. Some problems brought up by entrepreneurs were less focused on by scholars. These include competition growth in the region, unavailability of land for business expansion, activities of pressure groups, outflow of skilled laborers to metro cities, high production, threat from online shopping, threat to traditional businesses, people's mindset and religious influence.

Our analysis and the points made by the entrepreneurs regarding the benefits and problems of business growth in the NER present a pool of issues in both directions. The issues will be helpful in garnering good research for the betterment of the region. From the side of the union government, it could be said that the government is taking painstaking efforts for the development of the NER. Insight into the issues revealed in the research will provide the government with an edge in their constant effort for the development process.

REFERENCES

Aye, A. (2013). *Women entrepreneurship*. Tenth Biennial Conference on Entrepreneurship, 2, 944–949. Ahmedabad, Gujarat, India: Bookwell.

Barman, P., Goswami, S., & Sarmah, S. (2015). *Insights from Servuction Model based customer perspectives: A study in tourism enterprises in Kamrup (metropolitan) and Kamrup (rural) districts of Assam (India)*. Eleventh Biennial Conference on Entrepreneurship, 2, pp. 1295–1306. Ahmedabad, Gujarat, India: Bookwell.

Barua, I., & Devi, A. (2004). Women's market of Manipur: An anthropo-historical perspective. *Journal of Human Ecology, 15*(2), 129–133.

Baruah, S. (2013). *Tea tourism: An unexplored business opportunity in Assam* (pp. 1271–1278). Tenth Biennial conference on entrepreneurship.2. Ahmedabad, Gujarat, India: Bookwell.

Bhattacharjee, B. J., & Das, G. D. (2013). *Rural tourism entrepreneurs: Opportunities and challenges in North East Indian perspective*. Tenth Biennial Conference on Entrepreneurship, 2, pp. 1262–1270. Ahmedabad, Gujarat, India: Bookwell.

Chakravarty, E. (2013). The rural women entrepreneurial edge. *IOSR Journal of Humanities and Social Science, 10*(1), 33–36.

Chanu, Y. L., & Chanu, A. I. (2014). Women entrepreneurs of Manipur after MSME act, 2006: An analysis. *Journal of Entrepreneurship & Management, 3*(2), 37–43.

Chanu, A. I., & Chanu, L. (2015). *Branding and labelling of the products of women entrepreneurs of Manipur* (pp. 491–499). Eleventh Biennial conference on entrepreneurship.1, Ahmedabad, Gujarat, India: Bookwell.

Dadina, N., & Dey, N. B. (2015). *Agripreneurial barriers to fish farming in Manipur: An empirical study* (pp. 1200–1208). Eleventh Biennial conference on entrepreneurship.2. Ahmedabad, Gujarat, India: Bookwell.

Das, S. K. (2010). *India-ASEAN free trade agreement and development of North-East: Prospects and challenges*. CDS-IIFT-RIS-UNCTAD National seminar on India-ASEAN free trade agreement and way forward. Trivandrum: Center for Development Studies.

Das, I., & Ali, A. (2003). Tribal situation in North East India. *Studies of Tribes and Tribals, 1*, 141–148.

Das, M., & Goswami, N. (2017). *Entrepreneurial networks and small firm performance: A study of small enterprises in Kamrup, a district of Assam* (pp. 534–543). Twelfth Biennial conference on entrepreneurship.1. Ahmedabad, Gujarat, India: Bookwell.

Datt, G., & Ravallion, M. (1996). How important to India's poor is the sectoral composition of economic growth? *The World Bank Economic Review, 10*(1), 1–25.

Deb, S. (2013). *Role of village industries in socio-economic development of tribal people in Arunachal Pradesh with special reference to West Siang district: An empirical study* (pp. 606–619). Tenth Biennial conference on entrepreneurship.1. Ahmedabad, Gujarat, India: Bookwell.

Devi, M. K. (2014). Status of women entrepreneurship and micro finance: The Manipur experience. *Voice of Research, 3*(3), 24–27.

Devi, C. N. (2015). Women entrepreneurs in Manipur. *International Journal of Humanities and Social Science Studies, 2*(2), 150–156.

Devi, P. (2016). State of women entrepreneurship in Manipur: Study on molasses production. *International Journal of Humanities and Social Science Invention, 5*(9), 46–52.

Dey, B., & Sarma, M. K. (2010). Information source usage among motive-based segments of travelers to newly emerging tourist destinations. *Tourism Management, 31*(3), 341–344.

Goswami, K., Handique, K., & Hazarika, B. (2017). *Entrepreneurial settings for the development of handloom micro-entrepreneurs in North-East India.* Twelfth Biennial Conference on Entrepreneurship, 1, pp. 544–553. Ahmedabad, Gujarat, India: Bookwell.

Guha, P., & Adak, K. (2014). Gender influence on entrepreneurship: A case study of Aizawl district of Mizoram. *Journal of Entrepreneurship and Management, 3*(2), 9–13.

Hazarika, C., & Subramanian, S. R. (1999). Estimation of technical efficiency in the stochastic frontier production function model – An application to the tea industry in Assam. *Indian Journal of Agricultural Economics, 54*(2), 201–211.

Kabra, K. (2008). *Economic growth of Mizoram role of business and industry.* New Delhi: Concept Publishing Company.

Kalita, P. C., & Barman, P. (2013). *Tourism entrepreneurship in Assam: A study on the employment opportunities in tourism in Assam* (pp. 1288–1296). Tenth Biennial conference on entrepreneurship.2, Ahmedabad, Gujarat, India: Bookwell.

Kalita, P. C., & Bora, B. (2015). *Entrepreneurship education: A way to employment generation among the college students of Assam.* Eleventh Biennial Conference on Entrepreneurship, 1, pp. 250–259. Ahmedabad, Gujarat, India: Bookwell.

Khongsdier, R. (2005). BMI and morbidity in relation to body composition: A cross-sectional study of a rural community in North-East India. *British Journal of Nutrition, 93,* 101–107.

Kumar, M., Bohra, N. S., & Johari, A. (2010). Micro-finance as an antipoverty vaccine for rural India. *The International Review of Business and Finance, 2*(1), 29–35.

Kurbah, S. (2013). Role of women entrepreneurs in the economic development of Meghalaya: A north eastern state, India. *International Journal of Engineering, Business and Enterprise Applications, 13,* 175–181.

Lalhunthara. (2015). Entrepreneurship and gender: A case study of micro enterprises in Aizawl district, Mizoram. *The International Journal of Business and Management, 3*(8), 46–51.

Laskar, I. (2010). *Industrialization in Mizoram – Problems and prospects.* Kolkata: New Central Book Agency Pvt Ltd.

Lucas, R. E. (1988). On the mechanics of economic development. *Journal of Monetary Economics, 22*(1), 3–42.

Mazumdar, K. (1996). An analysis of causal flow between social development and economic growth: Social development index. *American Journal of Economics and Sociology, 55*(3). https://doi.org/10.1111/j.1536-7150.1996.tb02323.x

Mitra, A. (2008). The status of women among the scheduled tribes in India. *Journal of Socio-Economics, 37*(3), 1202–1217.

Mohan, R. (2003, December). Economic development of North East region: Some reflections. *Reserve Bank of India Bulletin.*

Paul, A. (2015). Tribal entrepreneurship through rural tourism and development: A case study of Hee Gaon, Sikkim. Eleventh Biennial Conference on Entrepreneurship, 2, pp. 937–947. Ahmedabad, Gujarat, India: Bookwell.

Planning Commission Data Table. (2014). Retrieved from http://planningcommission.nic.in/hindi/data/datatable/index.php?data=b_misdch.htm

Prabha. (2006). Problems of women entrepreneurs: A study of Imphal and Kamrup districts. In G. P. Prasain (Ed.), *Entrepreneurship and small scale industries* (pp. 280–287). New Delhi: Akansha Publishing House.

Preston, S. H. (1979). Urban growth in developing countries: A demographic reappraisal. *Population and Development Review, 5*(2), 195–216.

Ram, D., Singh, M. K., Chaudhary, K. P., & Jayarani, L. (2013). Entrepreneurship behaviour of women entrepreneurs in Imphal of Manipur. *Indian Research Journal of Extension Education, 13*(2), 31–35.

Saikia, B. K. (2015). *Development of indigenous entrepreneurship in Assam: Prospects and problems* (pp. 899–906). Eleventh Biennial conference on entrepreneurship.2, Ahmedabad, Gujarat, India: Bookwell.

Sharma, G. (2015). *Rural entrepreneurship: A pragmatic approach for socio-economic upliftment of women in Assam* (pp. 916–924). Eleventh Biennial conference on entrepreneurship.2, Ahmedabad, Gujarat, India: Bookwell.

Sharma, N. (2017). *Role of micro finance institutions in changing socio-economic status of women entrepreneurs: Evidence from Sonitpur district in Assam* (pp. 1283–1291). Twelfth Biennial conference on entrepreneurship.1, Ahmedabad, Gujarat, India: Bookwell.

Sharma, N., & Bora, B. (2015). *Role of microfinance in women entrepreneurship* (pp. 688–693). Eleventh Biennial conference on entrepreneurship.1, Ahmedabad, Gandhinagar, Gujarat: Bookwell.

Sievers, M., & Vandenberg, P. (2007). Synergies through linkages: Who benefits from linking micro-finance and business development services? *World Development, 35*, 1341–1358.

Singh, N. T. (2009). Micro finance practices in India: An overview. *International Review of Business Research Papers, 5*(5), 131–146.

Singh, E. N. (2016). *Financial management in women enterprises.* New Delhi: A Mittal Publication.

Singh, N. T., & Singh, P. C. (2012). Practices of marketing strategies in promotion of women entrepreneurs in Manipur. *Journal of Commerce and Trade, 2*, 47–55.

Singh, S. B., & Punitha, P. (2012). Entrepreneurship development through Anthurium flower – A case study of Mizoram, North-East India. *Indian Research Journal of Extension Education, 12*(3), 74–78.

Sorokhaibam, R. (2006). An overview of women entrepreneurs in Manipur. In G. P. Prasain (Ed.), *Entrepreneurship and small scale industries* (p. 248). New Delhi: Akansha Publishing House.

Thakur, S. S. (2017). *Role of youth in revolutionising entrepreneurship in the tribal state of Mizoram.* Twelfth Biennial Conference on Entrepreneurship, 2, pp. 1138–1144. Ahmedabad, Gujarat, India: Bookwell.

Tribal Health Bulletin. (2014). Retrieved from http://www.nirth.res.in/thrf/thb_special_issue2014.pdf

Upadhyay, A. P., & Barman, U. (2013). Identification of problems and formulation of extension strategies for upliftment of women agripreneurship in sericulture: An exploratory study in Garo hills of Meghalaya. *Journal of Academia and Industrial Research, 2*(6), 369–373.

PART II

Business Governance and Society: Mexico

CHAPTER 14

Relationship between Employee Mobility and Organizational Creativity to Improve Organizational Performance: A Strategic Analysis

Ananya Rajagopal

Introduction

Employees contribute significantly to the growth of an organization and its performance. Acquisition of high talents and retaining them is a major challenge for most organizations to grow competitive in the industry (Younge et al. 2015). Employees with high knowledge improve workplace environment and motivate work force with competitive knowledge and higher organizational efficiency (Younge et al. 2015). Organizations develop employee-oriented human resource strategies to discourage employee attrition, through mobility of employees within the organizational system or industry. Organizations encourage employees to enhance their knowledge and creativity to improve emotional stability within organizations (Hermann and Nadkarni 2014).

A. Rajagopal (✉)
EGADE Business School, Tecnologico de Monterrey,
Santa Fe, Mexico City, Mexico

© The Author(s) 2019
Rajagopal, R. Behl (eds.), *Business Governance and Society*,
https://doi.org/10.1007/978-3-319-94613-9_14

Inter-firm mobility occurs when an employee is moved to another organization, which may be the subsidiary of the parent organization, to acquire new dimensions of knowledge. Employee mobility encourages employees' intention to explore knowledge from other organizations, while the parent organizations aim at exploiting the enhanced knowledge of the employees who return to the parent organizations after spending time in other organizations. Cyert and March (1992) have argued that employees explore knowledge, while organizations exploit employees' talent. According to Cyert and March (1992), a firm encourages coalition of participants to exploit their knowledge and improve organizational performance.

Organizations assign different tasks to employees during intra-firm (within organization) mobility. To acquire knowledge of different areas within the organization, employees are encouraged to accept cross-functional assignments (Webster and Beehr 2013). Shipilov et al. (2017) argue that inter-firm mobility does not mean losing core employees of the organization to competitors. Mobility allows an organization to engage in external boundary-spanning activities. It may benefit the organization through access to external knowledge, but may also increase the risks of sharing knowledge and skills with competitors. Employee mobility is related to the benefits or risks associated with inter- and intra-organizational environments.

Destination mobility has been defined as employee willingness to accept mobility opportunities involving a geographical relocation to a workplace with specified characteristics (Noe and Barber 1993). Employee mobility to international destinations within the organizational system is encouraged under expatriate policy, which helps the employees gain more benefits on career prospects, share knowledge in an external business environment, and improve organizational performance (van der Heijden et al. 2009; Kansala et al. 2015). Employee relocation might happen due to two reasons—need for learning, and personal or organizational contingency (Shipilov et al. 2017). Employee relocation has been a conventional management practice to drive new experiences and share improved knowledge in organizations. This has been considered an effective way of managing career development, job mobility and relocation among industrial and commercial organizations since the 1990s (Forster 1990; Dai et al. 2015).

As explained by Xu and Payne (2016), inter-firm and intra-firm mobility are related. Such relationships are associated with causes and effects in reference to employee mobility within organizations. Often employees relocate to competing organizations for personal benefits. The employee behavior guides mobility factors over the stability and organizational attachment (Xu and Payne 2016). The causes and effects of employee mobility vary according to the objectives of the organization, and the knowledge acquired by the employee during his/her mobility within or outside the organization. Employees are mainly concerned about personal benefits in moving to other destinations (inter-firm and intra-firm mobility), whereas the organizations intend to achieve sustainable knowledge transfer through the employees for enhancing organizational performance (Ramirez et al. 2013). The organizational goals and objectives, and the causes and effects of employee mobility, should be understood when evaluating employees workplace knowledge (Kim and Choi 2010).

Firms may suffer from losing key employees to stronger or same-status organizations. Employee mobility is closely associated to organizational creativity (Lee and Corbett 2006; Jauhari and Singh 2013; Kumar et al. 2014). Companies hedge employee relationships by taking the risk of acquiring new talents, and work with heterogeneity in the workplace, to induce creation of competitive knowledge and distribution of employee values within organizations (Lieberman et al. 2017). Hedging employee relationships refers to the concept of recruiting potential employees with higher performance, against the existing employees who exhibit complex behavior and low performance. In this process, companies tend to overlook the low performance and complex behavior of the existing employees, as the new employees are expected to exhibit higher performance (Goulart et al. 2015).

Performance-based rewards harness sustainable innovations, creativity, and employee engagement in organizations, which enhances organizational performance (Baumann and Stieglitz 2014). The employee rewards linked to individual performance are beneficial for improving their commitment and job satisfaction. Such organizational policy has positive effect on an employee's perseverance to deliver high-quality results (Carbonell and Rodriguez-Escudero 2016). The performance-based reward system in organizations builds motivation, commitment and sustainable performance among employees, which positively contributes to the managerial relationships and organizational performance (Monteiro de Castro et al. 2016).

This study analyzes the attributes of relationships between employee mobility and creativity through the process of knowledge dissemination within organizations. Dissemination of creative ideas combined with applied knowledge in an organization motivates creativity among the employees. In addition, dissemination of creative knowledge through employee networks improves organizational performance. Dissemination of knowledge and creativity has significant positive influence on organizational performance (Wu et al. 2012). This conceptual study embeds the research question of how employee knowledge, creativity of employees, employee rewards, employee mobility and employee engagement contribute to organizational performance. This study critically examines the employee mobility across international companies in emerging markets in reference to the previous studies.

Literature Review

Inter- and intra-organization mobility (Lipparini et al. 2014; Lieberman et al. 2017; Kim and Steensma 2017) argues that the employee-organization performance can be improved by developing strategic convergence between employee behavior and organizational goals (Shinkle 2011). Convergence of external knowledge with inter-personal networks create knowledge hubs, which often generate new ideas in organizations contributing to creativity (Schilling and Fang 2014).

Hybrid knowledge can be stated as the blend of internal and external (exogenous) knowledge in an organization. The role of openness of the employees and sharing of hybrid knowledge enhances absorptive capacity among employees, which increases organizational creativity (de Castro 2015). The knowledge absorptive capacity in organizations plays a key and dynamic role in creating shared values (Campos-Climent and Sanchis-Palacio 2017). A study done by Inauen and Schenker-Wicki (2011) reveals that outside-in strategy induces openness towards knowledge building, creativity and innovative performance among employees. The openness and sharing of knowledge has a significant positive impact on organizational innovation activities as well (Inauen and Schenker-Wicki 2011). In an organization, exogenous knowledge is acquired from various formal sources and through employee mobility, enhancing creativity (Lwoga 2011). Developing hybrid knowledge repositories (also referred as knowledge bank, which documents the internal and external knowledge sources) not only enables external learning but also helps to overcome knowledge localization (Wagner et al. 2014).

Localization of employee's knowledge limits creativity, as they do not get the opportunity to learn about organizational experience beyond their own organization. There is a strong relationship between knowledge management practices and creativity in an organization, which helps in problem solving and enhancing organizational performance (Giampaoli et al. 2017). Knowledge and creativity are symbiotic, they develop awareness and motivation to increase organizational performance (Krylova et al. 2016). Knowledge creation is an intellectual evolution process for organizational creativity (Saulais and Ermine 2012). High level of creativity in an organization leads to enhanced organizational performance, as evidenced in Toyota's production system as an alignment of Kaizen (Watanabe 2011). Therefore, the research proposition can be formed as follows:

P_1: Acquiring knowledge from external sources leads to organizational creativity.

Organizational retreat is an approach in which organizations put employees in an environment different from their work place, to make them express liberally about their work culture. Companies plan and implement organizational retreat for employees, who have acquired competitors' knowledge, to induce new ideas to refine organizational tasks (Shipilov et al. 2017). A study by Shipilov et al. (2017) examines how social networks resulting from the external boundary-spanning ties of employees affect organizational creativity, and reveals that companies are most likely to benefit from diverse knowledge received from competing organizations. The study explains that employee mobility and knowledge-transfer process are interrelated. Thus, promoting employee mobility would help in enhancing the creative performance of an organization (Shipilov et al. 2017).

Organizational innovation, including technological innovation and business innovation, has direct as well as indirect effects on enhancing overall organizational performance (Lerro 2012; Dorson 2017). Knowledge building and creativity help employees to improve individual and collective performances, to contribute to the overall performance of an organization (Azar and Ciabuschi 2017). The findings of the study by Azar and Ciabuschi (2017) indicate that organizational innovation enhances performance both directly and indirectly by sustaining technological innovation.

The outside-in approach largely supports organizational innovation through sharing knowledge and stimulating creativity (Fu et al. 2015). The outside-in approach in companies is focused on creating and nurturing new knowledge, ideas and creativity. The outside-in approach of knowledge dissemination involves information and knowledge management to provide the employees timely and contextual knowledge, which enhances creativity and organizational performance. This process of knowledge management is determined as socialization of knowledge, which can be viewed in an organization through employee mobility (Apostolou et al. 2007). Knowledge dissemination through social networks has increased the knowledge socialization by motivating employees in promoting organizational creativity (Swift and Virick 2013). In view of the preceding discussion, the research proposition can be framed as follows:

P_2: The outside-in approach encourages organizational creativity.

Baumann and Stieglitz (2014) have observed that ideas emerging from employees act as a major source of value creation in firms. The empirical study revealed that firms could encourage employee creativity, and improve performance, by offering low-powered rewards (powered rewards indicate delegating power to employees with no economic benefits), and develop strategies for implementation of employee ideas to improve organizational performance (Baumann and Stieglitz 2014). The study argues that low-powered incentives provide a sufficient stream of good ideas, while the high-powered incentives (the powered incentives to employees refers to delegating power with economic benefits), in contrast, do not systematically translate into exceptional ideas (Baumann and Stieglitz 2014).

Economic incentives as rewards to the employees exhibit a direct positive relationship with work activity, improve satisfaction of the employees and engage them in creative contribution in the organizations (Tam 2015). Extrinsic rewards such as pay and promotions motivate employees, whereas the intrinsic rewards, such as satisfactory job description prompting employees to do more meaningful work, motivate organizational creativity (Stumpf et al. 2013). The findings of the study by Stumpf et al. (2013) reveal that intrinsic rewards (meaningfulness and choice) in an organization are positively related with employee satisfaction and creativity, which enhance organizational performance. Accordingly, the research proposition can be constructed as follows:

P_3: Rewarding employees in an organization increases organizational creativity.

The employee attributes in an organization include autonomy, creativity, job satisfaction, involvement in organizational leadership, and engagement in organizational performance (Zhao et al. 2016). Employee engagement is viewed as a long-term commitment between employees and organizations, which is critical to enhance creativity (Taneja et al. 2015). The study conducted by Taneja et al. (2015) reveals that employee engagement enhances creativity, which encourages organizations to retain quality employees in an increasingly competitive market place. Employee engagement builds emotional connectedness, and develops bonding across organizational culture to enhance organizational creativity (Kumar and Raghavendran 2015). The concept of employee engagement is important in companies to encourage knowledge sharing, motivate organizational creativity and work with new initiatives (Keating and Heslin 2015).

Employee engagement may be defined as "a positive, fulfilling, work-related state of mind that is characterized by vigor, dedication and absorption," as explained by Schaufeli and Bakker (2004). Employee engagement in a firm explains the knowledge-creation activities (Paruchuri and Awate 2017). An empirical study conducted by Paruchuri and Awate (2017) reveals that the firms consider building performance on their own knowledge, and draw conclusions for research on organizational knowledge and knowledge networks. This study reveals that collaboration among knowledge workers can improve the relationship between employee engagement and creativity in an organization (Paruchuri and Awate 2017). Hence, in view of the preceding discussion, the research proposition can be developed as follows:

P_4: Employee engagement strengthens organizational creativity.

Customer-centric companies engage customers in delivering knowledge and creativity in order to enhance the customer value (Day and Moorman 2011). As analyzed by Suarez-Barraza and Smith (2014), the Japanese automobile companies, such as Toyota and Suzuki, empower employees to express their ideas through the Kaizen management philosophy for improving the organizational performance. This is central to the generation of value-creating ideas involving employee engagement for creative output. The Kaizen approach in organizations is considered as an innovation boosting and knowledge enhancement tool. An empirical study reveals that allowing employees to express and implement their ideas within the organization's work culture enhances creativity and process innovation (Watanabe 2011; Suarez-Barraza and Smith 2014).

There is a direct relationship between organizational creativity and organizational performance, as organizations build coordination among superiors and subordinates to share knowledge and identify creative roles (Koseoglu et al. 2017). The employee creativity has been defined as developing products and processes that are both innovative and important determinants for organizations to innovate, survive and thrive in a competitive global marketplace (Koseoglu et al. 2017; Zhou and Shalley 2010). There is a significant positive impact of organizational creativity on organizational performance. Both dimensions are symbiotic, and are derived from the knowledge-management process in an organization (Shahzad et al. 2016). Hence, the research proposition can be structured as follows:

P_5: Organizational creativity enhances organizational performance.

In view of the preceding literature review and framework of hypotheses, I developed the research model as exhibited in Fig. 14.1. The model indicates the core dimensions and associated variables derived from the hypotheses and its supporting literature review.

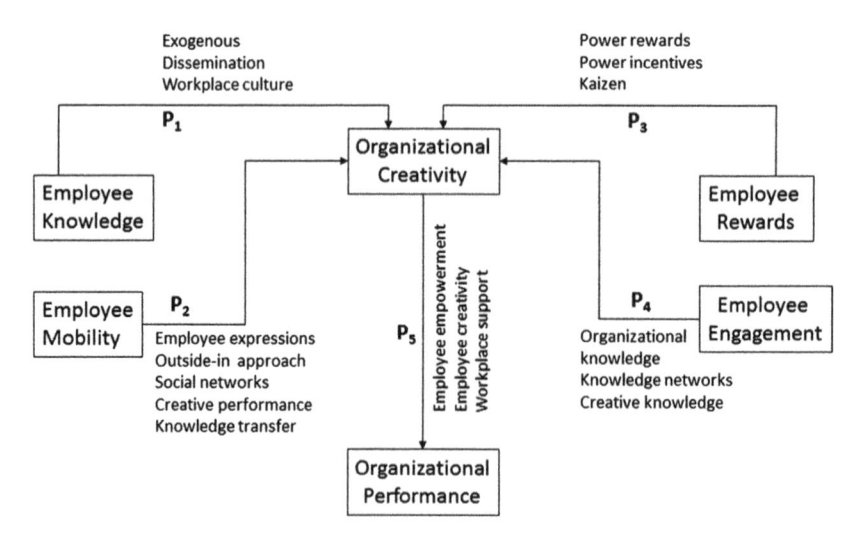

Fig. 14.1 Research model. Source: Author

General Discussion

It has been observed that multinational companies encourage employee mobility, cross-cultural workplace environment and creativity to increase organizational performance (Chiu et al. 2015; Ghosh et al. 2016; George and Zakkaryia 2015). Employee mobility and organizational creativity are closely related and deliver an impact on organizational performance. Leadership in an organization plays a significant role in motivating employee mobility to drive organizational creativity. Thus, transformation in the leadership in emerging organizations appears to be necessary in view of the changing organizational culture today.

Transformational leaders promote employee creativity, engaging immediate supervisors of employees and team leaders in this process. Most companies search for high-experience and high-caliber candidates, who have high mobility and potential of becoming a transformational leader. This would improve learning orientation of employees and yield positive results in the form of employee creativity, which would help organizations to generate sustainable competitive advantages for their organizations (Jyoti and Dev 2015). Large companies encourage employee creativity through mobility within the workplace. The high-performance work system influences employee creativity and critically analyzes the contingent factors in the relationship between perceived organizational support and employee creativity. In addition, an appropriate work-culture environment in an organization positively moderates the relationship between perceived organizational support and employee creativity (Tang et al. 2017).

Employee creativity and the extent to which psychological empowerment are interrelated in management context that contributes significantly towards employee creativity. The cognitive empowerment and rewards focus of employees significantly affect the ambidextrous work culture and employee creativity. Companies that adapt to open workplace culture and leadership styles tend to have employees with greater cognitive empowerment with a stronger promotion or rewards focus (Zacher and Rosing 2015; Tung 2016). However, workplace incivility, such as coworker and customer incivility, affects employees' creativity, by the way emotional exhaustion at work decreases their intrinsic motivation, and, in turn, damages service employees' creativity. Therefore, the workplace culture, co-worker behavior and leadership styles substantially affect the employee creativity as they often fail to transfer their knowledge for improving the organizational performance (Hur et al. 2016).

Future Research

This study addresses an interesting topic of relationship between employee mobility and creativity, which is an upcoming trend emerging out of globalization and followed by multi-national companies to improve organizational performance. This study opens opportunities for future research on various combinations of the dimensions considered in this study for developing focused studies with varied human resource perspectives within an organization. These dimensions may also be researched in future in the context of the upcoming small- and medium-sector organizations.

References

Apostolou, D., Avecker, A., & Mentzas, G. (2007). Harmonising codification and socialization in knowledge management. *Knowledge Management Research and Practice, 5*(4), 271–285.

Azar, G., & Ciabuschi, F. (2017). Organizational innovation, technological innovation, and export performance: The effects of innovation radicalness and extensiveness. *International Business Review, 26*(2), 324–336.

Baumann, O., & Stieglitz, N. (2014). Rewarding value-creating ideas in organizations: The power of low-powered incentives. *Strategic Management Journal, 35*(3), 358–375.

Campos-Climent, V., & Sanchis-Palacio, J. R. (2017). The influence of knowledge absorptive capacity on shared value creation in social enterprises. *Journal of Knowledge Management, 21*(5), 1163–1182.

Carbonell, P., & Rodriguez-Escudero, A. I. (2016). The individual and joint effects of process control and process based rewards on new product performance and job satisfaction. *Business Research Quality, 19*(1), 26–39.

Chiu, S. F., Lin, S. T., & Han, T. S. (2015). Employment status and employee service oriented organizational citizenship behavior; the mediating roles of internal mobility opportunity and job security. *Career Development International, 20*(2), 133–146.

Cyert, R., & March, J. (1992). *A behavioral theory of the firm* (2nd ed.). Cambridge, MA: Blackwell Business.

Dai, M., Keppo, J., & Maull, T. (2015). Hiring, firing and relocation under employment protection. *Journal of Economic Dynamics and Control, 56*(1), 55–81.

Day, G. S., & Moorman, C. (2011). An outside – in perspective to strategy. *Marketing Management,* Fall (Newsletter), pp. 22–29.

de Castro, G. M. (2015). Knowledge management and innovation in knowledge based and high-tech industrial markets: The role of openness and absorptive capacity. *Industrial Marketing Management, 47*(1), 143–146.

Dorson, T. A. (2017). Moderation-mediation effect of market demand and organizational culture on innovation and performance relationship. *Marketing Intelligence and Planning, 35*(2), 222–242.

Forster, N. S. (1990). Employee job mobility and relocation. *Personnel Review, 19*(6), 18–24.

Fu, N., Flood, P. C., Bosal, J., Morris, T., & O'Regan, P. (2015). How do high performance work systems influence organizational innovation in professional service firms? *Employee Relations, 37*(2), 209–231.

George, E., & Zakkaryia, K. A. (2015). Job related stress and job satisfaction: A comparative study among bank employees. *Journal of Management Development, 34*(3), 316–329.

Ghosh, P., Rai, A., Chauhan, R., Baranwal, G., & Srivastava, D. (2016). Rewards and recognition to engage private bank employees: Exploring the obligations dimension. *Management Research Review, 39*(12), 1738–1751.

Giampaoli, D., Ciambotti, M., & Bontis, N. (2017). Knowledge management, problem solving and performance in top Italian firms. *Journal of Knowledge Management, 21*(2), 355–375.

Goulart, M., da Costa, N. C. A., Andrade, E. B., & Santos, A. A. P. (2015). Hedging against embarrassment. *Journal of Economic Behavior and Organization, 116*(4), 310–318.

Hermann, P., & Nadkarni, S. (2014). Managing strategic change: The duality of CEO personality. *Strategic Management Journal, 36*(9), 1318–1342.

Hur, W. M., Moon, T., & Jun, J. K. (2016). The effect of workplace incivility on service employee creativity: The mediating role of emotional exhaustion and intrinsic motivation. *Journal of Services Marketing, 30*(3), 302–315.

Inauen, M., & Schenker-Wicki, A. (2011). The impact of outside-in open innovation on innovation performance. *European Journal of Innovation Management, 14*(4), 496–520.

Jauhari, H., & Singh, S. (2013). Perceived diversity climate and employee's organizational loyalty. *Equity, Diversity, and Inclusion: An International Journal, 32*(3), 262–276.

Jyoti, J., & Dev, M. (2015). The impact of transformational leadership on employee creativity: The role of learning orientation. *Journal of Asia Business Studies, 9*(1), 78–98.

Kansala, M., Makel, L., & Suutari, V. (2015). Career coordination strategies among dual career expatriate couples. *International Journal of Human Resource Management, 26*(17), 2187–2210.

Keating, L. A., & Heslin, P. A. (2015). The potential role of mindsets in unleasing employee engagement. *Human Resource Management Review, 25*(4), 329–341.

Kim, M. S., & Choi, J. N. (2010). Layoff victim's employment relationship with a new employer in korea: effect of unmet tenure expectations on trust and psychological contract. *International Journal of Human Resource Management, 21*(5), 781–798.

Kim, J. Y., & Steensma, H. K. (2017). Emloyee mobility, spin-outs, and knowledge spill-in: How incumbent firms can learn from new ventures. *Strategic Management Journal, 38*(8), 1626–1645.

Koseoglu, G., Liu, Y., & Shalley, C. E. (2017). Working with creative leaders: Exploring the relationship between supervisors and subordinates' creativity. *Leadership Quarterly, 28*(6), 798–811.

Krylova, K. O., Vera, D., & Crossan, M. (2016). Knowledge transfer in knowledge intensive organization: The crucial role of improvisation in transferring and protecting knowledge. *Journal of Knowledge Management, 20*(5), 1045–1064.

Kumar, H., & Raghavendran, S. (2015). Gamification, the finer art: Fostering creativity and employee engagement. *Journal of Business Strategy, 36*(6), 3–12.

Kumar, P., Dass, M., & Topaloglu, O. (2014). Understanding the drivers of job satisfaction of frontline service employees: Learning from the "Lost Employees". *Journal of Service Research, 17*(4), 367–380.

Lee, J., & Corbett, J. M. (2006). The impact of downsizing on employee's effective commitment. *Journal of Managerial Psychology, 21*(3), 176–199.

Lerro, A. (2012). Knowledge based perspective of innovation and performance improvement in healthcare. *Measuring Business Excellence, 16*(4), 3–13.

Lieberman, M. B., Castro, R. G., & Balasubramanian, N. (2017). Measuring value creation and appropriation in firms: The VCA model. *Strategic Management Journal, 38*(6), 1193–1211.

Lipparini, A., Lorenzoni, G., & Ferriani, S. (2014). From core to periphery and back: Study in the deliberate shaping of knowledge flows in inter-firm dyads and network. *Strategic Management Journal, 35*(4), 578–595.

Lwoga, E. T. (2011). Knowledge management approaches in managing agricultural indigenous and exogenous knowledge in Tanzania. *Journal of Documentation, 67*(3), 407–430.

Monteiro de Castro, M. L., Neto, M. T. R., Ferreira, C. A. A., & da Silva Gomes, J. F. (2016). Values, motivation, commitment, performance and rewards: Analysis model. *Business Process Management, 22*(6), 1139–1169.

Noe, R. A., & Barber, A. E. (1993). Willingness to accept mobility opportunities: Destination makes a difference. *Journal of Organizational Behavior, 14*(2), 159–175.

Paruchuri, S., & Awate, S. (2017). Organizational knowledge networks and local search: The role of intra-organizational inventor networks. *Strategic Management Journal, 38*(3), 657–675.

Ramirez, M., Li, X., & Chen, W. (2013). Comparing the impact of inter-and intra-regional labor mobility on problem solving in a Chinese Science Park. *Regional Studies: The Journal of Regional Studies Association, 47*(10), 1734–1751.

Saulais, P., & Ermine, J. L. (2012). Creativity and knowledge management. *VINE Journal of Information and Knowledge Management Systems, 42*(3–4), 416–438.

Schaufeli, W. B., & Bakker, A. B. (2004). Job demands, job resources and their relationship with burnout and engagement: A multi sample study. *Journal of Organizational Behavior, 25*(3), 293–315.

Schilling, M. A., & Fang, C. (2014). When hubs forget, lie and play favorite: Interpersonal network structure, information distortion and organizational learning. *Strategic Management Journal, 35*(7), 974–994.

Shahzad, K., Bajwa, S. U., Siddiqi, A. F. I., Ahmid, F., & Sultani, A. R. (2016). Integrating knowledge management strategies and processes to enhance organizational creativity and performance: An empirical investigation. *Journal of Modelling in Management, 11*(1), 154–179.

Shinkle, G. A. (2011). Organizational aspitarions, reference points and goals: Building on the past and aiming for the future. *Journal of Management, 38*(1), 415–455.

Shipilov, A., Godart, F. C., & Clement, J. (2017). Which boundaries? How mobility networks across countries and status groups affect the creative performance of organizations. *Strategic Management Journal, 38*(6), 1232–1252.

Stumpf, S. A., Walter, G. T., Favorito, N., & Smith, R. R. (2013). Employees and change initiatives: Intrinsic rewards and feeling valued. *Journal of Business Strategy, 34*(2), 21–29.

Suarez-Barraza, M. F., & Smith, T. (2014). The Kaizen approach with process innovation: Findings from a multiple case study in Ibero-American countries. *Total Quality Management and Business Excellence, 25*(9–10), 1002–1025.

Swift, M. L., & Virick, M. (2013). Perceived support, knowledge tacitness, and provider knowledge sharing. *Group and Organizational Management, 38*(6), 717–742.

Tam, L. (2015). The relationship between human capital, value creation and employee reward. *Journal of Intellectual Capital, 16*(2), 390–418.

Taneja, S., Sewell, S. S., & Odom, R. Y. (2015). A culture of employee engagement: A strategic perspective for global managers. *Journal of Business Strategy, 36*(3), 46–56.

Tang, G., Yu, B., Cooke, F. L., & Chen, Y. (2017). High-performance work system and employee creativity: The roles of perceived organisational support and devolved management. *Personnel Review, 46*(7), 1318–1334.

Tung, F. C. (2016). Does transformational, ambidextrous, transactional leadership promote employee creativity? Mediating effects of empowerment and promotion focus. *International Journal of Manpower, 37*(8), 1250–1263.

Van der Heijden, J., van Engen, M., & Paauwe, J. (2009). Expatriate career support: Predicting expatriate turnover and performance. *International Journal of Human Resource Management, 20*(4), 831–845.

Wagner, S., Hoisl, K., & Thoma, G. (2014). Overcoming localization of knowledge: The role of professional service firms. *Strategic Management Journal*, 35(11), 1671–1688.

Watanabe, R. M. (2011). Getting ready for Kaizen: Organizational and knowledge management enablers. *VINE Journal of Information and Knowledge Management Systems*, 41(4), 428–448.

Webster, J. R., & Beehr, T. A. (2013). Antecedents and outcomes of employee perceptions of the intra-organizational mobility channels. *Journal of Organizational Behavior*, 34(7), 919–941.

Wu, C. S., Lee, C. J., & Tsai, L. F. (2012). Influence of creativity and knowledge sharing on performance. *Journal of Technology Management in China*, 7(1), 64–77.

Xu, X., & Payne, S. C. (2016). Predicting retention duration from organizational commitment profile transitions. *Journal of Management*, 54(1), 159–181.

Younge, K. A., Tong, T. W., & Fleming, L. (2015). How anticipated employee mobility affects acquisition likelihood: Evidence from a natural experiment. *Strategic Management Journal*, 36(5), 686–708.

Zacher, H., & Rosing, K. (2015). Ambidextrous leadership and team innovation. *Leadership & Organization Development Journal*, 36(1), 54–68.

Zhao, X., Ghiselli, R., Law, R., & Ma, J. (2016). Motivating front line employees: Role of job characteristics in work and life satisfaction. *Journal of Hospitality and Tourism Management*, 27(2), 27–38.

Zhou, J., & Shalley, C. E. (2010). Deepening our understanding of creativity in the workplace. In S. Zedeck (Ed.), *APA Handbook of Industrial–Organizational Psychology* (Vol. 1, pp. 275–302). Washington, DC: American Psychological Association.

CHAPTER 15

Persuasion and Dissuasion via Social Networking Sites: The Influence of Word-of-Mouth on Consumer Activism

Andree Marie López-Fernández

INTRODUCTION

Today, more than ever, consumers have access to a vast amount of data and information regarding most anything. Internet access is the key to the world of information and social media the key to a boundless platform for both firms and consumers to have their voices heard. The Internet lets people around the world expand their real life network to a virtual one (Lee and Lee 2010); this is quite visible with the social connections and interactions that are possible via social media. The very existence of the latter has proven to be a game changer when it comes to consumer behavior, particularly within consumers' process of purchase decision making.

Consumers take to the Internet to gather information about products, services, brands, and firms to inform their decision making prior to purchase. Interestingly, consumers' preference for information sources has shifted from traditional mass media to social media. That is, they are finding that it is more accessible, has a lower cost (Gursoy and McCleary 2004),

A. M. López-Fernández (✉)
Universidad Panamericana, Mexico City, Mexico

© The Author(s) 2019
Rajagopal, R. Behl (eds.), *Business Governance and Society*,
https://doi.org/10.1007/978-3-319-94613-9_15

and they can obtain interesting information concerning business dynamics via social networking sites (SNSs); the latter enables users to interact with other consumers, customize their searches and content (Chung 2008), and actively participate in the conversation. Therefore, SNSs have become an important "information channel (Xiang and Gretzel 2010)" that successfully informs consumer behavior.

Regardless of the veracity of the information, the shared content and tone via social media, specifically on SNSs, is extremely powerful; there is no question about it, this information can influence, impact, and sway users' opinions, social media activity, and, ultimately, decisions. Further, it can have effects on politics, social activism (van Dijck and Poell 2013; Tufekci and Wilson 2012), and consumer activism (Lovejoy and Saxton 2012), amongst many others. Therefore, the information presented on social media is powerful, to say the least.

Persuasion and dissuasion practices via SNSs such as Facebook and Twitter influence the way consumers feel about a product, service, brand and firm, their behavior, including intentions to purchase, repurchase, and cognition leading to the rationalization of decision making. Informing consumers of business dynamics by means of such practices via social media may prove to have a direct influence on the development of consumer activism. Hence, the aim of this study is to analyze the effects of ongoing word-of-mouth via SNSs of persuasion and dissuasion of firm dynamics on consumer behavior. The study presents a series of propositions and a conceptual model to illustrate the proposed association of constructs and variables, as well as a discussion on the managerial implications of such association.

Literature Review

Consumer Behavior

The way consumers act, and the process behind their decision making, have interested a great many. Consumer behavior takes on the knowledge of other disciplines such as psychology, sociology, and economics (Solomon et al. 2013), amongst others. With information from the different areas of study, several models have been proposed and developed with the aim of understanding and, in some cases, controlling patterns of behavior (Horner and Swarbrooke 2016). Consumer behavior refers to much more than the actual purchase (Morales et al. 2017) of products and/or services, it includes the entire process of decision making prior to purchase, the impressions of purchase and consumption, as well as the effects of the latter; therefore, there is a vast amount of variables that surround consumer behavior.

A particular area of interest is the pre-purchase decision-making process. More specifically, the way data and information influence and impact purchase decision making. It is fair to say that consumers are currently highly informed (Clemons 2008), or may easily become informed with a few swift clicks. Because the Internet provides significant access to information, it not only impacts consumers' search behavior (Peterson and Merino 2003), but also allows consumers to become well versed in a product, service, brand, and/or firm by searching for information online. The amount of retrieved information notwithstanding, it ultimately influences and directly impacts consumer behavior, particularly purchase decision making. Furthermore, the source, nature, and veracity of the information may or may not play a significant role in decision making.

Social Media

Social media erupted in the midst of the information era and gave everyone with a communication device and Internet access a voice. It is true that information leads to knowledge, which, as we know, grants power. However, there is nothing that makes a person feel more powerful than having a voice and a limitless platform on which to use it. In fact, social media has provided both; in the sense that social media users are not only obtaining a vast amount of information on a daily basis, potentially becoming knowledgeable and powerful, but also have a means to have their voices heard, thus exercising power.

Social media are considered social websites, platforms, and applications based on the Web 2.0 foundations (Kaplan and Haenlein 2010) that enable users to connect, interact, participate, comment, and share information and opinions (Palmer and Koenig-Lewis 2009; Köksal and Özdemir 2013). Social media include blogs (Meraz 2009), micro blogs, podcasts, shared pictures and videos (Kaplan and Haenlein 2010), and SNSs (Elstad 2016). There are various SNSs, including Facebook, Twitter, Instagram, YouTube, Pinterest, amongst many others. According to Boyd and Ellison (2007), they make it possible for users to create their own profiles (semi-private or public), lists of users with whom they connect, and lists that intersect with that of other users/potential connections; such connections may be with people a user knows in real life or only online.

Facebook, founded in 2004, is one of the most popular SNSs (Greenwood et al. 2016) and accounts for the largest number of users, that is, more than two billion monthly active users (Facebook 2017). Twitter, founded two years later, is another popular SNS that has more than 300 million monthly active users (Aslam 2017). Therefore, there are billions of potential consumer users creating pages, accounts, and profiles to be virtually shared with the world. According to the Pew Research Center, social media users are those that utilize SNSs (Perrin 2015). SNSs are known and utilized not only by individuals but also by firms, institutions, and organizations (Alshaikh et al. 2014), which makes them mainstream (Keen 2007). According to Gilbert (2009), everyone using social media is treated the same; meaning that there is no distinction between those that the user actually knows and strangers. It also means there is no distinction made whether an individual, organization, politician, influencer, and so on in terms of treatment. The differences may lie in their number of friends and followers, as well as their objectives in social media use. Furthermore, users are also current and potential consumers who connect and interact with diverse communities, including brands (Koufaris 2002) and their respective firms. In addition, users have come to prefer SNSs as sources of information because they consider them to be credible and trustworthy (Reichelt et al. 2014). Therefore, social media has not only changed the way people interact (van Dijck and Poell 2013), but also the art of information retrieval and its impact on consumer behavior.

In regards to business dynamics, the number of firms utilizing SNSs to promote their efforts has increased significantly. This practice not only enhances visibility but it also increases brand awareness (Dong-Hun 2010; Edosomwan et al. 2011) and enables direct, real-time, communication with consumers (Aladwani 2014; VanMeter et al. 2015). Furthermore, because consumers share their thoughts on products, services, brands and firms, the latter has the possibility to learn about them and make effective and prompt decisions (Pookulangara and Koesler 2011). The use of social media also reduces costs (Kaplan and Haenlein 2010), it may influence consumer loyalty (Muniz and O'Guinn 2001; McAlexander et al. 2002; Lim et al. 2015), and significantly impact a brand's image (Bruhn et al. 2012), more specifically, consumers' perception of the brand. Therefore, it directly impacts corporate reputation (Lin et al. 2013; Slee 2011), growth (Chevalier and Mayzlin 2006; Singh and Sinha 2017), and the firm's survival (Kietzmann et al. 2011).

Word-of-Mouth

Perhaps one of the biggest differences between traditional media and social media is that the former is one-way communication while the latter is two-way, at least. The communication occurring on SNSs, also known as word-of-mouth (WOM) is limitless dialogue carried out by a massive number of users (Stauss 1997). Anything and everything posted on Facebook, or tweeted on Twitter, is potentially seen by at least the number of a user's friends and/or followers. The influence of WOM occurring via SNSs on consumer decision making has progressively increased (Steffes and Burgee 2009), reaching a greater number of current and potential consumers, because SNSs are naturally ubiquitous, and enabling direct communication with users (Jahng and Littau 2016). Thus, SNSs' users and consumers are not just viewing content, they are also creating it, commentating on it (Kietzmann et al. 2011), and, importantly, sharing it on boundless platforms.

One of the features that make SNSs interesting is the fact that their users take on a dual role; meaning that, they both generate the information and are simultaneously the audience (Dearstyne 2007) for information. Furthermore, the exchange of information is much more agile; in fact, it is done in real time and received simultaneously. Information is shared because those that possess it deem it useful to others (Berger and Milkman 2013), expect it to be beneficial (Lee et al. 2013), consider they are morally obligated to do so (Wasko and Faraj 2000), and/or are looking to advertise (Chu 2011; Okazaki and Taylor 2013) a product, service, brand, or firm.

There are three important facts that remain regarding information presented in SNSs: (1) it is not always sufficient, (2) it is not always accurate or verifiable, and (3) it is not always positive. There is usually insufficient information for adequate decision making. Granted, SNSs' users are continuously bombarded with information, but it usually is not the full story. Also, unfortunately, there is much information shared online that is either not accurate or not verifiable. On occasion, these are cases of miscommunication, lack of sufficient information and/or data, and in others, fabricated facts. The issue is that on social media, rumors can spread at high speed (Özdemir and Sarı 2014). Under these circumstances, consumer decision making is certainly influenced however inaccurate the information it is based on.

The more the information, WOM, is passed on from SNS user to user, the greater the possibility of information going viral. Virality, according to Guerini et al. (2011), is an indication of the amount of users that view content in a determined period of time. The question, then, is why does certain WOM spread throughout SNSs? That is, what elicits SNS activity, specifically sharing and/or retweeting? Godes et al. (2005) posit that news with negative content is likelier to be distributed. Hansen et al. (2011) analyzed the effects of news and non-news content on Twitter and found that although both positive and negative content propitiate sharing, negative news and positive non-news WOM are more likely to go viral. Swani et al. (2013) argue that inserting emotions in posts is a good strategy, as it is more likely to evoke a response. And, according to a study held by Berger and Milkman (2013), information may go viral when its content generates positive or negative emotions (i.e. happiness, amusement and anger, anxiety, respectively). Therefore, WOM that stimulates such emotions is more likely to be shared repeatedly, be trending, go viral, and, therefore, potentially reach millions of SNSs' users; hence, the research propositions can be framed as follows:

P_1 Emotional response to positive or negative SNS WOM prompts SNS activity.

P_2 Virality is derived from consumers' emotional response to positive or negative SNS WOM.

SNSs' users fully expect to arouse a response (French and Bazarova 2017) from other users to their updates, posts, comments, Tweets, retweets, and so on. That is, they may expect a comment, share, retweet, and, at least, a like. There are several actions that a SNS user may take once a post and/or tweet has been seen. These depend on the SNS and its features; for example, on Twitter, users have four options on each tweet, that is, they may comment, retweet, like (heart), and DM (direct message). On Facebook, each post includes three features or buttons that enable users to like a post, comment on it, and share it. Further, the feature for liking a post includes options such as like (thumbs up), love (heart), Haha (laughing face), Wow (amazed face), Sad (a tear on face), and Angry (heated, annoyed face). Therefore, these options communicate a consumers' emotional response to the WOM without having to write their negative or positive emotion. SNS activity is potentially seen by a user's friends and followers, and the number of views increases the more it is shared and/or retweeted. As such, even before the content of the WOM is verified, if at all, consumers that view information about products, services, brands, and firms are impacted by both the original content as well as previous users' SNS activity; that is, the emotional response of those that came across the WOM before; hence, the research proposition is structured as follows:

P_3 Consumer behavior is informed by personal emotional responses as well as previous SNS activity related to business dynamics WOM.

The WOM circulating via SNSs associated with a brand or firm and its products and/or services could be produced and posted and/or tweeted by the firm or a consumer. If a firm shares information regarding its operations, the content will intend to portray the firm in a positive light. However, there have been instances where collaborators have effectively tarnished the firm's reputation by making outrageous statements on the subject of their business operations. In 2015, the CEO of Dunkin Brands, Nigel Travis, took an interview with CNN's Poppy Harlow during which he stated that increasing the minimum wage to 15 dollars an hour was "absolutely outrageous," adding that living wage is sufficient to support a family (Wattles 2015). Needless to say, there was significant backlash as consumers took to social media to address the CEO's arguments and call for a boycott.

Consumers recount both positive and negative content in relation to firms' business dynamics. Of course, backlash is mostly strictly related to negative information. For instance, in 2014, the hashtag #WhyIStayed was trending on Twitter; it was created by Beverly Gooden after an incident of domestic abuse centered on NFL player Ray Rice that motivated people to ask why his fiancé had not left him (Kaplan 2014). As such, it was meant to encourage conversation on the subject matter. The company, DiGiorno's Pizza made a serious mistake when it took to Twitter for marketing purposes and utilized the hashtag, #WhyIStayed, and added: "you had pizza" (Petri 2014). The backslash was immediate, as consumers were enraged by the firm's overt display of insensitivity. The firm then took to Twitter again to apologize for their mistake and removed the offensive tweet. However, the damage had already been done, consumers worldwide were strongly taking this information into account for their purchase decision making.

The list of firms making such mistakes goes on and on; granted, human beings make mistakes, yet the difference is that they do not go unnoticed when placed on social media. Virality, in many cases, may be the objective of sharing content, although perception of the effects varies according to the emotional response evoked by the content. It is quite concerning to consider the firms and organizational leaders that take to social media and make outrageous statements that depict them as unethical, non-socially responsible, immoral, and so on. Further, consumers tend to wonder if they are willing to make such statements, what are they not saying, what are they holding back in relation to their policies, actions, and results? That said, according to Qualman (2011), positive comments should significantly surpass the negative ones; however, those firms that do not account for any negative comments tend to be outsold by brands that have at least a few, as they may be construed as inconsequential.

Consumer Activism

Activism refers to the intentions and efforts of the parties involved to affect change (Kozinets and Handelman 2004), and to impact and transform social order (Buechler 2000). Consumer activism is an act of solidarity (Glickman 2009) as it is carried out by groups of consumers with similar mindsets (Muniz and O'Guinn 2001), beliefs, principles, values, and so on. It creates a type of ethical agency (Glickman 2009) whose aim is to protect consumers (Hilton 2009; Holzer 2010). The collective action taken by consumers is meant to protest unfair, unethical, immoral, and questionable practices carried out by organizations. This may lead to a call to boycott, ban, and even a request to revoke their right to operate.

As was stated earlier, consumer behavior has been changing. There are consumers that increasingly base their purchase decision making on the firms' engagement in good and ethical practices, sustainability, and social responsibility. According to Creyer (1997), consumers are not only concerned with an organization's ethic stance, but are also willing to modify their purchase decision making on such basis. In such case, a consumer that finds an organization to be unethical may discard it from their lists of potential providers and deem it undesirable, no longer top of mind. For instance, some consumers have shown preference to purchase locally (Grebitus et al. 2017) from organizations that do not destroy the environment (Fields 2017), harm animals (Braunsberger and Buckler 2011), or exploit children (Auger et al. 2003) and collaborators (Brenton and Hacken 2006).

Activists are in the business of generating change, therefore, are agents of change. Consumer activists fervently protest the abovementioned with clear intentions of changing the manner in which businesses operate, their policies, standards, and norms that they deem inappropriate, distasteful, harmful, unethical, and immoral. As such, when they take to SNSs, they do so with the objective of changing the way firms, especially big businesses, and governments operate (Fields 2017), in order to protect those without a voice and to ensure that other consumers do not make a mistake by purchasing from these firms. That said, can negative WOM via SNSs instigate consumer activism? And, can consumer activists spreading content via SNSs influence consumer behavior and effectively persuade other consumers to become activists?

Consumer Behavior Persuasion and Dissuasion

Consumer persuasion through SNSs, such as Twitter (Mourao et al. 2015) and Facebook, are common practices that are characteristic of the platforms on which they are put forth. The two general types of business-associated WOM, positive and negative, overflow SNSs and actively influence consumer perception of the brand and firm; the effects of each type, however, vary. Positive information may influence consumer perceptions of the firm, which ultimately positively impacts the firm. For example, as information of a firm promoting equality, human and animal rights, sustainable practices, fair commerce practices, and so on erupts on social media, consumers that respond with positive emotions are likely to take one of two approaches: (1) current consumers may solidify their loyalty (Kim and Kim 2016; Martínez et al. 2014) towards the firm and (2) potential consumers may be persuaded to consider such firm for their next purchase. In both cases, consumers are expected to engage in SNS activity that directs the WOM on the path towards virality. Granted, there will certainly be SNS users that might attempt to disprove or devalue the information regardless of validity. However, consumer activists who see positive business-related WOM would strongly consider this information for their purchase decision making and take it as a cue to align their loyalty to that firm. In such cases, a positive effect on the firm's business growth is attainable. Furthermore, the more positive emotions are perceived through SNS activity, as it is indicative of social approval, the greater the persuasion to purchase. Therefore, the more WOM is shared across SNSs' users' pages and accounts, the greater the number of current and potential consumers whose purchase decision making is positively influenced; hence, the research proposition can be structured as follows:

P_4 Persuasion of brand loyalty is associated with positive viral WOM regarding business dynamics.

Negative information may influence consumer perceptions of the firm, which ultimately negatively impacts the firm. Firms that do not successfully conceal negative content, data, and/or decision making from the public, or even try to do so, lead current and potential consumers to question their overall ethics and moral compass. For instance, as content of a firm engaging in unethical or questionable practices, such as human rights violations, unequal pay, child labor, environmental destitution, animal cruelty, and so on blows up on social media, consumers that respond with negative emotions tend to take action in three different ways: (1) current consumers may significantly question their loyalty and be dissuaded from purchasing from the firm and may, ultimately, decide on switching brands (Zhang et al. 2015), (2) potential consumers may definitely be dissuaded from purchasing, and (3) current and potential consumers may be persuaded to become activists. In all cases, consumers are expected to engage in SNS activity that directs the WOM towards virality, especially since negative content is more likely to be spread on social media as well as evoke an emotional response.

The persuasion of consumer activism via SNSs may occur by two means: (1) current and potential consumers witness negative information regarding a firm's business dynamics that is perceived to be sufficiently severe that their tolerance zone (i.e. the point where the firm's actions have crossed a line and exceeded consumers' tolerance for questionable practices) has been reached—in a sense, these consumers have had enough—and (2) consumer activists take to SNSs to inform as many current and potential consumers as possible of the negative information they have come across with the intent to dissuade purchase and persuade activism.

Consumer activists have a tendency, however perfunctorily, to fact check the content they are witnessing via social media. Once information has been verified and confirmed to be true, a call for ban and boycott is to be expected. According to Friedman (1985), boycotts are efforts of one or more individuals, organizations, and so on to exhort other consumers to abstain from purchasing from the firm in question. Boycotts have served to pressure firms to conduct themselves to consumers' moral and ethical standards, and are frequently buzzing on SNSs. The greater the perceived severity of the actions, the more current and potential consumers are likely to participate in a boycott (Klein et al. 2004) requested via SNSs. Thus, consumer activists spreading negative business-related content on SNSs, by means of SNS activity, can influence consumer behavior and effectively persuade other consumers to become activists; hence, the research propositions can be formed as follows:

P_5 Dissuasion of consumption and switching behavior are associated with negative viral WOM regarding business dynamics.

P_6 Persuasion of consumer activism via SNS is associated with negative viral WOM regarding business dynamics.

Model Analysis: The Persuasion and Dissuasion of Consumer Behavior

A vast amount of information is unceasingly posted on Facebook and tweeted on Twitter in terms of products, services, brands, and firms on a daily basis. This information, WOM, is potentially being viewed by millions of active SNSs' users who interpret and classify it to shape their perceptions and ultimately make decisions regarding the information subject. The model illustrates how the WOM witnessed about a firm's business dynamics via SNSs influences consumer behavior and potentially impacts consumer loyalty, switching behavior, SNS activity, and even consumer activism (Fig. 15.1 illustrates the relation between SNSs persuasion and dissuasion and consumer behavior). As such, information, content, and tone are significant in the attempt to persuade and/or dissuade consumer behavior.

The model begins with the premise that there is WOM circulating on SNSs on the subject of business dynamics with both positive and negative content and tone. As stated earlier, positive information, or content that stimulates a positive emotion, that is repeatedly shared, potentially trending, and going viral, may be significantly beneficial for the parties involved. Conversely, any negative information or content that stimulates a negative emotion, and trends, may achieve virality. Under both circumstances, the emotional stimulation, in turn, inspires consumers to engage in SNS activity by liking, commentating, sharing, and/or retweeting the content. By doing so, the consumers' friends and followers are consequentially driven

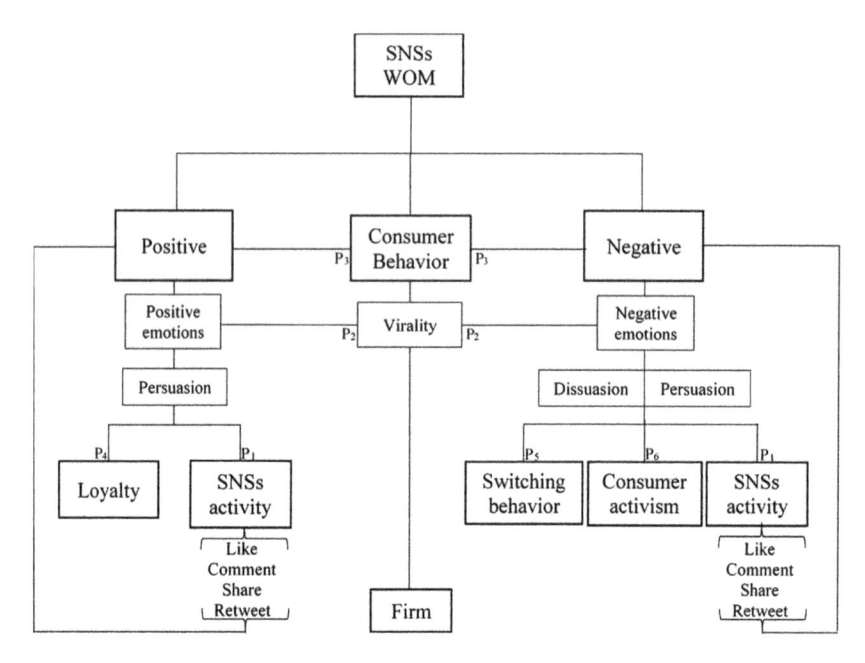

Fig. 15.1 Persuasion and dissuasion of consumer behavior via SNSs

to SNS activity further triggering virality (P_1 and P_2). Consumer behavior, particularly their purchase decision making, is influenced by the emotions they feel as they witness positive and negative content, and as they see the emotional responses of users that have viewed the information before them (P_3). Meaning that current and potential consumer purchase intentions may be effectively swayed by SNS content and activity.

The model then illustrates how persuasion and dissuasion of consumer behavior comes about. As each share and retweet further increases the potential number of SNS users that view the WOM. The greater the user access to information via SNSs, the greater the potential persuasion and dissuasion on consumer behavior. Consumer activism, WOM, SNS activity, loyalty, and switching behavior are all potential effects of persuasion and dissuasion derived from positive and negative information viewed on SNSs about business dynamics. As positive content persuades current and potential consumers towards brand loyalty (P_4), negative content dissuades consumption (P_5) and leads to switching behavior. Moreover, in accordance to the perceived severity of the negative content, SNS users may be persuaded towards consumer activism (P_6). Again, all forms of the effect of WOM on consumer behavior prompt SNS users to engage in SNS activity, further instigating virality.

Finally, any positive post and/or tweet about a product, service, brand, and/or firm that goes viral will certainly create positive effects for the firm in question, while negative content arousing negative emotions will most likely result in negative repercussions for the firm. Therefore, SNS WOM directly influences consumer behavior, which, in turn, directly impacts the firm. This ultimately occurs because the purchase decision making of SNS users, who are consumers, is continuously being shaped by viewed content. Thus, SNS WOM is key not only to consumer behavior but also to business growth and development.

Conclusions and Managerial Implications

Social media, particularly SNSs, have given users much more than games and apps; they have effectively provided both firms and consumers a boundless platform to put forth their ideas, opinions, and experiences. Consumer interest in business operations, policies, and results has gradually increased. More than ever, they are displaying concern for the way firms approach ethical and moral issues, sustainability, and social responsibility. It is not to say that consumers before had not been active in the pursuit of such knowledge, but that now it is much more visible or evident with the incessant activity on SNSs.

WOM occurring on SNSs is powerful; it can inform consumer behavior in the form of brand loyalty as well as switching behavior, motivate SNS activity, and even incite social movement and consumer activism. Without a doubt, consumers will take to SNSs to make their voices heard. No brand, firm, organization, institution, or individual is too big, too far, or too elite for consumers' insights. That is, they are certainly not intimidated by the world's magnates' "power," they are no longer, if they ever were, untouchable. Rather, they are merely separated by a device with internet access, a few passwords, and a couple of clicks. There is no reason to fear; the anonymity that social media offers empowers consumers to speak up. And, there is no reason to take the streets, as consumer activists can now take on the world on boundless social media platforms without leaving their homes, offices, or coffee shops.

SNSs, then, can be a remarkable advantage for businesses to promote their endeavors and achieve beneficial effects, and may pose a great disadvantage for businesses. Since the WOM occurring on social media can be produced by firms as well as current and potential consumers, there is no assurance of the type of content (i.e. positive and negative) that may potentially go viral. While positive content may positively influence consumer behavior, the issue is with negative content as it may be highly damaging to a firm's image and reputation as well as business growth and development. Thus, organizational leaders need not only be vigilant of the WOM but also of its imminent spread. Current and potential consumers, who are millions of SNSs' active monthly users, may engage in persuasion and dissuasion actions and practices on the basis of both factual and fictional data and information, so long as it evokes an emotional response.

Unfortunately, resisting content-related activity is not an option for any of the parties involved. Organizational leaders ought to be vigilant not only of their communications via SNSs, but also of those being held by current and potential consumers that may or may not be consumer activists. As such, it is important to appoint a special task force, also known as community managers (Saavedra et al. 2011), dedicated to the management of social media activity. Therefore, they should delegate managerial efforts towards prevention and preparation for adequately handling potential consumer misinformation and backlash as well as successfully managing the relationship with consumer activists.

Future Research Directions

Future research could test the suggested propositions and model with business-related content being spread on SNSs such as Facebook and Twitter. Furthermore, future research could focus on consumer behavior regarding limits of tolerance; that is, which are the lines that, if the firm should cross them, would render their products and/or services utterly undesirable? Moreover, future research could analyze if firms see this type of consumer activism via SNSs as a public relations nightmare or an opportunity for them to take a stance on the social issues that permeate society on a global scale. Finally, it would be interesting to evaluate the suggested propositions with the use of hashtags to analyze the impact of the content on consumer behavior to the firm.

References

Aladwani, A. M. (2014). Gravitating towards facebook (GoToFB): What it is? and how can it be measured? *Computers in Human Behavior, 33*(4), 270–278.

Alshaikh, F., Ramzan, F., Rawaf, S., & Majeed, A. (2014, July 14). Social Network Sites as a mode to collect health data: A systematic review. *Journal of Medical Internet Research, 16*(7), e171.

Aslam, S. (2017, August 12). *Twitter by the numbers: Stats, demographics & fun facts.* Retrieved November 15, 2017, from OMNICORE: https://www.omnicoreagency.com/twitter-statistics/.

Auger, P., Burke, P., Devinney, T. M., & Louviere, J. J. (2003, February). What will consumers pay for social product features? *Journal of Business Ethics, 42*(3), 281–304.

Berger, J., & Milkman, K. L. (2013, May). Emotion and virality: What makes online content go viral? *De Gruyter Insights, 5*(1), 18–23.

Boyd, D. M., & Ellison, N. B. (2007). Social network sites: Definition, history, and scholarship. *Journal of Computer-Mediated Communication, 13*(1), 210–230.

Braunsberger, K., & Buckler, B. (2011, January). What motivates consumers to participate in boycotts: Lessons from the ongoing Canadian seafood boycott. *Journal of Business Research, 64*(1), 96–102.

Brenton, S., & Hacken, L. T. (2006). Ethical consumerism: Are unethical labor practices important to consumers? *Journal of Research for Consumers, 11*, 1–11.

Bruhn, M., Schoenmueller, V., & Schäfer, D. B. (2012). Are social media replacing traditional media in terms of brand equity creation? *Management Research Review, 35*(9), 770–790.

Buechler, S. M. (2000). *Social movements in advanced capitalism: The political economy and cultural construction of social activism.* New York: Oxford University Press.

Chevalier, J. A., & Mayzlin, D. (2006, August). The effect of word of mouth on sales: Online book review. *Journal of Marketing Research, 43*(3), 345–354.

Chu, S.-C. (2011). Viral advertising in social media: Participation in Facebook groups and responses among college-aged users. *Journal of Interactive Advertising, 12*(1), 30–43.

Chung, D. (2008). Interactive features of online newspapers: Identifying patterns and predicting use of engaged readers. *Journal of Computer Mediated Communication, 13*(3), 658–679.

Clemons, E. K. (2008). How information changes consumer behavior and how consumer behavior determines corporate strategy. *Journal of Management Information Systems, 25*(2), 13–40.

Creyer, E. H. (1997). The influence of firm behavior on purchase intention: Do consumers really care about business ethics? *Journal of Consumer Marketing*, *14*(6), 421–432.

Dearstyne, B. W. (2007, July). Blogs! Mashups and Wikis: Oh, My! *Information Management Journal*, *41*, (4), 24–33.

Dong-Hun, L. (2010, October). Korean consumer & society: Growing popularity of social media and business strategy. *SERI Quarterly*, *3*(4), 112–1179.

Edosomwan, S., Sitalaskshmi, K. P., Kouame, D., Watson, J., & Seymour, T. (2011, July). The history of social media and its impact on business. *Journal of Applied Management and Entrepreneurship*, *16*(3), 79–91.

Elstad, E. (2016). Social networking sites, social media, and internet. In E. Elstad (Ed.), *Digital Expectations and Experiences in Education*. Rotterdam: SensePublishers.

Facebook. (2017, June 30). *Stats*. Retrieved November 17, 2017, from Newsroom. Company Info: https://newsroom.fb.com/company-info/.

Fields, Z. (2017). *Collective creativity for responsible and sustainable business practice*. Hershey: IGI Global.

French, M., & Bazarova, N. N. (2017, November). Is anybody out there?: Understanding masspersonal communication through expectations for response across social media platforms. *Journal of Computer-Mediated Communication*, *22*(6), 303–319.

Friedman, M. (1985). Consumer boycotts in the United States, 1970–1980: Contemporary events in historical perspective. *The Journal of Consumer Affairs*, *19*(1), 96–117.

Gilbert, E. (2009). Predicting tie strength with social media. *CHI '09 Proceedings of the SIGCHI Conference on Human Factors in Computing Systems* (pp. 211–220). Boston.

Glickman, L. B. (2009). *A history of consumer activism in America*. Chicago: University of Chicago Press.

Godes, D., Mayzlin, D., Chen, Y., Das, S., Dellarocas, C., Pfeiffer, B., et al. (2005). The firm's management of social interactions. *Marketing Letters*, *16*(3-4), 415–428.

Grebitus, C., Printezis, I., & Printezis, A. (2017, June). Relationship between consumer behavior and success of urban agriculture. *Ecological Economics*, *136*, 189–200.

Greenwood, S., Perrin, A., & Duggan, M. (2016, November 11). *Social media update*. Retrieved November 15, 2017, from Pew Research Center: http://www.pewinternet.org/2016/11/11/social-media-update-2016/pi_2016-11-11_social-media-update_0-01/.

Guerini, M., Strapparava, C., & Özbal, G. (2011). Exploring text virality in social networks. *Fifth International AAAI Conference on Weblogs and Social Media* (pp. 506–509). Barcelona: ICWSM.

Gursoy, D., & McCleary, K. W. (2004). An integrative model of tourists' information search behavior. *Annals of Tourism Research, 31*(2), 353–373.

Hansen, L. K., Arvidsson, A., Nielsen, F. A., Colleoni, E., & Etter, M. (2011). Good friends, bad news – Affect and virality in Twitter. In J. J. Park (Ed.), *Future information technology. Communications in computer and information science* (pp. 34–43). Berlin: Springer.

Hilton, M. (2009). *Prosperity for all: Consumer activism in an era of globalization*. Ithaca: Cornell University Press.

Holzer, B. (2010). *Moralizing the corporation*. Northampton: Edward Elgar Publishing.

Horner, S., & Swarbrooke, J. (2016). *Consumer behaviour in tourism*. New York: Routledge.

Jahng, M. R., & Littau, J. (2016). Interacting is believing: Interactivity, social cue, and perceptions of journalistic credibility on twitter. *Journalism & Mass Communication Quarterly, 93*(1), 38–58.

Kaplan, S. (2014, September 9). *#WhyIStayed: She saw herself in Ray Rice's wife, Janay, and tweeted about it. So did thousands of others*. Retrieved November 15, 2017, from The Washington Post: https://www.washingtonpost.com/news/morning-mix/wp/2014/09/09/whyistayed-she-saw-herself-in-ray-rices-wife-janay-and-tweeted-about-it-so-did-thousands-of-others/?utm_term=.c3e218a0c1d8.

Kaplan, A. M., & Haenlein, M. (2010, February). Users of the world, unite! The challenges and opportunities of Social Media. *Business Horizons, 53*(1), 59–68.

Keen, A. (2007). *The cult of the amateur: How today's Internet is killing our culture and assaulting our economy*. London: Nicholas Brealey Publishing.

Kietzmann, J. H., Hermkens, K., McCarthy, I. P., & Silvestre, B. S. (2011, May–June). Social media? Get serious! Understanding the functional building blocks of social media. *Business Horizons, 54*(3), 241–251.

Kim, S.-B., & Kim, D.-Y. (2016). The influence of corporate social responsibility, ability, reputation, and transparency on hotel customer loyalty in the U.S.: A gender based approach. *SingerPlus, 5*(1), 1537–1550.

Klein, J. G., Smith, N. C., & John, A. (2004, July). Why we boycott: Consumer motivations for boycott participation. *Journal of Marketing, 68*(3), 92–109.

Köksal, Y., & Özdemir, Ş. (2013). Bir İletişim Aracı Olarak Sosyal Medya'nın Tutundurma Karması İçerisindeki Yeri Üzerine Bir İnceleme. *Süleyman Demirel Üniversitesi İktisadi ve İdari Bilimler Fakültesi Dergisi, 18*(1), 323–337.

Koufaris, M. (2002, June). Applying the technology acceptance model and flow theory to online consumer behavior. *Information Systems Research, 13*(2), 205–223.

Kozinets, R. V., & Handelman, J. M. (2004, December). Adversaries of consumption: Consumer movements, activism, and ideology. *Journal of Consumer Research, 31*, 691–704.

Lee, J., & Lee, H. (2010, May). The computer-mediated communication network: Exploring the linkage between the online community and social capital. *New Media & Society, 12*(5), 711–727.

Lee, H., Park, H., & Kim, J. (2013, September). Why do people share their context information on Social Network Services? A qualitative study and an experimental study on users' behavior of balancing perceived benefit and risk. *International Journal of Human-Computer Studies, 71*(9), 862–877.

Lim, J. S., Hwang, Y., Kim, S., & Biocca, F. A. (2015). How social media engagement leads to sports channel loyalty: Mediating roles of social presence and channel commitment. *Computers in Human Behavior, 46*, 158–167.

Lin, C., Wu, Y.-S., & Chen, J.-C. V. (2013). Electronic word of mouth: The moderating roles of product involvement and brand image. *Proceedings of 2013 International Conference on Technology Innovation and Industrial Management* (pp. S3-29-S3-47). Phuket, Thailand: TIIM.

Lovejoy, K., & Saxton, G. D. (2012, April). Information, community, and action: How nonprofit organizations use social media. *Journal of Computer-Mediated Communication, 17*(3), 337–353.

Martínez, P., Pérez, A., & Rodríguez del Bosque, I. (2014). CSR influence on hotel brand image and loyalty. *Academia Revista Latinoamericana de Administración, 27*(2), 267–283.

McAlexander, J. H., Schouten, J. W., & Koenig, H. F. (2002, January). Building brand community. *Journal of Marketing, 66*(1), 38–54.

Meraz, S. (2009, April). Is there an elite hold? Traditional media to social media agenda setting influence in blog networks. *Journal of Computer-Mediated Communication, 14*(3), 682–707.

Morales, A. C., Amir, O., & Lee, L. (2017). Keeping it real in experimental research- Understanding when, where, and how to enhance realism and measure consumer behavior. *Journal of Consumer Research, 44*(2), 465–476.

Mourao, R. R., Yoo, J., Geise, S., Araiza, J. A., Kilgo, D. K., & Chen, V. Y. (2015). Online news, social media, and European Union attitudes: A multidimensional analysis. *International Journal of Communication, 9*, 3199–3222.

Muniz, A. M., & O'Guinn, T. C. (2001, March). Brand community. *Journal of Consumer Research, 27*(4), 412–432.

Okazaki, S., & Taylor, C. R. (2013). Social media and international advertising: Theoretical challenges and future directions. *International Marketing Review, 30*(1), 56–71.

Özdemir, G., & Sarı, Ö. (2014). Turist Destinasyonlarına Dönük Sosyal Medya Söylentileri Üzerine Bir Durum Çalışması. *İstanbul Ticaret Üniversitesi Sosyal Bilimleri Dergisi, 13*(25), 289–299.

Palmer, A., & Koenig-Lewis, N. (2009). An experiental, social network-based approach to direct marketing. *Direct Marketing: An International Journal, 3*(3), 162–176.

Perrin, A. (2015, October 8). *Social media usage: 2005–2015 65% of adults now use social networking sites-a nearly tenfold jump in the past decade*. Retrieved November 15, 2017, from Pew Research Center: http://www.pewinternet.org/2015/10/08/2015/Social-Networking-Usage-2005-2015/.

Peterson, R. A., & Merino, M. C. (2003, February). Consumer information search behavior and the internet. *Psychology & Marketing, 20*(2), 99–121.

Petri, A. (2014, September 9). #WhyIStayed, Digiorno, and other corporate disasters. Retrieved November 15, 2017, from The Washington Post: https://www.washingtonpost.com/blogs/compost/wp/2014/09/09/whyistayed-digiorno-and-other-corporate-disasters/?utm_term=.010da7f64100.

Pookulangara, S., & Koesler, K. (2011, July). Cultural influence on consumers' usage of social networks and its' impact on online purchase intentions. *Journal of Retailing and Consumer Services, 18*(4), 348–354.

Qualman, E. (2011). *Socialnomics: How social media transforms the way we live and do business*. Hoboken, NJ: John Wiley & Sons, Inc.

Reichelt, J., Sievert, J., & Jacob, F. (2014). How credibility affects eWOM reading: The influences of expertise, trustworthiness, and similarity on utilitarian and social functions. *Journal of Marketing Communications, 20*(1/2), 65–81.

Saavedra, J. L., Linero Sotillo, O. R., & Gutiérrez León, R. (2011). Community Manager y la marca como estrategia organizacional en las redes sociales online. *REDHECS, 10*(6), 168–181.

Singh, T. P., & Sinha, R. (2017, January–March). The impact of social media on business growth and performance in India. *International Journal of Research in Management & Business Studies, 4*(1), 36–40.

Slee, C. (2011, October). The impact of social media on corporate reputation. *VISTAS: Education. Economy and Community, 1*(2), 62–71.

Solomon, M., Russell-Bennett, R., & Previte, J. (2013). *Consumer behaviour. Buying, having, being*. Frenchs Forest: Pearson.

Stauss, B. (1997). Global word of mouth. *Marketing Management, 6*(3), 1–28.

Steffes, E. M., & Burgee, L. E. (2009). Social ties and online word of mouth. *Internet Research, 19*(1), 42–59.

Swani, K., Milne, G., & Brown, B. P. (2013). Spreading the word through likes on Facebook: Evaluating the message strategy effectiveness of Fortune 500 companies. *Journal of Research in Interactive Marketing, 7*(4), 269–294.

Tufekci, Z., & Wilson, C. (2012, April). Social media and the decision to participate in political protest: Observations from Tahir Square. *Journal of Communication, 62*(2), 363–379.

van Dijck, J., & Poell, T. (2013). Understanding social media logic. *Media and Communication, 1*(1), 2–14.

VanMeter, R. A., Grisaffe, D. B., & Chonko, L. B. (2015, November). Of "likes" and "pins": The effects of consumers' attachment to social media. *Journal of Interactive Marketing, 32*, 70–88.

Wasko, M. M., & Faraj, S. (2000, September). "It is what one does": Why people participate and help others in electronic communities of practice. *The Journal of Strategic Information Systems, 9*(2-3), 155–173.

Wattles, J. (2015, July 24). *Dunkin' CEO: $15 minimum wage is 'outrageous'*. Retrieved November 15, 2017, from CNN Money: http://money.cnn.com/2015/07/23/news/dunkin-ceo-minimum-wage/index.html.

Xiang, Z., & Gretzel, U. (2010). Role of social media in online travel information search. *Tourism Management, 31*(2), 179–188.

Zhang, H., Takanashi, C., Gemba, K., & Ishida, S. (2015, September). Empirical research on the influence of negative electronic word-of-mouth on brand switching behavior. *World Journal of Management, 6*(2), 46–61.

CHAPTER 16

Relationship between Exports and the BRICS Countries' Gross Domestic Product: A Bayesian Vector Autoregression Approach for the Period 1978–2016

José Antonio Núñez Mora and Leovardo Mata Mata

INTRODUCTION

Since 1978, China has been implementing various reforms aimed at free trade and towards the promotion of exports as an engine of economic development (Chow 1987; Chow and Lin 2002). Due to this, in the last 25 years the role of the Asian giant as the main exporter and importer has increased globally (Mah 2005; Mbaku 1989). Up to the year 2017, China's participation in both areas exceeds the annual average of 10% (Durán and Pellandra 2017).

The role of exports and imports in the growth of countries (Hye and Lau 2015) is a stylized fact that has been documented in literature in different ways (see for example Casanova and Ferreira (2016) and Tyler (1981)).

J. A. Núñez Mora (✉) • L. Mata Mata
EGADE Business School, Tecnologico de Monterrey, Mexico City, Mexico
e-mail: janm@itesm.mx; leovardo.mata@itesm.mx

Empirical evidence from different countries, in different time periods, has been obtained by regression models in two and three stages, Granger causality, cointegration, Autoregressive Distributed Lag (ARDL) models, Vector Error Correction (VEC) models, panel models with fixed effects, Vector Autoregressive (VAR) specifications and panel models with random effects, as indicated in Durán and Pellandra (2017). Montenegro et al. (2011) used regression models and found evidence to establish that the growth of the Chinese market was very useful for the Latin American countries at least until 2010. Moreover, at the global level, the imports from China to business partners in Latin America have not caused a displacement of China's imports from Latin American countries (Arize, 2002; Awokuse 2005). This fact is an argument to reinforce the idea of a bidirectional relationship between Gross Domestic Product (GDP) and exports between China and Latin America.

Previously, Bahmani-Oskooee and Alse (1993) found evidence of a bidirectional relationship between exports and real GDP for nine developed countries, just like Ahmad and Harnhirun (1995) found for the case of five Asian nations, and Ahmad and Kwan (1991) found for South Africa. The techniques used include regression models in time series and causality in the Granger sense. In fact, Luna (2014) pointed out the strategic importance that China plays in the economic activity inside the BRICS and analyzed the conformation process of this economic bloc as a coalition that has changed their initial goals, and nowadays the decisions do not respond to the initial economic expectations but strategic decisions for each member of the BRICS. In particular, China uses BRICS as a way to relieve the international stress and as manner of cooperation to complement its development policy.

Ramos (2001) found, through VEC models, that there is a bidirectional relationship between exports, imports and real GDP for Portugal. Awokuse (2007) proves the mentioned connection in the case of Bulgaria. In relation to the BRICS, there are studies that focus on the bilateral relationship with China, for example, Casanova and Ferreira (2016) develop an index of dependence between Latin America and the Asian giant, where it is noted that the dependence between the Asian giant and the Latin American countries has increased. Casanova and Ferreira (2016) identify sectors and countries with the highest exposure to the economic activity of China. They found evidence to affirm that the dependence between Latin America and China had increased drastically in the period 2008–2014, with four important products: soy, petroleum, copper and steel. Specifically, the most important countries related with China are Brazil, Argentina,

Chile, Peru, Colombia and Venezuela. Until 2014, 80% of exports of the aforementioned products went to China.

Hye and Lau (2015) find under ARDL models that China's total exports and imports have contributed, in both short and long term, to China's economic growth. Also, there are several studies that conclude bidirectional relationships between Latin America and China, such as Montenegro et al. (2011), Luna (2014) and Caputi et al. (2012). Specifically, Caputi et al. (2012) point out that the relationship with China has caused an increase in the exports of natural resources of Latin America, but this fact is against the industrialization of these countries (Hye and Siddiqui 2010). So, the challenge is the construction of commercial agreements for the development of the primary and secondary sectors in China and Latin America; otherwise, for Latin America, the exports will be based in the raw materials therefore stopping the industrial development of Latin America.

However, in the indicated works, Bayesian approaches are not used for the estimation of the causality between variables or for the calculation of the average effect, so the implementation of a Bayesian VAR to estimate the impulse-response functions and to measure the causal relationship between exports and economic growth is an area of opportunity presented in this work.

The methodology of a Bayesian VAR can be found using another economic variables, as in Jaramillo (2009), who applies this procedure to study the transmission mechanisms of the monetary policy toward the main macroeconomic variables of the Chilean economy. Compared with the traditional VAR, the goodness of fit is better for the Bayesian VAR.

Finally, this chapter is organized as follows: Sect. 2 presents the methodology used, Sect. 3 deals with the results and the estimations carried out as well as their interpretation, and Sect. 4 presents conclusions.

Methodology

In this work, annual data from 1978 to 2017 is used for exports from Brazil, Russia, China, India and South Africa. The information has been taken from the United Nations COMTRADE database. GDP and exports have been taken in dollars and at constant prices. The estimates were made by transforming the time series with a natural logarithm.

Then, the corresponding estimates were made under the following steps:

(a) The unit root test is performed under three different cases: augmented Dickey–Fuller (ADF), Phillips–Perron (PP) and Kwiatkowski–Phillips–Schmidt–Shin (KPSS). This exercise was carried out with the time series in levels and first difference.
(b) The number of optimal lags for the traditional VAR model (UVAR) and the Bayesian VAR model (BVAR) was calculated. The expression is

$$Y_t = C + \sum_{k=1}^{m} A(L_k) Y_{t-k} + B(L) X_t + u_t \qquad (16.1)$$

Where Y_t is a vector of endogenous variables, X_t is a vector of exogenous variables, u_t is a vector of random perturbations, and C, $A(L_k)$, $B(L)$ are lag matrices that must be calculated (Sims 1980).

(c) Based on the estimated VAR models, the impulse-response functions of the economic growth rate and the variation of exports are calculated. Based on the estimated time series of the impulse-response functions, the cumulative transfer elasticity (E) is calculated in the period τ as

$$E_\tau = \frac{\%\Delta Y_{t,\,t+\tau}}{\%\Delta E_{t,\,t+\tau}} \qquad (16.2)$$

Where $\%\Delta Y_{t,\,t+\tau}$ is the percentage change in real GDP τ periods after the shock, $\%\Delta E_{t,\,t+\tau}$ is the percentage change in exports in the same period. In this way, E_τ is an estimator for the average impact that exports have had on economic growth.

The BVAR model differs from the UVAR model in that the parameters θ to be determined are considered random variables, characterized by a multivariate normal distribution with known mean θ^* and covariance matrix given by Σ_θ (Jaramillo 2009).

In this way, the a priori density function is

$$f(\theta) = \left[\frac{1}{2\pi}\right]^{k^2 p/2} |\Sigma_\theta|^{-1/2} \exp\left[-\left(\frac{1}{2}\right)(\theta - \theta^*)' \Sigma_\theta^{-1} (\theta - \theta^*)\right] \qquad (16.3)$$

which implies a likelihood function given by

$$l(y|\theta) = \left(\frac{1}{2\pi}\right)^{kT/2} |I_T \otimes \Sigma|^{-1/2} \exp\left[-\frac{1}{2}(y-(X \otimes I_k)\theta)'(I_T \otimes \Sigma^{-1})\right] \quad (16.4)$$

where the vector of parameters θ is estimated and whose a posteriori probability density function is given by

$$f(\theta|y) \propto \exp\left[-\frac{1}{2}(\theta-\bar{\theta})'\bar{\Sigma}_\theta^{-1}(\theta-\bar{\theta})\right] \quad (16.5)$$

with

$$\bar{\theta} = \left[V_\theta^{-1} + (X'X \otimes \Sigma^{-1})\right]^{-1}\left[V_\theta^{-1}\theta^* + (X' \otimes \Sigma^{-1})y\right] \quad (16.6)$$

$$\bar{\Sigma}_\theta = \left[V_\theta^{-1} + (X'X \otimes \Sigma^{-1})\right]^{-1} \quad (16.7)$$

ESTIMATES AND RESULTS

The set of estimates are made under natural logarithm in each of the variables, since this transformation allows smoothing the time series, it allows the estimated coefficients to be interpreted as elasticities and it also relates the variables in percentage terms (Hye and Boubaker 2011).

The endogenous variables are exports and real GDP at constant prices of the BRICS countries for the period 1978–2017. This period was chosen because 1978 is the year when China began its process of opening its foreign trade.

Table 16.1 shows that exports and GDP, under natural logarithm, are non-stationary series, since the null hypothesis for the ADF and PP cases is not rejected, and it is rejected in all cases for KPSS. In contrast, in Table 16.2 we find evidence that the variations of the variables (first difference of the natural logarithm) are stationary time series.

Since the variables have had a logarithmic transformation, the first differences represent the growth rate and it is precisely these differences that will be taken into account for the estimation of the UVAR and BVAR models.

Table 16.1 Unit root test

Variable	ADF		PP		KPSS	
	t-statistic	p-value	t-statistic	p-value	t-statistic	p-value
Exports						
ln_exp_Brazil	2.24	0.197	0.59	0.860	0.18	0.000
ln_exp_Russia	2.01	0.281	0.06	0.901	0.26	0.000
ln_exp_india	0.71	0.840	0.94	0.980	0.24	0.000
ln_exp_China	2.37	0.150	0.19	0.930	0.27	0.000
ln_exp_South Africa	1.27	0.641	107	0.718	0.36	0.000
GDP						
ln_pib_Brazil	1.41	0.580	0.06	0.957	0.20	0.000
ln_pib_Russia	2.47	0.124	0.77	0.822	0.39	0.000
ln_pib_India	0.57	0.872	159	0.482	0.32	0.000
ln_pib_China	0.47	0.984	117	0.482	0.26	0.000
ln_pib_South Africa	0.88	0.988	124	0.651	0.18	0.000

GDP and exports in levels (natural logarithm). Source: Authors analysis

Table 16.2 Unit root test

Variable	ADF		PP		KPSS	
	t-statistic	p-value	t-statistic	p-value	t-statistic	p-value
Exports						
ln_exp_Brazil	14.33	0.000	12.32	0.000	0.50	0.107
ln_exp_Russia	13.04	0.000	10.82	0.000	0.80	0.115
ln_exp_India	4.11	0.001	3.29	0.000	0.61	0.103
ln_exp_china	11.2	0.000	9.74	0.000	0.72	0.147
ln_exp_South Africa	4.24	0.001	3.99	0.000	0.92	0.173
GDP						
ln_pib_Brazil	10.32	0.000	8.57	0.000	0.63	0.148
ln_pib_Russia	9.45	0.000	8.22	0.000	0.94	0.158
ln_pib_India	8.42	0.000	6.82	0.000	0.84	0.140
ln_pib_china	7.33	0.000	6.01	0.000	0.72	0.146
ln_pib_South Africa	5.23	0.000	4.55	0.000	0.52	0.181

GDP and exports in first difference (natural logarithm). Source: Authors analysis

Table 16.3 shows the election of the optimal number of lags for the VAR model, with the lag chosen being equal to 1, since the values of the information criteria acquire a minimum value for that case.

Table 16.4 presents the Granger causality test for exports and the economic growth rate of the countries that make up the BRICS group. Given

Table 16.3 Optimal lags for VAR models

Lags	AIC	SC	HQ
0	−13.97324	−13.70598	−13.86591
1	−14.44133	**−13.96075**[a]	**−14.24863**[a]
2	−14.47163	−13.77674	−14.19256
3	−14.53029	−13.62159	−14.16536
4	−14.66219	−13.53968	−14.21139
5	−14.64346	−13.30714	−14.10679
6	−14.65502	−13.10488	−14.03248
7	−14.62161	−12.85766	−13.9132
8	−14.61994	−12.64218	−13.82567
9	−14.60476	−12.41319	−13.72462
10	−14.62503	−12.21965	−13.65902
11	−14.98809	−12.36889	−13.93621
12	**−15.24384**[a]	−12.41083	−14.10610

Source: Authors analysis

AIC Akaike information criterion; BIC Schwarz information criterion; HQ Hannan-Quinn information criterion

[a]Indicates the optimum lag selected by the information criterion

Table 16.4 Granger cause

Exports	Statistical F	p-value
Dln_exp_Brazil does not cause in Granger sense Dln_pib_Brazil	2.128	0.0190
Dln_exp_Russia does not cause in Granger sense Dln_pib_Russia	1.836	0.0486
Dln_exp_India does not cause in Granger sense Dln_pib_India	1.703	0.0451
Dln_exp_China does not cause in Granger sense Dln_pib_China	2.078	0.0550
Dln_exp_South Africa does not cause in Granger sense Dln_pib_South Africa	2.158	0.0571
GDP		
Dln_pib_Brazil does not cause in Granger sense Dln_exp_Brazil	1.912	0.0571
Dln_pib_Russia does not cause in Granger sense Dln_exp_Russia	1.576	0.0471
Dln_pib_India does not cause in Granger sense Dln_exp_India	1.683	0.0503
Dln_pib_China does not cause in Granger sense Dln_exp_China	1.812	0.0541
Dln_pib_South Africa does not cause in Granger sense Dln_exp_South Africa	1.573	0.0470

Source: Authors calculation

the p-value of the test, it can be affirmed that bidirectional causality exists, in the Granger sense, between all the variables.

Now, using the variables in first difference, two autoregressive vectors are estimated: a traditional VAR and a Bayesian VAR. The objective is to estimate the cumulative effect of exports on the economic growth rate for the BRICS. Using the information criteria of Akaike, Schwarz and Hanna-Quinn, it is found that the goodness of fit for the time series in the period 1978–2017 is higher when estimating a Bayesian VAR.

Table 16.5 shows the following points:

(a) A 1% increase in China's exports to Brazil contribute 0.59% to China's economic growth rate. This value is the largest and it indicates how relevant Brazil is to China, in relation to Russia, India and South Africa. The rest of the figures in the first column are interpreted similarly.
(b) A 1% increase in China's economic growth rate implies a 1.64% increase in exports to Brazil. This value is the largest effect and it reflects the key role that the Asian giant has within the BRICS. The rest of the figures in column 2 are interpreted in a similar way.

Additionally, Table 16.5 shows that the results obtained measure the average cumulative effect of exports on the economic growth rate of each country. The effect is positive for each member of the BRICS, although the magnitudes are different: the greatest effect is between China and Brazil, while the smaller impact occurs between South Africa and India.

Table 16.5 Percentage relationship between GDP and exports for the BRICS

Variables	Cumulative average effect of exports on the economic growth rate (%)	Cumulative average effect of the economic growth on the variation of exports (%)
Brazil to China	0.10	1.09
Russia to China	0.13	1.11
India to China	0.17	1.34
South Africa to China	0.06	1.04
China to Brazil	0.59	1.64
China to Russia	0.46	1.28
China to India	0.52	1.19
China to South Africa	0.38	1.11

Source: Own elaboration

The set of estimates made offers an indirect measure of the dependence of the BRICS countries and it provides empirical evidence to indicate the benefits of free trade and trade liberalization.

Conclusions

This study examines the relationship between the exports and the GDP in the case of the BRICS. The procedure used is a traditional VAR model and a Bayesian VAR model. Both specifications coincide in the sense of the effects between the variables, but UVAR tends to underestimate the impact, in relation to BVAR. The BVAR model has a superior goodness of fit for the data set, according to the tests performed.

According to the estimations carried out, it can be affirmed that there is a bidirectional relationship between exports and economic growth for BRICS countries. This result is compatible with what is indicated in the literature for other countries and other time periods.

The magnitude of the effects is greater between Brazil and China, both on exports and on GDP. This indicates indirect evidence of greater dependence between these two nations.

The areas of opportunity and future lines of research that can be pointed out are the estimation with a larger sample of countries, in different time periods. The exercise could also be carried out by distinguishing by sector or commercialized product, in such a way that the effect of the variables can be established in disaggregated terms.

References

Ahmad, J., & Harnhirun, S. (1995). Unit roots and cointegration in estimating causality between exports and economic growth: Empirical evidence from the ASEAN countries. *Economics Letters, 49*, 329–334.

Ahmad, J., & Kwan, A. C. C. (1991). Causality between exports and economic growth: Empirical evidence from Africa. *Economics Letters, 37*, 243–248.

Arize, A. (2002). Imports and exports in 50 countries: Tests for cointegration and structural breaks. *International Review of Economics and Finance, 11*(1), 101–115.

Awokuse, T. O. (2005). Exports, economic growth and causality in Korea. *Applied Economics Letters, 12*(11), 693–696.

Awokuse, T. O. (2007). Causality between exports, imports, and economic growth: Evidence from transition economies. *Economics Letters, 94*(3), 389–395.

Bahmani-Oskooee, M., & Alse, J. (1993). Export growth and economic growth: An application of cointegration and error correction modelling. *Journal of Developing Areas, 27*(4), 535–542.

Caputi, M., Moreira, A., & Gomes de Lima, M. (2012). *Revista CEPAL, 106*(1), 57–77.

Casanova, C., & Ferreira, R. (2016). Measuring Latin America's export dependency on China. *Journal Chinese Economic and Foreign Trade Studies, 9*(3), 213–233.

Chow, P. C. Y. (1987). Causality between export growth and industrial development: Empirical evidence from the NICs. *Journal of Development Economics, 26*(1), 55–63.

Chow, G., & Lin, A. L. (2002). Accounting for economic growth in Taiwan and Mainland China: A comparative analysis. *Journal of Comparative Economics, 30*(3), 507–530.

Durán, J., & Pellandra, A. (2017). *La irrupción de China y su impacto sobre la estructura productiva y comercial de América Latina y el Caribe.* Serie Comercio Internacional. Santiago de Chile: CEPAL.

Hye, Q. M. A., & Boubaker, H. B. H. (2011). Exports, imports and economic growth: An empirical analysis of Tunisia. *The IUP Monetary Economics, 9*(1), 6–21.

Hye, Q. M. A., & Siddiqui, M. M. (2010). Are imports and exports cointegrated in Pakistan? A rolling window bound testing approach. *World Applied Sciences Journal, 9*(7), 708–711.

Hye, Q. M. A., & Lau, W. Y. (2015). Trade openness and economic growth: Empirical evidence from India. *Journal of Business Economics and Management, 16*(1), 188–205.

Jaramillo, P. (2009). Estimación de VAR Bayesianos para la Economía Chilena. *Revista de Análisis Económico, 24*(1), 101–126.

Luna, L. (2014). La C de los BRICS: el rol de China en la consolidación del grupo. *Oasis, 19*(1), 53–66.

Mah, J. S. (2005). Export expansion, economic growth and causality in China. *Applied Economics Letters, 12*(2), 105–107.

Mbaku, J. M. (1989). Export growth and economic performance in developing countries: Further evidence from Africa. *Journal of Economic Development, 14*, 127–142.

Montenegro, C., Pereira, M., & Soloaga, I. (2011). El efecto de China en el comercio internacional de América Latina. *Estudios de Economía, 38*(2), 341–368.

Ramos, F. F. R. (2001). Exports, imports, and economic growth in Portugal: Evidence from causality and cointegration analysis. *Journal of Economic Modeling, 18*(4), 613–623.

Sims, C. (1980). Macroeconomics and reality. *Econometrica: Journal of the Econometric Society, 48*, 1–48.

Tyler, W. (1981). Growth and export expansion in developing countries: Some empirical evidence. *Journal of Development Economics, 9*(1), 121–130.

CHAPTER 17

Consumer Behavior on Social Media: A Thematic Exploration and an Agenda for Future Inquiry

Alberto Lopez and Raquel Castaño

INTRODUCTION

The Internet has completely renovated the way consumers behave in many different marketing settings (Sharma and Sheth 2004). Specifically, Internet-based social media has increased the power of consumers in their relationships with brands. Consumers are now able to interact with their brands from their own cellphones, they can also spread positive or negative word-of-mouth to their friends on social media (e-WOM), and even influence the value of the firm in the financial markets just by sharing a video on social media, just to name a few examples.

According to recent estimations, by 2017 almost half of the worldwide population has at least one social media account (Kemp 2017). Moreover, in developed countries like the United States, about 65% of adults use social media in their everyday lives. More importantly, the social media usage rate among young consumers from 18 to 29 years old is 90% (Perrin 2015). These technological and sociological developments influence how

A. Lopez (✉) • R. Castaño
Tecnologico de Monterrey, EGADE Business School, Monterrey, NL, Mexico
e-mail: rcastano@itesm.mx

© The Author(s) 2019
Rajagopal, R. Behl (eds.), *Business Governance and Society*,
https://doi.org/10.1007/978-3-319-94613-9_17

marketing managers create and implement their strategies by presenting both new challenges and opportunities. Given the great impact of these new digital environments on how consumers behave and interact with brands, as well as on how marketers develop and implement their strategies to target their consumers, in the last decade a substantial body of research has been published in marketing journals, attempting to describe and explain how consumers behave in social media environments.

This chapter carries out an extensive review of all this previous literature on the phenomenon of consumer behavior on social media. The purpose is to organize the academic literature on this topic and to propose an integrative model that describes and helps explain how consumers behave on social media and how they interact with brands in these new digital environments. Finally, we suggest areas of greatest potential for future research. To our knowledge, this is the first attempt to review the academic literature on consumer behavior on social media, and therefore this work makes a significant contribution to the fields of consumer behavior and social media marketing.

Methodology

Identifying the Papers

In order to guarantee the validity of this review, we followed a systematic process. To gather the initial pool of papers, we conducted extensive searches in the top academic databases, such as Academic Search Premier, EBSCO, and The Web of Science. We searched a large set of keywords, such as social media, online social networks, and online communities. We then analyzed abstracts in order to determine the fit with our research purpose. After several rounds of filtering, we selected 103 final papers that met the following criteria: (1) the paper is published in a peer-reviewed journal, (2) the research focus or/and the unit of analysis is the consumer, (3) the paper is published in a marketing journal, (4) the paper is entirely written in the English language, and (5) the paper was published between 2010 and 2017. Table 17.1 shows the total of published papers on the topic by journal. It is interesting to note that while our review includes papers from more than 20 marketing journals, only five journals make up more than 50% of all published papers (*Journal of Interactive Marketing*, *Journal of Consumer Research*, *Journal of Marketing Research*, *Psychology and Marketing*, and *International Journal of Research in Marketing*).

Table 17.1 Number of published papers by Journal

Journal	Papers published
Journal of Interactive Marketing	20
Journal of Consumer Research	10
Journal of Marketing Research	8
Psychology and Marketing	7
International Journal of Research in Marketing	7
Journal of the Association for Consumer Research	6
International Journal of Advertising	6
Journal of Research in Interactive Marketing	5
Journal of Services Marketing	4
Journal of Marketing	4
Journal of Business Research	4
European Journal of Marketing	4
International Journal of Consumer Studies	3
Qualitative Market Research: An International Journal	2
Marketing Science	2
Marketing Letters	2
Journal of Consumer Psychology	2
Journal of Consumer Marketing	2
Quantitative Marketing and Economics	1
Journal of the Academy of Marketing Science	1
Journal of Consumer Behavior	1
Journal of Brand Management	1
Electronic Commerce Research and Applications	1
Total	103

Classifying the Papers

Each of the 103 papers previously identified was entirely read and classified according to its main findings and contributions to the literature. Authors analyzed the 103 papers in an iterative manner (Spiggle 1994); the papers were read several times in order to identify the themes, sub-themes, and codes. These categorizations were changed many times as new themes emerged from the data. The authors finished analyzing the data when they stopped seeing new themes emerging. This endeavor was conducted with the aid of the software NVivo (version 11). Based on these results, we identified the main themes and propose a model to integrate and illustrate the state of the art of this topic.

Results

Years of Publication

All the analyzed papers were published from 2010 to 2017. Most of them were published in the last three years (2015–2017). It is also interesting to note that overall, the number of papers published on this topic has been increasing year by year, which indicates just how much interest this topic is garnering right now. Due to the relevance of this phenomenon, it is very likely that this tendency will remain and even increase in the next years (Fig. 17.1).

Counting Analysis of the Most Prominent Words

Using the content analysis tools of NVivo, we conducted an exploratory analysis of the 103 papers. The most prominent words are brand, consumers, social, and media, in concordance with the purpose of our study. Furthermore, these words appear combined with other prominent words on a secondary level, such as online, advertising, network, motivations, e-WOM, Facebook, relationships, reviews, and so on.

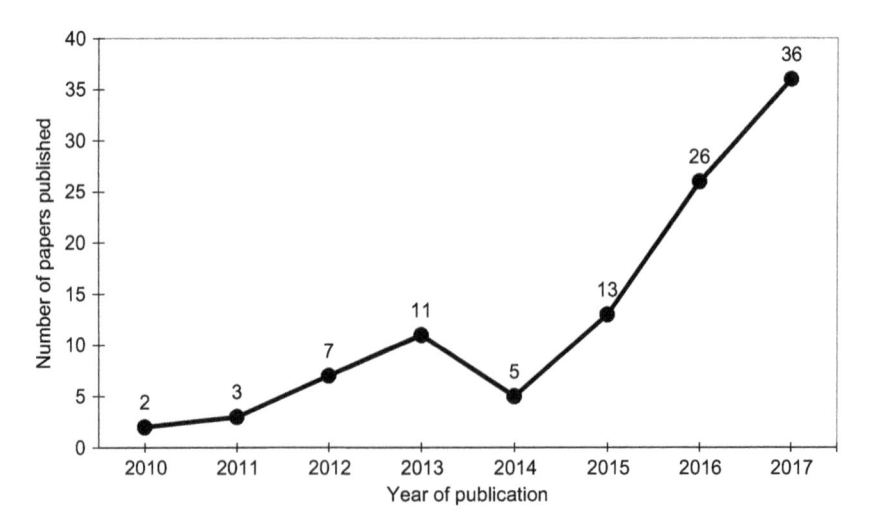

Fig. 17.1 Number of papers published by year

Emerging Themes

During the coding process, five major themes emerged from the data of which each of the 103 papers could be assigned to one. Most of the themes also have sub-themes and some of them also have sub-codes:

1. Motivators to follow brands on social media
   (a) Brand antecedents
   (b) Looking for benefits
   (c) Personality traits
2. Demotivators to follow brands on social media
   (a) Consumer privacy and security concerns
3. Consumer-brand interactions on social media
   (a) Consumer complaint and service recovery
   (b) Consumer-generated content
      (i) Consumer only
      (ii) Co-created
   (c) Conspicuous consumption display
   (d) Advertising
      (i) Virality
      (ii) Message composition
4. Effects of following brands on social media
   (a) Brand evaluations
   (b) Actual/intentional purchase
   (c) e-WOM (word of mouth)
   (d) Stock price
5. Interpersonal relationships and social media

We propose that the current research on the topic of consumer behavior on social media can be integrated into these five broad themes. Table 17.2 shows an exploratory analysis of the most and least researched topics in this phenomenon.

State of the Art of Consumer Behavior on Social Media

We unified the previous presented themes and sub-themes into an integrative model, which illustrates and summarizes the state of the art of the current literature on consumer behavior on social media. Figure 17.2 shows

Table 17.2 Number of published papers by theme and sub-themes

Theme	Frequency
1. Motivators to follow brands on social media	**14**
1.1 Brand antecedents	6
1.2 Looking for benefits	7
1.3 Personality traits	1
2. Demotivators to follow brands on social media	**4**
2.1 Consumer privacy and security concerns	4
3. Consumer-brand interactions on social media	**36**
3.1 Consumer complaint and service recovery	3
3.2 Consumer-generated content	10
3.3 Conspicuous consumption display	6
3.4 Advertising	17
4. Effects of following brands on social media	**39**
4.1 Brand evaluations	9
4.2 actual/intentional purchase	5
4.3 e-WOM	23
4.4 Stock price	2
5. Interpersonal relationships and social media	**10**
Total	103

Consumer Behavior in Social Media

Interpersonal Relationships

Motivators to Follow Brands in Social Media
- Brand antecedents
- Looking for benefits
- Personality traits

Demotivators to Follow Brands in Social Media
- Consumer privacy and security concerns

Consumer–Brand Interactions in Social Media
- Consumer complaint and service recovery
- Consumer-generated content
  – Consumer only
  – Co Created
- Conspicuous consumption display
- Advertising
  – Virality
  – Message composition

Effects of Following Brands in Social Media
- Brand evaluations
- Actual/intentional Purchase
- e–WOM (Word of Mouth)
- Stock price

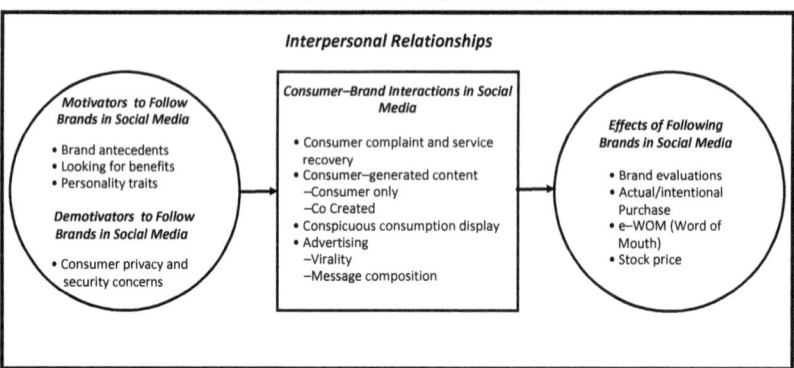

Fig. 17.2 Conceptual model of consumer behavior on social media

the proposed conceptual model. Overall, we propose that the whole body of literature can be grouped into five big categories: (1) motivators for consumers to follow brands on social media, (2) demotivators for consumers to follow brands on social media, (3) the interactions that consumers have with brands on social media, (4) the effects of following brands on social media, and (5) interpersonal relationships on social media, which we argue are an important contextual factor that affects all the previous models. Next, we explain in more detail our conceptual model.

1. Motivators to Follow Brands on Social Media

The motivators for consumers to follow brands on social media represent the antecedents or drivers that make consumers more prone to engage or to get in touch with brands on social media. These motivators can be categorized into brand antecedents, looking for benefits, and personality traits. Table 17.3 shows a systematic summary of the reviewed articles regarding this theme.

1.1 Brand antecedents. Previous research has found that warm brand personalities make consumers more prone to endorse them on social media. Moreover, brand symbolism makes this relationship stronger (Bernritter et al. 2016). Brand trust, brand reputation, brand loyalty, previous attitudes towards the brand, and brand attachment have also been identified as precursors of social media engagement (Chahal and Rani 2017; Chu et al. 2016a; Rapp et al. 2013).

1.2 Looking for benefits. This refers to the benefits obtained by consumers for following brands on social media, that is, the gratifications they receive, such as brand information seeking, entertainment, sales promotions, customer

Table 17.3 Motivators to follow brands on social media: systematic summary of reviewed articles

Sub-theme	References
1.1 Brand antecedents	(Bernritter et al. 2016), (Chahal and Rani 2017), (Chu et al. 2016a), (Rapp et al. 2013), (VanMeter et al. 2015), (Dimitriu and Guesalaga 2017)
1.2 Looking for benefits	(Azar et al. 2016), (Bernritter et al. 2017), (Hamilton et al. 2016a), (Rohm et al. 2013), (Whiting and Williams 2013), (Pöyry et al. 2013), (Heinonen 2011)
1.3 Personality traits	(Chu et al. 2016b)

service, expression of opinion, and personalization or exclusivity (Azar et al. 2016; Hamilton et al. 2016a; Whiting and Williams 2013). More importantly, research has found that consumers follow brands on social media in order to signal their identity with their own followers on social media (Bernritter et al. 2017).

1.3 Personality traits. Consumers who are high on the personality traits of materialism and self-construal have been associated with a higher use of social media (Chu et al. 2016b).

2. Demotivators to Follow Brands on Social Media

Previous research has found that consumer's concerns about their privacy and security make them less likely to follow brands and share their personal information with companies on social media (Mosteller and Poddar 2017; Tucker 2014). Table 17.4 shows a systematic summary of the reviewed articles regarding this theme.

3. Consumer-Brand Interactions on Social Media

Once consumers have decided to follow brands on social media, they can interact with them in several ways. Our model proposes there are four main types of consumer-brand interactions on social media: (1) consumer complaint and service recovery, (2) consumer-generated content, (3) conspicuous consumption display, and (4) advertising. Table 17.5 shows a systematic summary of the reviewed articles regarding this theme.

3.1 Consumer complaint and service recovery. Previous research has found that in response to online complaining, firms must show sincerity and avoid generic recovery messages or efforts. A highly adaptive response is the best recovery for online complaining (Abney et al. 2017). Customers

Table 17.4 Demotivators to follow brands on social media: systematic summary of reviewed articles

Sub-theme	References
2.1 Consumer privacy and security concerns	(Hille et al. 2015), (Mosteller and Poddar 2017), (Pagani and Malacarne 2017), (Tucker 2014)

Table 17.5 Consumer-brand interactions on social media: systematic summary of reviewed articles

Sub-theme	Sub-code	References
3.1 Consumer complaint and service recovery		(Abney et al. 2017), (Ma et al. 2015), (McGraw et al. 2015)
3.2 Consumer-generated content	3.2.1 Consumer only	(Hautz et al. 2014), (Jalali and Papatla 2016), (Kao et al. 2016), (Presi et al. 2016), (Smith et al. 2012)
	3.2.2 Co-created	(Arvidsson and Caliandro 2016), (Kull and Heath 2014), (Liu and Gal 2011), (Singh and Sonnenburg 2012), (Kao et al. 2016)
3.3 Conspicuous consumption display		(Bellezza et al. 2017), (Duan and Dholakia 2017), (Hollenbeck and Kaikati 2012), (Pounders et al. 2016), (Taylor and Strutton 2016), (John et al. 2017)
3.4 Advertising	3.4.1 Virality	(Akpinar and Berger 2017), (Huang et al. 2013), (Koch and Benlian 2015), (Shehu et al. 2016), (Shen et al. 2016), (Zhang et al. 2017a), (Joshi and Trusov 2017), (Fossen et al. 2017)
	3.4.2 Message composition	(Belanche et al. 2017), (Boerman et al. 2017), (Colliander et al. 2015), (De Veirman et al. 2017), (Humphrey et al. 2017), (Kumar et al. 2016), (Luangrath et al. 2017), (Zhang and Mao 2016), (Gretry et al. 2017)

are mainly looking for redress when they complain. Interestingly, redress seeking is not always beneficial for the company since it encourages more complaints later, even if they are not valid complaints (Ma et al. 2015). Previous literature has also explored the tone of complaints on social media. Specifically, it has been found that humorous complaints benefit consumers who want to warn, entertain, and make a favorable impression on others. Nevertheless, since being humorous suggests that a dissatisfying situation is okay, humorous complaints are less likely to elicit redress or sympathy from others than non-humorous complaints (McGraw et al. 2015).

3.2 Consumer-generated content. Consumers sometimes decide to create their own content regarding their brands and share such content on their social media accounts with their own followers. There are two types of consumer-generated content on social media: content created only by the consumer, such as videos, reviews, and even brand selfies (Hautz et al. 2014; Presi et al. 2016), and content co-created between the consumer and the company, such as brand communities and cause-related marketing strategies (Arvidsson and Caliandro 2016; Kull and Heath 2014).

3.3 Conspicuous consumption display. Consumers "show off" their physical possessions and their lifestyles in order to signal their own status among their followers. Previous research has found that consumers show certain brands in order to reflect their ideal self (Hollenbeck and Kaikati 2012). More importantly, it has been found that posting purchases on social media increases happiness (Duan and Dholakia 2017).

3.4 Advertising. This refers to all promotional efforts that consumers see and interact with on social media. Research in this specific matter covers two main topics: (1) the aspects that make a brand message go viral (Joshi and Trusov 2017; Koch and Benlian 2015) and (2) the composition of the message in order to increase its persuasive effects on social media (Gretry et al. 2017; Luangrath et al. 2017).

4. Effects of Following Brands on Social Media

Once consumers have decided to follow brands and have interacted with them on social media, there are several effects for having done so. Our model proposes four broad effects: brand evaluations, actual or intentional purchase, e-WOM (word-of-mouth), and the stock price of the firm in the financial markets. Table 17.6 shows a systematic summary of the reviewed articles regarding this theme.

4.1 Brand evaluations. Previous research has found that social media is associated with enhanced brand evaluations such as brand equity, brand engagement, and even brand love (Beukeboom et al. 2015; Hollebeek et al. 2014; John et al. 2017).

4.2 Actual/Intentional purchase. Previous research has explored the role of social media on actual sales and on purchase intention declared by the consumer. Research in this regard has found mixed results; some studies have found a direct relationship between social media and purchase, while other studies have not found such a relationship or have found a not-so-straightforward effect (Naylor et al. 2012; Zhang et al. 2017b)

4.3 e-WOM. It has also been established that social media is related to a higher willingness to share word-of-mouth on social media (e-WOM) (Chen 2017; Chu and Kim 2011). Moreover, since written communication gives people more time to construct and refine what to say, consumers

Table 17.6 Effects of following brands on social media: systematic summary of reviewed articles

Sub-theme	References
4.1 Brand evaluations	(Beukeboom et al. 2015), (Godey et al. 2016), (Hollebeek et al. 2014), (Hudson et al. 2016), (John et al. 2017), (Chung and Cho 2017), (Ramadan 2017), (Chung and Cho 2017), (Hoffman et al. 2017)
4.2 Actual/intentional purchase	(Hamilton et al. 2016b), (Naylor et al. 2012), (Saboo et al. 2016), (Zhang et al. 2017b), (Kozinets et al. 2017)
4.3 e-WOM	(Amezcua and Quintanilla 2016), (Babić Rosario et al. 2016), (Berger and Iyengar 2013), (Chakravarty et al. 2010), (Chen 2017), (Chu and Kim 2011), (Colliander and Hauge Wien 2013), (Dubois et al. 2016), (Eisingerich et al. 2015), (Hamilton et al. 2017), (Homburg et al. 2015), (Liu et al. 2017), (Marchand et al. 2017), (Poddar et al. 2017), (Prado-Gascó et al. 2017), (Punj 2013), (Rossmann et al. 2016), (Toubia and Stephen 2013), (Wang et al. 2012), (You et al. 2015), (Zhu et al. 2012), (Eelen et al. 2017), (Moore and McFerran 2017)
4.4 Stock price	(McAlister et al. 2012), (Piñeiro-Chousa et al. 2017)

use this opportunity to mention more interesting things when spreading e-WOM than traditional WOM (Berger and Iyengar 2013). Regarding the motivations that make consumers spread e-WOM on their social media accounts, it has been found that social risk is a demotivator for consumers to spread e-WOM but not for traditional WOM (Eisingerich et al. 2015).

4.4 Stock price. Surprisingly, the effect of social media on the stock price of the holding firm has also been studied. Previous literature has found that social media chatter and sentiment influences stock markets (McAlister et al. 2012; Piñeiro-Chousa et al. 2017).

5. Interpersonal Relationships and Social Media

Lastly, our model shows that interpersonal relationships are a major contextual factor that has an important impact on the behavior of consumers on social media. Table 17.7 shows a systematic summary of the reviewed articles regarding this theme. Social media provide a participatory media environment based on the interactive platform; this feature makes social media an effective tool for mobilizing people to participate in social movements. Indeed, previous research has found that participation intent in social movements was higher among those individuals who were more involved with social media (Hwang and Kim 2015). Unfortunately, there

Table 17.7 Interpersonal relationships and social media: systematic summary of reviewed articles

Sub-theme	References
5.1 Interpersonal relationships	(Belk 2013), (Hwang and Kim 2015), (de la Peña and Quintanilla 2015), (Shmargad and Watts 2016), (Wilcox and Stephen 2013), (Barasch et al. 2017), (Bélisle and Bodur 2010), (Park et al. 2015), (David and Roberts 2017), (Ward et al. 2017)

are also negative effects for consumers for using social media. There is evidence suggesting that greater social network use is associated with a higher body mass index, higher levels of credit card debt, and lower levels of self-esteem (Wilcox and Stephen 2013).

Moreover, taking pictures with the intention to share them via social media reduces enjoyment of experiences due to self-presentational concerns (Barasch et al. 2017). Additionally, individuals who are engaged in a conversation and are being ignored by their counterpart for using their cellphone experience a sense of social exclusion, which leads to a heightened need for attention and results in individuals attaching to social media in hopes of regaining a sense of inclusion (David and Roberts 2017). Surprisingly, cellphone and social media usage have also been associated with fewer cognitive resources available for consumers (Ward et al. 2017).

Future Research

We now present the areas of greatest potential for future exploration in this topic. In Table 17.2, we can see that e-WOM leads the investigation in this phenomenon with 23 papers published, followed by advertising, effects of following brands on social media, and motivators to follow brands on social media. The least investigated themes, which still have a lot to offer to the discipline, are conspicuous consumption display on social media, consumer privacy and security concerns, and consumer complaint and service recovery on social media.

We also note that the current literature treats social media as a unique digital environment. Nevertheless, there are several social networking sites with different characteristics and purposes (Meyer Foundation 2015), from chatting to photos to job seeking and even to finding a date. Future research should explore the differences for marketing and brands across all these different sites. Our analysis showed there are mixed results regarding the relationship between social media and purchasing behavior. We believe such relationship is more complex, so further research should apply sophisticated statistical techniques that could reveal a not-so-direct relationship between these two variables.

Wearable tech devices, such as smart watches, have increased in popularity among consumers in recent years (Pitt et al. 2017). Nevertheless, no single research paper has studied the effect of instant social media notifications and feeds on such devices. Future research should explore how social media usage on those devices affects consumers regarding their interactions with brands. Research in the topic of advertising in social media has focused on the advantages. However, we believe there are also several disadvantages for such type of advertising. Consumers, for example, can be annoyed by brands that force them to watch an ad before they can watch a video on YouTube. Future research should address the possible disadvantages for brands when they advertise on social media.

Researchers should also explore the synergies between social media and traditional media. Consumers experience these two environments simultaneously, for example, they can interact with a brand on social media and in a traditional store. Researchers have neglected to study these two environments simultaneously; they have focused only on one environment at a time. Cultural differences are a major topic of interest in consumer behavior (Richard and Habibi 2016). Nevertheless, no previous research has explored how consumer's usage of social media varies across cultures. Future research should study how culture moderates the relationships and frameworks we propose in our model.

The purchasing decision process is perhaps one of the most studied topics in the consumer behavior literature (Hoyer 1984). We believe that social media has strongly impacted this process. Consumers can now access multiples reviews online, ask for opinions on their social media, and even compare brands and prices instantly. Future research should address how social media has changed the purchase decision process. Regarding methodological aspects, we propose that more naturalistic research is necessary (Morales et al. 2017). Our review revealed that experimental research has relied on laboratory experimental designs that seem unrealistic. Future research should take advantage of technology and use a more naturalistic experimental design. Also, we identified that there is a lack of longitudinal research. What is the effect of social media over time? Finally, we found that there are very few qualitative papers on this topic. We argue that more qualitative research is needed in order to fully understand possible underlying mechanisms and contextual factors.

Conclusion

Given the rising amount of research on the topic of consumer behavior on social media, we carried out a systematic review of the literature regarding this marketing phenomenon. Over the past seven years, consumers have experienced a major change in their consumption behaviors due to the increased usage of social media in their everyday lives. After identifying and reviewing 103 academic papers regarding this topic, we conducted a coding analysis and identified five broad themes. We then proposed an integrative model that illustrates and summarizes the state of the art of the current literature on the topic of consumer behavior on social media.

Our proposed conceptual model focuses on how consumers and brands interact in these new digital environments. We conclude this chapter by affirming that social media has been and will continue to be an important medium that has changed how consumers behave. Our hope is that our research provides useful insights about the way consumers behave on social media and inspires more research on this topic in order to fully understand how consumers behave on social media.

References

Abney, A. K., Pelletier, M. J., Ford, T.-R. S., & Horky, A. B. (2017). #IHateYourBrand: Adaptive service recovery strategies on twitter. *Journal of Services Marketing, 31*(3), 281–294.

Akpinar, E., & Berger, J. (2017). Valuable virality. *Journal of Marketing Research, 54*(2), 318–330.

Amezcua, B., & Quintanilla, C. (2016). When eWOM becomes cynical. *International Journal of Consumer Studies, 40*(3), 290–298.

Arvidsson, A., & Caliandro, A. (2016). Brand public. *Journal of Consumer Research, 42*(5), 727–748.

Azar, S. L., Machado, J. C., Vacas-De-Carvalho, L., & Mendes, A. (2016). Motivations to interact with brands on Facebook – Towards a typology of consumer-brand interactions. *Journal of Brand Management, 23*(2), 153–178.

Babić Rosario, A., Sotgiu, F., De Valck, K., & Bijmolt, T. H. A. (2016). The effect of electronic word of mouth on sales: A meta-analytic review of platform, product, and metric factors. *Journal of Marketing Research, 53*(3), 297–318.

Barasch, A., Zauberman, G., & Diehl, K. (2017). How the intention to share can undermine enjoyment: Photo-taking goals and evaluation of experiences. *Journal of Consumer Research, 44*(6), 1220–1237.

Belanche, D., Flavián, C., & Pérez-Rueda, A. (2017). Understanding interactive online advertising: Congruence and product involvement in highly and lowly arousing, skippable video ads. *Journal of Interactive Marketing, 37*, 75–88.

Bélisle, J. F., & Bodur, H. O. (2010). Avatars as information: Perception of consumers based on their avatars in virtual worlds. *Psychology and Marketing, 27*(8), 741–765.

Belk, R. W. (2013). Extended self in a digital world: Table 1. *Journal of Consumer Research, 40*(3), 477–500.

Bellezza, S., Paharia, N., & Keinan, A. (2017). Conspicuous consumption of time: When busyness and lack of leisure time become a status symbol. *Journal of Consumer Research, 44*(1), 118–138.

Berger, J., & Iyengar, R. (2013). Communication channels and word of mouth: How the medium shapes the message. *Journal of Consumer Research, 40*(3), 567–579.

Bernritter, S. F., Verlegh, P. W. J., & Smit, E. G. (2016). Why nonprofits are easier to endorse on social media: The roles of warmth and brand symbolism. *Journal of Interactive Marketing, 33*, 27–42.

Bernritter, S. F., Loermans, A. C., Verlegh, P. W. J., & Smit, E. G. (2017). "We" are more likely to endorse than "I": The effects of self-construal and brand symbolism on consumers' online brand endorsements. *International Journal of Advertising, 36*(1), 107–120.

Beukeboom, C. J., Kerkhof, P., & de Vries, M. (2015). Does a virtual like cause actual liking? How following a brand's facebook updates enhances brand evaluations and purchase intention. *Journal of Interactive Marketing, 32*, 26–36.

Boerman, S. C., Willemsen, L. M., & Van Der Aa, E. P. (2017). "This post is sponsored": Effects of sponsorship disclosure on persuasion knowledge and electronic word of mouth in the context of Facebook. *Journal of Interactive Marketing, 38*, 82–92.

Chahal, H., & Rani, A. (2017). How trust moderates social media engagement and brand equity. *Journal of Research in Interactive Marketing, 11*(3), 312–335.

Chakravarty, A., Liu, Y., & Mazumdar, T. (2010). The differential effects of online word-of-mouth and critics' reviews on pre-release movie evaluation. *Journal of Interactive Marketing, 24*(3), 185–197.

Chen, Z. (2017). Social acceptance and word of mouth: How the motive to belong leads to divergent WOM with strangers and friends. *Journal of Consumer Research, 44*(3), 613–632.

Chu, S. C., & Kim, Y. (2011). Determinants of consumer engagement in electronic word-of-mouth (eWOM) in social networking sites. *International Journal of Advertising, 30*(1), 47–75.

Chu, S. C., Chen, H. T., & Sung, Y. (2016a). Following brands on twitter: An extension of theory of planned behavior. *International Journal of Advertising, 35*(3), 421–437.

Chu, S. C., Windels, K., & Kamal, S. (2016b). The influence of self-construal and materialism on social media intensity: A study of China and the United States. *International Journal of Advertising*, *35*(3), 569–588.

Chung, S., & Cho, H. (2017). Fostering parasocial relationships with celebrities on social media: Implications for celebrity endorsement. *Psychology and Marketing*, *34*(4), 481–495.

Colliander, J., & Hauge Wien, A. (2013). Trash talk rebuffed: Consumers' defense of companies criticized in online communities. *European Journal of Marketing*, *47*(10), 1733–1757.

Colliander, J., Dahlén, M., & Modig, E. (2015). Twitter for two: Investigating the effects of dialogue with customers in social media. *International Journal of Advertising*, *34*(2), 181–194.

David, M. E., & Roberts, J. A. (2017). Phubbed and alone: Phone snubbing, social exclusion, and attachment to social media. *Journal of the Association for Consumer Research*, *2*(2), 155–163.

De Veirman, M., Cauberghe, V., & Hudders, L. (2017). Marketing through instagram influencers: The impact of number of followers and product divergence on brand attitude. *International Journal of Advertising*, *36*(5), 798–828.

Dimitriu, R., & Guesalaga, R. (2017). Consumers??? Social media brand behaviors: Uncovering underlying motivators and deriving meaningful consumer segments. *Psychology and Marketing*, *34*(5), 580–592.

Duan, J., & Dholakia, R. (2017). Posting purchases on social media increases happiness: The mediating roles of purchases' impact on self and interpersonal relationships. *Journal of Consumer Marketing*, *34*(5), 404–413.

Dubois, D., Bonezzi, A., & De Angelis, M. (2016). Sharing with friends versus strangers: How interpersonal closeness influences word-of-mouth valence. *Journal of Marketing Research*, *53*(5), 712–727.

Eelen, J., Özturan, P., & Verlegh, P. W. J. (2017). The differential impact of brand loyalty on traditional and online word of mouth: The moderating roles of self-brand connection and the desire to help the brand. *International Journal of Research in Marketing*, *34*, 872–891.

Eisingerich, A. B., Chun, H. E. H., Liu, Y., Jia, H. M., & Bell, S. J. (2015). Why recommend a brand face-to-face but not on Facebook? How word-of-mouth on online social sites differs from traditional word-of-mouth. *Journal of Consumer Psychology*, *25*(1), 120–128.

Fossen, B., Andrews, M., & Schweidel, D. (2017). Sociodemographic versus geographic proximity in the diffusion of online conversations. *Journal of the Association for Consumer Research*, *2*(2), 246–266.

Foundation, M. (2015). *Social media platform comparison*. Washington, DC: Meyer Foundation Press.

Godey, B., Manthiou, A., Pederzoli, D., Rokka, J., Aiello, G., Donvito, R., & Singh, R. (2016). Social media marketing efforts of luxury brands: Influence on brand equity and consumer behavior. *Journal of Business Research*, *69*(12), 5833–5841.

Gretry, A., Horváth, C., Belei, N., & van Riel, A. C. R. (2017). "Don't pretend to be my friend!" when an informal brand communication style backfires on social media. *Journal of Business Research, 74*, 77–89.

Hamilton, M., Kaltcheva, V. D., & Rohm, A. J. (2016a). Hashtags and handshakes: Consumer motives and platform use in brand-consumer interactions. *Journal of Consumer Marketing, 33*(2), 135–144.

Hamilton, M., Kaltcheva, V. D., & Rohm, A. J. (2016b). Social media and value creation: The role of interaction satisfaction and interaction immersion. *Journal of Interactive Marketing, 36*, 121–133.

Hamilton, R. W., Schlosser, A., & Chen, Y.-J. (2017). Who's driving this conversation? Systematic biases in the content of online consumer discussions. *Journal of Marketing Research, 54*(4), 540–555.

Hautz, J., Füller, J., Hutter, K., & Thürridl, C. (2014). Let users generate your video ads? The impact of video source and quality on consumers' perceptions and intended behaviors. *Journal of Interactive Marketing, 28*(1), 1–15.

Heinonen, K. (2011). Consumer activity in social media: Managerial approaches to consumers' social media behavior. *Journal of Consumer Behaviour, 10*(6), 356–364.

Hille, P., Walsh, G., & Cleveland, M. (2015). Consumer fear of online identity theft: Scale development and validation. *Journal of Interactive Marketing, 30*, 1–19.

Hoffman, D. L., Novak, T. P., & Kang, H. (2017). Let's get closer: Feelings of connectedness from using social media, with implications for brand outcomes. *Journal of the Association for Consumer Research, 2*(2), 216–228.

Hollebeek, L. D., Glynn, M. S., & Brodie, R. J. (2014). Consumer brand engagement in social media: Conceptualization, scale development and validation. *Journal of Interactive Marketing, 28*(2), 149–165.

Hollenbeck, C. R., & Kaikati, A. M. (2012). Consumers' use of brands to reflect their actual and ideal selves on Facebook. *International Journal of Research in Marketing, 29*(4), 395–405.

Homburg, C., Ehm, L., & Artz, M. (2015). Measuring and managing consumer sentiment in an online community environment. *Journal of Marketing Research, 52*(5), 629–641.

Hoyer, W. D. (1984). An examination of consumer decision making for a common repeat purchase product. *Journal of Consumer Research, 11*(3), 822.

Huang, J., Su, S., Zhou, L., & Liu, X. (2013). Attitude toward the viral ad: Expanding traditional advertising models to interactive advertising. *Journal of Interactive Marketing, 27*(1), 36–46.

Hudson, S., Huang, L., Roth, M. S., & Madden, T. J. (2016). The influence of social media interactions on consumer-brand relationships: A three-country study of brand perceptions and marketing behaviors. *International Journal of Research in Marketing, 33*(1), 27–41.

Humphrey Jr., W. F., Laverie, D. A., & Rinaldo, S. B. (2017). Brand choice via incidental social media exposure. *Journal of Research in Interactive Marketing*, *11*(2), 110–130.

Hwang, H., & Kim, K.-O. (2015). Social media as a tool for social movements: The effect of social media use and social capital on intention to participate in social movements. *International Journal of Consumer Studies*, *39*(5), 478–488.

Jalali, N. Y., & Papatla, P. (2016). The palette that stands out: Color compositions of online curated visual UGC that attracts higher consumer interaction. *Quantitative Marketing and Economics*, *14*(4), 353–384.

John, L. K., Emrich, O., Gupta, S., & Norton, M. I. (2017). Does "liking" lead to loving? The impact of joining a brand's social network on marketing outcomes. *Journal of Marketing Research*, *54*(1), 144–155.

Joshi, A. M., & Trusov, M. (2017). Are you a "viral star"? Conceptualizing and modeling inter-media virality. *Journal of the Association for Consumer Research*, *2*(2), 196–215.

Kao, T.-Y., Yang, M.-H., Wu, J.-T. B., & Cheng, Y.-Y. (2016). Co-creating value with consumers through social media. *Journal of Services Marketing*, *30*(2), 141–151.

Kemp, S. (2017). Number of social media users passes 3 billion with no signs of slowing. Retrieved from https://thenextweb.com/contributors/2017/08/07/number-social-media-users-passes-3-billion-no-signs-slowing.

Koch, O. F., & Benlian, A. (2015). Promotional tactics for online viral marketing campaigns: How scarcity and personalization affect seed stage referrals. *Journal of Interactive Marketing*, *32*, 37–52.

Kozinets, R., Patterson, A., & Ashman, R. (2017). Networks of desire: How technology increases our passion to consume. *Journal of Consumer Research*, *43*(5), 659–682.

Kull, A. J., & Heath, T. B. (2014). You decide, we donate: Strengthening consumer-brand relationships through digitally co-created social responsibility. *International Journal of Research in Marketing*, *33*(1), 78–92.

Kumar, A., Bezawada, R., Rishika, R., Janakiraman, R., & Kannan, P. K. (2016). From social to sale: The effects of firm-generated content in social media on customer behavior. *Journal of Marketing*, *80*(1), 7–25.

de la Peña, A. S., & Quintanilla, C. (2015). Share, like and achieve: The power of Facebook to reach health-related goals. *International Journal of Consumer Studies*, *39*(5), 495–505.

Liu, W., & Gal, D. (2011). Bringing us together or driving us apart: The effect of soliciting consumer input on consumers' propensity to transact with an organization. *Journal of Consumer Research*, *38*(2), 242–259.

Liu, X., Hu, J., & Xu, B. (2017). Does eWOM matter to brand extension? *Journal of Research in Interactive Marketing*, *11*(3), 232–245.

Luangrath, A. W., Peck, J., & Barger, V. A. (2017). Textual paralanguage and its implications for marketing communications. *Journal of Consumer Psychology, 27*(1), 98–107.

Ma, L., Sun, B., & Kekre, S. (2015). The squeaky wheel gets the grease – An empirical analysis of customer voice and firm intervention on twitter. *Marketing Science, 34*(5), 627–645.

Marchand, A., Hennig-Thurau, T., & Wiertz, C. (2017). Not all digital word of mouth is created equal: Understanding the respective impact of consumer reviews and microblogs on new product success. *International Journal of Research in Marketing, 34*(2), 336–354.

McAlister, L., Sonnier, G., & Shively, T. (2012). The relationship between online chatter and firm value. *Marketing Letters, 23*(1), 1–12.

McGraw, A. P., Warren, C., & Kan, C. (2015). Humorous complaining. *Journal of Consumer Research, 41*(5), 1153–1171.

Moore, S., & McFerran, B. (2017). She said, she said: Differential interpersonal similarities predict unique linguistic mimicry in online word of mouth. *Journal of the Association for Consumer Research, 2*(2), 229–245.

Morales, A. C., Amir, O., & Lee, L. (2017). Keeping it real in experimental research-understanding when, where, and how to enhance realism and measure consumer behavior. *Journal of Consumer Research, 44*(2), 465–476.

Mosteller, J., & Poddar, A. (2017). To share and protect: Using regulatory focus theory to examine the privacy paradox of consumers' social media engagement and online privacy protection behaviors. *Journal of Interactive Marketing, 39*, 27–38.

Naylor, R. W., Lamberton, C. P., & West, P. M. (2012). Beyond the "like" button: The impact of mere virtual presence on brand evaluations and purchase intentions in social media settings. *Journal of Marketing, 76*(6), 105–120.

Pagani, M., & Malacarne, G. (2017). Experiential engagement and active vs. passive behavior in mobile location-based social networks: The moderating role of privacy. *Journal of Interactive Marketing, 37*, 133–148.

Park, M. S., Shin, J. K., & Ju, Y. (2015). A taxonomy of social networking site users: Social surveillance and self-surveillance perspective. *Psychology and Marketing, 32*(6), 601–610.

Perrin, A. (2015). *Social media usage*. Washington, DC: Pew Research Center.

Piñeiro-Chousa, J., Vizcaíno-González, M., & Pérez-Pico, A. M. (2017). Influence of social media over the stock market. *Psychology & Marketing, 34*(1), 101–108.

Pitt, L., Kietzmann, R., Robson, K., Plangger, K., Treen, E., Paschen, J., & Hannah, D. (2017). Understanding the opportunities and challenges of wearable technology. In *Creating marketing magic and innovative future marketing trends* (pp. 139–141). Cham: Springer.

Poddar, A., Banerjee, S., & Sridhar, K. (2017). False advertising or slander? Using location based tweets to assess online rating-reliability. *Journal of Business Research*, 0–1. Retrieved from https://www.sciencedirect.com/science/article/abs/pii/S0148296317302941.

Pounders, K., Kowalczyk, C. M., & Stowers, K. (2016). Insight into the motivation of selfie postings: Impression management and self-esteem. *European Journal of Marketing, 50*(9/10), 1879–1892.

Pöyry, E., Parvinen, P., & Malmivaara, T. (2013). Can we get from liking to buying? Behavioral differences in hedonic and utilitarian Facebook usage. *Electronic Commerce Research and Applications, 12*(4), 224–235.

Prado-Gascó, V., Calabuig Moreno, F., Añó Sanz, V., Núñez-Pomar, J., & Crespo Hervás, J. (2017). To post or not to post: Social media sharing and sporting event performance. *Psychology and Marketing, 34*(11), 995–1003.

Presi, C., Maehle, N., & Kleppe, I. A. (2016). Brand selfies: Consumer experiences and marketplace conversations. *European Journal of Marketing, 50*(9/10), 1814–1834.

Punj, G. N. (2013). Do consumers who conduct online research also post online reviews? A model of the relationship between online research and review posting behavior. *Marketing Letters, 24*(1), 97–108.

Ramadan, Z. (2017). Examining the dilution of the consumer-brand relationship on Facebook: The saturation issue. *Qualitative Market Research: An International Journal, 20*(3), 335–353.

Rapp, A., Beitelspacher, L. S., Grewal, D., & Hughes, D. E. (2013). Understanding social media effects across seller, retailer, and consumer interactions. *Journal of the Academy of Marketing Science, 41*(5), 547–566.

Richard, M. O., & Habibi, M. R. (2016). Advanced modeling of online consumer behavior: The moderating roles of hedonism and culture. *Journal of Business Research, 69*(3), 1103–1119.

Rohm, A., Kaltcheva, V. D., & Milne, G. R. (2013). A mixed-method approach to examining brand-consumer interactions driven by social media. *Journal of Research in Interactive Marketing, 7*(4), 295–311.

Rossmann, A., Ranjan, K. R., & Sugathan, P. (2016). Drivers of user engagement in eWoM communication. *Journal of Services Marketing, 30*(5), 541–553.

Saboo, A. R., Kumar, V., & Ramani, G. (2016). Evaluating the impact of social media activities on human brand sales. *International Journal of Research in Marketing, 33*(3), 524–541.

Sharma, A., & Sheth, J. N. (2004). Web-based marketing: The coming revolution in marketing thought and strategy. *Journal of Business Research, 57*(7), 696–702.

Shehu, E., Bijmolt, T. H. A., & Clement, M. (2016). Effects of likeability dynamics on consumers' intention to share online video advertisements. *Journal of Interactive Marketing, 35*, 27–43.

Shen, G. C.-C., Chiou, J.-S., Hsiao, C.-H., Wang, C.-H., & Li, H.-N. (2016). Effective marketing communication via social networking site: The moderating role of the social tie. *Journal of Business Research, 69*(6), 2265–2270.

Shmargad, Y., & Watts, J. K. M. (2016). When online visibility deters social interaction: The case of digital gifts. *Journal of Interactive Marketing, 36*, 1–14.

Singh, S., & Sonnenburg, S. (2012). Brand performances in social media. *Journal of Interactive Marketing, 26*(4), 189–197.

Smith, A. N., Fischer, E., & Yongjian, C. (2012). How does brand-related user-generated content differ across YouTube, Facebook, and twitter? *Journal of Interactive Marketing, 26*(2), 102–113.

Spiggle, S. (1994). Analysis and interpretation of qualitative data in consumer research. *Journal of Consumer Research, 21*(3), 491.

Taylor, D. G., & Strutton, D. (2016). Does Facebook usage lead to conspicuous consumption? *Journal of Research in Interactive Marketing, 10*(3), 231–248.

Toubia, O., & Stephen, A. T. (2013). Intrinsic vs. image-related utility in social media: Why do people contribute content to twitter? *Marketing Science, 32*(3), 368–392.

Tucker, C. E. (2014). Social networks, personalized advertising, and privacy controls. *Journal of Marketing Research, 51*(5), 546–562.

VanMeter, R. A., Grisaffe, D. B., & Chonko, L. B. (2015). Of "likes" and "pins": The effects of consumers' attachment to social media. *Journal of Interactive Marketing, 32,* 70–88.

Wang, X., Yu, C., & Wei, Y. (2012). Social media peer communication and impacts on purchase intentions: A consumer socialization framework. *Journal of Interactive Marketing, 26*(4), 198–208.

Ward, A. F., Duke, K., Gneezy, A., & Bos, M. W. (2017). Brain drain: The mere presence of one's own smartphone reduces available cognitive capacity. *Journal of the Association for Consumer Research, 2*(2), 140–154.

Whiting, A., & Williams, D. (2013). Why people use social media: A uses and gratifications approach. *Qualitative Market Research: An International Journal, 16*(4), 362–369.

Wilcox, K., & Stephen, A. T. (2013). Are close friends the enemy? Online social networks, self-esteem, and self-control. *Journal of Consumer Research, 40*(1), 90–103.

You, Y., Vadakkepatt, G. G., & Joshi, A. M. (2015). A meta-analysis of electronic word-of-mouth elasticity. *Journal of Marketing, 79*(2), 19–39.

Zhang, J., & Mao, E. (2016). From online motivations to ad clicks and to behavioral intentions: An empirical study of consumer response to social media advertising. *Psychology & Marketing, 33*(3), 155–164.

Zhang, Y., Moe, W. W., & Schweidel, D. A. (2017a). Modeling the role of message content and influencers in social media rebroadcasting. *International Journal of Research in Marketing, 34*(1), 100–119.

Zhang, Y., Trusov, M., Stephen, A. T., & Jamal, Z. (2017b). Online shopping and social media: Friends or foes? Journal of Marketing, *81* (November), jm.14, 0344.

Zhu, R., Dholakia, U. M., Chen, X., & Algesheimer, R. (2012). Does online community participation foster risky financial behavior? *Journal of Marketing Research, 49*(3), 394–407.

CHAPTER 18

Diffusion of Reverse Innovations across Markets: An Agent-Based Model

Pável Reyes-Mercado

THE NEED TO UNDERSTAND THE DIFFUSION OF REVERSE INNOVATIONS ACROSS MARKETS

The analysis of business efforts to internationalize the sales of novel products is pervasive across practitioners and academics. The traditional business perspective stands that innovative products are conceptualized and designed in a developed country. The further diffusion process in which Multi-National Companies (MNC) have relied is to find new market segments outside of the original country, that is, in developing countries. Reverse innovations have the potential of disrupting the way business operates and commerce is exchanged around the world, but it is not clear how such an innovation diffuses across countries. For example, research is needed to understand how products like 'chotuKool', an affordable, low-energy-consumption portable cooler that was firstly launched in India to attend to the needs of rural families (WIPO 2013), can diffuse to developed countries. The typical family in the rural landscape in India cannot afford large refrigerators due mainly to two restrictions. The first of them is price. While urban families may have enough

---

P. Reyes-Mercado (✉)
Anahuac University, Mexico City, Mexico

© The Author(s) 2019
Rajagopal, R. Behl (eds.), *Business Governance and Society*,
https://doi.org/10.1007/978-3-319-94613-9_18

family income to afford large, branded, high-energy consumption refrigerators, rural families may not be able to access such appliances. However, they can afford a product like chotuKool, which has a price point of less than one third of a commercial refrigerator. The second reason is electricity coverage. While India has doubled electricity overage since 2000 (The Hindu 2017), there are still 240 million who lack access to electricity (Bloomberg 2017). This limits the diffusion of new mainstream products. Other innovative products, often regarded as reverse innovations or frugal innovations, have been launched in emerging countries, such as China. Academic literature has gathered case studies on frugal and reverse innovation. Such is the example of Hang et al. (2010) who discuss how four innovative products that fall into the category of disruptive innovations diffused from developing countries to developed countries. In the literature, there are also frameworks aimed to understand how innovations flow across borders. For example, Hossain et al. (2016) argue that frugal innovations—affordable, sustainable, easy-to-use new products built in business environments under scarce resources—start to diffuse locally and then flow towards closely related business spaces. If successful, the innovation reaches places that are more distant and finally, it reaches a stage of reverse diffusion when the product lands in a developed country.

The concept of reverse innovation has recently received attention from researchers and practitioners. As reverse innovations have similar patters to frugal innovations (both are born in an emerging country and then jump into more developed ones), there is a need to understand how such innovation diffuses across two very different markets with contrasting socio-economic, cultural, and behavioral settings. This chapter analyzes the two-stage diffusion pattern, first in a developing economy and then in developed countries using controlled (paid advertising messages) and uncontrolled marketing influences (word of mouth) as diffusion leverages. Specifically, this chapter aims to analyze two intertwined phenomena:

1. Simulated adoption decisions of a reverse innovation of consumers in a developing and a developed country, and
2. the temporal diffusion patterns of a reverse innovation in a developing and a developed country.

This chapter is one of the first attempts to gain knowledge on how reverse innovation diffusion may flow from a developing country towards a developed country. Most studies on adoption of innovation follow the standard methodological focus of linear transversal studies, but the diffusion patterns are inherently non-linear. Results from this study reveal that the differentiated reverse diffusion patterns across countries call for the implementation of ambidexterity commercialization strategies.

The following section discusses the theoretical and empirical aspects of existing literature on reverse innovation. Section "Methodological Approach" details the underlying logic of an agent-based model and explains the parameters utilized to tune it. Section "Complexities Unveiled in the Diffusion of Reverse Innovations" discusses the results of the experiments performed using the ABM. Finally, section "The Need for an Ambidexterity Strategy" discusses the managerial implications of the insights. Finally, section "Conclusion" closes with some study limitations and proposes some avenues for further research.

What We Know So Far on Reverse Innovations

Similarities and Differences Among Innovations Born in Developing Countries

Research on the stream of diffusion of innovations analyzes how new products, messages, and social practices spread in a given market over time. As a sociologically coined concept, diffusion of innovations (Rogers 2010) draws on a broad range of social influences that goes from social influences, endogenous conditions, and normative beliefs to marketing practices. Diffusion of innovations departs from the critical aspect that social interactions drive adoption of products or practices.

The rising growth of markets in developing countries has attracted the attention of academics who have proposed a number of frameworks to analyze the business stages of development of an innovation, launch to market, consumer adoption, and further diffusion. In this way, disruptive innovation theory (Christensen 1997), frugal innovation (Zeschky et al. 2011), and reverse innovation (Immelt et al. 2009) were born. All these theories have as a commonality the design and development of products for a market that focuses mainly on price rather than performance. What is also noteworthy is that these theories call for a change of commerce patterns between developing and developed countries. Furthermore, many other concepts have been coined. For example, resource constrained innovation (Ray and Ray 2011), cost innovation (Zeng and Williamson 2007), and Gandhian innovation (Prahalad and Mashelkar 2010). The wide number of concepts shows that the academic debate on how innovations are coined and framed is not over. Rather, many products may fit into more than one of the definitions and, therefore, become interchangeable.

A reverse innovation is a low-price, low-performance product first developed and adopted in a developing country to then encroach to more developed countries (Immelt et al. 2009). When these academics coined the term reverse innovation, they realized that a low price for a reverse innovation in a developing country does not necessarily imply that it lacks technological development or that it is a low-performance product. The challenging aspect for reverse innovation to be adopted in two contrasting markets is that while it may be adopted and diffused in a developing country, the product may present challenges when being marketed in more developed countries. The concept of reverse innovation seems similar to the term 'disruptive innovation' (Christensen et al. 2015) in that both refer to low cost, low performance, and high user-friendliness. Furthermore, both innovations initiate in unattended, fringe, and unprofitable markets in which consumers' preferences tend to favor ease of use over complexity, as the latter product feature is commonly associated with higher price points (Christensen 1997). The difference between concepts lies in the fact that disruptive innovations move from a fringe to a mainstream market with the consequence of creating new value networks whereas a reverse innovation departs from markets with economic, legal, environmental, and business structural gaps to developed, mature markets with more affluent sophisticated consumers in different countries. The preceiding suggests that the diffusion patterns may run at different paces, depending on consumers' perceptions of the reverse innovation's attributes (Kapoor et al. 2014). When developing countries liberalized their energy, manufacturing, and banking industries, the attention of MNCs emphasized the mergers and acquisitions to gain access to low cost of labor and inputs. However, under the perspectives of disruptive innovation, frugal innovation, and reverse innovation, the implication for commerce is that flow is changed in a way that MNCs in developing countries are now able to push products towards developed countries in a more autonomous way.

To clarify the theoretical discussion in this chapter, we adhere to the definitions of reverse innovation and frugal innovation as argued by Nunes and Breene (2011). While a product designed from the perspective of frugal innovation refers to innovations explicitly designed for low-income market segments, the focus of a reverse innovation lies in the fact that such product is afterwards altered to suit the needs of market segments in a developed country (Nunes and Breene 2011). The following Bass model utilizes this definition of reverse innovation.

The Bass Model

Diffusion of innovations relies heavily on the Bass model (Bass et al. 1994), which introduces the influences of mass media and word of mouth on individual adoption decisions. At the market level, individual decisions take the shape of S-curves. While the original Bass model refers to aggregate responses, using ABMs allows for substantiating the role of external influences on consumers' decisions. A conceptual model for the Bass model is presented in Fig. 18.1, in which the consumer receives influences of mass media and word of mouth before deciding the adoption of a reverse innovation. Recent academic attention (Peres et al. 2010) to continue the use of such mathematical models proposes the use of agent-based models to analyze the diffusion of innovation across markets. Specifically, cross-country influences, growth differences across countries, and competition and growth (Peres et al. 2010).

Fig. 18.1 Conceptual model for adoption of reverse innovations. Source: Adapted from Delre et al. (2010)

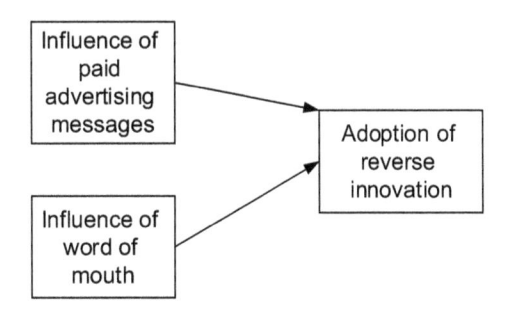

Methodological Approach

The study of diffusion of innovations has followed two main research streams. The first of them involves the use of cross-sectional, one-time studies that analyze the exogenous and endogenous antecedents that lead to innovation adoption. While these studies commonly involve the use of structural models, the temporal dimension is absent. Hence, little can be known on how an innovation diffuses in time. Under this perspective, the researcher needs a clear picture of the diffusion stages the innovation is into. Otherwise, results only show small effects of antecedent variables on adoption. The second stream refers to mathematical modelling of social phenomena, which has gained academic attention since the 1960s. The Bass model (Bass et al. 1994) depicts the diffusion of any given innovation as an epidemiological (contagion) process under the influence of external influences. While the Bass model provides a differential-equation generalization of the diffusion process at the aggregate level, it lacks the features that permit the analysis of direct consumer decisions. Besides, performing experiments with such simultaneous mathematical formulas becomes complex.

Departing from the mainstream economic perspective that assumes consumer homogeneity, equilibrium-like conditions, and highly rational consumers, ABMs have the capacity of modelling temporal heterogeneous consumer behaviors subject to external influences and embedded in evolving complex adaptive systems (Kiesling et al. 2012). ABM models heterogeneous consumers as well as external influences. Different types of social networks can be used to understand innovation diffusion in varying social settings. ABMs have been used mainly in marketing to analyze individual-level models that can be scaled to explain collective phenomena. Specifically, ABMs are useful to analyze the heterogeneous decision making on adoption decisions as well as how these decisions diffuse in different structures of social networks. Hence, the technique is suitable to analyze the adoption of new products.

Framing the ABM

As the focus of this chapter is to understand the interactions between heterogeneous consumers' decisions, other consumers' messages, and paid advertising messages, as well as a high number of consumers and interactions, ABMs represents one of the best model methods to answer the research question. Another motive to select ABM is that this chapter focuses also on the analysis of temporal patterns embedded in complex social networks.

The following methodological discussion addresses all aspects of ABM rigorous modelling. In this discussion, we followed the guidelines of Macal and North (2010) regarding the simulation steps and from Rand and Rust (2011) for the application to marketing, that is, to the adoption decision. In the proposed ABM, the consumer is related to many other consumers as they all participate in a defined social network and they exchange word-of-mouth messages. The ABM assumes two geographically distant countries: one developed country and one developing country in which a reverse innovation is first launched in the developing country to then be launched in a developed country. The environment in which consumers are embedded is a social network in which the consumers interact, and was modelled as a preferential attachment network. This network is scale-free, that is, the number of links for each consumer follows a power law (Barabási and Albert 1999). The types of social networks have only very recently started to be included in analyses of adoption and diffusion despite the existence of analytical techniques that have been around for a long time (Delre et al. 2010). There are influential consumers who can interrelate to other consumers and have an effect on regular consumer's decisions. As consumers are modelled as agents who take the decision of adopting a reverse innovation, their observable behaviour is adoption.

We formulated an ABM based on the Bass model in a sequential two-stage computational experiment design, one for a developing country in which the reverse innovation is born, and the other for launching of such reverse innovation in a developed country. For sake of parsimony, the ABM does not consider other influences as those internal to the consumer (personality traits, impulsiveness, etc.) and interaction effects with other products and decisions. Agents in the ABM refer to consumers in a developing country and consumers acting in a developed country. In modelling the number of agents, a proxy on the populations of the developing and developed countries were be considered (imagine 1000 consumers for a 1 billion population like India and 300 consumers for a country like the United States or Europe). A small amount of consumers represents early adopters with influence upon other consumers. That is, there are some consumers who spread word of mouth about the innovation and other consumers who receive the messages and so their adoption decision is influenced. Each agent in the model is subject to develop an adoption probability, based on word of mouth and paid advertising messages. Consumers exchange messages with adjacent consumers in the social network. Agents make an adoption decision, which is a function of the mass media influence and the number of adjacent consumers and early adopters in the social network. The environment in which consumers interact is a simulated social network and was modelled as a preferential attachment network. This network is scale free, that is, the number of links (connections between two consumers) follows a power law. To create this network, new consumers and links are added to the existing ones, so the consumers with more connections with other consumers are more likely to receive new connections (Barabási and Albert 1999). This type of network was selected because it resembles the way people interact on the Internet.

The inputs for the ABM represent the simulated parameters for word of mouth, paid advertising messages, and the type of networks. The output data represents the count of adopters per each time step. The ABM is run using discrete time steps in which agents interact with other agents and their environment according to the previous pre-specified rules. In each time step, a number of agents are initialized and the network created; the agent decides if it will adopt the reverse innovation due to the influence of word of mouth or mass media or, alternatively, if it will not adopt it at all. If the agent adopts, the agents' properties will be updated so in the next time step, adjacent agents can know if their neighbors have adopted. This process repeats until all agents have adopted.

Constructing the ABM

During initialization, the number of agents is set and then they are interconnected in the type of network according to a parameter of density. The parameters of word of mouth and paid advertising messages are also set. Initially, agents have not adopted. Agents who have not yet adopted decide whether to adopt if a randomly generated variable is lower than the value set for the influence of paid advertising messages or if the value of another random variable is lower than the weighted influence of word of mouth from neighbour agents (adopters and non-adopters). The number of adopters is stored at each time step. The iterative process is continued and terminated when all agents have adopted. The ABM was implemented using NetLogo 6.0.2 with default settings. The pseudocode and source code for the AMB is available upon author request. Figure 18.2 presents a flowchart for the ABM.

Fig. 18.2 Agent-Based Model implementation for adoption of reverse innovations. Source: Author

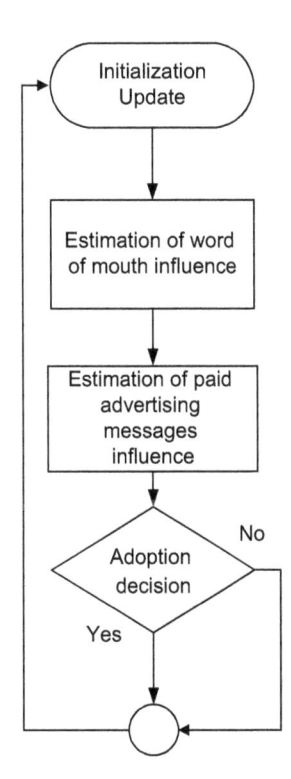

Verification of the ABM

Before utilizing the model for experimental purposes, verification and validation should be addressed. Verification refers to assuring that the ABM corresponds to the conceptual model. To conduct the verification assessment, the complete model was documented; several code walkthroughs were performed to ensure each routine in the code. Finally, the code was tested using extreme cases. For example, paid advertising messages and word of mouth influences were set to zero, so the model resulted in zero adopters. Separate incremental values of word of mouth and paid advertising messages (in 0.1 steps starting from 0.0 and finishing at 1.0) were carried out and results in adopters were consistent with the Bass model's formulation. Hence, the model can be considered as verified.

Validating the ABM

Validation refers to how well the ABM represents reality. Validations procedures are performed for each parameter of the model as well as the overall patterns. Similarly, an empirical comparison of input and output data against the real world completes the validation assessment. The proposed ABM uses the influence of word of mouth and paid advertising messages in terms of probabilities that range from 0 to 1. As the ABM is parameterized into such range, each of the parameters is valid (micro face validation). The overall response of the model refers to S-curves of diffusion, which is consistent with the mathematical formulation of the Bass model (macro face validation).

COMPLEXITIES UNVEILED IN THE DIFFUSION OF REVERSE INNOVATIONS

For the diffusion of a reverse innovation in the developing country, this study assumed 1000 consumers with a density of relationships of 0.1. Two free ABM parameters were modelled: word of mouth and paid advertising. For the developed country, 300 consumers were included in the simulations with a density of relationships of 0.7. The same two free parameters of the developing country were used as well as a preferential attachment network. To generate consumer heterogeneity, ABMs rely on random seeds so, each time an experiment is run, different results are obtained. So, for this study, the model for each country is run 100 times. On the basis of the previous ABM experiments for both countries, developing and developed, we built diffusion graphs that depict the temporal patterns of reverse innovation diffusion. The marketing mix (social influence and paid advertising messages) differ across markets given consumer densities and the individual weight of social influence and paid advertising messages.

After validating the model, we are now able to interpret the results of the experiments performed for the developing and developed countries. We ran 1000 experiments for each of the experimental variables (word of mouth, paid advertising messages, and network density). While experimenting with changes in word of mouth influence, we kept the influence of paid advertising messages and network density without changes. We maintained the same experimental conditions when analyzing each experimental variable. In all, three experiments were run for the developing country and three for the developed country.

Diffusion in a Developing Country

In the first experiment for the developing country, word of mouth influence was varied from 0.0 to 1.0 (that is, from 0.0% to 100%), while influence of paid advertising messages and network density were unchanged. The results show that the aggregated diffusion due to word of mouth influence is similar to the original Bass model: the higher the influence of the social environment, the faster the reverse innovation adoption. These results are depicted in Fig. 18.4. The second experimental condition was to vary paid advertising messages' influence and to keep word of mouth influence and network density constant. In the third experiment, only network density was unchanged. Depicting all diffusion variables for the three experiments would be very extensive in space and difficult to interpret, so the results from the 1000 runs for each of the three experiments were aggregated and descriptive statistics were calculated for each time step. Figure 18.3 groups all the results of the experiments. Influence of paid

Difusion pattern. Developing country. 1,000 consumers

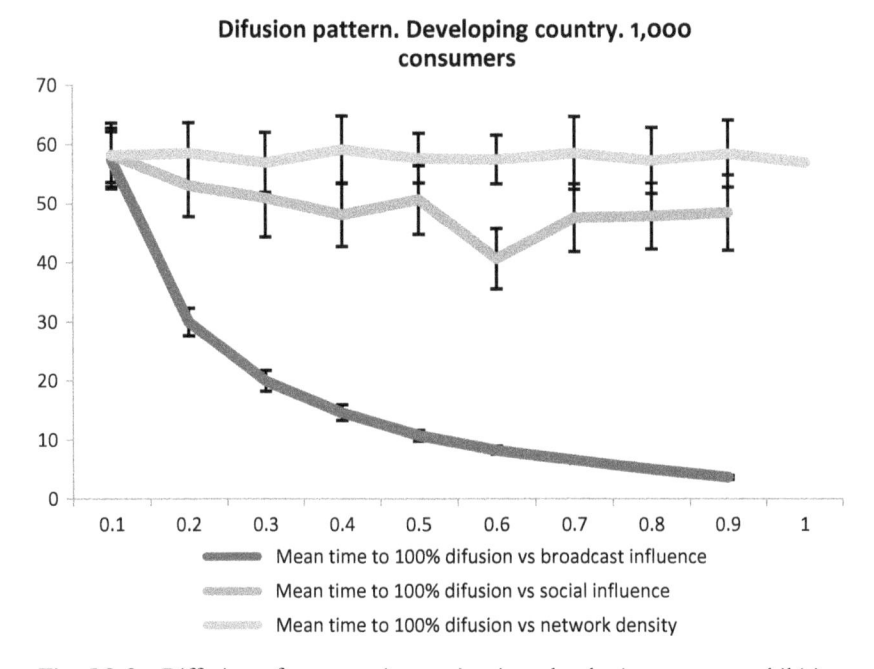

— Mean time to 100% difusion vs broadcast influence
— Mean time to 100% difusion vs social influence
— Mean time to 100% difusion vs network density

Fig. 18.3 Diffusion of a reverse innovation in a developing country exhibiting one influence at a time. Source: Author

Diffussion pattern. Developed country. 300 consumers.

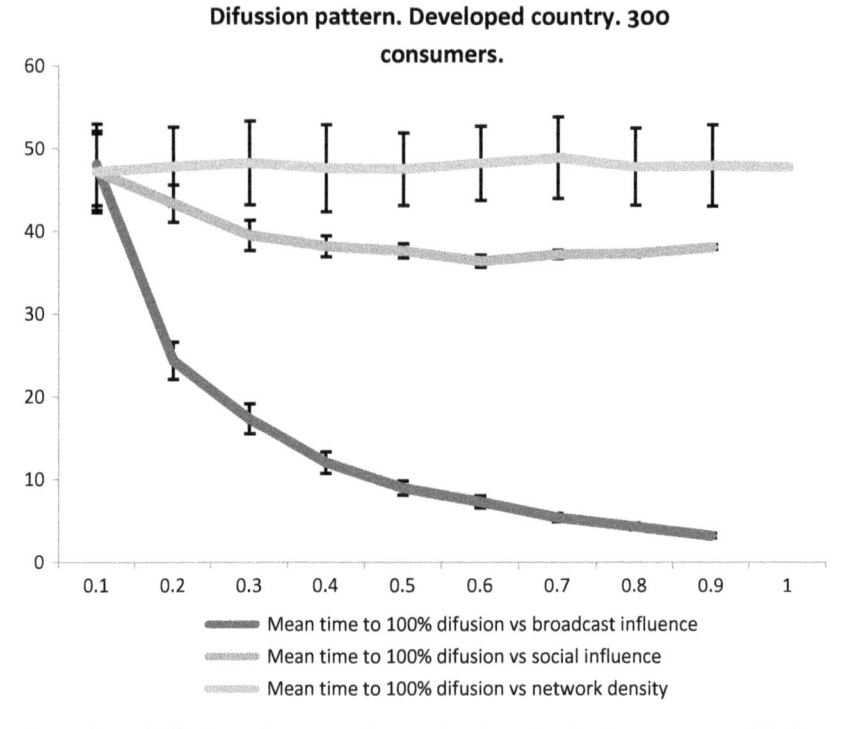

— Mean time to 100% difusion vs broadcast influence
— Mean time to 100% difusion vs social influence
— Mean time to 100% difusion vs network density

Fig. 18.4 Diffusion of a reverse innovation in a developing country exhibiting one influence at a time. Source: Author

advertising messages was modelled as a variable with high weight on consumers' adoption decisions. First, consistent with the Bass model, the high-slope line in Fig. 18.4 means that the time quickly decreases to reach 100 per cent of diffusion the developing country. The second aspect to note is that as word of mouth influence was modelled with less weight in consumers' decisions, the speed to which the innovation diffuses is slower. Third, varying the network density exhibits only a small influence on diffusion speed. The modelled network refers a preferential attachment in there are clusters of highly linked consumers. When network density is low, consumers who have adopted the innovation spread the message through their social circles. An important feature of these experiments is that it takes 60 time steps to reach a simulated market of 1000 consumers to adopt the reverse innovation.

Diffusion in a Developed Country

A similar approach to the developing country was performed to analyze the diffusion of the reverse innovation in a developed country. For purposes of comparison, the weights of word of mouth influence and influence of paid advertising messages were maintained as the same. Similarly, the type of social network in which the consumers are embedded was the same preferential attachment. Figure 18.4 presents the aggregate descriptive results for each experimental condition in the developed country. The interpretation of the graph is quite similar to the one of the developing country. Noteworthy, it takes 50 time steps for a reverse innovation to reach 100% diffusion. While this timeframe seems to be similar to the developing country, the maximum diffusion only reaches a simulated market of 300 consumers—about one third the size of the market in the developing country.

THE NEED FOR AN AMBIDEXTERITY STRATEGY

Existing theory in reverse innovations focuses mainly on strategic and market entrance issues, but focus on actual consumption has been disregarded. This study aims to close this gap by modelling consumer adoption decisions. Results present some implications for theory development. First, by using ABMs, researchers have an additional modelling tool available to test and measure the influence of external and internal factors, including the temporal dimension. This is an enhancement to the current cross-sectional frameworks broadly available in consumer behaviour research. Second, sensibility analyses can be performed to understand variations in the weights of the variables in experimental ABM settings. This enables researchers to achieve higher degrees of accuracy when forecasting consumer responses towards new products. Third, although ABMs have been criticized because external validation is challenging, research benefits are clear in that such modelling technique extends the traditional statistical techniques range.

Results show that diffusion speeds vary between the country origin of the reverse innovation and the developed country towards which it encroaches. First, diffusion speed achieves 100% of total diffusion in the developing market in an average of 60 steps and eventually reaches 1000 simulated consumers. The influence of paid advertising messages has more weight on adoption decisions than word-of-mouth influence and network density. Managers who design innovations in developing countries need to be aware of the influence of paid advertising messages as a critical factor that leads to a faster pace in diffusion. Managers could allocate resources to paid advertising as a fundamental way to push diffusion of new products. As word-of-mouth influence was modelled with a relatively low weight, this factor has little influence on consumers' decisions. Network structure was used as a proxy for the actual social circle of consumers. Managers need to understand the features of social networks as they involve the relationships among consumers since they become another influence factor. Managers may engage in attracting influential consumers (bloggers, YouTubers, etc.) as a tactic to influence other consumers to whom they are related. Second, the results show that the average time to reach a simulated segment of 300 consumers (full diffusion) is 50 steps. To maintain a fair comparison between the two countries, word of mouth and influence of paid advertising messages were modelled alike. Although this modelling limitation cannot properly resemble the actual situations in emerging and developed countries, it exhibits that consumers are heavily influenced by paid advertising messages. As the developed country was modelled, only 300 consumers are involved in the social network. Managers in developed countries may face additional pressure to reach higher diffusion rates if compared with the developing country.

As the segment in the developed country is smaller than the one in the developing country, concerns about profit levels may also arise. Clear expectations about the total addressable market as well as speed of diffusion should be shared across the value network so management across borders remain proactive. Third, a final implication of the previous observations is that international marketers need to be aware of the fact that diffusing a reverse innovation calls for use of an ambidexterity marketing strategy (Zimmermann et al. 2015; Koryak et al. 2018) given the different features of developing and developed markets. This refers mainly to exploration and exploitation of business opportunities. While developed countries offer consumer segments characterized by their wealth, risk proneness, and preferences of products based on performance rather than prices, developing countries exhibit a critical mass of rising middle-class consumers more inclined to favour price over performance. Therefore, an ambidexterity strategy would enable MNCs to implement exploitation strategies in which the headquartered office of an MNC may focus on price, ease of use, and sustainability to achieve high rates of product diffusion. In the case of a developed country, an MNC would expect lower levels of reverse diffusion in a market; this call for an exploration strategy in which the MNC leads efforts to gain a better understanding of the market at the consumer level before engaging in heavy plans of commercialization of reverse innovations. Although consumer features were not modelled in this study, there are also differences on socio-economic, psychographic, and risk attitudes between countries.

Conclusion

A rather simple ABM has been presented to illustrate how external factors to the consumer influence diffusion of reverse innovation in two countries. While it is difficult to model both internal and external consumer influences, the ABM advanced in this chapter provides an initial illustration of how diffusion may occur. The model shows parsimony, so researchers are able to observe aggregate adoption results in two different markets at a consumer level. The ABM allowed for studying the market at the micro level, a scope that, in absence of secondary data, becomes almost unfeasible. This chapter has surpassed this limitation by simulating consumer decisions under two external influences. As many of the existing theory is focused on strategic and market entrance issues, ABM allows for understanding and measuring the impact of factors affecting reverse innovation diffusion. Moreover, as data on reverse innovation diffusion becomes available, ABM can be fine-tuned accordingly. Further studies can also pursue the fit between the theoretical ABM to real data from identified reverse innovations that are already being commercialized in markets. Although the ABM aims to replicate consumer density and number of consumers in the two countries, models that are more sophisticated can be used to depict the broader reality of markets. This limits the power of the explanatory forecasting of this study. However, in absence of such data, validation of further ABMs can be accomplished using standard statistical techniques, such as structural equation modelling or conjoint analysis experiments.

References

Barabási, A. L., & Albert, R. (1999). Emergence of scaling in random networks. *Science, 286*(5439), 509–512.

Bass, F. M., Krishnan, T. V., & Jain, D. C. (1994). Why the Bass model fits without decision variables. *Marketing Science, 13*(3), 203–223.

Bloomberg. (2017). Living in the dark: 240 million Indians have no electricity. *Bloomberg News Website*. Retrieved January 12, 2018, from https://www.bloomberg.com/news/features/2017-01-24/living-in-the-dark-240-million-indians-have-no-electricity.

Christensen, C. (1997). *The innovator's dilemma: When new technologies cause great firms to fail*. Boston, MA: Harvard Business Review Press.

Christensen, C. M., Raynor, M. E., & McDonald, R. (2015). What is disruptive innovation. *Harvard Business Review, 93*(12), 44–53.

Delre, S. A., Jager, W., Bijmolt, T. H., & Janssen, M. A. (2010). Will it spread or not? The effects of social influences and network topology on innovation diffusion. *Journal of Product Innovation Management, 27*(2), 267–282.

Hang, C. C., Chen, J., & Subramian, A. M. (2010). Developing disruptive products for emerging economies: Lessons from Asian cases. *Research-Technology Management, 53*(4), 21–26.

Hossain, M., Simula, H., & Halme, M. (2016). Can frugal go global? Diffusion patterns of frugal innovations. *Technology in Society, 46*(1), 132–139.

Immelt, J. R., Govindarajan, V., & Trimble, C. (2009). How GE is disrupting itself. *Harvard Business Review, 87*(10), 56–65.

Kapoor, K., Dwivedi, Y., & Williams, M. (2014). Innovation adoption attributes: A review and synthesis of research findings. *European Journal of Innovation Management, 17*(3), 327–348.

Kiesling, E., Günther, M., Stummer, C., & Wakolbinger, L. M. (2012). Agent-based simulation of innovation diffusion: A review. *Central European Journal of Operations Research, 20*(2), 183–230.

Koryak, O., Lockett, A., Hayton, J., Nicolaou, N., & Mole, K. (2018). Disentangling the antecedents of ambidexterity: Exploration and exploitation. *Research Policy, 47*(2), 413–427.

Macal, C. M., & North, M. J. (2010). Tutorial on agent-based modelling and simulation. *Journal of Simulation, 4*(3), 151–162.

Nunes, P. F., & Breene, T. S. (2011). *Jumping the S-Curve. How to beat the growth cycle, get on top, and stay there*. Boston, MA: Harvard Business Review Press.

Peres, R., Muller, E., & Mahajan, V. (2010). Innovation diffusion and new product growth models: A critical review and research directions. *International Journal of Research in Marketing, 27*(2), 91–106.

Prahalad, C. K., & Mashelkar, R. A. (2010). Innovation's holy grail. *Harvard Business Review, 88*(7-8), 132–141.

Rand, W., & Rust, R. T. (2011). Agent-based modeling in marketing: Guidelines for rigor. *International Journal of Research in Marketing, 28*(3), 181–193.

Ray, S., & Ray, P. (2011). Product innovation for the people's car in an emerging economy. *Technovation, 31*(5–6), 216–227.

Rogers, E. M. (2010). *Diffusion of innovations*. New York: Simon and Schuster.

The Hindu. (2017). India to achieve 'electricity for all' by early 2020: IEA. *The Hindu Business Website*. Retrieved January 12, 2018, from http://www.thehindu.com/business/india-to-achieve-electricity-for-all-by-early-2020s-iea/article21291173.ece.

WIPO. (2013). Chotukool: Keeping things cool with frugal innovation. *WIPO Magazine*. Retrieved January 12, 2018, from http://www.wipo.int/wipo_magazine/en/2013/06/article_0003.html.

Zeng, M., & Williamson, P. J. (2007). *Dragons at your door: How Chinese cost innovation is disrupting global competition*. Boston, MA: Harvard Business Review Press.

Zeschky, M., Widenmayer, B., & Gassmann, O. (2011). Frugal innovation in emerging markets. *Research-Technology Management, 54*(4), 38–45.

Zimmermann, A., Raisch, S., & Birkinshaw, J. (2015). How is ambidexterity initiated? The emergent charter definition process. *Organization Science, 26*(4), 1119–1139.

CHAPTER 19

Relationship Lending and Entrepreneurial Behavior: Analyzing Empirical Evidences

Fernando A. Moya Dávila

INTRODUCTION

It is often complex for the financial institution to explore effective and ineffective incentives for entrepreneurs. Effective incentives for entrepreneurs include, for example, the decrease of the cost of credit and the decrease of the value of the collateral while a good incentive for a financial institution is a decrease of the probability of default of entrepreneurs. As relationship lending increases, more favorable conditions of the credit for the borrower (the entrepreneurs) are granted. The cost of credit decreases, the probability of pledging collateral decreases and value of collateral with respect of the credit decreases as well. In addition, as relationship lending increases, the bank will be rewarded as the probability of default for the entrepreneurs decreases. As the relationship gets stronger, the entrepreneur will be willing to pay the loan back to banks at any circumstances. If the entrepreneur is in distress, they will seek out other financial sources to avoid default. The probability of default decreases when the strength of the relationship increases. The moral hazard problem that banks used to

F. A. Moya Dávila (✉)
Tecnologico de Monterrey, EGADE Business School, Mexico City, Mexico
e-mail: fernando.moya@itesm.mx

© The Author(s) 2019
Rajagopal, R. Behl (eds.), *Business Governance and Society*,
https://doi.org/10.1007/978-3-319-94613-9_19

have with entrepreneurs will be diminished when entrepreneurs exert high effort to the project that the bank is financing. An entrepreneur is comfortable exerting high effort rather than low effort when the bank monitors his or her daily activities. Additionally, entrepreneurs have more incentives to interact with banks using the relationship lending technique because the cost of credit decreases when the strength of the relationship increases. As time passes, the conditions for future credits get friendlier. The probability of pledging collateral as well as the value of the requested collateral decreases as the strength of the relationship increases.

Empirical Research Review of Relationship Lending

Turning to the empirical evidence, in the United States, various papers have analyzed small firm financing, using data from the National Survey of Small Business Finance. Petersen and Rajan (1994) found indications that, ceteris paribus, older firms, or firms dealing with a relatively small number of banks, benefit from easier access to bank credit and from lower interest rates; the length of the relationship has a positive and significant effect on credit availability, whereas its impact on the cost of credit is positive but insignificant. The results of Petersen and Rajan (1994) are in line with those of previous studies as far as credit availability is concerned irrespective of the length of the relationship. The determinants of the borrowing rate for young businesses show a lower cost of credit in less competitive markets, where the bank can more easily internalize the value of the customer relationship. Contrary to Petersen and Rajan's findings, Berger and Udell (1995) found that for firms maintaining longstanding relationships with banks the cost of borrowing on previously negotiated credit lines is smaller and collateral is less frequently required. Berger and Udell (1995) used lines of credit to prove that if relationship increases, the cost of credit decreases. Cole (1998) finds that a lender is less likely to grant credit to a firm if the customer relationship has lasted for one year or less, or if the firm deals with other financial counterparts.

D'Auria and Foglia (1997), working on a panel of large firms, find a positive effect of their proxy for the length of the relationship on the cost of credit. Angelini et al. (1998) find that with banks other than cooperative banks, lending rates tend to increase with the length of the relationship for all customers, whereas with local cooperative banks (CCBs) this is the case for non-member customers only; by contrast, long-standing relationships have no significant effect on lending rates for CCBs' own members. This evidence is in line with bank capture theories, which may not apply to CCB members. They also find that CCB members enjoy easier access to credit, unlike non-member customers. Elsas and Krahnene (1998) studied the nature of relationship lending by analyzing the role of collateral. They found that aspects of relationship lending and renegotiation mainly drive the use of collateral in loan contracts. Relationship lenders do require more collateral from their debtors than normal lenders, thereby increasing the borrower's lock-in as well as strengthening the bank's bargaining power in future renegotiations.

This research is in line with Berger and Udell (1995). A big difference is that I test how the value of the collateral decreases as the strength of the relationship increases. In addition, as the relationship gets stronger, the probability of default by the entrepreneurs decreases, creating value to the bank. This chapter argues that relationship lending creates an incentive to both the entrepreneurs and banks to interact. It contributes to the existing literature responding to the question of how entrepreneurs benefit from the relationship with financial institutions. This study also investigates the crux of monetary gain for banks if the relationship with the entrepreneurs is built effectively.

The Data

I use a unique dataset based on credit files obtained from a Mexican leading bank (Banorte) in this study. It contains credits granted to 8928 clients considered entrepreneurs by Banorte. Credits run from the third quarter of 2002 to the second quarter of 2004. One client can receive more than one credit and be registered on different quarters. The database includes a total of 96,872 observations. It contains the following fields:

1. Client id—Identification of client.
2. Credit id—Identification of credit. One client can have more than one credit.
3. The date that client started a relationship with the bank—Date that the client was registered on the bank's files. Date when the relationship starts.
4. Date that credit was granted—Date when bank delivers the credit to the client.
5. The date that credit ends—Date when the credit expires.
6. Amount of credit granted—Pesos, US dollars or UDIS
7. Type of credit
    (a) Simple (lines of credits)—Simple credits are conditional credits that request special conditions for the credit to be granted. There is no clear definition of what a simple credit is. It may or may not require collateral or guarantee. They are also called current account credits. The use of the loan is not specified in the covenants.

(b) Fixed assets—The use of the loan is specified in the contract. It requires the borrower to buy fixed assets. Commonly it requires collateral.
(c) Mortgage—Home owner.
(d) Personal—Personal credit.
(e) Working Capital—The use of the loan is specified in the contract. It requires to buy raw materials or to be used to pay salaries or other expenses. It is specifically granted to invest on working capital. Commonly, collateral is required.
(f) Direct loans—It considers personal characteristics of the borrower such as moral and economic solvency for the loan to be granted.
(g) Restructured credits
(h) Sold for less
(i) Other (Renewed credits)
8. Type of credit
    (a) Floating rate
    (b) Fixed rate
9. Currency
    (a) Mexican Peso
    (b) USD
    (c) 50. UDI (virtual currency; its value is indexed to inflation)
10. Type of credit technology used
    (a) Credit Score
    (b) Balance (Financial Statements)
11. Industry
    (a) Electricity
    (b) Commerce
    (c) Services
    (d) Transportation
    (e) Manufacturing
    (f) Financial Services
    (g) Agriculture
    (h) Mining
    (i) Construction
12. Assets/Personal Guarantee—If credit score technology was used to grant the credit it represents the percentage of personal guarantee with respect to the credit size. The value of the guarantee is declared by the borrower. If financial statement technology was used to grant the credit it represents the assets of the company.

13. Debt/Assets/Personal Guarantee—If credit score technology was used to grant the credit it represents a percentage of personal guarantee with respect to the credit size (not real estate). The guarantee can be a financial backer. The guarantee can be bonds or stock. If financial statement technology was used to grant the credit it represents the leverage ratio of the company (Debt/Assets).
14. EBIT/Guarantee—If credit score technology was used to grant the credit it represents a percentage of a guarantee (not real estate) with respect to the credit size. It can be an inventory of raw materials or finished goods. If financial statement technology was used to grant the credit it represents earnings before interest rate and taxes.
15. Sales/Mortgage—If credit score technology was used to grant the credit it represents a percentage of collateral (real estate) with respect to the credit size. If financial statement technology was used to grant the credit it represents the sales of the company.

Descriptive Statistics

The dataset was analyzed using SPSS. Of the 96,782 observations, 45,594 were the first observation of the credit granted to the entrepreneurs (FirstCredit) and 41,278 credits were part of FirstCredits, but in different quarters (see Table 19.1); data from 9910 observations were lost. The same borrower can receive a credit more than once. Banorte classified companies as entrepreneurs. All credits fall under Banorte's category of entrepreneur loans.

The 45,594 credits are divided into credits granted in Mexican pesos (45,041), US dollars (539), and UDIS (14). UDI is a virtual currency that is indexed to the Mexican inflation rates (see Table 19.2). In order to test the hypothesis, only credits granted in Mexican pesos have been considered in the analysis.

The bank uses two transaction-lending technologies to grant credits—credit score and financial statement of lending. Under credit scoring, consumer data on the owner of the firm is drawn from the consumer credit bureaus and combined with data on the firm from financial statements and/or commercial credit bureaus—42,836 credits were granted using this lending technology (see Table 19.3). These data are processed in a model to give a credit score, or summary statistic about the borrower's expected future loan performance. Unlike financial statement lending and asset-based lending, under entrepreneur credit scoring, both the owner and the firm are viewed as sources of repayment for the loan and are

Table 19.1 FirstCredit

Credit	Frequency	Percentage	Valid percentage	Cum percentage
FirstCredit	45,594	52.5	52.5	100.0
Total	86,872	100.0	100.0	

Cum Percentage stands for cumulative percentage

Table 19.2 Currency

Currency	Frequency	Percentage	Valid percentage	Cum percentage
Peso	45,041	98.8	98.8	98.8
USD	539	1.2	1.2	100.0
UDI	14	0.0	0.0	100.0
Total	45,594	100.0	100.0	

Cum Percentage stands for cumulative percentage

viewed as inseparable from a credit perspective. Under financial statement lending, bankers focus on standard financial statement analysis. That is, they utilize financial ratios to analyze historical financial statements, to analyze projected financial statements and to analyze pro forma financial statements, which estimate the impact of proposed actions.

This study found that 2758 credits were granted using a lending technology. Number of credits granted at a *floating rate* is 35,328 (77.5%) and credits granted at a *fixed rate* is 10,266 (22.5%) (see Table 19.4).

Nine types of credit are included in the database (see Table 19.5). The most common one is Simple Credit (lines of credit). It is also the most relationship-oriented credit (Berger and Udell, 94). The Fixed Asset and Mortgage Credits are the most transactional-oriented credits (Berger and Udell, 94).

In addition, nine industries are represented in my database (see Table 19.6). The most common industry is commerce (25,201 credits) followed by manufacturing (9209 credits) and services (5336 credits).

Descriptive statistics of variables for FirstCredit regression are shown on Table 19.7. I used ordinary least square regression and logistics regressions to test my hypothesis. Mean size loan is $766,319.20 pesos (CreditSize). In the regressions, I use the natural log of CreditSize called LnCredit (see Table 19.8). Only credits granted in pesos are analyzed. Loans that are registered with 0 pesos (1560 credits) were taken out of the sample; only loans greater than $1000 pesos were used. The proxy for interest rate used is the premium paid over the TIIE (Equilibrium Interbank Lending Rate). It is

Table 19.3 Credit technology

Credit technology	Frequency	Percentage	Valid percentage	Cum percentage
Credit score	42,836	94.0	94.0	94.0
Financial statements	2758	6.0	6.0	100.0
Total	45,594	100.0	100.0	

Cum Percentage stands for cumulative percentage

Table 19.4 Type of interest rates

Credit rate	Frequency	Percentage	Valid percentage	Cum percentage
Floating	35,328	77.5	77.5	77.5
Fixed	10,266	22.5	22.5	100.0
Total	45,594	100.0	100.0	

Cum Percentage stands for cumulative percentage

Table 19.5 Credit type

Credit type	Frequency	Percentage	Valid percentage	Cum percentage
Other	13	0.0	0.0	0.0
Simple	41,572	91.2	91.2	91.2
Fixed assets	252	0.6	0.6	91.8
Mortgage	197	0.4	0.4	92.2
Personal	1288	2.8	2.8	90
Working capital	381	0.8	0.8	99
Direct loan	1840	4.0	4.0	99.9
Restructured	12	0.0	0.0	99.9
Sold to less	39	0.1	0.1	100.0
Total	45,594	100.0	100.0	

Cum Percentage stands for cumulative percentage

Table 19.6 Industry

Industry type	Frequency	Percentage	Valid percentage	Cum percentage
Electricity	365	0.8	0.8	0.8
Commerce	25,201	53	53	56.1
Services	5336	11.7	11.7	67.8
Transportation	2680	9	9	73.7
Manufacturing	9209	20.2	20.2	93.9
Financial services	988	2.2	2.2	96.0
Agriculture	216	0.5	0.5	96.5
Mining	135	0.3	0.3	96.8
Construction	1464	3.2	3.2	100.0

Cum Percentage stands for cumulative percentage

Table 19.7 Descriptive statistics

	N statistic	Min statistic	Max statistic	Mean statistic	Std. dev statistic	Var statistic	Kurtosis Statistic	Error
Credit size	45,041	0	6,229,779,000	743,212.99	36,307,247.142	1.31821620E+15	210,59.877	0.023
Premio_i	45,041	−0.0903	0.8014	0.0914	0.0424	0.002	9.372	0.023
Years relation	43,593	0.00	21.12	1.8619	2.21494	4.906	14.019	0.023
Rel index ($N = 0.25$ and $w = 0.3$)	43,593	0.00	0.25	0.1046	0.07865	0.006	−1.188	0.023
N v álido	43,593							

similar to the US prime rate. The dataset contains the interest rate charged every quarter for a particular loan. I calculated the average TIIE for the particular quarter and subtracted it from the interest rate charges. This variable is identified in this study as *premio_i*, which has been used as proxy for the interest rate. The mean for *premio_i* in the dataset is 9.6%. A dummy variable for industry and credit type as control variables has also been used

Table 19.8 Definition of explanatory variables

Variable name	Description
Credit characteristic:	
Premio_i	Cost of credit above TIIE of the same period
LnCredit	Natural log of size of credit.
Floating rate	=1 if credit charges floating rate, else fixed.
Simple credit	=1 if credit was granted as simple credit (line of credit)
Fixed asset credit	=1 if credit was granted as fixed asset credit
Home ownership credit	=1 if credit was granted as mortgage credit
Personal credit	=1 if credit was granted as a personal credit
Working capital credit	=1 if credit was granted as working capital credit
Direct credit	=1 if credit was granted as a direct credit
Restr credit	=1 if credit was granted as restructured credit
Sold for less credit	=1 if credit was granted as a sold to less credit
Industry characteristics:	
Commerce	=1 if in commerce industry
Services	=1 if in service industry
Transport	=1 if in transportation industry
Manufact	=1 if in manufacturing industry
Finservices	=1 if in financial services industry
Agricult	=1 if in agricultural industry
Mining	=1 if in mining industry
Construction	=1 if in construction industry
Electr	=1 if in electricity industry
Credit technology:	
Credit Tecn	=1 if credit score technology was used, else financial statements technology
Default	=1 if borrower defaulted the loan
Collateral:	
Mortgage collateral	=1 if bank pledge collateral (mortgage)
Mortgage (value)	Value of collateral with respect to credit
Relationship characteristics:	
Rel Index (N = 0.25 and w = 0.3)	Relationship index with an N = 0.25 and w = 0.3, t = years of the relationship $$\Re i = \left[1 - \left(\frac{1}{e^{(e^{wt}-1)}}\right)\right] N$$

in the analysis. The most common proxy used for a relationship is years of the relationship. I use a new approach to measuring relationship, the relationship index (*Rel Index*), which has been generated in this study with the available dataset on entrepreneurial credit.

The mean size of years of relationship in my data set is 1.86 years, ranging from 0 years to 283 years. The relationship index is used with N of 0.25 and w of 0.3. (Later, the convenience of the relationship index is discussed instead of years of the relationship. Both indicators demonstrate that they are strong and equivalent.) The speed (w) of the relationship refers to how fast the interaction becomes stronger. The limit (N) of the relationship refers to the cap that government regulations set to avoid fully relationship loans and to the bank preferences and policies to never let the interest rate be 0 even tough a long-lasting relationship with the entrepreneur. The index is fully explained in Moya (2018). The index was used to run all the OLS and logistic regressions to prove the hypothesis.

Econometric Specification and Test Results

In my empirical analysis, I test the joint hypothesis that:

1. relationship lending decreases interest rates,

$$Premio\_i = \beta_0 + \beta_1 \left(\text{Credit characteristics}\right) + \beta_2 \left(\text{Industry}\right) + \beta_3 \left(\text{Credit technology}\right) + \beta_4 \left(\text{Relationship index}\right) + \varepsilon$$

2. relationship lending decreases the probability of default,

$$\text{Prob}\left(\text{Default} = 1\right) = \beta_0 + \beta_1 \left(\text{Credit charact}\right) + \beta_2 \left(\text{Industry}\right) + \beta_3 \left(\text{Credit techology}\right) + \beta_4 \left(\text{Relationship index}\right) + \varepsilon$$

3. relationship lending decreases the probability of pledging collateral requirement,

$$\text{Prob}\left(\text{Pledge collateral} = 1\right) = \beta_0 + \beta_1 \left(\text{Credit charact}\right) + \beta_2 \left(\text{Industry}\right) + \beta_3 \left(\text{Relationship index}\right) + \varepsilon$$

4. relationship lending decreases the value of the collateral,

$$\text{Value collateral}(X) = \beta_0 + \beta_1(\text{Credit charact}) + \beta_2(\text{Industry}) + \beta_3(\text{Relationship index}) + \varepsilon$$

To prove that my relationship index is a reliable proxy for relationship lending, I ran regressions for the first hypothesis (see Tables 19.9 and 19.10).

$$Premio\_i = \beta_0 + \beta_1(\text{Credit characteristics}) + \beta_2(\text{Industry}) + \beta_3(\text{Credit technology}) + \beta_4(\text{Relationship index}) + \varepsilon$$

Using the relationship index with different values for w and N and comparing them with the same regression but using years as a proxy for relationship lending.

$$Premio\_i = \beta_0 + \beta_1(\text{Credit characteristics}) + \beta_2(\text{Industry}) + \beta_3(\text{Credit technology}) + \beta_4(\text{Years of relationship}) + \varepsilon.$$

In all cases, the regressions were statistically significant and with the same negative sign.

Table 19.9 Relationship index VS premium

			N		
w	0.1	0.2	0.3	0.4	0.5
0.1	−0.062	−0.031	−0.021	−0.016	−0.012
	(−8.203)	(−8.203)	(−8.203)	(−8.203)	(−8.203)
0.2	−0.051	−0.026	−0.017	−0.013	−0.010
	(−9.913)	(−9.913)	(−9.913)	(−9.913)	(−9.913)
0.3	−0.048	−0.024	−0.016	−0.012	−0.010
	(−10.926)	(−10.926)	(−10.926)	(−10.926)	(−10.926)

β the coefficient of Ri with different levels of w and N

Table 19.10 Years VS premium

β	−0.0004214
t statistic	(6.921)

β the coefficient of years

The advantage of using relationship index is that N and w can be modified. N is the limit of the relationship and w is the speed of the relationship. In other words, any bank will let the entrepreneurs start a relationship, but will decide how fast the relationship can go (w). In addition, a bank will limit the relationship until a convenient level (N). For the present research, w of 0.3 and N of 0.2 have been used for analysis. However, for the future, N and w can be subjects of further research. They can be compared between banks and be calculated using simultaneous equations.

Relationship Lending and the Cost of Credit

The entrepreneurs have to perceive that there is a direct benefit if nurturing a relationship with a bank. A good incentive for entrepreneurs to build a relationship with a bank is that there is direct evidence that the cost of credit will decrease if the strength of the relationship is increased. Why might this happen? As a bank knows better the characteristics of the entrepreneurs, the information asymmetries will be alleviated and the risk associated to such asymmetries is lowered. Lower risk decreases the cost of credit.

The first regression tests analyzed 43,474 cases (see Table 19.11) and exhibit how the relationship index is related to the cost of credit using all types of credits (simple credits, fixed assets, mortgages, etc.). A R^2 of 0.14 resulted from the regression. It is a good R^2 as compared to Berger and Udell (1995). The regression model is significant with an F of 355 meaning that at least one independent variable is significant. The *Rel_index* (N = 0.25 and w = 0.3) coefficient shows a negative and significant sign of −0.019, which means that if relationship index increases by 1, the premium of the cost of credit will decrease by 1.9%. As relationship index is limited to grow up to 0.25, an increase of 0.1 will decrease the premium of the cost of credit to 0.19%. There is value created by the entrepreneurs with a greater relationship index, as their cost of credit is less than the cost of credit for a lower relationship index and is an incentive for the entrepreneurs to build strong relationships.

Control variables that were statistically significant on this regression were *LnCredit* and *CreditTecn*. The size of the credit affects the cost of credit. The bigger the credit is, the less it costs. This can be interpreted as straight economies of scale. Also, I observe that for loans in which credit score technology was used, the cost of credit is larger. In the regression, the dummy variable *CreditTecn* has a value of 1 if credit score is used and

Table 19.11 Descriptive statistics of first credit[b]

	Mean	Std dev.	N
Premio_i (Dep. Var.)	0.0971[a]	0.0296	43,474
Credit Tecnology:			
CreditTecn	0.94	0.238	43,474
Relationship index:			
Rel Index (N = 0.25 and w = 0.3)	0.1046	0.07864	43,474
R^2 = 0.140			

Regression analysis

	Non-standardized coefficients		Standardized coefficients	t	Sig. (p)
	B	Error	Beta		
Rel Index (N = 0.25 and w = 0.3)	−0.019[c]	0.002	−0.050	−10.926	0.000

[a]dependent variable: *premio_i*; [b]Only First credit cases; [c]Statistically Significant at a 5% level

0 if financial statement technology is used. A positive and significant coefficient of 0.024 can be interpreted as a 2.4% difference on the cost of credit between financial statement loans and credit score loans. Credit score seems to be a more reliable transaction technology to be used for detecting entrepreneurs' risk associated to the credit. In the sample, 42,836 credits were granted using credit score and 2758 using financial statements. This technology assigns a higher risk to the entrepreneurs and it has a natural impact on the cost of credit. Financial statement technology is not frequently used in this sample. Only 6% of the credits used this technology. It has been written that the entrepreneurs do not have reliable financial statements (Berger and Udell 1995). This explains why banks prefer a credit score. It is harder to explain why loans that used financial statements as credit technology have a lower interest rate. Intuition tells me that the bank was very selective in using financial statements. They used this technology only for those entrepreneurs they knew had correct and reliable financial statements. If this is true, this explains why the cost of credit is lower.

$$Premio\_i = \beta_0 + \beta_1 \left(\text{Credit characteristics}\right) + \beta_2 \left(\text{Industry}\right)$$
$$+ \beta_3 \left(\text{Credit technology}\right) + \beta_4 \left(\text{Relationship index}\right) + \varepsilon$$

Petersen and Rajan (1994) found that there was no significant causality between relationship and cost of credit. Berger and Udell (1995) argued that they did not find any causality because they use in their sample a large number of no lines of credit loans (fixed assets loans). Fixed assets loans are more transaction driven compared to simple loans (lines of credits). In my sample, simple loans dominate the entire loan pool.

In the next regression (see Table 19.12), I used only simple loans to test the causality between relationship index and cost of credit. In all, I analyzed 39,634 credits. R^2 for the regression is 0.137. Results are consistent with the original hypothesis. Beta coefficient for *Rel Index* ($w = 0.3$ and $N = 0.25$) is -0.021 with a t statistic of -12.328. Simple credits make up the majority of the relationship loans in the whole pool of credits. This is reflected in the size of the coefficient and t statistics. The absolute value for both numbers increased if only analyzing simple credits. This means that if *Rel Index* ($w = 0.3$ and $N = 0.25$) increases by 0.1, the cost of credit will decrease to 0.21%.

$$Premio\_i = \beta_0 + \beta_1 \left(\text{Credit characteristics}\right) + \beta_2 \left(\text{Industry}\right)$$
$$+ \beta_3 \left(\text{Credit technology}\right) + \beta_4 \left(\text{Relationship index}\right) + \varepsilon$$

To check robustness of the results, I ran an analysis with fixed assets loans only and excluded other types of loans. The results are consistent with Berger and Udell (1995). Fixed assets loans are not relationship loans. They are more transaction-driven loans. Look at the coefficient of *Rel Index* ($N = 0.25$ and $w = 0.3$) in Table 19.13; it is negative at -0.034, but with a not significant t statistic of -0.776. The relationship is not relevant on loans given to finance fixed assets.

$$Premio\_i = \beta_0 + \beta_1 \left(\text{Credit characteristics}\right) + \beta_2 \left(\text{Industry}\right)$$
$$+ \beta_3 \left(\text{Credit technology}\right) + \beta_4 \left(\text{Relationship index}\right) + \varepsilon$$

In the preceding analysis, I found no significant problems with including fixed rate credits in my regressions because interest rates in those quar-

Table 19.12 Interest rates and relationship index, $N = 0.25$ and $w = 0.3$ (first credit, only simple credits)

Descriptive statistics[b]

	Mean	Std dev.	N
Premio_i (Dep. Var)	0.0974[a]	0.02782	39,634
Credit technology:			
CreditTecn	0.94	0.231	39,634
Relationship index:			
Rel Index ($N = 0.25$ and $w = 0.3$)	0.1036	0.07783	39,634

$R^2 = 0.137$

Regression analysis

	Non-standardized coefficients		Standardized coefficients	t	Sig. (p)
	B	error.	Beta		
Rel Index ($N = 0.25$ and $w = 0.3$)	−0.021[c]	0.002	−0.059	−12.328	0.000

Selection made only for cases that Credit Type = Simple

[a]Dependent variable: *premio_i*; [b]Selection only for cases that Credit Type = Simple; [c]Statistically Significant at a 5% level

ters where very small and had little volatility. Using only floating rates, considering the problems detected by Berger and Udell (1995), my conclusions are the same. R^2 increased to 0.27. The beta coefficient for the *Rel Index* ($N = 0.25$ and $w = 0.3$) for floating rates credits is −0.10, with a significant t statistic of −6.456. If the relationship index increases by 0.1, the cost of credit will drop to 0.10% (see Table 19.14).

$$Premio\_i = \beta_0 + \beta_1 \left(\text{Credit characteristics} \right) + \beta_2 \left(\text{Industry} \right) + \beta_3 \left(\text{Credit technology} \right) + \beta_4 \left(\text{Relationship index} \right) + \varepsilon$$

Table 19.13 Interest rates and relationship index, $N = 0.25$ and $w = 0.3$ (first credit, fixed assets credit)[c]

Descriptive statistics[a]

	Mean	Std dev.	N
Premio_i (Dep.Var)	0.1049[b]	0.0405	243
Electr	0.00	0.064	243
Credit technology:			
CreditTecn	0.89	0.310	243
Relationship index:			
Rel Index ($N = 0.25$ and $w = 0.3$)	0.0342	0.05830	243
$R = 0.421$; $R^2 = 0.177$			

Regression analysis

	Non-Standardized coefficients		Standardized coefficients	t	Sig. (p)
	B	Error	Beta		
Rel Index ($N = 0.25$ and $w = 0.3$)	−0.034[d]	0.043	−0.048	−0.776	0.439

[a]Section made only for cases that Credit Type = Fixed Assets; [b]dependent variable: *premio_i*; [c]Selection made only for cases that Credit Type = Fixed assets; [d]Statistically Significant at a 5% level

Table 19.14 Interest rates and relationship index, $N = 0.25$ and $w = 0.3$ (first credit, floating rate)[c]

Descriptive statistics[a]

	Mean	Std dev.	N
Premio_i (Dep Var)	0.0964[b]	0.024	33,819
Credit charact:			
Credit technology:			
CreditTecn	0.94	0.243	33,819
Relationship index:			
Rel Index ($N = 0.25$ and $w = 0.3$)	0.1092	0.07614	33,819
$R = 0.525$; $R^2 = 0.275$			

Regression analysis

	Non-standardized coefficients		Standardized coefficients	t	Sig. (p)
	B	Error típ.	Beta		
Rel Index ($N = 0.25$ and $w = 0.3$)	−0.010[d]	0.001	−0.030	−6.456	0.000

[a]Selection for cases that FloatingRate = floating rate; [b]Dependent variable: *premio_i*; [c]Selection only made for cases thatFloatingRate = floating rate; [d]Statistically significant at a level of 5%

Relationship Lending and Probability of Default

In Mexico, a loan is classified as non-performing after 90 days of missing a payment, or in the case of a one-payment loan, after 30 days of missing the payment (La Porta et al. 2003). Banorte coded each credit per quarter as 1 if the client defaulted and 0 if the client paid normally. In all, 79,946 observations were included in the analysis. The number of observations is different from the first regression (cost of credit) because it includes the performance of each credit through time. This means that the first credit granted to the client lasted, in most of the cases, more than one quarter. The observations include the payment behavior of each client through the end of the credit life. For example, a credit might have a length of eight quarters. The client might have defaulted, let's say, in the third quarter and this means that two out of eight observations were coded with a 1 (defaulted) and the rest with a 0.

I used the following logit regression model:

$$\text{Prob}(\text{Default} = 1) = \beta_0 + \beta_1 (\text{Credit charact}) + \beta_2 (\text{Industry}) + \beta_3 (\text{Credit techology}) + \beta_4 (\text{Relationship index}) + \varepsilon$$

Of the 79,946 valid observations, 75,829 were paid on time and 4117 credits defaulted. A Wald test is used to test the statistical significance of each coefficient (β) in the model. A Wald test calculates a Z statistic, which is:

$$z = \frac{\hat{B}}{SE}$$

This z value is then squared, yielding a Wald statistic with a chi-square distribution. However, several authors have identified problems with the use of the Wald statistic. Menard (1995) warns that for large coefficients, the standard error is inflated, lowering the Wald statistic (chi-square) value. Agresti (1996) states that the likelihood ratio test is more reliable for small sample sizes than the Wald test. The Wald statistic (equivalent to the F stat) is 33,144.127. This means that at least one independent variable is significant and has a relationship with the dependent variable (1 = defaulted, 0 = not defaulted).

The likelihood ratio test uses the ratio of the maximized value of the likelihood function for the full model (L_1) over the maximized value of the likelihood function for the simpler model (L_0). The likelihood ratio test statistic equals:

$$-2\log\left(\frac{L_0}{L_1}\right) = 2\left[\log(L_0) - \log(L_1)\right] = -2(L_0 - L_1)$$

This log transformation of the likelihood functions yields a chi-squared statistic. This is the recommended test statistic to use when building a model through backward stepwise elimination. The $-2LL$ for the logit regression is 30,768 (significant) and the Cox and Snell R^2 is 0.021 while the Nagelkerke R^2 is 0.062. Cox and Snell's R^2 is an attempt to imitate the interpretation of multiple R^2 based on likelihood, but its maximum can be less than 1, making it difficult to interpret. Nagelkerke's R^2 is a further modification of Cox and Snell's coefficient to assure it can vary from 0 to 1. That is, Nagelkerke's R^2 divides Cox and Snell's R^2 by its maximum in order to achieve a number that ranges from 0 to 1.

The relationship index has been used with a $w = 0.3$ and $N = 0.2$. It has been observed that the relationship index increases the probability of default decreases. Beta coefficient for *Rel Index* is -1.545 with a Wald statistic of 47.446 (Table 19.15). This makes the coefficient significant or not different from zero. What does a coefficient of -1.545 mean? Suppose that a certain client has a probability of default of 15%, which is the same as having an 85% probability of paying. The odds ratio for such client is $15/85 = 0.176$. The odds ratio coefficient for the regression model is $e^{-1.545} = 0.21331187$. The new odds of the dependent variable is $0.176*0.21331187 = 0.03764$. Let assume X is the new probability of default and $1-X$ the new probability of payment: $X/1-X = 0.03764$. Solving for new $X = 0.03627766$. This means that for every unit that *Rel Index* ($N = 0.25$ and $w = 0.3$) increases, the probability of default for a client with a probability of 15% will decrease to 3.6277%. Relationship index that does not increase or decrease can take a value that goes from 0 to 0.2 instead of using 1 as an increase or decrease of the relationship index I will now use 0.1. This means that an increase of 0.10 in the relationship index will make the probability of default of the client decrease from 15% to 13.1347%.

Table 19.15 Probability of default and relationship index, $N = 0.25$, and $w = 0.3$ (all credits)

Summary of cases

		N	Percentage
Selected cases	Included in the analysis	79,946	100.0
	Lost cases	34	0.0
	Total	79,980	100.0
Not selected cases		0	0.0
Total		79,980	100.0

Variables of the equation

		B	E.T.	Wald	df	Sig. (p)	Exp(B)
Step 0	Constant	−2.913	0.016	33,144.127	1	0.000	0.054

Summary of the model

Step	−2 log likelihood	R-squared Cox and Snell	R-squared Nagelkerke
1	30,768.265	0.021	0.062

Variables of the equation

	B	E.T.	Wald	df	Sig. (p)	Exp(B)
Credit charact:						
Premio_i	6.559[a]	0.489	179.623	1	0.000	70,532
Credit technology:						
CreditTecn(1)	−0.536[a]	0.100	28.652	1	0.000	0.585
Relationship index:						
Rel index	−1.545[a]	0.224	47.446	1	0.000	0.213
Constante	10.163[a]	2.53	16.136	1	0.000	25928.404

[a]Statistically significant at a level of 5%

$$\text{Prob}(\text{Default} = 1) = \beta_0 + \beta_1 (\text{Credit charact}) + \beta_2 (\text{Industry}) + \beta_3 (\text{Credit techology}) + \beta_4 (\text{Relationship index}) + \varepsilon$$

As in the previous analysis, only simple credits (70,075 observations) were used to analyze cost of credit regression, leading to the same results. The beta coefficient of *Rel Index* ($N = 0.25$ and $w = 0.3$) is −1.627 with a

Wald statistic of 49.304 (sig. 000). See Table 19.16. Simple credits are more relationship oriented compared to fixed asset credits measured by the significance of the coefficients. The magnitude of the change has to be bigger when isolating simple credits. For a client with a probability of default of 15%, an increase of the relationship index ($N = 0.25$ and $w = 0.3$) of 1 decreases the probability of default to 3.334%. Nevertheless, as rela-

Table 19.16 Probability of default and relationship index, $N = 0.25$ and $w = 0.3$ (simple credits)

Summary of cases

		N	Percent
Selected cases	Included in the analysis	70,075	87.6
	Lost cases	29	0.0
	Total	70,104	87.7
Not selected cases			12.3
Total			100.0

Variables of the equation

		B	E.T.	Wald	df	Sig. (p)	Exp(B)
Step 0	Constant	−2.937	0.017	28,907.522	1	0.000	0.053

Summary of the model

Step	−2 log likelihood	R-squared Cox and Snell	R-squared Nagelkerke
1	27,401.134	0.008	0.025

Variables of the equation

	B	E.T.	Wald	df	Sig. (p)	Exp(B)
Credit charact:						
Premio_i	9.866[a]	0.581	288.617	1	0.000	19,258.665
LnCredit	−0.001	0.008	0.018	1	0.893	0.999
Credit technology:						
CreditTecn(1)	−0.366[a]	0.107	11.668	1	0.001	0.693
Relationship index:						
Rel index	−1.627[a]	0.232	49.304	1	0.000	0.196
Constante	159[a]	2.521	4.187	1	0.041	173.962

[a]Statistically significant at 5% level

tionship index is limited to 0.25 if relationship index increases by 0.1, the probability of default will decrease to 13.04%.

Fixed assets credits are more transaction-driven credits compared to simple credits. Beta coefficient for fixed asset credits is expected to be lower and not significant compared to beta coefficient for simple credits. When the regression was run for only fixed assets credits, I found a significant coefficient turned as a bigger causality; a beta coefficient of −6.601 (Table 19.17) for relationship index with a Wald statistic of 974 (sign. 0.015). The results reveal that the increase in this coefficient compared to simple credits as a commitment behavior of the entrepreneurs to pay more of loan back as the relationship is strengthened. Another interpretation is

Table 19.17 Probability of default and relationship index, $N = 0.25$ and $w = 0.3$ (fixed assets credits)

Summary of cases			N	Percent
Selected cases	Included in the analysis		1361	1.7
	Lost cases		0	0.0
	Total		1361	1.7
Not selected cases				98.3
Total				100.0

Summary of the model			
Step	−2 log likelihood	R-squared Cox and Snell	R-squared Nagelkerke
1	841.608	0.098	0.190

Variables of the equation	B	E.T.	Wald	df	Sig. (p)	Exp(B)
Credit charact:						
Premio_i	8.918[a]	2.125	17.617	1	0.000	7462.646
Credit	−8.026[a]	2.022	1753	1	0.000	0.000
Credit technology:						
Credit tech(1)	−0.464	0.542	0.725	1	0.394	0.630
Relationship index:						
Rel index	−6.601[a]	2.701	974	1	0.015	0.001
Constante	113.901	16,347,273	0.000	1	0.999	2.929E+49

[a]Statistically significant at a 5% level

that the entrepreneurs fear how the bank will cash the collaterals that the entrepreneurs put up if the loan is not paid back. For a client with 15% of probability of default, a −6.601 coefficient means that if *Rel Index* ($N = 0.25$ and $w = 0.3$) increases by 0.1 the probability of default will drop to 8.36% on fixed assets credits.

For both floating and fixed rates, an interesting behavior of borrowers was found. There is a smaller beta coefficient on the *Rel Index* independent variable of −0.879 for floating rate credits contrasted with a −2.06 beta coefficient for the fixed rates credits. Both coefficients are significant. A possible explanation for this difference is that, on one hand, as borrowers have a stronger relationship with the bank, borrowers feel committed to paying the bank back and find it easier to do so due to the certainty of the interest rate when granted a fixed rate credit. On the other hand, borrowers find it more difficult to pay the credit back due to the uncertainty of the interest rate when granted a floating rate credit.

Note that $Premio\_i$ for floating rate credit regression is not significant while the fixed rate credit regression is significant. The greater the $Premio\_i$ the greater the probability of default for fixed rates. $Premio\_i$ for floating rates moves in the same direction as TIIE, so it is not a relevant variable to default. $Premio\_i$ for fixed rates increases or decreases as TIIE moves down or up making it relevant to default.

Relationship Lending and Probability of Asking for Collateral

As Berger and Udell (1995) did, I analyzed whether the amount of required collateral is greater or less for borrowers with long-standing relationships. A logit regression is used to calculate the probability of a bank asking for collateral from entrepreneurs. In the study, only collateral that is secured legally is considered. Usually, this type of collateral is real estate. It has to be registered with government officials and cannot be sold or transferred to third parties during the life of the credit. The beta coefficient for *Rel Ind* ($N = 0.25$, $w = 0.3$) is negative and significant. A −2.4 beta coefficient (see Table 19.18) and a Wald statistic of 274.833 make me accept the hypothesis that as the relationship increases, the probability of asking for collateral decreases. The results are online with the theoretical model and with Berger and Udell (1995) and Boot and Thakor (1994). If the probability of asking a borrower for real estate collateral is 15%, an increment of 1 on *Rel Index* ($N = 0.25$, $w = 0.3$) will decrease this

Table 19.18 Probability of asking for collateral and relationship index, $N = 0.25$, $w = 0.3$ (all first credits)

Summary of cases

		N	Percent
Selected cases	Included in the analysis	46,853	100.0
	Lost cases	15	0.0
	Total	46,868	100.0
Not selected cases			0.0
Total			100.0

Summary of the model

Step 0	−2 log likelihood	Cox and Snell R-squared	Nagelkerke R squared
1	47683.732(a)	0.061	0.082

Variables in the equation

	B	E.T.	Wald	df	Sig. (p)	Exp(B)
Credit charact:						
Premio_i	−1.601	0.414	14.977	1	0.000	0.202
LnCredit	0.159	0.009	323.331	1	0.000	1.173
Relationship index:						
Rel index	−2.400	0.145	274.833	1	0.000	0.091
Constante	−2.393	1.096	4.766	1	0.029	0.091

probability to 1.57%. As the relationship index increases from 0 to 0.25, a 0.1 increase of the index decreases the probability of asking for collateral from 15% to 12.19% ($e^{-0.24} = 0.7866$, $0.7866*0.15/0.85 = 0.1388$). The new odds ratio is 0.1388 and is equal to $x/(1-x)$, where x is a new probability. Solving for x, $0.1388 = x/(1-x)$, $x = 12.19\%$.

$$\text{Prob}(\text{Pledge collateral} = 1) = \beta_0 + \beta_1(\text{Credit charact}) + \beta_2(\text{Industry}) + \beta_3(\text{Relationship index}) + \varepsilon$$

If the regressions, in which the probability of asking for collateral is the dependent variable, are run selecting only simple credits and fixed assets credits, it is observed once more that simple credits are more relationship-oriented credits than fixed assets credits are. The coefficient for the relationship index is −2.406 with a Wald statistic of 261.334. This means that if the relationship index increases, the probability of the bank asking for collateral decreases. Suppose an entrepreneur has a probability of being asked for collateral of 15%. As the entrepreneur increases his relationship index with the bank by 0.1, the probability he will be asked for collateral decreases to 12.18%—$e^{-0.2406} = 0.7861, 0.7861*0.15/0.85 = 0.1387, x/(1-x) = 0.1387, x = 0.1387/1.1387, x = 12.18\%$. The data has been analyzed where the regression includes the probability of pledging collateral and relationship index, only, this time, fixed asset credits were selected. A negative causality between both is observed but with no significance. A Wald statistic of 0.051 is consistent with the hypothesis, as the coefficient for *Rel Index* equals zero. It has been found again that fixed asset credits are not guided by relationship lending. This type of credit is guided by transaction-based lending.

Relationship Lending and Value of the Collateral

In a durable relationship, a bank can reduce the hardship to subsidize the borrowers through time by reducing the amount of requested collateral. As described in my theoretical model, collateral value was inversely related to the relationship index by the model $C = J(1-Ri)L$. As the relationship index increases, the value of the collateral decreases. The simple credits (lines of credits) given to the entrepreneurs to test this hypothesis are analyzed in Table 19.19. Only simple credits have been used because these types of credit are more relationship-oriented credits compared to the rest (fully demonstrated with fixed assets). Empirical results are again consistent with theory. Credit score technology was used to grant the credit. The database given by Banorte only included information for collaterals when credit score technology was used. The coefficient of *Rel Ind* ($N = 0.25, w = 0.3$) is negative and significant. The beta coefficient of *Rel Ind* is −1.303 with a *t* statistic of −9.157. This number can be interpreted that as the relationship index increases by 1, the value of collateral with respect to the credit decreases by 1.303. The relationship index goes from 0 to 0.25, so, the coefficient can be also interpreted as if the index increases by 0.1, the value of collateral decreases to 0.1303. Let's assume that a borrower asks for a loan of $100,000 pesos. Suppose that the bank asks for collateral with a value of $200,000 pesos. The value of collateral with respect the credit is 2. If the borrower increases the relationship index by

Table 19.19 Value of collateral and relationship index, $N = 0.25$, $w = 0.3$ (simple credits or lines of credit)

Descriptive statistics

	Mean	Std dev.	N
Sales/mortgage	1.40	1.996	33,853
Premio_i	0.09953754818970	0.026069651683161	33,853
LnCredit	12.0123	1.30495	33,853
Rel Index ($N = 0.25$ and $w = 0.3$)	0.1030	0.07740	33,853
$R = 0.129$; $R^2 = 0\,0.17$			

Regression analysis

	Not standardized coefficients		Standardized coefficients	t	Sig. (p)
	B	error.	Beta		
Premio_i	−0.858	0.427	−0.011	−2.011	0.044
LnCredit	0.068[a]	0.009	0.044	7.771	0.000
FloatingRate	−0.534[a]	0.031	−0.096	−17.238	0.000
Relationship index: Rel Index ($N = 0.25$ and $w = 0.3$)	−1.303[a]	0.142	−0.051	−9.157	0.000

[a]Statistically significant at a 5% level

0.1, the value of the collateral decreases to 0.1303. In other words, the bank will ask for collateral with a value of 2–0.1303 = 1.8697 times the loan or $186,970 pesos ($100,000 × 1.8697). Elsas and Kranhen (2002) found that relationship lenders do require more collateral from their debtors than normal lenders. The results reveal that both variables, relationship and value of collateral, are inversely related. Intuition tells me that as the relationship is built, trust and commitment is developed between borrower and lender. Collateral becomes less important to the bank, and management competency and business practice developed by the entrepreneurs and observed by banks becomes more important.

$$\text{Value collateral}(X) = \beta_0 + \beta_1(\text{Credit charact}) + \beta_2(\text{Industry}) + \beta_3(\text{Relationship index}) + \varepsilon$$

Summary

Four hypotheses tested in this chapter include (1) as relationship lending increases the cost of credit decreases, (2) as relationship lending increases, the probability of pledging collateral decreases, (3) as relationship lending increases, the probability of default decrease and (4) as relationship lending increases, the value of collateral decreases. Using multiple regressions and logistic regressions, it was found during the study that relationship has an effect on the cost of credit, default and collateral. Not surprisingly, the results are consistent with previous literature. The beauty of this approach is that it uses a new proxy for a relationship: the relationship index. In addition, it uses a dataset of loans given by a Mexican bank to Mexican entrepreneurs. Even though government regulations and bank policies limit the relationship, it is clear that relationship lending is present on the bank-entrepreneurs interaction and has the very same effects as those in other countries. These effects are good reasons (create incentives) for both economic agents (bank and entrepreneurs) to interact.

References

Agresti, A. (1996). *An introduction to categorical data analysis.* New York: Wiley & S Sons.

Angelini, P., Salvo, R. D., & Ferri, G. (1998). Availability and cost of credit for small businesses: Customer relationships and credit cooperatives. *Journal of Banking & Finance, 22*(6), 925–954.

Berger, A. N., & Udell, G. F. (1995). Relationship lending and lines of credit in small firm finance. *Journal of Business, 68*, 351–381.

Boot, A. W. A., & Thakor, A. V. (1994). Moral hazard and secured lending in an infinitely repeated credit market game. *International Economic Review, 35*, 899–920.

Cole, R. (1998). The importance of relationships to the availability of credit. *Journal of Banking & Finance, 22*(6–8), 959–977.

Elsas, Ralf, & Krahnen, Jan Pieter (2002). Collateral, relationship lending and financial distress: An empirical study on financial contracting, CFS Working Paper, No. 2002/17, Goethe University, Center for Financial Studies (CFS), Frankfurt a. M. Retrieved from http://nbn-resolving.de/urn:nbn:de:he bis:30-53001.

D'auria, C., & Foglia, A. (1997). *Le determinanti del tasso di interesse sui crediti alle imprese.* Temi di discussione, n. 293. Roma: Banca d'Italia.

Elsas, R., & Krahnen, J. P. (1998). Is relationship lending special? Evidence from creditfile data in Germany. *Journal of Banking and Finance, 22*, 1283–1316.

La Porta, R., Lopez de Silanes, F., & Zamarripa, G. (2003). Related lending. *Quarterly Journal of Economics, 118*, 231–268.

Menard, C. (1995). Markets as institutions versus organizations as markets: Disentangling some fundamental concepts. *Journal of Economic Behavior & Organization, 28*(2), 161–182.

Moya, F. A. (2018). Relationship lending and entrepreneurial behavior: A game-theoretic-based modeling. In A. Rajagopal & R. Behl (Eds.), *Start-up enterprises and contemporary innovation strategies in the global marketplace* (pp. 65–86). Hershey, PA: IGI Global. http://dx.doi.org/10.4018/978-1-5225-4831-7.ch006

Petersen, M. A., & Rajan, R. G. (1994). The benefits of lending relationships: Evidence from small businesses. *Journal of Finance, 49*, 3–37.

PART III

Business Governance and Society: Nepal

CHAPTER 20

The Impact of Corporate Governance on Efficiency of Nepalese Commercial Banks

Radhe S. Pradhan, Mukesh Kumar Shah, Nabin Bhandari, Nagendra Prasad Mahato, Namaraj Adhikari, and Nirajan Bam

INTRODUCTION

Corporate governance has been increasingly popular in recent years. From the 1997 Asian financial crisis to the Enron and WorldCom scandals in the United States, the main reason for these problems was poor corporate governance. Corporate governance is considered as one of the most critical factors influencing firm performance. Corporate governance in the banking sector is particularly important. This is because the banking sector plays a special role in the economic system as it facilitates capital allocations and the risk management of the business. Thus, the corporate governance arrangements of banks are very important for the business of the banks and their business customers.

Corporate governance is the key to the global integrity of corporate institutions especially financial institutions and other sectors. It cannot

R. S. Pradhan (✉) • M. K. Shah • N. Bhandari • N. P. Mahato
• N. Adhikari • N. Bam
Uniglobe College, Thribhuvan University, Kathmandu, Nepal
e-mail: rspradhan@uniglobe.edu.np

© The Author(s) 2019
Rajagopal, R. Behl (eds.), *Business Governance and Society*,
https://doi.org/10.1007/978-3-319-94613-9_20

occur in the absence of accountability and transparency. These bring development, growth and lasting corporate performance in monetary and operational terms. For this reason, the quality of corporate governance principles in place affects the performance of individual institutions and that of the economy as a whole in terms of growth and development. The impact of corporate governance on firm performance has received enormous attention in economic and finance literature in recent years. This attention was motivated by financial scandals that rocked the US economy in early and late 2000 and the Asian financial crisis of late 1990s. Despite a number of studies having been undertaken on the subject matter, there is still much debate on the relationship between corporate governance and firm performance and more soon on the relationship between corporate governance and performance of commercial banks (Marimuthu 2008).

The banking sector plays a crucial financial intermediary role in any economy. The 1997–1998 economic crises in the Asian countries highlighted the importance of corporate governance. The corporate governance of banks is more important than of other industries. Poor corporate governance of banks can drive the market to lose confidence in the ability of banks, leading to economic crisis in a country and inviting systemic risk (Poudel and Hovey 2013). In contrast, good corporate governance strengthens property rights, minimizes transaction costs and the costs of capital, and leads to capital market development. Corporate governance is viewed as a whole set of measures taken within an enterprise to favor the economic agents to take part in the productive process, in order to generate some organization surplus and to set up a fair distribution between the partners, taking into consideration what they have brought to the organization (Tornyeva and Wereko 2012). The literature from four complementary theoretical perspectives is reviewed.

One of the theoretical principles underlying the issue of corporate governance is the agency theory of separation of ownership and control (Tornyeva and Wereko 2012). Agency theory is defined as the relationship between the principles. In this theory, shareholders who are the owners or principles of the company hire the agents to perform work (Wanyama and Olweny 2013). Principles delegate the running of business to the directors or managers who are shareholder agents. Agency problem arises because the action of managers does not always promote the interest of the financier; in fact, some of their actions are very detrimental to the financier (Tornyeva and Wereko 2012).

Jensen revealed the consumption of perquisites by managers and other types of empirical building. Agency theory suggests that employees or manager in organizations can be self-interested. It also states that shareholders expect the agents to act and make decisions in the best interest of the principals. On the contrary, agents may not necessarily make decisions in the best interest of the principals. An agent may succumb to self-interest and opportunistic behavior and fall short of congruence between the aspirations of the principal and the agent's pursuits. The agents are controlled by principal-made rules with the aim of maximizing shareholders' values. Thus, agency theory can be employed to explore the relationship between ownership and management.

The theory is based on the assumption that the interest of shareholders and the interest of management are aligned; therefore, management is motivated to make decisions that maximize performance and the total value of the company (Tornyeva and Wereko 2012). Donaldson and Davis found that one who protects and maximizes shareholders' wealth through firm performance maximizes steward utility functions (Wanyama and Olweny 2013). The theory believes that there is greater utility in cooperative rather than individualistic behavior, hence whilst the action of management maximizes shareholder wealth it also meets management's personal needs (Tornyeva and Wereko 2012). Managers protect and maximize shareholders' wealth through firm performance, because by so doing, their utility functions are maximized. Moreover, stewardship theory suggests unifying the role of the CEO and the chairman so as to reduce agency costs and to have greater role as steward in the organization. It was evident that there would be better safeguard of the interest of the shareholder.

The resource dependency theory was developed with the objective of emphasizing the important role played by the board of directors in providing access to resources that would enhance the company performance and protect it against externalities (Tornyeva and Wereko 2012). Resource dependency theory focused on the role that directors play in providing or securing essential resources to an organization through their linkage to the external environment. Directors bring essential resources to the company in the form of information, skills, legitimacy, and access to key constituents such as suppliers, buyers, the public, policymakers and social groups. Customers influence the financial performance of banking organizations (Tornyeva and Wereko 2012). Johnson et al. agreed that the theory provides focus on the appointment of representatives of independent organizations as a means of gaining accessibility to resources critical to the organization's success (Tornyeva and Wereko 2012).

Moreover, this theory can be defined as any group or individual who can affect or is affected by the achievement of the organization's objectives. Stakeholder theory suggests that managers in an organization have a network of relationships to serve, which includes the suppliers, employees and business partners. It has been argued that this network of relationships is more important than the owner-manager-employee relationship as in agency theory. Stakeholder theory, like resource dependency theory, also proposed for the representation of the various interest groups on the organization's board in order to ensure consensus building and to avoid conflict. The board therefore serves as arbitration over the conflicting interest of the stakeholders and brings about cohesion needed for the achievement of the organizational objectives.

Jensen (2001) observed a theory for adopting a single-valued objective of maximizing wealth of stakeholders. According to him, the performance of an organization is not only measured by returns to stakeholders but also by the management of information in the organization with particular reference to vertical communication, inter-personal relationships in the organization and the working environment. Due to the complex nature of the stakeholder relationship and the need for better management of the various stakeholders, it was determined that stakeholder theory cannot be a single theory but rather should be categorized into three different approaches: descriptive, instrumental and normative (Donaldson and Preston 1995).

In the context of Nepal, corporate governance reforms are of great significance for gaining sustained effort to attract foreign direct investment and foreign portfolio management, and to mobilize greater saving through the capital market. Specifically, the central bank of Nepal reported severe lapses in corporate governance in every bank. Despite issuing directives to strengthen corporate governance in 2005, the results were not improved. Therefore, the objectives of this research are to fill a gap as the first in-depth study on the role of corporate governance in efficiency of Nepalese commercial banks. Interestingly, the findings of the research are consistent with the previous studies conducted in various countries (Poudel and Hovey 2013). This study will focus on how banks choose their corporate structures and strategies that will in turn affect their performance.

The preceding discussion reveals that there is no consistency in the findings of various studies concerning the impact of corporate governance on efficiency of Nepalese commercial banks.

The main objective of the study is to find the impact of corporate governance on firm performance of Nepalese commercials banks. It also measures the corporate governance practices in Nepal and it examines the impact of corporate governance on the ratio of non-performing loans. The preceding discussion reveals that there is no consistency in the findings of various studies concerning capital adequacy, cost income and bank performance. Therefore, this study has been conducted to analyze the effect of capital adequacy and cost income on the performance of Nepalese commercial banks. More specifically, it examines the effects of capital adequacy ratio, cost income ratio, debt to equity ratio, equity capital to assets, bank size and liquid ratio on the performance of Nepalese commercial banks.

The remainder of this study is organized as follows: Section "Methodological Aspects" describes the sample, data and methodology. Section "Result and Discussion" presents the empirical results and the final section draw conclusions and discuss the implications of the study findings.

METHODOLOGICAL ASPECTS

The study is based on the secondary data gathered from 18 commercial banks in Nepal for the period 2010–2011to 2015–2016. The main sources of data are annual reports and websites of the selected commercial banks.

Table 20.1 shows the number of commercial banks selected for the study along with the study period and number of observations.

The Model

The model estimated in this study assumes that the non-performing loan depends on several corporate governance variables. The corporate governance variables include board size, independent director, audit committee member, domestic ownership, female director, board meeting, bank age, and foreign ownership and CEO duality. Therefore, the model takes the following form:

Efficiency (EY) = f(board size, number of independent director on the board, number of audit committee member, foreign ownership, domestic ownership, CEO duality, bank age, number of female director in the board, number of board meetings, bank size).

Table 20.1 List of sample banks selected for the study alone with the study period and number of observations

S. no.	Name of commercial banks	Study period	Observations
1	Agriculture Development Bank Limited	2010/11–2015/16	6
2	Nabil Bank Limited	2010/11–2015/16	6
3	Nepal Investment Bank Limited	2010/11–2015/16	6
4	Standard Chartered Bank Nepal Limited	2010/11–2015/16	6
5	Himalayan Bank Limited	2010/11–2015/16	6
6	Nepal SBI Bank	2010/11–2015/16	6
7	Everest Bank Limited	2010/11–2015/16	6
8	Kumari Bank Limited	2010/11–2015/16	6
9	Bank of Kathmandu Limited	2010/11–2015/16	6
10	Laxmi Bank Limited	2010/11–2015/16	6
11	Citizens Bank International Limited	2010/11–2015/16	6
12	Prime Commercial Bank Limited	2010/11–2015/16	6
13	Sunrise Bank Limited	2010/11–2015/16	6
14	NMB Bank Nepal Limited	2010/11–2015/16	6
15	NIC Asia Bank Limited	2010/11–2015/16	6
16	Machhapuchchhre Bank Limited	2010/11–2015/16	6
17	Sanima Bank Limited	2010/11–2015/16	6
18	Siddhartha Bank Limited	2010/11–2015/16	6
Total number of observations			108

More specifically, the given model is segmented into the following models:

Model 1

$$\text{NPLS} = \beta_0 + \beta_1 \text{BS} + \beta_2 \text{ID} + \beta_3 \text{ACM} + \beta_4 \text{FO} + \beta_5 \text{DO} \\ + \beta_6 \text{CEOD} + \beta_7 \text{BA} + \beta_8 \text{FD} + \beta_9 \text{BM} + \beta_{10} \text{BAS} + \varepsilon_{it} \dots \quad (20.\text{i})$$

Model 2

$$\text{CE} = \beta_0 + \beta_1 \text{BS} + \beta_2 \text{ID} + \beta_3 \text{ACM} + \beta_4 \text{FO} + \beta_5 \text{DO} \\ + \beta_6 \text{CEOD} + \beta_7 \text{BA} + \beta_8 \text{FD} + \beta_9 \text{BM} + \beta_{10} \text{BAS} + \varepsilon_{it} \dots \dots \quad (20.\text{ii})$$

where,

NPLS = Efficiency is defined as the ratio of non-performing loan to total loan, in percentage.

CE = Cost-efficiency is defined as the ratio of total operating expenses to total assets, in percentage.

BS = Board size is defined as the number of directors on the board.

ID = Independent directors are defined as the number of independent directors on the board.

ACM = Audit committee is defined as the number of audit committee members.

FO = Foreign ownership is defined as the proportion of foreign ownership in the firm.

DO = Domestic ownership is defined as the proportion of domestic ownership in the firm.

CEOD = CEO duality is defined as the combination of responsibility of board chairperson; CEO = 0 for the different role of CEO and chairman, 1 otherwise.

BA = Bank age is defined as duration of operation until current year.

FD = Female directors is defined as the number of female directors on the board.

BM = Board meeting is defined as the number of board meetings held in the given year.

BAS = Bank size is defined as total assets of the bank.

Board Size

Agency theory assumes that a smaller board is recommended to minimize the agency cost by effective control over the management whereas larger boards might increase a large number of potential interactions and conflicts among the group members (Yoshikawa and Phan 2003). Bussoli and Marisa (2015) explored the relationship between corporate governance and banks' loans performance and empirically stated that board size negatively influences the quality of loans and resulted in higher non-performing loans. They empirically concluded that the larger the board size, the less the efficiency of the banks. Similarly, Simpson and Gleason (1999) and Belkhir revealed that larger board size is linked to lower performance of banking and a larger number of non-performing loans. Conversely, there is an another school of thought in favor of larger board size that believes that firms with larger board size have the ability to push the managers to track lower costs of debt and increase performance because creditors view these firms as having more effective monitors of their financial accounting process. Jensen and Ruback (1983) argued that the size of the board should be limited to seven or eight members. Based on the codes of corporate governance in Nepal, the board of directors consists of five to nine members. Some studies have suggested smaller boards are better for improving firm performance (Lipton and Lorsch 1992). While some other studies provide a positive relationship between board size and firm performance (Zahra and Pearce 1989). However, Ghabayen (2012) found no relationship between board size and a firm's performance. Moreover, if performance is measured in return on assets (ROA) and return on equity (ROE), the impact of board size has a positive significance with firm performance. In view of the above discussion, the hypothesis has been structured as

H_1 *There is a negative relationship between board size and efficiency.*

Board Independence

The empirical findings on board independence and bank performance are mixed. Prior studies show that a majority of independent directors are necessary for better bank governance (Crespi-Cladera and Gispert 2003). A strand of literature revealed the importance of board independence and concluded that higher board independence is linked with higher efficiency of banks. Jensen found that independent directors are more likely to protect the shareholders' rights. Others find there is an inverted U-shaped relation between outsider and bank performance. In this study, we emphasize that an independent board of directors has fewer conflicts of interest when monitoring managers. Thus, when the monitoring function is prevalent, we expect that adding new independent directors to the board will improve the supervision of management and reduce the conflicts of interest among stakeholders. However, we expect that too many independent directors will destroy bank value because of problems with coordination and decision-making. Accordingly, a board should have an optimum mix of executive and independent directors, which is more adequate for creating value for banks than excessively independent boards. Thus, based on this, the following hypothesis is examined:

H_2 *There is positive relationship between board independence and bank efficiency.*

Number of Audit Committee Members

Al-Smadi (2013) found that committee of the board of the directors has a significant impact only on bank performance. Agency theory suggests that shareholders require protection because management (agents) may not always act in the interest of the corporation's owners (principals). The main role of the audit committee is to improve the quality of the financial reporting, which leads to improved firm performance (Pincus et al. 1989). The Cadbury Commission suggested that the audit committee should consist of three members. It is likely that larger audit committees have better resources than smaller audit committees. The decision-making literature has argued that increasing the number of people involved in an activity substantially increases group performance and decreases the chance for wrongdoing because collusion becomes more difficult. Boubakri et al. (2005) showed that the degree to which audit clients were confronted with agency conflicts influences their choice of audit quality. The articles also indicated that the negative effect of audit committee size on bank performance could be attributed to the audit committee members' lack of expertise in helping the board in the governance of the bank. There are mixed results regarding audit committee size and a firm's performance. Klein (2002) and Coleman-Kyereboah revealed a positive relationship between audit committee size and a firm's performance. However, other researchers reported no relation between audit committee size and performance. Accordingly, the hypothesis has been structures as

H_3 *There is a positive relationship between the size of the audit committee and bank efficiency.*

Foreign Ownership

Foreign ownership has a positive impact on banks' soundness. Brealey and Kaplanis (1996) reported that the presence of foreign banks may enhance foreign direct investment in the non-financial sector. Besides, foreign ownership improves human capital through the presence of foreign managers that bring better skills and technologies, in particular in developing countries (Lensink and Hermes 2004). This international expertise will also lead to improved local competencies through training and knowledge transfer. Empirically, Barth et al. (2002) found a negative effect of foreign ownership on non-performing loans in a cross-country analysis. They highlight that foreign banks raise loan quality in a country and this may lead to improved credit quality of domestic banks. In a sample of 81 banks from 22 developing countries, Boubakri et al. (2005) showed that foreign participation reduces the level of risk taken amongst banks. Finally, Micco et al. found that foreign-controlled banks are more preferred than domestic ones for a panel of emerging countries. Relevant literature on corporate governance provides much attention to the issue of shareholder identity (Shleifer and Vishny 1997). There is a number of research into the relationship between ownership and bank profitability. It is accepted that foreign ownership plays a crucial role in a firm's performance, particularly in developing and transitional economies (Gorg and Greenaway 2004). Most of these studies were carried out in industrial and developing countries (Bonin and Wheeler 2005). Clarke et al. argued that foreign banks are more profitable than domestic ones in developing countries and less profitable in industrial countries. The above discussion on literature review suggest structuring the following hypothesis

H_4 There is a positive relationship between foreign ownership and bank efficiency.

Domestic Ownership

Increased domestic ownership (DO) presence adversely affects capital allocation efficiency. Increases in DO are associated with increased lending to less productive economic sectors and to industries that are not dependent on external finance, suggesting a misallocation of funds by domestic shareholder-controlled banks. These findings are consistent with the looting view, a pessimistic assessment of related lending practices by banks (La Porta et al. 2003). The main finding from the study is that DO has a significant impact on a bank's performance and non-performing loans (Al-Smadi 2013). The large domestic shareholders of banks (e.g. local companies, wealthy individuals) typically have substantial interests in non-financial firms as well; banks controlled by these domestic shareholders usually direct a significant portion of their lending activities to related parties (e.g. firms controlled by relatives), even when these firms are inefficient. La Porta et al. (2003) observed that developing countries with poor governance could adversely affect capital allocation efficiency. Hence, the hypothesis has been formed as stated below

H_5 There is a negative relationship between domestic ownership and bank efficiency.

CEO Duality

The board is a governance mechanism in agency framework for strategic decision-making and setting an organization's vision by the supposition that when the shareholders have the information to verify and influence supervision deeds, the executives are more likely to act in the interests of the shareholders. Moreover, agency theorists put forward one key monitoring feature, which is the separation between the roles of the CEO and chairman. El-Chaarani (2014) found that there is a significant and negative relationship between CEO duality and bank performance. Daily and Dalton (1993) explained that duality may light the board's ability to watch for executive opportunism because the powerful chief executive is able to control the board. Moreover, agency theorists claim that a powerful leader holding both the CEO and board chairman positions will tend to pursue his personal interests more willingly than for the benefit of the principal. On one hand, an individual with dual positions will tend to operate ceremonially, communicate poorly and "rubber-stamp" the executive's verdicts (Chen and Michael 2009). On the other hand, the separation of CEO and chairman positions sends positive signals to corporate lenders and investors, hence increasing the chances of raising additional capital that reduces the risk of bankruptcy (Yermack 1996). Ehikioya and Benjamin discovered that for firms in which their CEO and board chairman are separated, stakeholders are likely to gain confidence in the firms' ability to raise additional capital and hence there are less chances of bankruptcy. In view of the above discussion, the hypothesis has been structured as stated below

H_6 There is a positive relationship between CEO duality and bank efficiency.

Bank Age

As a firm ages, it is expected to gain experience in production processes, handling of customers, understanding needs of employees and adopting with whole stakeholders. In studying the relationship between firm age and profitability, we want to differentiate the possible influence of age on profitability by going back to previous studies. Segarra et al. found evidence that firms improve with age, because ageing firms are observed to have steadily increasing levels of productivity and higher profits. While most of the studies proved the existence of a significant negative relationship between age and profitability, bank age, duration of the loan and credit policy were found to be significant determinants of non-performing loans (Ikram et al. 2016). Other studies also concluded no significant relationship between age and profitability. However, the nature of banks may be different somehow, because as bank grows in age, they gain customer loyalty and benefit from the experience curve. Our seventh hypothesis is stated as follows:

H_7 *There is a positive correlation between a bank's age and its efficiency.*

Female Directors

Virtanen (2012) suggested that "women (like external shareholders, ethnic minorities, and foreigners often bring a fresh perspective on complex issues, and this can help correct informational biases in strategy formation and problem solving." Adams and Funk (2012) provided evidence that generalizing from the population to the executive ranks may be misleading. In a survey of the population of directors in Sweden, they show that women on boards of publicly listed firms are different both from women in the general population and from male directors in the values they emphasize. Female directors are more open to change and less conservation-oriented than both their population counterparts and male directors. A recent Finnish study reports that female board members are, compared to their male counterparts, more likely to take an active role on their boards (Virtanen 2012). Resource dependency theory is a second guiding perspective as female directors bring unique and valuable resources and relationships to their boards. In the case of networks, early work revealed that compared to male managers, female managers generally have more diverse networks (Ibarra 1992). Eagly suggested that an individual gender determines behavior and its effectiveness with respect to influence. Furthermore, the theory suggests that male and female behaviors are assessed in terms of how they ascribe (or diverge) from expectations of the respective gender. Individuals who use tactics that are aligned to their gender tend to be perceived better by others. For example, women are expected to ascribe to more feminine traits such as sympathy and gentility. In contrast, men are expected to be more assertive and aggressive. Another gender role associated with women is flexibility, which leads to greater ability to manage ambiguous situations. The researcher confirmed that the gender of a co-op bank board of director's president had significant influence on the bank's effectiveness, and when that position was held by a woman it had a positive effect on the bank's condition, which implies a positive relationship between board gender diversity and firm performance (Balina 2017). Hence, hypothesis has been formed as stated below

H_8 *There is a positive relationship between female director and bank efficiency.*

Number of Board Meetings

Capital adequacy ratio (CAR) and non-performing loans are not statistically significantly related with number of board meetings (Lai and Choi 2014). Relconger et al. suggested that the board meeting is an important resource in improving the effectiveness of the board. It helps directors to stay informed and keep abreast of the development of the organization (Marimuthu 2008). Regular meetings also allow directors to sit and strategize on how to move the organization forward. Lipton and Lorsch (1992) revealed that regular meetings enable directors to interact thereby creating and strengthening cohesive bonds among them. However, the opposing view of board meetings is that they are costly in terms of travel expenses, refreshments and sitting allowance to be paid to directors. Board meetings are not necessarily useful because the limited time directors meet outside is not used for meaningful exchange of ideas between themselves and management. Instead, the time is preoccupied with routine tasks and meeting formalities (Jensen 1993). This reduces the amount of time the board has to monitor management (Lipton and Lorsch 1992). The hypothesis has been structured as

H_9 *There is a positively relationship between the board meetings and bank efficiency.*

Bank Size

Pandey defined the size of the organization in the form of the assets that it holds. Large firms are less disposed to insolvency; this is because such firms have diversified their investment segments and hence lowered their risks. Hauner (2005) found that the relationship between bank size and efficiency is positive. Pasiouras et al. (2007) showed that bank size is positively associated with bank cost-efficiency. Low levels of bankruptcy allow larger firms to access high amounts of debt. Large firms may reduce the level of information asymmetry in the market by taking advantage of opportunities in the market that enhance performance. Large firms are more stable compared to smaller firms because they have capacity to satisfy their financial duties and hence have a high degree of information exposure. Large banks meet the customers' financial demands as a result of their wide network of branches; this has a greater impact on large banks compared to small banks that do not service these markets. Willison and Hong argued that efficiencies induced by bank growth are determined by bank size because economies of scale differ based on a range of possible sizes of bank operations. Larger firms have better market experiences and well-defined networks and hence stand a better chance compared to younger banks that are still struggling to establish themselves in the market. Ammar et al. (2003) assessed the factors that affected profitability of a bank prior to and during the financial crisis in Switzerland. The results found that both large and small banks were positively related to profitability. Further, it was revealed that big and smaller banks were profitable compared to medium-sized banks prior to the crisis. One of the reasons given why larger banks were profitable was because they had more efficient services since they adopted modern technologies. The banks had diversified their products and services to minimize risks, by handling bulky products and services and having complex systems and processes enabling the banks to enjoy economies of scale. Accordingly, the hypothesis is developed as stated below

H_{10} *There is a positive relationship between bank size and bank efficiency.*

Results and Discussion

Descriptive Statistics

Table 20.2 presents the descriptive statistics of selected dependent and independent variables during the period 2010–2011 to 2015–2016.

The board size ranges from a minimum of five directors to a maximum of 11 directors giving an average 7.907 percent. The number of independent directors ranges from a minimum of one to a maximum of four, giving an average 2.343 percent. The number of audit committee members ranges from a minimum of two members to a maximum of five members, giving an average of 3.546 percent. Percentage of foreign ownership

Table 20.2 Descriptive statistics

Variables	Minimum	Maximum	Mean	S.D.
CE	0.02	0.65	0.08	0.10
NPL	0.00	8.60	1.81	1.62
BS	5.00	11.00	7.90	1.31
ID	1.00	4.00	2.34	0.84
ACM	2.00	5.00	3.54	0.71
FO	0.00	75.00	12.93	22.59
DO	25.00	100.00	87.06	22.59
CEOD	0.00	1.00	0.05	0.23
BA	3.00	48.00	17.16	10.20
FD	0.00	2.00	0.34	0.61
BM	6.00	56.00	17.64	8.99
BAS	2.10	127.30	48.65	27.47

Table 20.2 presents the descriptive statistics of selected dependent and independent variables during the period 2010–2011 to 2015–2016. Dependent variables are NPLs (non-performing loans is defined as non-performing loan divided by total loan), NPL/TA (non-performing loan to total assets is defined as non-performing loan divided by total assets), CE (cost-efficiency is defined as the ratio of total operating expenses to total assets, in percentage). Independent variables are BS (board size is defined as number of board members in a commercial bank), BM (board meeting is defined as number of board meetings held in a year), ID (independent directors is defined as the number of independent directors on the board), CEOD (CEO duality is defined as the combination of responsibility of board chairperson and CEO), BA (bank age is defined as duration of operation until current year), FO (foreign ownership is defined as percentage of ownership occupied by foreign investors), DO (domestic ownership is defined as percentage of ownership occupied by national investors), ACM (composition of audit committee is defined as number of members formed from different wings of the bank on the audit committee), BAS (bank size is defined as total assets of the bank), BM (board meeting is defined as the number of board meetings held in the given year), and FD (female directors is defined as the number of female directors on the board)

ranges from a minimum of 0 percent to a maximum of 75 percent, giving an average 12.939 percent. Percentage of domestic ownership ranges from a minimum of 25 percent to a maximum of 100 percent, giving an average of 86.135 percent. CEO duality ranges from a minimum of 0 to the maximum of 1, giving an average of 0.056 percent. Bank age ranges from a minimum of three years to a maximum of 48 years, giving an average 17.16 percent. The number of female directors ranges from a minimum of 0 to a maximum of two, giving an average of 0.34 percent. The number of board meetings ranges from a minimum of six meetings to a maximum of 56 meetings, giving an average of 17.64 percent. Bank size ranges from a minimum of 2.12 to a maximum of 129.78, giving an average of 49.112 percent.

Correlation Analysis

Having indicated the descriptive statistics, we compute the Pearson correlation coefficients for commercial banks and present them in Table 20.3. The table shows that there is a positive relationship between board size and non-performing loans of the commercial banks, which means the larger the board, the higher the ratio of non-performing loans. Similarly, independent directors, audit committee members, domestic ownership, bank age, female director and bank size also have a positive relation with the ratio of non-performing loans. In contrast, foreign ownership and CEO duality have a negative relation with the ratio of non-performing loans.

Regression Analysis

Having indicated the Pearson's correlation coefficients, we carried out the regression analysis and present them in Table 20.4. More specifically, it shows the regression results of board size, number of independent directors on the board, number of audit committee members, foreign ownership, domestic ownership, CEO duality, bank age, number of female directors on the board, number of board meetings, and bank size.

Table 20.4 shows that beta coefficients are positive and significant for board size. This indicates that larger the board, the higher the inefficiency of Nepalese commercial banks. This finding is consistent with the findings of Lipton and Lorsch (1992). The results also show that beta coefficients are positive and significant for board independence. This indicates that the higher the number of independent members on the board, the higher the inefficiency of Nepalese commercial banks. This finding is consistent with the findings of Anderson. Similarly, beta coefficients are positive and significant for audit committee members. This indicates that the larger the size of the audit committee, the higher the inefficiency of Nepalese commercial banks. This finding is opposite to the findings of Pathak and Zigli. Furthermore, the results show that beta coefficients are negative and significant for foreign ownership. This indicates that the higher the percentage of foreign ownership in the commercial bank, the higher the efficiency of the bank. This result is consistent with the findings of Clarke et al. Conversely, results show that beta coefficients are positive

Table 20.3 Pearson correlation matrix for the selected Nepalese commercial banks

Variables	CE	NPL	BS	ID	ACM	FO	DO	CEOD	BA	FD	BM	BAS
CE	1											
NPL	0.05	1										
BS	−0.05	0.25**	1									
ID	−0.19*	0.49**	0.61**	1								
ACM	0.03	0.45**	0.23*	0.27**	1							
FO	−0.21*	−0.27**	−0.36**	−0.17	0.09	1						
DO	0.21*	0.27**	0.36**	0.17	−0.06	−1.00**	1					
CEOD	−0.13	−0.19*	−0.35**	−0.09	0.04	0.69**	−0.69**	1				
BA	−0.02	0.43**	−0.12	0.09	0.59**	0.36**	−0.36**	0.22*	1			
FD	0.07	0.26**	0.14	0.13	0.29**	0.95**	−0.95**	0.19*	0.40**	1		
BM	−0.07	0.19*	0.37**	0.34**	0.10	−0.04**	0.34**	−0.11	−0.21*	−0.12	1	
BAS	−0.12	0.020*	−0.04	0.02	0.59**	0.26**	−0.26**	0.03	0.75**	0.136	−0.14	1

Note: The asterisk signs (**) and (*) indicate that correlations are significant at 1 percent and 5 percent levels respectively

The table shows the correlation of dependent and independent variables of selected Nepalese enterprises from 2010–2011 to 2015–2016. Dependent variables are NPLs (non-performing loan to total assets is defined as non-performing loan divided by total assets, in percentage) and CE (cost-efficiency is defined as the ratio of total operating expenses to total assets, in percentage). Independent variables are BS (board size is defined as number of board members in a commercial bank), ID (independent directors is defined as the number of independent directors on the board), ACM (composition of audit committee is defined as number of members formed from different wings of the bank on the audit committee), FO (foreign ownership is defined as percentage of ownership occupied by foreign investors), DO (domestic ownership is defined as percentage of ownership occupied by national investors), CEOD (CEO duality is defined as the combination of responsibility of board chairperson and CEO), BA (bank age is defined as duration of operation until current year), FD (female directors is defined as the number of female directors on the board), BM (board meeting is defined as the number of board meetings held in the given year), and BAS (bank size is defined as total assets of the bank)

Table 20.4 Regression of corporate governance and dependent variable of non-performing loan

Model	Intercept	BS	ID	ACM	FO	DO	CEOD	BA	FD	BM	BAS	Adj.R^2	SEE	F
1	−1.34 (1.47)	0.38 (3.41)**										0.09	1.54	11.64
2	−0.56 (1.41)		0.97 (6.08)**									0.25	1.40	37.05
3	−2.67 (4.00)**			1.24 (6.72)**								0.29	1.36	45.21
4	1.9 (11.13)**				−0.01** (−2.59)**							0.05	1.58	6.73
5	0.22 (0.39)					0.01 (2.76)						0.05	1.57	7.63
6	1.79 (11.31)**						−1.26 (1.87)					0.02	1.60	3.51
7	1.00 (3.92)**							0.04 (3.48)**				0.09	1.54	12.17
8	1.45 (8.487)**								0.788 (3.21)**			0.08	1.55	10.32

9	0.99 (2.95)**						0.041 (2.42)*		0.04	1.58	5.89
10	0.95 (3.123)**							0.016 (2.88)**	0.06	1.57	8.39
11	−2.18 (−2.38)*	0.39 (3.60)**						0.01 (3.11)**	0.159	1.48	11.13
12	−3.44 (5.33)**	0.74 (5.10)**	0.92 (4.61)**			0.08 (0.73)**			0.42	1.23	27.34
13	−0.75 (0.55)			−0.01 (1.25)	0.008 (0.58)		0.91 (4.21)**	0.038 (2.54)*	0.022 (4.35)**	0.31	1.345	10.74

Notes: (a) Figures in parenthesis are *t*-values; (b) The asterisk signs (**) and (*) indicate that the results are significant at 1 percent and 5 percent levels, respectively; (c) Non-performing loan is a dependent variable

The results are based on panel data of 18 banks with 108 observations during the period 2010–2011 to 2015–2016, by using regression model. The model is, NPLS = β_0 + β_1BS + β_2ID + β_3ACM + β_4FO + β_5DO + β_6CEOD + β_7BA + β_8FD + β_9BM + β_{10}BAS + ε_{it}. Dependent variable are NPLs (non-performing loan to total assets is defined as non-performing loan divided by total assets, in percentage). Independent variables are BS (board size is defined as number of board members in a commercial bank), ID (independent directors is defined as the number of independent directors on the board), ACM (composition of audit committee is defined as number of members formed from different wings of the bank on the audit committee), FO (foreign ownership is defined as percentage of ownership occupied by foreign investors), DO (domestic ownership is defined as percentage of ownership occupied by national investors), CEOD (CEO duality is defined as the combination of responsibility of board chairperson and CEO), BA (bank age is defined as duration of operation until current year), FD (female directors is defined as the number of female directors on the board), BM (board meeting is defined as the number of board meetings held in the given year), and BAS (bank size is defined as total assets of the bank) and significant for domestic ownership. This indicates that higher the percentage of domestic ownership, the higher the inefficiency of Nepalese commercial banks. This finding is similar to the findings of La Porta et al. (2003). Moreover, the result also shows that beta coefficients for CEO duality are negative. This indicates that if the roles of board chairman and CEO are not separated, the commercial bank will experience greater efficiency. This finding is consistent with the findings of Daily and Dalton (1993). The result also shows that beta coefficients are positive and significant for bank age. This indicates that the older the bank, the higher its inefficiency. This finding is consistent with the findings of Majudmar. The result also shows that beta coefficients are positive and significant for female directors. This indicates that an increase in the number of female directors on the board increases the inefficiency of Nepalese commercial banks. This finding is opposite to the finding of Ibarra (1992). Furthermore, the result shows that beta coefficients are positive and significant for board meetings. This indicates that the higher the number of board meetings, the higher the inefficiency of Nepalese commercial banks. The finding is in contrast to the finding of Jensen and Meckling (1976). The result also showed that beta coefficients are positive and significant for bank size. This indicates that the larger the size of the bank, the greater its inefficiency. This finding is in contrast to the finding of Deis and Guffey.

Table 20.5 shows the regression results of board size, number of independent directors on the board, number of audit committee members, foreign ownership, domestic ownership, CEO duality, bank age, number of female directors on the board, number of board meetings, and bank size of Nepalese enterprises.

Table 20.5 shows that beta coefficients for board size, number of independent directors, foreign ownership, CEO duality, bank age, number of board meetings and bank size are all negative. The greater these variables, the lower the bank's cost-efficiency. Beta coefficients for number of audit committee members, domestic ownership and number of female directors is positive. The greater these variables, the higher the bank's cost-efficiency.

Table 20.5 Regression of corporate governance and dependent variable of cost efficiency

Mode	Intercept	BS	ID	ACM	FO	DO	CEOD	BA	FD	BM	BAS	Adj. R^2	SEE	F
1	0.12 (2.14)*	−0.04 (0.56)										0.03	0.10	0.31
2	0.14 (4.94)**		−0.02 (1.98)*									0.02	0.10	3.95
3	0.08 (1.27)			0.10 (0.03)								0.00	0.10	0.01
4	0.10 (9.04)**				−0.01 (2.23)*							0.03	0.09	5.75
5	0.04 (0.14)					0.01 (2.25)*						0.03	0.09	5.75
6	0.09 (9.01)**						−0.05 (1.36)					0.08	0.12	1.48
7	0.08 (4.66)**							−0.21 (0.02)				0.000	0.10	0.00
8	0.08 (7.73)**								0.03 (0.17)			−0.09	0.10	0.03
9	0.09 (4.34)**									0.03 (0.33)**		−0.08	0.10	0.14
10	0.11 (5.57)**										−0.00 (1.33)	0.01	0.10	1.79
11	0.01 (0.04)	−0.01 (0.13)	−0.03 (2.09)	0.05 (1.55)		0.01 (2.28)	−0.04 (0.24)					0.06	0.09	2.49
12	0.13 (1.93)*			−0.05 (0.35)	−0.01 (1.96)		−0.10 (0.18)	−0.01 (0.84)				0.06	0.10	1.44
13	0.18 (0.20)	−0.02 (0.18)	−0.03 (2.37)*	0.19 (1.12)		0.01 (1.50)	−0.02 (0.47)	−0.03 (1.75)	0.02 (0.91)	−0.04 (0.18)	−0.01 (2.15)*	0.08	0.09	2.05

(continued)

Table 20.5 (continued)

Notes: (a) Figures in parenthesis are t-values; (b) The asterisk signs (**) and (*) indicate that the results are significant at 1 percent and 5 percent level respectively; (c) Cost-efficiency is dependent variable

The results are based on panel data of 18 banks with 108 observations during the period 2010–2011 to 2015–2016, by using regression model. The model is, $(CE) = \beta_0 + \beta_1 BS + \beta_2 ID + \beta_3 ACM + \beta_4 FO + \beta_5 DO + \beta_6 CEOD + \beta_7 BA + \beta_8 FD + \beta_9 BM + \beta_{10} BAS + \varepsilon_{it}$.

The dependent variable is CE (cost-efficiency is defined as the ratio of total operating expenses to total assets, in percentage). Independent variables are BS (board size is defined as number of board members in a commercial bank), ID (independent directors is defined as the number of independent directors on the board), ACM (composition of audit committee is defined as number of members formed from different wings of the bank on the audit committee), FO (foreign ownership is defined as percentage of ownership occupied by foreign investors), DO (domestic ownership is defined as percentage of ownership occupied by national investors), CEOD (CEO duality is defined as the combination of responsibility of board chairperson and CEO), BA (bank age is defined as duration of operation until current year), FD (female directors is defined as the number of female directors on the board), BM (board meeting is defined as the number of board meetings held in the given year), and BAS (bank size is defined as total assets of the bank)

Summary and Conclusion

Corporate governance has a relationship pattern between management and stakeholders, and management and board of directors. These relationships are based on ethics, corporate culture and corporate value, and are supported by systems, processes, working procedures and the organization in achieving maximum performance. Non-performing loans are an important subject for the corporate body as they show the efficiency and effectiveness of the organization.

This study attempts to examine the effect of corporate governance variables on non-performing loans to assets. This study is based on secondary data of 18 commercial banks with 108 observations for the period of 2010–2011 to 2015–2016.

The major conclusion of the study is that board size, number of independent directors, number of audit committee members, domestic ownership, bank age, number of female directors and bank size all have a positive relationship with the ratio of non-performing loans. This means that the greater these variables, the higher the ratio of non-performing loans and hence the lower the bank's efficiency. Conversely, foreign ownership and CEO duality have a negative relationship with the ratio of non-performing loans, which indicates that the ratio of non-performing loans will decrease thus increasing the bank's efficiency.

References

Adams, R. B., & Funk, P. C. (2012). Is corporate governance different for bank holding companies? *Economic Policy Review, 9*(1), 123–142.

Al-Smadi, M. O. (2013). Examining the relationship between corporate governance and banks' performance, and risk in Saudi Arabia. *European Journal of Economics, Finance and Administrative Sciences, 16*(2), 59–62.

Ammar, A., Hanna, A. S., Nordheim, E. V., & Russell, J. S. (2003). Indicator variables model of firm's size-profitability relationship of electrical contractors using financial and economic data. *Journal of Construction Engineering and Management, 129*(2), 192–197.

Balina, R. (2017). Does the gender of a bank's president have an effect on financial performance? A case study of Poland's cooperative bank sector. *Journal of Corporate Responsibility and Leadership, 3*(2), 9–22.

Barth, J. R., Dopico, L. G., Nolle, D. E., & Wilcox, J. A. (2002). Bank safety and soundness and the structure of bank supervision: A cross-country analysis. *International Review of Finance, 3*(4), 163–188.

Bonin, D., & Wheeler, J. V. (2005). Bank performance, efficiency and ownership in transition countries. *Journal of Banking & Finance, 19*(1), 31–53.

Boubakri, N., Cosset, J. C., & Guedhami, O. (2005). Post privatization corporate governance: The role of ownership structure and investor protection. *Journal of Financial Economics, 76*(2), 369–399.

Brealey, R. A., & Kaplanis, E. C. (1996). The determination of foreign banking location. *Journal of International Money and Finance, 15*(4), 77–97.

Bussoli, G., & Marisa, B. T. (2015). The impact of corporate governance on banks performance and loan quality: Evidence from Italian cooperative banks. *Chinese Business Review, 14*(8), 390–401.

Chen, Y. Y., & Michael, N. Y. (2009). Cross-border mergers and acquisitions by Chinese listed companies: A principal–principal perspective. *Asia Pacific Journal of Management, 27*(3), 523–539.

Crespi-Cladera, R., & Gispert, C. (2003). Total board compensation, governance and performance of Spanish listed companies. *Labour, 17*(1), 103–126.

Daily, C. M., & Dalton, D. R. (1993). Board of directors' leadership and structure: Control and performance implications. *Entrepreneurship: Theory and Practice, 17*(3), 65–82.

Donaldson, T., & Preston, L. E. (1995). The stakeholder theory of the corporation: Concepts, evidence, and implications. *Academy of Management Review, 20*(1), 65–91.

El-Chaarani, H. (2014). The impact of corporate governance on the performance of Lebanese banks. *The International Journal of Business and Finance Research, 8*(5), 35–46.

Ghabayen, M. A. (2012). Board characteristics and firm performance: Case of Saudi Arabia. *International Journal of Accounting and Financial Reporting, 2*(2), 168–178.

Gorg, H., & Greenaway, D. (2004). Much ado about nothing? Do domestic firms really benefit from foreign direct investment? *The World Bank Research Observer, 19*(2), 171–197.

Hauner, D. (2005). Explaining efficiency differences among large German and Austrian banks. *Applied Economics, 37*(9), 969–980.

Ibarra, H. (1992). Homophile and differential returns: Sex differences in network structure and access in an advertising firm. *Administrative Science Quarterly, 24*(8), 422–447.

Ikram, A., Su, Q., Ijaz, F., & Fiaz, M. (2016). Determinants of non-performing loans: An empirical investigation of bank-specific microeconomic factors. *Journal of Applied Business Research, 32*(6), 1723–1736.

Jensen, M. C. (1993). The modern industrial revolution, exit, and the failure of internal control systems. *Journal of Finance, 48*(3), 31–80.

Jensen, M. C. (2001). Value maximization, stakeholder theory, and the corporate objective function. *Journal of Applied Corporate Finance, 14*(3), 8–21.

Jensen, M. C., & Meckling, W. H. (1976). Theory of the firm: Managerial behavior, agency costs and ownership structure. *Journal of Financial Economics, 3*(4), 305–360.

Jensen, M. C., & Ruback, R. S. (1983). The market for corporate control: The scientific evidence. *Journal of Financial Economics, 11*(1–4), 5–50.

Klein, A. (2002). Audit committee, board of director characteristics, and earnings management. *Journal of Accounting and Economics, 33*(3), 375–400.

La Porta, R., Lopez-de-Silanes, F., & Zamarripa, G. (2003). Related lending. *The Quarterly Journal of Economics, 118*(1), 231–268.

Lai, P. F., & Choi, O. N. (2014). Corporate governance and financial performance of bank in Asian regions and recommendations. *Asian Journal of Finance & Accounting, 6*(2), 377–406.

Lensink, R., & Hermes, N. (2004). The short-term effects of foreign bank entry on domestic bank behavior: Does economic development matter? *Journal of Banking & Finance, 28*(3), 553–568.

Lipton, M., & Lorsch, J. W. (1992). A modest proposal for improved corporate governance. *The Business Lawyer, 22*(8), 59–77.

Marimuthu, M. (2008). Ethnic diversity on boards of directors and its implications on firm financial performance. *Journal of International Social Research, 1*(4), 44–56.

Pasiouras, F., Sifodaskalakis, E., & Zopounidis, C. (2007). Estimating and analyzing the cost efficiency of Greek cooperative banks: An application of two-stage data envelopment analysis. *University of Bath Working Paper, 2*(3), 3–15.

Pincus, K., Rusbarsky, M., & Wong, J. (1989). Voluntary formation of corporate audit committees among NASDAQ firms. *Journal of Accounting and Public Policy, 8*(4), 239–265.

Poudel, R. P., & Hovey, M. (2013). Corporate governance and efficiency in Nepalese commercial banks. *International Review of Business Research Papers, 9*(4), 53–64.

Shleifer, A., & Vishny, R. W. (1997). A survey of corporate governance. *The Journal of Finance, 52*(2), 737–783.

Simpson, W. G., & Gleason, A. E. (1999). Board structure, ownership, and financial distress in banking firms. *International Review of Economics and Finance, 8*(4), 281–292.

Tornyeva, K., & Wereko, T. (2012). Corporate governance and firm performance: Evidence from the insurance. *European Journal of Business and Management, 4*(13), 95–112.

Virtanen, A. (2012). Women on the boards of listed companies: Evidence from Finland. *Journal of Management and Governance, 16*(4), 571–593.

Wanyama, D. W., & Olweny, T. (2013). Effects of corporate governance on financial performance of listed insurance firms in Kenya. *Public policy and Administration Research, 3*(4), 96–120.

Yermack, D. (1996). Higher market valuation of companies with a small board of directors. *Journal of Financial Economics, 40*(2), 185–211.

Yoshikawa, T., & Phan, P. H. (2003). The performance implications of ownership-driven governance reform. *European Management Journal, 21*(6), 698–706.

Zahra, S. A., & Pearce, J. A. (1989). Boards of directors and corporate financial performance: A review and integrative model. *Journal of Management, 15*(2), 291–334.

CHAPTER 21

Impact of Corporate Governance on Dividend Policy of Nepalese Enterprises

Nar B. Bista, Nitesh Raj Bartaula, Om Shrestha, Pooja Gnawali, Poshan Lamichhane, and Pratiksha Parajuli

INTRODUCTION

Corporate governance is the process that facilitates the creation of shareholder value, protection of the individual and collective interests of all stakeholders. The concept of corporate governance is defined as dealing with the ways in which governance of suppliers of finance to corporations has a positive impact on organizational performance (Claessen, 2009). Corporate governance has become a contemporary issue because of its enormous contribution to the economic growth and development of nations. Effective governance is critical to all economic relations especially in emerging and transition economies (Dharwardkar 2000).

N. B. Bista (✉) • N. R. Bartaula • O. Shrestha • P. Gnawali
• P. Lamichhane • P. Parajuli
Uniglobe College, Thribhuvan University, Kathmandu, Nepal
e-mail: nbbista@uniglobe.edu.np

© The Author(s) 2019
Rajagopal, R. Behl (eds.), *Business Governance and Society*,
https://doi.org/10.1007/978-3-319-94613-9_21

Good corporate governance helps in enhancing a firm's performance. This is evident by the increasing attention being given to matters of corporate governance by governments, regulatory bodies, regional bodies and private institutions. Corporate governance refers to the way an organization is directed, administrated or controlled. It includes the set of rules and regulations that affect managerial decisions and contribute to the way a company is perceived by the current and potential stakeholders.

The corporate governance structure specifies the distribution of rights and responsibilities among different participants in the corporation, such as boards, managers, shareholders and other stakeholders, spells out the rules and procedures, and provides decision making assistance in corporate affairs (Thuraisingam 2013). Corporate governance refers to the set of rules and incentives by which the management of a company is directed and controlled (Velnampy 2013). While the objective of the corporation's shareholder is a return on their investment, managers are likely to have other goals, such as power and prestige the come with running a large and powerful organization, or entertainment perquisites of their position. In this situation, managers' superior access to inside information, and the relatively powerless position of the numerous and dispersed shareholders, means that managers are likely to have the upper hand (Jensen 1983).

Corporate governance is seen as an essential mechanism helping the company to attain its corporate objectives and monitoring its performance in achieving these objectives (Mallin et al. 2013). Good corporate governance maximizes the profitability and long-term value of the firm for the shareholders (Heenetigala 2011). The concept of corporate governance presumes a fundamental tension between shareholders and corporate managers (Meckling 1976). Dividend payment is a major component of stock return to shareholders. Dividend payment could provide a signal to the investors that the company is complying with good corporate governance practices (Jo and Pan 2009).

Lee (2009) found that there is a positive relationship between the bank's profitability, bank's size and the dividend payout. Likewise, the profitability, leverage, changes in dividends and collateral capacity had a positive significant impact on the dividend policies of banks in Ghana. Similarly, Ekanayake and Parantham (2010) stated that there is a positive impact of CEO duality on a firm's dividend policy and there is a negative impact of ownership structure on a firm's dividend policy. It was found that firm size and profitability explain firm dividend policy. Firm size has a negative relationship with the dividend payout ratio and dividend yield.

It indicates the larger the firm, the more likely it is to retain cash to pay off its liabilities (Bushra and Mishra 2015).

Likewise, there is a negative relationship between managerial ownership and dividend payout (Rozeff 1982; Jensen et al. 1992; Eckbo and Verma 1994). This means that firms with higher managerial ownership tend to increase internal funds at the expense of low dividend payouts in order to finance investments. The managers are reluctant to pay dividends (Jensen 1986). However, both managerial ownership and dividends resolve agency problems (Chen and Steiner 1999a, b). Similarly, Jensen et al. (1992) found a negative relationship between leverage and dividends. A firm acquiring debt will have fixed financial charges, interests and repayment of principals thus leading the firm into liquidation. Consequently, the firm has a tendency to pay lower dividends to maintain a good liquidity position and cash flow. There is a significant positive relationship between total foreign ownership and dividend policy and a significant negative relationship between managerial ownership and dividend policy (Aydin and Cavdar 2015).

According to Kulathunga (2017), there is a significant relationship between corporate governance variables and dividend policy. Board independence, CEO duality and return on assets have significant positive impact on dividend policy, and size of the board has a negative impact on dividend policy. Foreign investors with strong monitoring incentives lead firms to pay more dividends (Gong 2015). The independent and non-executive directors, board size, CEO, proportion of family members and ownership pattern in the organizations are interrelated (Shehu 2015). Board size, board composition, CEO tenure and management equity have weak negative relationships with dividend payout (Ikunda et al. 2016).

Further, the study found that board composition and managerial equity holding were found to have no statistical significant impact on the dividend payout. Board size, board independence, CEO duality, return on assets (ROA) and debt-to total assets variables align with the corporate governance and dividend policy (Ajanthan 2013). The results of the study suggested that only CEO duality is negatively related to dividend payout whereas board size, board independence, ROA and debt-to-total assets do not appear to be significantly related to the dividend payout. In the Nepalese context, Pradhan (2003) examined that a major motive for paying cash dividends is to convey information to shareholders about favorable prospects of the enterprise. Pradhan and Balampaki (2004) found that the board size has a negative impact on dividend yield. Dhungel (2011) revealed that it is unclear about the relationship between market price per share (MPS) and dividend per share in the context of Nepal.

According to Adhikari, size and liquidity are major determinants of corporate dividend payout in Nepal. This study also reveals that there is sector-specific importance of the determinants of corporate dividend payout in Nepal. Manandhar (1998) revealed that dividend per share and return on equity (ROE) have a positive impact on market capitalization while earnings per share, price earnings ratio, and dividend yield have a negative impact. The study found that there is a positive relationship between dividend and stock price. Dividend per share is a motivating factor in the Nepalese financial sector. It is strong enough to increase MPS of the banking and non-financial firms (Joshi 2011). The preceding discussion reveals that there is no consistency in the findings of various studies concerning the impact of corporate governance on dividend policy.

The major objective of this study is to assess the relationship between corporate governance and dividend policy in Nepalese enterprises. More specifically, it examines the impact of *firm size, liquidity, CEO duality, ROA, foreign ownership, gender diversity on board, managerial ownership and leverage on dividend policy of Nepalese enterprises*. The remainder of this study is organized as follows: Section "Methodological Aspects" describes the sample, data and methodology. Section "Results and Discussion" presents the empirical results and the final section draw conclusions and discuss the implications of the study findings.

Methodological Aspects

This study is based on secondary data collected from 14 commercial banks and seven insurance companies in Nepal. The main sources of data are the banks' and insurance companies' annual reports. Table 21.1 shows the list of banks and non-banks selected for the study along with the study period and number of observations.

The Model

The model estimated in this study assumes that the dividend policy depends on bank- and insurance-specific macro variables. Therefore, the study uses following model:

Dividend policy = f (firm size, liquidity, CEO duality, ROA, foreign ownership, gender diversity on board, managerial ownership, institutional ownership and leverage).

Table 21.1 Number of commercial banks and insurance companies selected for the study along with study period and number of observations

S. No.	Name of enterprises	Study period	Observations
1	Nabil Bank Limited	2010/11–2015/16	6
2	Nepal SBI Bank Limited	2010/11–2015/16	6
3	Nepal Bangladesh Bank Limited	2010/11–2015/16	6
4	Everest Bank Limited	2010/11–2015/16	6
5	Himalayan Bank Limited	2010/11–2015/16	6
6	Kumari Bank Limited	2010/11–2015/16	6
7	Machhapuchchhre Bank Limited	2010/11–2015/16	6
8	Laxmi Bank Limited	2010/11–2015/16	6
9	Nepal Investment Bank Limited	2010/11–2015/16	6
10	Standard Chartered Bank Limited	2010/11–2015/16	6
11	Citizens International Bank Limited	2010/11–2015/16	6
12	Siddhartha Bank Limited	2010/11–2015/16	6
13	Global IME Bank Limited	2010/11–2015/16	6
14	Nepal Bank Limited	2010/11–2015/16	6
15	Sagarmatha Insurance	2010/11–2015/16	6
16	Shikhar Insurance	2010/11–2015/16	6
17	LIC Insurance	2010/11–2015/16	6
18	Premier Insurance	2010/11–2015/16	6
19	Himalayan General Ltd.	2010/11–2015/16	6
20	Asian Insurance	2010/11–2015/16	6
21	Gurans Life Insurance	2010/11–2015/16	6
Total observations			126

More specifically, the given model is segmented into the following models:

Model I

$$DPR = \beta_0 + \beta_1 MO + \beta_2 LIQ + \beta_3 CEOD + \beta_4 FORTOT + \beta_5 FS + \beta_6 BGD + \beta_7 IO + \beta_8 LEV + \beta_9 ROA + e$$

Model II

$$DY = \beta_0 + \beta_1 MO + \beta_2 LIQ + \beta_3 CEOD + \beta_4 FORTOT + \beta_5 FS + \beta_6 BGD + \beta_7 IO + \beta_8 LEV + \beta_9 ROA + e$$

shere,

DPR = Dividend payout ratio is defined as dividend per share to earnings per share.
DY = Dividend yield is defined as dividend per share divided by market per share.
GD = Gender diversity refers to the number of women directors on a board.
FS = Firm size of the banks refers to the total assets of firms.
IO = Institutional ownership represents shares held by institutional investors, such as banks and insurance companies.
FORTOT = Total foreign ownership is defined as the ownership of foreign investors in Nepalese enterprise.
LEV = Total debt to total shareholders' equity.
CEOD = 1 if CEO is chairman as well and 0 if otherwise.
MO = Managerial ownership is defined as the total percentage of equity held by inside shareholders that take part in the company's management.
LIQ = Liquidity is defined as the degree to which an asset or security can be bought or sold in the market without affecting the asset price.
ROA = Return on assets is defined as net profit after tax to total assets.

Firm Size

Total assets are used as a measure of firm size. Lintner revealed that firm size has a negative impact on a company's dividend policy. Similarly, there is a negative relationship between firm size and dividend payout ratio. Likewise, Asghar et al. stated that firm size negatively influences dividend policy. However, Nasir et al. found that firm size is positively related to dividend payout ratio. Based on these findings, we develop the following hypothesis:

H_1 *There is a negative relationship between firm size and a company's dividend policy.*

Liquidity

Liquidity refers to the ease with which an investment asset (stocks, bonds and mutual funds) can be converted into cash in a short period of time without a significant decrease in its value. Jensen and Meckling (1976) found that higher liquidity leads to higher dividend payment. Likewise, Ho found that liquidity is positively related to dividend policy. Similarly, Alli and Ramirez found that dividend payments dependent upon cash flow and current earnings do not really reflect a firm's ability to pay dividends. Based on these findings, we develop the following hypothesis:

***H₂** There is a positive relation between liquidity level and a company's dividend policy.*

Foreign Ownership

Foreign ownership in a bank is the portion of the bank owned by a person or company from another country. Foreign ownership (FO) has a significant positive association with dividend payout ratio. Hence, the greater the percentage of foreign ownership in a firm, the higher the dividend payment. La Porta et al. (2000) found that foreign ownership has a positive impact on dividend payment. The study reveals the importance of foreign shareholding on the dividend policy that a company adopts. However, Lam et al. (2012) found that foreign ownership has a significantly negative effect on cash dividends. Baba showed that if a firm has paid dividends, it will have a higher proportion of foreign ownership. This means that if a firm increases its dividend payments, foreign ownership will increase and vice versa. Based on these findings, this study develops the following hypothesis:

***H₃** There is a positive relationship between foreign ownership and a company's dividend policy.*

Gender Diversity on Board

Women on the board bring different perspectives and points of view on issues, hence bringing with them the potential to increase the value for shareholders, according to the work of Vera and Campbell (2007). Both Terjesen et al. and Luckerath-Rovers (2013) found a positive relationship between the number of women on the board and a firm's performance. Likewise, Adams (2008) argued that presence of diversity in gender may also increase the efficiency of banks. Female directors on the board are more likely to prevent management's opportunistic behaviors by supporting more dividend payouts. Bilimoria (2000) revealed that female directors are valued as board members for their productive discourse. Based on these findings, we develop the following hypothesis:

***H₄** There is a positive relationship between gender diversity on a board and a company's dividend policy.*

CEO Duality

According to Asamoah (2005), CEO duality means the situation when the CEO also holds the position of chairman of the board. The board of directors is appointed to monitor managers, such as the CEO, on the behalf of the shareholders. Abor and Fiador (2013) found a negative relationship between CEO duality and dividend payout. When a CEO doubles as board chair, the CEO is afforded a greater opportunity to influence the decisions made by the board. Based on these findings, we develop the following hypothesis:

H_5 There is a negative relationship between CEO duality and a company's dividend policy.

Institutional Ownership

Institutional ownership refers to shares held by institutional investors, such as banks and insurance companies. Eckbo and Verma (1994) found that institutional investors prefer free cash flow to be distributed in the form of dividends. However, institutional owners are expected to have a negative effect on both dependent variables mainly because such firms tend to pay dividends in order to reduce the cost of agency conflict (Jensen 1986; Rozeff 1982). Similarly, Renneboog and Szilagyi (2008) found that highly concentrated institutional ownership has a negative effect on dividend payouts. Similarly, According to Shleifer and Vishny (1986), institutional ownership creates incentives to monitor management, thereby overcoming the free-rider problem. Similarly, Wiberg (2008) found a positive relationship between institutional ownership and dividend policy. Based on these findings, we develop the following hypothesis:

H_6 There is a negative relationship between institutional ownership and a company's dividend policy.

Managerial Ownership

Managerial ownership refers to the total percentage of equity held by inside shareholders that take part in the company's management. Jensen (1986) found a positive relationship between managerial ownership and dividend policy. However, Chen et al. found a negative relationship between managerial ownership and dividend policy. Similarly, Jensen et al. (1992) show that insider ownership is associated with lower dividend payouts. Likewise, there is a negative relationship between insider ownership and dividend payout (Rozeff 1982). However, Abdullah et al. (2012) found concentrated ownership has a significant positive influence on dividend policy. Based on these findings, we develop the following hypothesis:

H_7 There is a negative relationship between managerial ownership and a company's dividend policy.

Return on Assets

According to Asamoah (2005), ROA is an indicator of how profitable an organization is relative to its total assets. ROA provides information regarding how efficient management is at using its assets to generate earnings. Belanes et al. found that ROA is positively related to dividend yield. Based on these findings, we develop the following hypothesis:

H_8 There is a positive relationship between managerial ownership and a company's dividend policy.

Leverage

Leverage represents a firm's leverage, measured by short-term and long-term debt divided by total assets. It is assumed that leverage, that is, total debt to total assets, plays a significant role in determining firm performance. Bhaduri (2002) found that leverage is positively related to dividend policy. However, Al-Malkawi (2007), Patra et al. and Al-Najjar and Hussainey (2009) found that leverage is negatively related to dividend payments because firms with more debt prefer to retain more in order to repay loans instead of paying more dividends. Similarly, Jensen et al. (1992) found a negative relationship between leverage and dividends. Based on these findings, we develop the following hypothesis:

H_9 There is a negative relationship between leverage and a company's dividend policy.

Results and Discussion

Descriptive Statistics

Table 21.2 presents the descriptive statistics of selected dependent and independent variables during the period 2010–2011 to 2015–2016.

Table 21.2 shows that average dividend yield has a minimum value of 0 percent and a maximum value of 16.93 percent with an average value of 1.29 percent. The average value of dividend payouts is 4.56 percent with a minimum value of 0 percent and a maximum value of 45.94 percent. Firm size varies from a minimum of Rs.18.95 million to a maximum value of Rs.25.59 million, leading to an average of Rs.23.33 million. Liquidity varies from a minimum value of 0.05 times to a maximum value of 0.56 times, leading to an average value of 0.19 percent. The average value of leverage is 0.74 percent with a minimum value of 0.04 percent and maximum value of 1.08 percent. Average value of managerial ownership is 0.31 percent with a minimum value of 0 percent and a maximum of 1 percent. Average value of total foreign ownership is 14.28 percent with a minimum value of 0 percent and a maximum of 75 percent. Average value of ROA assets is 1.16 percent with a minimum value of −0.07 percent and a maximum value of 4.01 percent. Average value of gender diversity on board is 0.17 percent with a minimum value of 0 percent and a maximum value of 2 percent. Average value of institutional ownership of selected companies during the study period is 19.95 percent with a minimum value of 0 percent and a maximum value of 80 percent.

Correlation Analysis

Having indicated the descriptive statistics, we computed Pearson's correlation coefficients and present them in Table 21.3.

The results show that liquidity, firm size and foreign ownership are positively related to dividend yield. The greater the value of these variables, the higher the dividend yield. Conversely, managerial ownership, institutional ownership, CEO duality, gender diversity and ROA are negatively related to dividend yield. An increase in managerial and institutional ownership leads to a decrease in dividend yield. Having a different CEO and chairman of the board leads to a high dividend yield. The smaller the

Table 21.2 Descriptive statistics

Variables	Minimum	Maximum	Mean	Std. deviation
DY	0.00	16.93	1.29	2.73
DPR	0.00	45.94	4.56	10.13
FS	0.17	129.89	37.48	33.07
MO	0.00	1.00	0.31	0.46
LIQ	0.04	0.56	0.19	0.12
GD	0.00	2.00	0.17	0.43
IO	0.00	80.00	19.95	21.42
FORTOT	0.00	75.00	14.28	23.06
ROA	−0.07	4.01	1.16	0.97
LEV	0.04	1.08	0.74	0.29

This table shows the descriptive statistics of dependent, independent and control variables of commercial banks and insurance companies for the study period of 2010–2011 to 2015–2016. DPR (Dividend payout ratio is defined as dividend per share to earnings per share, in percentage), DY (Dividend yield is defined as dividend per share divided by market per share, in percentage), GD (Gender diversity refers to the number of women directors on a board), FS (Firm size of the banks refers to the total assets of firms, in billion rupees), IO (Institutional ownership represent shares held by institutional investors such as banks and insurance companies, in percentage), FORTOT (Total foreign ownership is defined as the ownership of foreign investors in Nepalese enterprise, in percentage), LEV (Leverage is defined as total debt to total shareholders' equity, in percentage), CEOD (1 if CEO is chairman as well and 0 if otherwise), MO (Managerial ownership is defined as the total percentage of equity held by inside shareholders that take part in the company's management, in percentage), LIQ (Liquidity is defined as the degree to which an asset or security can be bought or sold in the market without affecting the asset price, in times), and ROA (Return on assets is defined as net profit after tax to total assets, in percentage)

number of women directors on a board, the higher the dividend yield. Similarly, the lower the ROA and leverage, the higher the dividend yield.

The table shows that liquidity and institutional ownership are negatively related to dividend payout ratio. This indicates that that higher the liquidity and institutional ownership, the lower the dividend payout ratio. However, the result also shows that firm size is positively correlated to dividend payout ratio. This means that the larger the firm size, the higher the dividend payout ratio. The same is true for managerial ownership and foreign ownership. Similarly, CEO duality is also positively related to dividend payout ratio. It implies that a firm with the same person serving as both CEO and chairman of the board has a high dividend payout ratio. Gender diversity is also positively related to dividend payout ratio. The more female directors on the board, the higher the dividend payout. The same is true for ROA and leverage.

Table 21.3 Pearson's correlation coefficients matrix for enterprises

Variables	DY	DPR	FS	MO	LIQ	CEOD	GD	IO	FORTOT	ROA	LEV
DY	1										
DPR	0.096	1									
FS	0.287**	0.304**	1								
MO	−0.189*	0.212*	0.410**	1							
LIQ	0.235**	−0.188*	−0.418**	−0.297**	1						
CEOD	−0.094	0.376**	0.414**	0.111	−0.305**	1					
GD	−0.108	0.120	0.142	0.298**	−0.198*	0.157	1				
IO	−0.110	−0.127	0.251**	−0.015	−0.086	0.120	0.057	1			
FORTOT	0.098	0.523**	0.551**	0.548**	−0.303**	0.513**	0.352**	0.008	1		
ROA	−0.236**	0.548**	0.695**	0.524**	−0.413**	0.440**	0.237**	0.045	0.652**	1	
LEV	−0.311**	0.245**	0.599**	0.383**	−0.431**	0.305**	0.233**	0.266**	0.363**	0.663**	1

Note: The asterisk signs (**) and (*) indicate that the results are significant at 1 percent and 5 percent level respectively

This table shows the Pearson correlation coefficients of dependent and independent variables of selected Nepalese commercial banks and insurance companies for the study period of 2010–2011 to 2015–2016. DPR (Dividend payout ratio is defined as dividend per share to earnings per share, in percentage), DY (Dividend yield is defined as dividend per share divided by market per share, in percentage), FS (firm size of bank refers to the total assets of firms, in billion rupees), GD (Gender diversity refers to the number of women directors on a board), IO (Institutional ownership represents shares held by institutional investors such as banks and insurance companies, in percentage), FORTOT (Total foreign ownership is defined as the ownership of foreign investors in Nepalese enterprise, in percentage), LEV (Leverage is defined as total debt to total shareholder's equity, in percentage), CEOD (1 if CEO is chairman as well as 0 if otherwise), MO (Managerial ownership is defined as the total percentage of equity held by inside shareholders that take part in the company's management, in percentage), LIQ (Liquidity is defined as the degree to which an asset or security can be bought or sold in the market without affecting the asset price, in times), ROA (Return on assets is defined as net profit after tax to total assets, in percentage)

Regression Analysis

Having indicated the correlation coefficients, we performed regression analysis and present the results in Table 21.4.

Table 21.4 shows that the beta coefficient for firm size is positive, which means that the smaller the firm size, the smaller the dividend payout ratio. The beta coefficient for managerial ownership is positive, indicating that the lower the managerial ownership, the lower the dividend payout ratio. Likewise, the beta coefficient for CEO duality is also positive. A firm with the same person serving as both CEO and chairman of the board has a high dividend payout ratio.

The beta coefficient for liquidity is negative, which indicates that the lower the liquidity, the higher the dividend payout ratio. The beta coefficient for gender diversity on a board is positive. It indicates that the greater the number of female directors on a board, the higher the dividend payout ratio. This finding is similar to the findings of Adams (2008). Likewise, the beta coefficient for ROA is positive. This means that the higher the ROA, the higher the dividend payout ratio.

Similarly, beta coefficients for foreign ownership and leverage are positive, indicating that the greater the percentage of foreign ownership of a company and the more leveraged the firm is, the higher the dividend payout ratio. Conversely, the beta coefficient for institutional ownership is negative. It implies that higher the institutional ownership of the company, the lower the dividend payout ratio. Table 21.5 shows the regression results of firm size, liquidity, CEO duality, and return on assets, foreign ownership, and gender diversity on board, managerial ownership, institutional ownership and leverage on dividend yield of Nepalese enterprises.

Table 21.5 shows that the beta coefficient for liquidity is positive. This means that higher the liquidity, the higher the dividend yield. This finding is similar to the findings of Ho. The beta coefficient for foreign ownership is also positive, which shows that the greater the percentage of foreign ownership of the company, the higher the dividend yield.

However, the beta coefficients for managerial ownership and institutional ownership are negative. The greater the value of these variables, the lower the dividend yield. Likewise, the beta coefficient for CEO duality is negative. It indicates that a firm with a different person each serving as CEO and chairman of the board has a high dividend yield. The beta coefficient for gender diversity on board is also negative. This means that the lesser the number of female directors on a board, the higher the dividend

Table 21.4 Estimated regression results of FS, MO, LIQ, CEOD, GD, IO, FORTOT, ROA and LEV on dividend payout ratio

Model	Intercept	FS	MO	LIQ	CEOD	GD	IO	FORTOT	ROA	LEV	Adj R^2	SEE	F-value
1	1.07 (-0.82)	0.09 (3.56)**									0.85	9.69	12.66
2	3.13 (2.94)**		4.63 (2.42)*								0.04	9.94	5.85
3	7.54 (4.59)**			-15.34 (-2.12)*							0.03	9.99	4.52
4	2.58 (2.72)**				9.25 (4.51)**						0.13	9.43	20.38
5	4.09 (4.25)**					2.8 (-1.34)					0.006	10.1	1.81
6	5.76 (4.68)**						-0.06 (-1.42)				0.008	10.09	2.02
7	1.28 (-1.41)							0.23 (6.83)**			0.27	8.67	46.72
8	-2.04 (-1.73)								5.7 (7.29)**		0.29	8.51	53.16
9	-1.75 (-0.72)									8.54 (2.81)**	0.05	9.87	7.9
10	3.86	0.1 (3.47)**		-5.57 (-0.74)			-0.1 (-2.48)*				0.12	9.51	6.64
11	-1.66 (-0.74) / -1.35 (-0.62)	-0.04 (-1.08)		3.87	5.11 (2.49)*		0.07 (-1.86)		5.88 (5.24)**		0.33	8.27	13.54
12	-0.46 (-0.21)	-0.004 (-0.12)	-2.84 (-1.38)	-0.57				0.25 (5.58)**		3.38 (-0.99)	0.26	8.69	12.27

Notes: (a) Figures in parentheses are t-values; (b) The asterisk signs (**) and (*) indicate that the results are significant at 1 percent and 5 percent level respectively; (c) Dependent variable is dividend payout ratio

The results are based on pooled cross-sectional data of 14 commercial banks and seven insurance companies with 126 observations by using linear regression model. The results are based on time series data of Nepalese enterprises for the six years from 2010 to 2016 by using the linear regression model. The model is DPR = β_0 + β_1MO + β_2LIQ + β_3CEOD + β_4FORTOT + β_5FS + β_6BGD + β_7IO + β_8LEV + β_9ROA + ϵ. Dividend payout ratio and dividend yield both refer to dividend policy. DPR (Dividend payout ratio is defined as dividend per share to earnings per share, in percentage), DY (Dividend yield is defined as dividend per share divided by market per share), GD (Gender diversity refers to the number of women directors in a board, in percentage), FS (firm size of bank refers to the total assets of firms, in billion rupees), IO (Institutional ownership represent shares held by institutional investors such as banks and insurance companies, in percentage), FORTOT (Total foreign ownership is defined as the ownership of foreign investors in Nepalese enterprise, in percentage), LEV (Leverage is defined as total debt to total shareholder's equity, in percentage), CEOD (1 if CEO is chairman as well as 0 if otherwise), MO (Managerial ownership is defined as the total percentage of equity held by inside shareholders that take part in the company's management, in percentage), LIQ (Liquidity is defined as the degree to which an asset or security can be bought or sold in the market without affecting the asset price, in times), and ROA (Return on assets is defined as net profit after tax divided by total assets, in percentage)

Table 21.5 Estimated regression results of FS, MO, LIQ, CEOD, GD, IO, FORTOT, ROA and LEV on dividend yield

Model	Intercept	Regression									Adj R^2	SEE	F
		FS	MO	LIQ	CEOD	GD	IO	FORTOT	ROA	LEV			
1	2.19 (6.16)**	−0.02 (−3.34)**									0.75	2.62	11.2
2	1.64 (5.69)**		−1.11 (−2.14)*								0.028	2.69	4.57
3	0.32 (−0.75)			5.18 (2.70)**							0.048	2.66	7.27
4	1.43 (5.22)**				−0.62 (−1.05)						0.001	2.73	1.1
5	1.41 (5.52)**					−0.68 (−1.21)					0.004	2.72	1.46
6	1.58 (4.74)**						−0.01 (−1.23)				0.004	2.72	1.51
7	1.46 (5.12)**							−0.01 (−1.10)			0.02	2.73	1.21
8	2.06 (5.58)**								−0.66 (2.70)**		0.048	2.66	7.29
9	3.46 (5.44)**									−2.934 (−3.65)**	0.9	2.6	13.3
10	1.53 (2.29)*	−0.02 (−1.64)	−0.37 (−0.62)	2.83 −1.33					−0.03 (−0.08)		0.73	2.63	3.45
11	3.30 (4.99)**	−0.02 (−1.54)						0.01 −0.90	−0.06 (−0.15)	−2.00 (−1.72)	0.08	2.61	3.26

Notes: (a) Figures in parenthesis are t-values; (b) The asterisk signs (**) and (*) indicate that the results are significant at 1 percent and 5 percent level respectively; (c) Dividend yield is dependent variable

The results are based on pooled cross-sectional data of 14 commercial banks and seven insurance companies with 126 observations by using linear regression model. The results are based on time series data of Nepalese enterprises for the six years from 2010 to 2016 by using the linear regression model. The model is DPR = $\beta_0 + \beta_1$MO + β_2LIQ + β_3CEOD + β_4FORTOT + β_5FS + β_6BGD + β_7IO + β_8LEV + β_8ROA + ε.

DPR (Dividend payout ratio is defined as dividend per share divided per share to earnings per share), DY (Dividend yield is defined as dividend per share divided by market per share), GD (Gender diversity refers to the number of women directors on a board), FS (firm size of bank refers to the total assets of firms), IO (Institutional ownership represent shares held by institutional investors such as banks and insurance companies), FORTOT (Total foreign ownership is defined as the ownership of foreign investor in Nepalese enterprise), LEV (Leverage is defined as total debt to total shareholder's equity), CEOD (A binary that equal one if the CEO is chairman of the board and zero otherwise), MO (Managerial ownership is defined as the total percentage of equity held by inside shareholders that take part in the company's management), LIQ (Liquidity is defined as the degree to which an asset or security can be bought or sold in the market without affecting the asset price), and ROA (Return on assets is defined as net profit after tax to total assets) yield. Beta coefficients for ROA and leverage are negative as well. The lower the ROA, the higher the yield, and the higher the company's leverage, the lower its dividend yield. This finding is similar to the findings of Patra et al.

Summary and Conclusion

The dividend per share and dividend yield are attractive tools for both existing and potential investors. High rates of both are not only demanded by high-class investors, but they also attract the interest of small investors. High rates of dividend per share and dividend yield pushes the investors to invest in stocks, but many of them do not have much knowledge about operations and factors affecting a company's dividend policy as there are various internal and external factors that influence it. The financial performance of companies is the most essential factor for investors. Selecting companies with winning portfolios helps investors garner reliable and consistent returns.

This study attempts to examine the relationship between a firm's performance and its dividend policy in Nepalese commercial banks and insurance companies. This study is based on secondary data of 14 commercial banks and seven insurance companies with 126 observations for the period of 2010–2011 to 2015–2016.

The study shows that firm size and foreign ownership are positively related to dividend payout ratio and dividend yield. The larger the firm size and the greater the percentage of foreign ownership, the higher the dividend payout ratio. It also indicates that the smaller the firm size and the lesser the percentage of foreign ownership, the smaller the dividend yield. The regression results show that institutional ownership has a negative impact on the dividend payout ratio and dividend yield.

References

Abdullah, N. M. H., Ahmad, Z., & Roslan, S. (2012). The influence of ownership structure on the firms' dividend policy based Lintner model. *International Review of Business Research Papers, 8*(6), 71–88.

Abor, J., & Fiador, V. (2013). Does corporate governance explain dividend policy in sub-Saharan Africa? *International Journal of Law and Management, 55*(3), 201–225.

Adams, G. (2008). A cultural analysis of the experiment and an experimental analysis of culture. *Social Psychology and Personality Compass, 2*(1), 1895–1912.

Ajanthan, A. (2013). The relationship between dividend payout and firm. *International Journal of Scientific and Research Publication, 3*(6), 2250–3153.

Al-Malkawi, H. (2007). Determinants of corporate dividend policy in Jordan: An application of the Tobit model. *Journal of Economic and Administrative Sciences, 23*(2), 44–70.

Al-Najjar, B., & Hussainey, K. (2009). The association between dividend payout and outside directorships. *Journal of Applied Accounting Research, 10*(1), 4–19.

Asamoah, G. N. (2005). Corporate governance and dividend policy: An evidence from Ghana. *SSRN Electronic Journal, 3*(2), 1–22.

Aydin, A. D., & Cavdar, S. C. (2015). Corporate governance and dividend policy: An empirical analysis from borsa Istanbul corporate governance index. *Accounting and Finance Research, 4*(3), 66–74.

Bhaduri, S. N. (2002). Determinants of corporate borrowing: Some evidence from the Indian corporate structure. *Journal of Economics and Fiance, 26*(2), 200–215.

Bilimoria, D. (2000). Building the business case for women corporate directors. *Women on Corporate Boards of Directors, 18*(1), 25–40.

Bushra, A., & Mishra, N. (2015). The determinants of corporate dividend policy in Pakistan. *The Lahore Journal of Economics, 20*(2), 14–24.

Chen, C., & Steiner, T. (1999a). Managerial ownership and agency conflict: A non-linear simultaneous approach. *Journal of Banking and Finance, 34*(3), 897–924.

Chen, C. R., & Steiner, T. L. (1999b). Managerial ownership and agency conflicts: A nonlinear simultaneous equation analysis of managerial ownership, risk taking, debt policy, and dividend policy. *Financial Review, 34*(1), 119–136.

Claessen, S. (2009). What happens during recessions, crunches and busts? *Economic Policy, 60*(1), 653–700.

Dharwardkar, R. (2000). Privatization in emerging economies: An agency theory perspective. *Academy of Management Journal, 25*(1), 650–669.

Dhungel, A. (2011). Impact of dividend on share pricing of nepal. *Banking Journal, 3*(2), 21–36.

Eckbo, B. E., & Verma, S. (1994). Managerial shareownership, voting power, and cash dividend policy. *Journal of Corporate Finance, 1*(1), 33–62.

Ekanayake, H. L., & Parantham, T. (2010). The impact of corporate governance on firms' dividend policy: Evidence from the listed SandP SL20 companies in the Colombo stock exchange. *Journal for Accounting Researchers and Educators, 7*(1), 14–23.

Gong, J. (2015). The corporate governance structure and dividend policy. *Advanced Science and Technology Letters, 84*(1), 118–121.

Heenetigala, K. (2011). Corporate governance practices and firm performance of listed companies in Sri Lanka. *Journal of Financial Economics, 4*(3), 14–26.

Ikunda, C., Muiru, M., & Kamau, S. M. (2016). The impact of corporate governance on dividend payout of exchange. *Journal of Finance and Accounting, 4*(5), 254–261.

Jensen, E. F. (1983). Separation of ownership and control. *Journal of Law and Economics, 26*(2), 301–325.

Jensen, M. C. (1986). Agency costs of free cash flow, corporate finance. *The American Economic Review, 76*(2), 323–329.

Jensen, M. C., & Meckling, W. H. (1976). Theory of the firm: Managerial behavior, agency costs and ownership structure. *Journal of Financial Economics, 3*(4), 305–360.

Jensen, G. R., Solberg, D. P., & Zorn, T. S. (1992). Simultaneous determination of insider ownership, debt, and dividend policies. *Journal of Financial and Quantitative Analysis, 27*(2), 247–263.

Jo, H., & Pan, C. (2009). Why are firms with entrenched managers more likely to pay dividends? *Review of Accounting and Finance, 8*(1), 87–116.

Joshi, P. (2011). Diffusion of management accounting practices in gulf cooperation council countries. *Accounting Prespectives, 10*(1), 23–53.

Kulathunga, K. (2017). Corporate governance and dividend policy: A study of listed manufacturing companies in Sri Lanka. *International Journal of Scientific Research and Innovative Technology, 4*(2), 64–81.

La Porta, R., Lopez-de-Silanes, F., Shleifer, A., & Vishny, R. (2000). Investor protection and corporate governance. *Journal of Financial Economics, 58*(1), 3–27.

Lam, C. K., Sami, H., & Zhou, H. (2012). The roles of cross-listing, foreign ownership and state ownership in dividend policy in as emerging market. *China Journal of Accounting Research, 5*(3), 199–216.

Lee, D. S. (2009). Training, wages, and sample selection: Estimating sharp bounds on treatment effects. *Review of Economics Studies, 76*(3), 1071–1102.

Luckerath-Rovers, M. (2013). Women on boards and firm performance. *Journal of Management and Governance, 17*(2), 491–509.

Mallin, C., Michelon, G., & Raggi, D. (2013). Monitoring intensity and stakeholders' orientation: How does governance affect social and environmental disclosure? *Journal of Business Ethics, 114*(1), 29–43.

Manandhar, K. (1998). A study of dividend policy and value of the firm in small stock market: A case of Nepal. *Management Dynamics, 8*(1), 15–20.

Meckling, M. C. (1976). Theory of the firm: Managerial behavior, agency costs and ownership structure. *Journal of Financial Economics, 3*(4), 305–360.

Pradhan, R. S. (2003). A survey of dividend policy and practices of Nepalese enterprises. *Research in Nepalese Finance, 1*(1), 220–250.

Pradhan, R. S., & Balampaki, D. R. (2004). Fundamentals of stock returns in Nepal. *SEBO Journal, 1*(1), 8–24.

Renneboog, L., & Szilagyi, P. G. (2008). Corporate restructuring and bondholder wealth. *European Financial Management, 14*(4), 792–819.

Rozeff, M. (1982). Growth, beta and agency costs as the determinants of dividend payout ratios. *Journal of Financial Research, 5*(3), 249–259.

Shehu, M. (2015). Board characteristics and dividend payout: Evidence from Malaysian public listed companies. *Research Journal of Finance and Accounting, 3*(2), 6–16.

Shleifer, A., & Vishny, R. W. (1986). Large shareholders and corporate control. *Journal of Political Economy, 94*(1), 461–488.

Thuraisingam, R. (2013). The effects of corporate governance on company performance: Evidence from Sri Lankan financial services industry. *Journal of Economics and Sustainable Development, 4*(17), 103–110.

Velnampy, T. (2013). Corporate governance and firm performance: A study of SriLankan manufacturing companies. *Journal of Economics and Sustainable Development, 4*(3), 228–235.

Vera, C., & Campbell, K. (2007). *The influence of gender on spanish boards of directors: An emperical analysis*, 1–31. Valencia: Instituto Valenciano de Investigaciones Económicas (IVIE).

Wiberg, D. (2008). Ownership, dividends, R&D and retained earnings are institutional owners short-term oriented? *The Royal Institute of technology. Centre of Excellence for Science and Innovation Studies (CESIS), 4*(3), 1–11.

CHAPTER 22

Impact of Ownership Structure and Corporate Governance on Capital Structure of Nepalese Listed Companies

Raj Kumar Bajagai, Ravi Kumar Keshari, Pratikshya Bhetwal, Radhe Shyam Sah, and Rajnish Nath Jha

INTRODUCTION

Corporate governance is a process that creates shareholder value by managing corporate affairs. Corporate governance is the system by which businesses are directed and controlled (Cadbury 1992). Melvin and Hirt (2005) described the concept of corporate governance as referring to corporate decision making and control, particularly the structure of the board and its working procedures. It is a set of relationships between a company's management, its board, shareholders and stakeholders. Corporate governance is defined as the process and structure used to direct and manage business affairs of a company towards enhancing prosperity and corporate

R. K. Bajagai (✉) • R. K. Keshari • P. Bhetwal • R. S. Sah • R. N. Jha
Department of Management, Uniglobe College, Thribhuvan University, Kathmandu, Nepal
e-mail: rspradhan@uniglobe.edu.np

accounting with the ultimate objective of realizing long-term shareholder value. Corporate governance has become one of the most discussed topics in business administration due to balance sheet manipulations or even collapse of some public corporations like Enron, WorldCom and so on. After these financial crises, corporate governance has been undergoing a reform process. The enormous consequences, namely catastrophic losses of financial firms that almost led to a collapse of the financial system followed by the deep global recession, emphasize the importance of corporate governance (Lang and Jagtiani 2010).

Strategic decisions like external financing can be influenced by sound corporate principles as such decisions are taken at the board level. Good corporate governance practices have a significant influence on the strategic decisions of a company taken at the board level, such as external financing, cost of financing, and so on. Corporate governance has been defined as the relationship among shareholders, the board of directors and the top management in determining the direction and performance of a corporation (Jensen 1993). Therefore, corporate governance variables like board size, board composition, board skills and chief executive officer (CEO)/chair duality may have a direct impact on capital structure or leverage decisions.

Capital structure decisions are affected by corporate governance variables and ownership structure variables. Capital structure refers to the different options used by a firm in financing its assets (Bhaduri 2002). Modigliani and Miller (1958) were the first ones to landmark the topic of capital structure and they argued that capital structure was irrelevant in determining a firm's value and its future performance. Capital structure is also referred to as financial structure of a firm. It is the mix of debt and equity capital maintained by a firm. The capital structure of a firm is very important since it is related to the ability of the firm to meet the needs of its stakeholders.

Imam and Malik stated that the need for corporate governance arises from the potential conflicts of interest among participants (stakeholders) in the capital structure. Boodhoo (2009) found that there exists a positive relationship between the capital structure and ownership structure of a firm. Rehman et al. (2010) investigated the relationship between corporate governance and capital structure of 19 randomly selected banks in Pakistan from 2005–2006. They found a positive relationship between board size and capital structure. Berger et al. (1997), Wen et al. (2002) and Abor and Biekpe (2004) discussed the influence of corporate governance on the capital structure decisions of firms for developed and emerging markets. Their results revealed that there exists a positive relationship between corporate governance and capital structure.

Owusu et al. (2014) argued that corporate governance and ownership structure plays an important role in a firm's capital mix determination. This gives confidence to the general public and other lenders resulting in favorable borrowing terms by the company. Dalton and Dan (2005) found that boards with more outsiders outperformed other firms, but that a majority of independent directors was not necessary to ensure above average value. Heng and Azrbaijani (2012) emphasized that board of directors' features, such as CEO/chair duality, presence of non-executive directors, board size and presence of independent directors, may have direct influence on the firm's capital structure decisions. The result also revealed that there is a significant positive linkage between the presence of independent directors on the board and a firm's capital structure. Emamgholipour et al. (2013) investigated the effect of CEO duality on the capital structure of listed companies on the Tehran Stock Exchange. The results showed that there is a significant and positive relationship between CEO duality and capital structure of companies, which indicates that existence of one person as CEO and chairman of the board has a positive effect on capital structure.

Lubatkin and Chatterjee (1994) found that there exists a positive relationship between capital structure and firm value. According to Titman and Wessels (1988), size of companies is positively related to debt. Pfeffer and Salancik (1978) and Lipton and Lorsch (1992) found that there is a significant relationship between board size and capital structure. If board meetings are held frequently, more discussions will be held on problems and prospects of business and business can be expected to run more efficiently. Kajananthan (2012) examined the effect of corporate governance on the capital structure of manufacturing companies in Sri Lanka and results show that there exists a positive relationship between leverage and board size, board meeting and proportion of non-executive directors. Short et al. (2002) examined the influence of ownership structure on the financial structure of UK firms. Results revealed that there exists a positive relationship between management ownership and leverage ratio whereas a negative relationship is observed between large external equity holder ownership and financial leverage. However, the relationship between management ownership and leverage ratio is not significant in the presence of large outside equity holders.

Pfeffer and Salancik (1978) emphasized that independent director plays an essential role in enhancing the capability of a company to get recognition from external stakeholders. Thus, leading to reduction in uncertainty about the company and enhancing the ability of the company to raise funds. Heng and Azrbaijani (2012) showed that board size and presence of independent directors on the board have a significant negative correlation with debt-to-asset ratio, respectively. Wen et al. (2002) revealed that outside directors tend to monitor managers more actively, causing these managers to adopt lower leverage for getting improved performance results. The research also found that the firm with a higher proportion of outside director tends to pursue low financial leverage with a high market value of equity.

In the context of Nepal, Sharma et al. (2014) found that there is a positive impact of corporate governance on capital structure in financial institutions, mainly commercial banks, and concluded that the impact of board size and firm size are positively significant with capital structure. The result further revealed that good corporate governance contributes to sustainable economic development by enhancing performance of companies and increasing their access to outside capital. Thagunna and Poudel (2013) revealed that there is no significant relationship between efficiency level and ownership structure of banks and there are no notable differences in the efficiency levels of banks according to their asset size.

Pradhan (2014) found that there is a significant impact of corporate governance on return on assets (ROA) as well as return on equity (ROE) in financial institutions, mainly commercial banks. Rai et al. (2015) revealed that there is a significant impact of corporate governance on leverage. The findings also specify that elements of corporate governance, such as the presence of firm size, have a positive effect on capital structure. Likewise, Joshi et al. (2016) showed that there is a significant impact of board size and number of audit committee members on ROA. Thapa et al. (2016) showed that there is significant impact of corporate governance on ROA. Pradhan (2014) and Pandey (2014) confirmed that leverage ratios increase with firm size, and decrease with profitability significantly. The preceding discussion reveals that there is a consistency in the findings of various studies concerning the impact of corporate governance and ownership structure on capital structure of companies in Nepal.

The major objective of this study is to examine the impact of corporate governance and ownership structure on capital structure of Nepalese companies. More specifically, it examines the impact of board size, board composition, CEO duality, women director, number of board meetings, institutional shareholdings, managerial shareholdings, age of the firm, size of the firm and profitability of the firm. The remainder of this study is organized as follows. Section "Methodology Aspect" describes the sample, data and methodology. Section "Results and Discussions" presents the empirical results and the final section draws conclusion and discuss the implications of the study findings.

METHODOLOGY ASPECT

The study is based on secondary data of 20 enterprises consisting of 15 commercial banks and five insurance companies with 100 observations for the period 2011–2012 to 2015–2016. We collected the from the banking and financial statistics, and Bank Supervision Report published by Nepal Rastra Bank, and annual reports of the selected enterprises. We collected data on financial leverage, long-term debt, board size, board composition, CEO duality, women director, number of board meetings, managerial shareholding, institutional shareholding, firm size, age of firm, ROA and industry dummies of banking and insurance sectors.

Table 22.1 shows the list of commercial banks selected for the study along with study period and number of observations.

Table 22.1 Number of enterprises selected for the study along with study period and number of observations

S. No.	Name of firms	Study period	No. of observations
Commercial banks			
1	Bank of Kathmandu	2011/12–2015/16	5
2	Sunrise Bank	2011/12–2015/16	5
3	Sanima Bank	2011/12–2015/16	5
4	Nabil bank	2011/12–2015/16	5
5	Kumari Bank	2011/12–2015/16	5
6	Everest bank	2011/12–2015/16	5
7	Siddhartha Bank	2011/12–2015/16	5
8	Standard chartered Bank	2011/12–2015/16	5
9	SBI Bank	2011/12–2015/16	5
10	Himalayan Bank	2011/12–2015/16	5
11	Global IME Bank	2011/12–2015/16	5
12	Nepal Bangladesh Bank	2011/12–2015/16	5
13	Machhapuchare Bank	2011/12–2015/16	5
14	Nepal investment bank	2011/12–2015/16	5
15	NMB Bank	2011/12–2015/16	5
Insurance companies			
16	Sagarmatha insurance co.	2011/12–2015/16	5
17	Shikhar insurance co.	2011/12–2015/16	5
18	Nepal insurance	2011/12–2015/16	5
19	Premier insurance	2011/12–2015/16	5
20	Himalayan insurance ltd	2011/12–2015/16	5
Total observations			100

The Model

As a first approximation, the models estimated in this study assume that the capital structure (CS) depends on corporate governance variables (CG) and ownership structure (OS). Therefore, the model takes the following form:

$$CS = f(CG \text{ and } OS).$$

More specifically, the given model is segmented into the following models:

Model I

$$\begin{aligned}LEV_{it} &= \beta_0 + \beta_1 (BODCOMP)_{it} + \beta_2 (WD) + \beta3 (\%INSTSH) \\ &+ \beta_4 (MANGSH)_{it} + \beta_5 (NB) + \beta_6 (CEO)_{it} + \beta_7 (BS)_{it} + \beta_8 (SZ)_{it} \\ &+ \beta_9 (ROA)_{it} + \beta_{10} (AGE)_{it} + \varepsilon_t.\end{aligned}$$

Model II

$$\begin{aligned}LTD\_TA_{it} &= \beta_0 + \beta_1 (BS)_{it} + \beta_2 (BODCOMP)_{it} + \beta_3 (CEO)_{it} \\ &+ \beta_4 (WD) + \beta_5 (\%INSTSH) + \beta_6 (MANGSH)_{it} + \beta_7 (NB) \\ &+ \beta_8 (SZ)_{it} + \beta_9 (ROA) + \beta_{10} (AGE)_{it} + \varepsilon_t.\end{aligned}$$

Where,
LEV = leverage is defined as the ratio of total debts to total equity.
LTD_TA = Long-term debt to total assets is defined as the ratio of total long-term debt to total assets.
BS = Board size is defined as total number of directors on the board.
BODCOMP = Board composition is defined as total number of outside directors.
DUALITY = CEO/chair duality is represented by dummy variable 1 if CEO and chairman are the same person, and 0 if CEO and chairman are different persons.
WD = Women director is defined as the total number of women directors on a board of directors.

NB = Board meeting is the total number of board meetings held by the board.

MANGSH = Managerial shareholding is defined as the total shares in percentage held by management team of the firm.

INSTSH = Institutional shareholding is defined as the total shares in percentage held by outside entities.

SZ = Size of firm is defined as the book value of the total assets.

ROA = Return on assets is defined as the net profit as a percentage of total assets.

AGE = Age of firm is defined as the number of years between observation year and year of incorporation.

Board Size

Board size is defined as total number of directors on the board. According to Pfeffer and Salancik (1978) and Lipton and Lorsch (1992), there is a significant positive relationship between board size and capital structure. Berger et al. (1997) found that firm with larger board members have low leverage or debt ratio. Jensen (1986) argued that firms with larger boards have high leverage or debt ratio. Similarly, Wen et al. (2002), and Abor and Biekpe (2004) revealed that there exists a positive relationship between board size and leverage. Based on these findings, we develop the following hypothesis:

H_1 *There is a positive relationship between board size and capital structure.*

Board Composition

Board composition is defined as the total number of outside directors on the board. Jensen (1986) and Berger et al. (1997) found that companies with relatively higher independent directors have higher gearing levels whereas companies with lower representation of independent directors experience lower leverage. Similarly, Wen et al. (2002) revealed that there exist a significantly negative relationship between number of outside directors on the board and leverage. However, Abor and Biekpe (2004) argued that firms with relatively more outside directors have higher leverage, while firms with low percentage of outside directors experience lower leverage. Based on these findings, we develop the following hypothesis:

H_2 *There is a positive relationship between board composition and capital structure.*

CEO Duality

CEO duality is the situation when the CEO also holds the position of the chairman of the board. For the purpose of the study, CEO/chair duality is included as a dummy variable. It is taken as 1 if CEO is chairman, otherwise it is taken as 0. Emamgholipour et al. (2013) revealed that there exists a positive relationship between CEO duality and capital structure of the companies listed in the Theran Stock Exchange. Fosberg (2004) found that firms with separate chairman and CEO employ the optimal amount of debt in their capital structure, which revealed that a firm with a separate CEO and chairman generally has higher financial leverage. Abor and Biekpe also argued that there is a positive relationship between gearing level and CEO duality. Based on these findings, we develop the following hypothesis:

H_3 *There is a positive relationship between CEO duality and capital structure.*

Women Director

Women director is the total number of women/female directors on the board. Adams and Ferriera (2009) reported that female directors have a strong effect on board input and output. On the contrary, Abobakr and Elgiziry (2015) revealed that female members on the board and capital structure are negatively related, that is, the greater the number of female members on a board, the lower the capital structure of the firm. Alvas et al. (2014) analyzed the association between composition of board of directors and capital structure and findings revealed that a firm with more board diversity will have a capital structure composed of more long-term sources of financing. Based on these findings, we develop the following hypothesis:

H_4 *There is a positive relationship between women directors and capital structure.*

Board Meeting

Board meeting is defined as the total number of board meetings held by the company. According to Finch and Shivdasani (2006), a board that meets more frequently is valued less by the market. On the contrary, Carcello et al. (2002) and Karamanou and Vefeas (2005) reported a positive relationship between the frequency of board meetings and capital structure. Similarly, Kajananthan (2012) revealed that there exists a positive relationship between capital structure and board meetings. Based on these findings, we develop the following hypothesis:

H_5 *There is a positive relationship between the number of board meetings and capital structure.*

Institutional Shareholding

Institutional shareholding is measured in terms of the percentage of total shares held by outside entities. According to Krivogorky (2006), more than 50% of shareholding in the listed industrial companies in Australia, Belgium, Germany and Italy are held by large blockholders. The result also revealed that the presence of institutional shareholding in a company helps it to raise long-term finance at an advantageous cost. Kyereboah-Coleman (2007) revealed that institutional shareholding is the signal to other investors of the potential profitability of the firm, which could lead to increased demand for the firm's shares and improve its market valuation. The result also showed that there exists a positive relationship between institutional shareholding and capital structure of the firm. Butt and Hasan (2009) revealed that institutional ownership has a positive relationship with capital structure. Based on these findings, we develop the following hypothesis:

H_6 *There is a positive relationship between institutional shareholding and capital structure.*

Managerial Shareholding

Managerial shareholding is measured in terms of total shares held by the management team of a firm. Fredrick revealed that managerial ownership is negatively related to capital structure, which indicates that increased managerial ownership aligns the interest of managers with the interest of outside shareholders and reduces the role of debt as a tool to mitigate agency problems. However, Abobakr and Elgiziry (2015) revealed that there exists a positive relationship between managerial ownership and capital structure. Nyamweya (2015) examined the relationship between the board of directors' characteristics and the capital structures of companies listed in the Nairobi Securities Exchange and found that there is a positive relationship between managerial shareholding and capital structure. Based on these findings, we develop the following hypothesis:

H_7 There is a positive relationship between managerial shareholding and capital structure.

Firm Size

Firm size is measured as the total assets possessed by the company. Titman and Wessels (1988) stated that large firms do not consider the bankruptcy costs in deciding the level of leverage as these are just a small percentage of the total value of the firm. Therefore, large firms may prefer to use a higher level of gearing. Friend and Lang (1988) and Marsh (1982) found a positive relationship between firm size and leverage levels. Thippayana revealed that leverage ratios increase with firm size. Based on these findings, we develop the following hypothesis:

H_8 There is a positive relationship between size and capital structure.

Age of Firm

Age is the number of years since the establishment of a company. Ahmad and Aris (2015) stated that the age of a firm is considered as an important determinant of capital structure in most financial literature. The longer the company is in business, the higher is its ability in taking on more debt and therefore there is a positive relationship between the age and leverage of the firm. Rafael et al. (1999) found that bank age has a positive effect on the capital structure of the firm. Based on these findings, we develop the following hypothesis:

H_9 There is a positive relationship between age of firm and leverage.

Return on Assets

ROA is defined as the ratio of net profit to total assets. Myers and Majluf (1984) found that profitable firms generally have low gearing levels because these firms prefer internally generated funds over external financing. Devinaga (2010) revealed that there is a positive relationship between profiatability and capital structure of the firm. According to Titman and Wessels (1988), profitability firms are better able to raise funds from the general public. Based on these findings, we develop the following hypothesis:

H_{10} *There is a positive relationship between ROA and capital structure.*

RESULTS AND DISCUSSIONS

Descriptive Statistics

Table 22.2 presents the descriptive statistics of selected dependent and independent variables during the period 2011–2012 to 2015–2016.

Correlation Analysis

Having indicated the descriptive statistics, we computed Pearson's correlation coefficients and present them in Table 22.3. More specifically, it shows the correlation coefficients of dependent and independent variables of Nepalese commercial banks and insurance organizations.

Table 22.3 shows the negative relationship of board size with capital structure. This indicates that an increase in board size leads to a decrease in capital structure. However, the results show a positive relationship of board composition and CEO duality with capital structure, which means that an increase in board composition and CEO duality leads to an increase in capital structure. Women directors and board meeting have a positive relationship with capital structure. This reveals that an increase in the number of board meetings and number of women directors on the board leads to an increase in capital structure. Similarly, institutional shareholding and managerial shareholding show a positive relationship with capital structure. This means that an increase in institutional shareholding and managerial shareholding leads to an increase in capital structure. Firm size, age of firm and ROA also have a positive relationship with capital structure. An increase in these variables leads to an increase in capital structure.

Table 22.2 Descriptive statistics

Variables	Minimum	Maximum	Mean	Std. deviation
LEV	5.29	95.23	81.91	19.55
LTD_TA	5.19	82.97	67.35	15.24
BS	5.00	11.00	7.61	1.30
BODCOMP	0.00	4.00	1.67	0.99
CEO	0.00	1.00	0.01	0.10
WD	0.00	2.00	0.13	0.37
NB	9.00	39.00	15.26	6.28
INSTSH	0.00	80.00	16.91	20.89
MANGSH	0.00	1.00	0.33	0.47
SZ	0.39	116.37	35.37	27.50
Age	4.00	32.00	17.65	6.80
ROA	−0.08	4.13	1.34	1.01

This table shows the descriptive statistics of dependent and independent variables. Dependent variables are LEV (leverage defined as ratio of total debt to total assets, in percentage) and LTD_TA (total long-term debt to total assets defined as ratio of total long term debt to total assets, in percentage). Independent variables are BS (board size defined as total number of members on a board), BODCOMP (board composition defined as ratio of outside directors to the number of directors), DUALITY (CEO duality is defined as dummy variable 1 if CEO and chairman are the same person, and 0 if CEO and chairman are different persons), INSTSH (institutional shareholding is defined as percentage of shares held by institutions as disclosed by annual financial report), MANGSH (managerial shareholding is defined as percentage of shares held by managers of board disclosed in annual financial report), WD (women director is defined as total number of director positions held by women), NB (board meeting is defined as total number of board meetings held by the board), AGE (age of a firm is defined as number of years between observation year and year of incorporation), SZ (firm size is defined as total assets in billions), ROA (return on assets is defined as net profit as a ratio of total assets, in percentage). The descriptive statistics are based on data from 20 Nepalese enterprises consisting of 10 banks and five insurance companies with 100 observations for the period 2011–2012 to 2015–2016

Regression Analysis

Having indicated the Pearson's correlation coefficients, we carried out the regression analysis and present the results in Table 22.4. More specifically, the table shows the regression results of leverage on board composition, board size, CEO duality, women director, number of board meetings, institutional shareholding, managerial shareholding, firm size, ROA and age of firm.

Table 22.4 shows that the beta coefficients for board composition are positive. It reveals that the higher the board composition, the higher the leverage. This finding is similar to the findings of Lipton and Lorsch (1992). The beta coefficient for women director is positive, indicating that the greater the number of women directors, the higher the leverage. This

Table 22.3 Pearson's correlation coefficients matrix for Nepalese commercial banks

	LEV	LTD	BS	BODCOMP	CEO	WD	NB	INSTSH	MANGSH	SZ	Age	ROA
LEV	1											
LTD	0.971**	1										
BS	−0.010	−0.021	1									
BODCOMP	0.336**	0.396**	0.237*	1								
CEO	0.063	0.052	0.030	0.034	1							
WD	0.194	0.186	−0.062	−0.132	−0.036	1						
NB	0.287**	0.279**	0.281**	0.256*	−0.052	−0.120	1					
INSTSH	0.213*	0.151	−0.038	−0.406**	−0.031	0.122	0.033	1				
MANGSH	0.371**	0.340**	0.047	0.366**	−0.071	0.041	0.073	−0.105	1			
SZ	0.591**	0.476**	−0.149	0.012	0.040	0.191	0.141	0.387**	0.386**	1		
Age	0.260**	0.211	−0.197*	−0.132	0.005	0.205*	−0.160	0.366**	−0.011	0.520**	1	
ROA	0.605**	0.521**	−0.318**	0.034	0.077	0.185	0.036	0.377**	0.178	0.682**	0.477**	1

Note: The asterisk signs (**) and (*) indicate that coefficients are significant at 1 percent and 5 percent levels respectively

This table reveals the bivariate Pearson correlation coefficients of different dependent and independent variables. The coefficients are based on data from 20 Nepalese enterprises (15 banks and five insurance companies) with 100 observations for the period 2011–2012 to 2015–2016. Dependent variables are LEV (leverage defined as ratio of total debt to total assets, in percentage) and LTD_TA (total long-term debt to total assets defined as ratio of total long-term debt to total assets, in percentage). Independent variables are BS (board size defined as total number of members on a board), BODCOMP (board composition defined as ratio of outside directors to the number of directors), DUALITY (CEO duality is defined as dummy variable 1 if CEO and chairman are the same person, and 0 if CEO and chairman are different persons), INSTSH (institutional shareholding is defined as percentage of shares held by institutions as disclosed by annual financial report), MANGSH (managerial shareholding is defined as percentage of shares held by managers of board disclosed in annual financial report), WD (women director is defined as total number of director positions held by women), NB (board meeting is defined as total number of board meetings held by the board), AGE (age of a firm is defined as number of years between observation year and year of incorporation), SZ (firm size is defined as total assets in billions), ROA (return on assets is defined as net profit as a ratio of total assets, in percentage)

Table 22.4 Estimated regression of LEV on BS, BOCOM, CEO, WD, NB, INSTSH, MANGSH, SZ, ROA, and AGE

Model	Intercept	Regression coefficients of										Adj R^2	SEE	F-Value
		BODCOMP	WD	INSTSH	MANGSH	NB	CEO	BS	SZ	ROA	AGE			
1	70.79 (19.36)**	6.67 (3.54)**										0.1	18.5	12.46
2	80.57 (39.37)**		10.4 (1.96)*									0.08	19.3	3.83
3	78.54 (31.53)**			0.02 (2.2)*								0.04	19.2	4.68
4	76.85 (34.47)**				15.34 (3.95)**							0.13	18.25	16.61
5	68.29 (13.74)**					0.89 (2.96)**						0.07	18.8	8.76
6	81.79 (41.49)**						12.33 -0.63					0.004	19.61	0.39
7	83.1 (7.095)**							-0.154 (-0.102)				0.01	19.65	0.1
8	67.039 (25.88)**								0.42 (7.26)**			0.34	15.8	52.72
9	66.34 (25.54)**									11.7 (7.52)**		0.36	15.7	56.45
10	68.73 (12.98)**										0.75 (2.67)**	0.058	19	7.11
11	67.917 (18.92)**	5.321 (2.751)**	11.654 (2.408)**		10.898 (2.724)**							0.26	17.421	9.565
12	51.9 (13.71)**	8.324 (5.113)**	7.125 (1.783)	0.166 (2.00)*					0.35 (6.01)**			0.48	14.2	23.35
13	46.355 (7.86)**	4.567 (1.29)	0.527 (2.23)*	8.1 (0.6)		0.15 (1.89)	6.99 (3.71)**	-0.08 (-0.32)	5.87 (3.46)**	7.119 (1.88)	0.106 (1.32)	0.54	13.3	13.94

Note: The asterisk signs (**) and (*) indicate that coefficients are significant at 1 percent and 5 percent levels respectively

finding is similar to the findings of Adam and Ferriera (2009). Similarly, the beta coefficient for institutional shareholding is also positive. This denotes that the higher the institutional shareholding, the higher the leverage. This finding is similar to the findings of Butt and Hasan (2009). The beta coefficient for managerial shareholding is positive, indicating the higher the shareholding, the higher the leverage. This finding is similar to the findings of Pamba. In addition, the beta coefficient for board meeting is positive. The greater the number of board meetings, the greater the leverage. This finding is similar to the findings of Karamanou and Vefeas (2005). The beta coefficient for CEO duality is also positive. This shows that the higher the CEO duality value, the higher the leverage. This finding is similar to the findings of Emamgholipour et al. (2013). However, the beta coefficient for board size is negative. The larger the board size, the higher the leverage. This finding is not consistent with the findings of Lipton and Lorsch (1992). The beta coefficient for firm size is positive, meaning the larger the firm size, the higher the leverage. This finding is similar to the findings of Friend and Lang (1988). The beta coefficients for age of the firm and ROA are positive as well. The older the firm, the higher the leverage, and the higher the ROA, the higher the leverage. This finding is similar to the findings of Devinaga (2010).

The estimated regression results of BS, BOCOM, CEO, WD, NB, INSTSH, MANGSH, SZ, ROA, and AGE on LTD_TA are presented in Table 22.5.

In the Table 22.5 the results are is based on 20 enterprises (15 banks and five insurance companies) with 100 observations for the period of 2011–2012 to 2015–2016 by using the regression model. The model is $LTD\_TA_{it} = \beta_0 + \beta_1 (BS)_{it} + \beta_2 (BODCOMP)_{it} + \beta_3 (CEO)_{it} + \beta_4 (WD) + \beta_5 (\%INSTSH) + \beta_6 (MANGSH)_{it} + \beta_7 (NB) + \beta_8 (SZ)_{it} + \beta_9 (ROA) + \beta_{10} (AGE)_{it} + \varepsilon_t$.

The dependent variable is LTD_TA (total long-term debt to total assets defined as ratio of total long term debt to total assets, in percentage). Independent variables are BS (board size defined as total number of members on a board), BODCOMP (board composition defined as ratio of outside directors to the number of directors), DUALITY (CEO duality is defined as dummy variable 1 if CEO and chairman are the same person, and 0 if CEO and chairman are different persons), INSTSH (institutional shareholding is defined as percentage of shares held by institutions as disclosed by annual financial report), MANGSH

Table 22.5 Estimated regression of LTD_TA on BS, BOCOM, CEO, WD, NB, INSTSH, MANGSH, SZ, ROA, and AGE

Model	Intercept	Regression Coefficients of LTD_TA									Adj R^2	SEE	F-Value
		BS	BODCOMP	CEO	WD	INSTSH	MANGSH	NB	SZ	ROA	AGE			
1	69.22 (7.58)**	−0.25 (−0.21)										0	15.32	0.043
2	57.13 (20.56)**		6.13 (4.26)**									0.148	14.07	18.208
3	67.27 (43.75)**			7.95 (0.52)								0.03	15.29	0.27
4	66.35 (41.52)**				7.7 (−1.87)							0.025	15.05	3.5
5	65.5 (33.56)**					0.11 (1.5)						0.013	15.14	2.27
6	63.03 (36.22)**						10.98 (3.58)**					0.107	14.4	12.84
7	57.01 (14.68)**							0.68 (2.87)**				0.068	14.72	8.27
8	58.02 (26.35)**								0.26 (5.37)**			0.219	13.47	28.74
9	56.88 (26.22)**									7.83 (6.048)**		0.264	13.072	46.58
10	59.02 (14.11)**										0.47 (2.14)*	0.035	14.97	4.55
11	45.32 (16.32)**		6.18 (5.3)**	5.26 (0.47)	5.6 (1.7)	0.09 (1.3)	3.26 (1.09)	0.402 (1.99)*	0.12 (2.11)*	5.02 (3.24)**	0.09 (−0.4)	0.439	11.42	20.33
12	39.47 (7.87)**		5.76 (3.99)**	−0.45 (0.47)	6.46 (2.03)*				0.06 (0.8)	5.1 (3.18)**	0.011	0.45	11.29	10.07
13	42.17 (4.93)**	−0.399 (−0.39)	5.91 (3.94)**	5.61	6.54 (2.01)*	0.09 (1.34)	3.29 (1.09)	0.42 (2.025)*	−0.804	4.87 (2.84)**	−0.049	0.44	11.34	8.99

Note: The asterisk signs (**) and (*) indicate that coefficients are significant at 1 percent and 5 percent levels respectively

(managerial shareholding is defined as percentage of shares held by managers of board disclosed in annual financial report), WD (women director is defined as total number of director positions held by women), NB (board meeting is defined as total number of board meetings held by the board), AGE (age of a firm is defined as number of years between observation year and year of incorporation), SZ (firm size is defined as total assets in billions), ROA (return on assets is defined as net profit as a ratio of total assets, in percentage).

Table 22.5 shows that the beta coefficients for board composition are positive. It reveals that the higher the board composition, the higher the total long-term debt to total assets. This finding is similar to the findings of Jensen (1986). The beta coefficient for women director is positive, indicating that the greater the number of women directors, the higher the long-term debt to total assets. This finding is similar to the findings of Adam and Ferriera (2009). Similarly, the beta coefficient for institutional shareholding is positive. This denotes that the higher the institutional shareholding, the higher the total long-term debt to total assets. This finding is similar to the findings of Kyereboah-Coleman (2007). The beta coefficient for managerial shareholding is also positive. Again, a higher value for this variable means higher total long-term debt to total assets. This finding is similar to the findings of Mohamed and Khairy. In addition, the beta coefficient for board meeting is positive, indicating the greater the number of board meetings, the higher the total long-term debt to total assets. This finding is similar to the findings of Karamanou and Vefeas (2005). The beta coefficient for CEO duality is positive as well. This shows that the higher the value of CEO duality, the higher the total long-term debt to total assets. This finding is similar to the findings of Abor and Biekpe. Conversely, the beta coefficient for board size is negative. This means that the larger the board, the higher the total long-term debt to total assets. This finding is not consistent with the findings of Wen et al. (2002).

Likewise, the beta coefficient for firm size is positive, indicating the larger the firm size, the higher the total long-term debt to total assets. This finding is similar to the findings of Friend and Lang (1988). Finally, the beta coefficients for age of the firm and ROA are also positive. The older the firm and the higher the ROA, the higher the long-term debt to total assets. This finding is similar to the findings of Devinaga (2010).

Summary and Conclusion

Corporate governance is the process that facilitates the creation of shareholder value, and protection of the individual and collective interests of all stakeholders. Corporate governance is generally associated with the existence of agency problems and its roots can be traced back to separation of ownership and control of a firm. Capital structure is one of the most important effective parameters on the valuation and direction of economic enterprises in the capital market. The changing evaluation environment affects the capital structure and strategic planning of the companies towards maximizing the shareholder wealth (Drobetz and Fix 2003). According to Saleem and Rafique (2013), capital structure of a firm is defined as the various financing alternatives of its assets used by the firm.

This study attempts to examine the impact of corporate governance and ownership structure on the capital structure of companies in Nepal. This study is based on secondary data from 20 listed companies consisting of 15 commercial banks and five insurance companies with 100 observations for the period of 2011–2012 to 2015–2016. The variables that examine the impact of corporate governance and ownership structure on capital structure are board size, board composition, CEO duality, women director, number of board meetings, managerial shareholding, institutional shareholding, firm size, age of firm and ROA.

The study shows that board composition and CEO duality have a positive and significant impact on capital structure. The higher the board composition and value of CEO duality, the higher the capital structure. The study also reveals that there is a positive impact of number of board meetings and managerial shareholding on capital structure. Similarly, firm size, age and ROA also have a positive and significant impact on capital structure, which indicates that the greater the value of these variable, the greater the capital structure.

References

Abobakr, G. M., & Elgiziry, K. (2015). The effect of board characteristics and ownership structure on the corporate financial leverage. *Journal of Accounting and Finance, 5*(1), 1–14.

Abor, J. Y., & Biekpe, N. (2004). Does corporate governance affect the capital structure decisions of Ghanaian SMEs? *International Journal of Business in Society, 4*(1), 21–27.

Adams, B. R., & Ferreira, D. (2009). Women in the boardroom and their impact on governance and performance. *Journal of Financial Economics, 94*(1), 291–309.

Ahmad, N., & Aris, B. W. (2015). Does age of the firm determine capital structure decision? Evidence from Malaysian trading and services sector. *International Business Management, 9*(3), 200–207.

Alvas, F. P., Berger, C. E., & Paulo, F. (2014). Board of director's composition and capital structure. *Research in International Business and Finance, 35*(2015), 1–32.

Berger, P. G., Ofek, E., & Yermack, D. L. (1997). Managerial entrenchment and capital structure decisions. *The Journal of Finance, 52*(4), 1411–1438.

Bhaduri, S. N. (2002). Determinants of corporate borrowing: Some evidence from the Indian corporate structure. *Journal of Economics and Finance, 26*(2), 200–215.

Boodhoo, R. (2009). Capital structure and ownership structure: A review of literature. *The Journal of Online Education, 4*(5), 65–70.

Butt, S. A., & Hasan, A. (2009). Impact of ownership structure and corporate structure on capital structure of Pakistani listed companies. *International Journal of Business and Management, 4*(2), 50–57.

Cadbury, A. (1992). Report of the committee on the financial aspects of corporate governance. *London Gee Publishing, 7*(4), 24–50.

Carcello, J. V., Neal, R. A., Riley, R. A., & Hermanson, D. R. (2002). Board characteristics and audit fees. *Contemporary Accounting Research, 19*(2), 365–384.

Dalton, M. C., & Dan, R. D. (2005). Board of directors: Utilizing empirical evidence in developing practical prescription. *British Journal of Management, 16*(1), 91–97.

Devinaga, R. (2010). Theoretical framework of profitability as applied to commercial banks in Malaysia. *European Journal of Economics, Finance and Administrative Sciences, 19*(4), 74–88.

Drobetz, W., & Fix, R. (2003). What are the determinants of the capital structure? Some evidence for Switzerland. *Journal of Business, 5*(6), 75–88.

Emamgholipour, M., Ramezani, A., Behzadnia, Z., & Rekabdarkolaei, E. A. (2013). The effect of CEO duality on the capital structure: Evidence from the Tehran stock exchange. *International Journal of Basic Sciences and Applied Research, 2*(4), 332–336.

Finch, E. M., & Shivdasani, A. (2006). Are busy boards effective monitors. *Journal of Finance, 51*(2), 689–724.

Fosberg, R. H. (2004). Agency problems and debt financing: Leadership structure effects, corporate governance. *The International Journal of Business in Society, 4*(1), 31–38.

Friend, I., & Lang, L. H. (1988). An empirical test of the impact of managerial self-interest on corporate capital structure. *The Journal of Finance, 43*(2), 271–281.

Heng, T. B., & Azrbaijani, S. (2012). Board of directors and capital structure: Evidence from leading Malaysian companies. *Journal of Asian Social Science, 8*(3), 123–136.

Jensen, M. C. (1986). Agency costs of free cash flow, corporate finance, and takeovers. *The American Economic Review, 76*(2), 323–329.

Jensen, M. C. (1993). The modern industrial revolution, exit, and the failure of internal control system. *The Journal of Finance, 48*(3), 831–880.

Joshi, A., Basel, A., Maskey, A., Khadka, B., & Pandey, B. (2016). Impact of corporate governance on firm performance in unstable economic and political environment in Nepal. *Nepalese Journal of Business, 3*(1), 15–25.

Kajananthan, R. (2012). Effect of corporate governance on capital structure: Case of the Sri Lankan listed manufacturing companies. *Journal of Arts, Science and Commerce, 3*(4), 63–71.

Karamanou, I., & Vafeas, N. (2005). The association between boards, audit committees, and management earnings forecasts: An empirical analysis. *Journal of Accounting Research, 43*(3), 453–486.

Krivogorky, V. (2006). Ownership, board structure and performance in continental Europe. *The International Journal of Accounting, 4*(1), 176–197.

Kyereboah-Coleman, A. (2007). *Corporate governance and firm performance in Africa: A dynamic panel data analysis.* Paper presented at the international conference on corporate governance in emerging market, Sabanci University, Istanbul, Turkey.

Lang, W., & Jagtiani, J. (2010). The mortgage financial crises: The role of credit risk management and corporate governance. *Atlantic Economic Journal, 38*(3), 295–316.

Lipton, M., & Lorsch, J. W. (1992). A modest proposal for improved corporate governance. *The Business Lawyer, 4*(1), 59–77.

Lubatkin, M., & Chatterjee, S. (1994). Extending modern portfolio theory into the domain of corporate diversification: Does it apply? *Academy of Management Journal, 3*(7), 109–136.

Marsh, P. (1982). The choice between equity and debt: An empirical study. *The Journal of Finance, 37*(1), 121–144.

Melvin, C., & Hirt, H. (2005). Corporate governance and performance: A brief review and assessment of the evidence for a link between corporate governance and performance. *Journal of Business and Finance, 8*(6), 269–278.

Modigliani, F., & Miller, M. H. (1958). The cost of capital, corporation finance and the theory of investment. *The American Economic Review, 4*(8), 261–297.

Myers, S. C., & Majluf, N. S. (1984). Corporate financing and investment decision when firms have information that investors do not have. *Journal of Financial Economics, 13*(2), 187–221.

Nyamweya, S. A. (2015). Relationship between the board of directors' characteristics and the capital structures of companies listed in Nairobi securities exchange. *Journal of Business and Management, 17*(2), 104–109.

Owusu, A., Agyei, K., & Richard, A. (2014). The effect of ownership structure and corporate governance on capital structure of Ghanaian listed manufacturing companies. *International Journal of Academic Research in Accounting, Finance and Management Sciences, 4*(1), 109–118.

Pandey, P. (2014). Determinants of capital structure in Nepal. *Nepalese Journal of Management, 1*(4), 74–77.

Pfeffer, J., & Salancik, G. R. (1978). *The external control of organisations: A resource-dependence perspective.* New York: Harper and Row.

Pradhan, R. S. (2014). Corporate governance and bank performance in Nepal. *Journal of Management and Development Economics, 3*(1), 1–14.

Rafael, P. L., Pfeffer, F. L., & Sheleifer, A. (1999). Corporate ownership around the world. *The Journal of Finance, 54*(2), 471–517.

Rai, P., Ojha, P., Singh, P., Gyawali, R., & Gupta, R. (2015). Corporate governance and bank performance: Empirical evidence from Nepal. *Nepalese Journal of Management, 2*(2), 94–104.

Rehman, M. A. U., Rehman, R. U., & Raoof, A. (2010). Does corporate governance lead to achangein the capital structure? *American Journal of Social and Management Sciences, 3*(4), 63–71.

Saleem, F., & Rafique, B. (2013). The determination of capital structure of a gas firms listed on Karachi stock exchange in Pakistan. *Interdisciplinary Journal of Contemporary Research in Business, 9*(2), 225–235.

Sharma, G., Pant, M., & Thapa, N. (2014). Role of corporate governance on bank performance: A case of Nepalese banks. *Nepalese Journal of Corporate Governance, 1*(1), 15–26.

Short, H., Wen, Z. H., & Keasey, P. (2002). The link between dividend policy and institutional ownership. *Journal of Corporate Finance, 8*(5), 105–122.

Thagunna, K. S., & Poudel, S. (2013). Measuring bank performance of Nepali banks: A data envelopment analysis (DEA). *International Journals of Economis and Financial, 3*(1), 54–65.

Thapa, P. J., Gurung, P., Shrestha, R., Kshetri, R. R., & Shrestha, R. (2016). Impact of board characteristics on firm's performance: A case of Nepalese commercial banks. *Nepalese Journal of Business, 1*(3), 124–134.

Titman, S., & Wessels, R. (1988). The determinants of capital structure choice. *The Journal of Finance, 4*(3), 1–19.

Wen, Y., Rwegasira, K., & Bilderbeek, J. (2002). Corporate governance and capital structure decisions of the Chinese listed firms. *An International Review, 10*(2), 75–83.

Effect of Board Diversity and Corporate Governance Structure on Operating Performance: Evidence from the Nepalese Enterprises

Ritu Kumari Gupta, Rupa Chand, Sabeena Sadaula, Sangita Saud, and Sapana Ambai

Introduction

Corporate governance is defined as the set of procedures laws, policies and institutions influencing the way corporation is administered or managed. Corporate governance has been referred to as a collective group of people united as one body with power and authority to direct, control and rule an organization (Ruin 2001). Corporate governance is the system by which businesses are directed and controlled (Cadbury 1992). It is a set of relationships between a company's management, its board, its shareholders and stakeholders. Hill and Jones (2001) asserted that corporate governance from a managerial perspective refers to the control used to ensure

---

R. K. Gupta (✉) • R. Chand • S. Sadaula • S. Saud • S. Ambai
Department of Management, Uniglobe College, Thribhuvan University, Kathmandu, Nepal
e-mail: rspradhan@uniglobe.edu.np

that managers' actions are consistent with the interest of key constituent shareholders. The conflicts of interest among the contractual parties in a firm are a main focus of corporate governance literature.

According to Jensen and Meckling (1976), the three main parties with the potential for such a conflict are the directors, the shareholders and debtors. The aim of corporate governance is to protect the shareholders from self-interest of the directors so that they can get fair return on their investment. There will be greater agency problem where corporate governance mechanisms are weak (Guli et al. 2012). According to Kang et al. (2007) and Ferreira (2010), corporate board structure along with demographic diversity such as gender, age, ethnicity and so on is efficient in better protecting the interest of the shareholders and other stakeholders and adds value to the performance of the firm. Board diversity as a corporate governance concept has recently caught the attention of policymakers, managers, directors, shareholders and academia (Johansen 2008).

Shrader et al. (1997) examined firm financial performance with gender diversity at the middle and upper management, and at the board of director levels for large firms. The result found that there is positive relationship of board diversity on operating performance. Kang and Shivdasan (1995) examined the role of corporate governance mechanisms during top executive turnover in Japanese corporations. They found that the likelihood of non-routine turnover is significantly related to industry-adjusted return on assets, excess stock returns and negative operating income, but is not related to industry performance.

Burke (2000) found significant correlation coefficients between the number of women directors and revenue, assets and profit margins for Canadian firms. Fondas (2000) argued that the presence of women directors helps a board execute its strategic function because their experience is often closely aligned with company needs. Farrell and Hersch (2005) found that women tend to serve on better-performing firms. Smith et al. (2006) revealed that the proportion of women in top management tends to have positive effects on firm performance. Adams and Ferreira (2009) found that female directors have a positive impact on board inputs and firm outcomes. According to Jensen (1993) and Yermack, as the board size increases there arises the problem of communication and coordination and decreased ability of the board to control management, thereby leading to agency problems. The result also found that larger boards can make coordination, communication and decision making more cumbersome than smaller boards. Sami et al. (2011) found that composite measure of corporate governance is positively and significantly associated with firm performance and valuation.

Dalton et al. (1998) revealed mixed findings on the relationship between board independence and CEO duality and firm performance. The result revealed that neither board composition (proportion of independent directors) nor board leadership structure (CEO duality) has been consistently linked to firm performance. Rhoades et al. (2001) found a significant relationship between CEO duality and firm performance. Chen et al. examined the relationship between the partnership structure, company performance and dividend policies in companies operating in Hong Kong and found a negative relation between duality and Tobin Q (for large companies). But no relation has been found between duality and return on assets (ROA) or return on equity (ROE). Abdul et al. (2006) argued that a lesser number of audit committee meetings improves a firm's financial performance as it reduces the additional cost incurred with every meeting.

Majumdar (1997) revealed that there is a negative and significant relationship between leverage and corporate performance. Peni and Vahamaa (2012) investigated that firm size has a significant positive influence on firm profitability. Burson (2007) found a negative relationship between firm size and profitability. Shleifer and Vishny (1997) argued that large block shareholders have a positive effect on firm value and are an effective device for monitoring management. Javid and Robina (2007) found that there is a positive relationship between ownership concentration and firm performance. Finch and Shivdasani (2006) revealed that boards that meet more frequently are valued less by the market. Mangena and Tauringana (2008) argued that there is a positive relationship between the frequency of board meetings and a firm's corporate performance. Further, frequent meetings intermingled with informal sideline interactions can create and strengthen cohesive bonds among directors and thereby impact positively on corporate performance (Lipton and Lorsch 1992). Adnan (2011) found that among the corporate governance variables, smaller board size and higher ratio of block ownership seem to consistently lead to better efficiency. However, the rest of the corporate governance variables do not seem to have a significant and consistent impact on efficiency.

In the context of Nepal, Pradhan and Adhikari (2009) showed that there exists a positive relationship between corporate governance practice and firm performance. Shah et al. (2013) found that bigger board and audit committee size and lower frequency of board meetings and lower proportion of institutional ownership lead to better efficiency in commercial banks. Poudel and Hovey revealed a positive relationship between audit committee size and bank efficiency. The result also explained a positive relationship between board size and bank efficiency, and a negative relationship between board meetings and bank efficiency. Silwal (2011) revealed that corporate governance has a significant impact on firm performance based on ROA as well as board size, and leverage has a negative and significant effect on firm performance. However, age of the firm and audit committee have positive effects on firm performance based on ROE. Guragain et al. (2016) argued that firm size has a positive significant impact on ROA in financial institutions in Nepal. Sharma et al. (2014) found that there is a positive impact of corporate governance on ROE in financial institutions, mainly commercial banks, and concluded that the impact of board size and firm size are positively significant with ROE.

Lama et al. (2015) concluded leverage has a negative impact on ROE, whereas board size has a positive impact on ROE. Thapa et al. (2013) argued that leverage has a positive relationship with ROA while it has a negative relationship with the ROE in Nepalese enterprises. Thagunna and Poudel (2013) revealed that there were no differences in the efficiency levels of banks according to their asset size. The preceding discussion reveals that there is no consistency in the findings of various studies concerning the impact of board diversity and corporate governance on operating performance. The major objective of this study is to find out the impact of board diversity and corporate governance on operating performance. More specifically, it examines the impact of duality, outside directors, board diversity, board size, audit committee, board meeting, block shareholders, firm size and leverage on operating performance.

The remainder of this study is organized as follows. Section "Methodology" describes the sample, data and methodology. Section "Result and Discussions" presents the empirical results and the final section draws conclusions and discusses the implications of the study's finding.

Methodology

The study is based on secondary data of 20 enterprises consisting of 10 banking and 10 insurance companies with 100 observations for the period 2011–2012 to 2015–2016 in Nepal. The data are collected from the

Table 23.1 Number of enterprises selected for the study along with study period and number of observations

S. No.	Name of enterprises	Study period	Observation
	Insurance companies		
1	National Premier Insurance Company	2011/12–2015/16	5
2	Himalayan general insurance company	2011/12–2015/16	5
3	Asian insurance company	2011/12–2015/16	5
4	Guras life insurance company	2011/12–2015/16	5
5	NB National Insurance	2011/12–2015/16	5
6	Shikhar insurance company	2011/12–2015/16	5
7	Sagarmatha insurance company	2011/12–2015/16	5
8	Surya Insurance company	2011/12–2015/16	5
9	Nepal life insurance company	2011/12–2015/16	5
10	National Life Insurance Company	2011/12–2015/16	5
	Commercial banks		
11	NMB Bank limited	2011/12–2015/16	5
12	Laxmi Bank limited	2011/12–2015/16	5
13	Nabil Bank limited	2011/12–2015/16	5
14	SBI Bank limited	2011/12–2015/16	5
15	Nepal investment Bank limited	2011/12–2015/16	5
16	Bank of Kathmandu limited	2011/12–2015/16	5
17	Everest Bank limited	2011/12–2015/16	5
18	Sanima Bank limited	2011/12–2015/16	5
19	Himalayan Bank limited	2011/12–2015/16	5
20	Kumari Bank limited	2011/12–2015/16	5
	Total		100

Banking and Financial Statistics and Bank Supervision Report published by Nepal Rastra Bank and annual reports of selected Nepalese enterprises. We collected data on board size, board meeting, audit committee, board diversity, block shareholders, CEO duality, leverage and firm size. Table 23.1 shows the list of enterprises selected for the study along with study period and number of observations.

The Model

As the first approximation, the model estimated in this study assumes that operating performance depends on several independent variables. Therefore, the model takes the following form:

Model 1

$$\text{ROE} = \beta_0 + \beta_1 \text{BDV}_{it} + \beta_2 \text{BSIZE}_{it} + \beta_3 \text{AUCOM}_{it} + \beta_4 \text{BMET}_{it}$$
$$+ \beta_5 \text{BHS}_{it} + \beta_6 \text{DUAL}_{it} + \beta_7 \text{FMZ}_{it} + \beta_8 \text{LEV}_{it} + e_{it}$$

Model 2

$$\text{MPS} = \beta_0 + \beta_1 \text{BDV}_{it} + \beta_2 \text{BSIZE}_{it} + \beta_3 \text{AUCOM}_{it}$$
$$+ \beta_4 \text{BMET}_{it} + \beta_5 \text{BHS}_{it} + \beta_6 \text{DUAL}_{it} + \beta_7 \text{FMZ}_{it} + \beta_8 \text{LEV}_{it} + e_{it}$$

Where,

ROE = Return on equity is defined as net income to shareholder equity.

MPS = Market price per share is defined as average of beginning and ending year market price per share.

BDV = Board diversity is defined as the proportion of women directors to the number of directors on the board of a company.

BSIZE = Board size is defined as the absolute number of directors on the board of a company.

AUCOM = Audit committee is defined as the number of members on an audit committee.

BMET = Board meeting is defined as the absolute number of meetings held by a board of directors.

BHS = Block shareholders is defined as the proportion of board members who have at least 5% of a company's shares to the number of directors on the board.

DUAL = Duality is defined as 1 if the CEO and chairman are the same or 0 if they are different.

FMZ = Firm size is defined as the total assets of a company.

LEV = Leverage is defined as the ratio of total debt to total equity.

Board Diversity

Board diversity is defined as the proportion of women directors to the number of directors on the board of companies. Erhardt et al. (2003) argued that correlation and regression analyses of board diversity are positively associated with the financial indicators of firm performance. Adler

(2001) showed a strong correlation between women-friendly firms and high profitability. Carter et al. (2003) found a positive relationship between board diversity (in terms of women and minorities) and firm value. Based on these findings, this study develops the following hypothesis:

H_1 *There is a positive relationship between board diversity and operating performance.*

Board Size

Board size is defined as the absolute number of directors on the board of a company. Jensen (1994) revealed that a large board is less effective than a small board. Gill and Mathur (2011) found a negative association between board size and firm performance. However, Johl et al. (2015) indicated that board size is positively related to firm performance. Dalton et al. showed a positive relationship between board size and firm performance. Nuryanah and Islam (2011) showed that the larger the board size the better the firm's performance. Based on these findings, this study develops the following hypothesis:

H_2 *There is a positive relationship between board size and operating performance.*

Audit Committee

Audit committee is defined as the number of members on an audit committee. DrorParnesa (2011) found that an effective audit committee measured by a high number of experts on the committee enhances reporting quality. Abbott and Parker (2000) showed a significant inverse relationship between audit committee and firm performance. Kyereboah-Coleman (2008) established favourable outcomes of frequent audit committee meetings on market measures of firm performance. Based on these findings, this study develops the following hypothesis:

H_3 *There is a positive relationship between audit committee and operating performance.*

Board Meeting

Board meeting is defined as the absolute number of meetings held by a board of directors. Ntim (2009) found that a higher frequency of board meetings can result in a higher quality of managerial monitoring and thereby impacts positively on corporate financial performance. Peng et al. (2007) revealed that regular meeting attendance is considered a hallmark of the conscientious director. Karamanou and Vafeas (2005) found a positive association between board meeting frequency and the accuracy of management earnings forecasts. Based on these findings, this study develops the following hypothesis:

H_4 *There is a positive relationship between board meeting and operating performance.*

Block Shareholders

Block shareholders are defined as the proportion of board members who have at least 5% of a company's shares to the number of directors on the board. Block holders are shareholders owning a large amount of stock; they are generally institutional investors. Shleifer and Vishny (1997) found that firm performance is positively related to the presence of larger shareholders. The result also revealed that large block shareholders have a positive effect on firm value and are an effective device for monitoring management. Shleifer and Wolfenson (2002) showed that concentration of ownership is considered as a solution to solve agency conflicts. Agrawal and Mandelker (1990) explained that firm performance could be improved by merging ownership and managerial interests through concentration of ownership. Based on these findings, this study develops the following hypothesis:

H_5 *There is a positive relationship between block shareholders and operating performance.*

CEO Duality

CEO duality is defined as 1 if the CEO and chairman are the same and 0 if they are different. Sheikh et al. (2013) found no significant difference in performance of companies with and without role duality. The results were found to be mixed in sign and statistically insignificant. Brickley et al.

(1997) also found no systematic link between duality status and organizational performance or market value. Abdullah (2004) showed that no relation has been found between duality and company performance. Velnampy and Pratheepkanth (2012) revealed that duality has a negative effect on company performance in a section of the study concerning the structure of corporation leadership. Based on these findings, this study develops the following hypothesis:

H_6 *There is a negative relationship between CEO duality and operating performance.*

Firm Size

Firm size is defined as the total assets of a company. Majumdar (1997) investigated the impact that firm size has on profitability and productivity of a firm and found that firm size has a positive impact on performance. Burson (2007) revealed that firm size has a positive significant relationship with ROA (firm performance). Ekwe and Duru (2012) argued that there is a strong positive relationship between firm size and financial performance. Based on these findings, this study develops the following hypothesis:

H_7 *There is a positive relationship between firm size and operating performance.*

Leverage

Leverage is defined as the ratio of total debt to total equity. Abor (2007) indicated a positive relationship between corporate governance and leverage and identified that firms with good corporate governance practices have more chances to get debt financing than those firms that do not implement good corporate governance practices. The result also found that firms with good corporate governance are able to pay off their dues, interest and debt on time. Kyereboah-coleman and Biekpe (2006) found that leverage has a positive and significant association with performance. Based on these findings, this study develops the following hypothesis.

H_8 *There is a positive relationship between leverage and operating performance.*

RESULT AND DISCUSSIONS

Descriptive Statistics

Table 23.2 presents the descriptive statistics of selected dependent and independent variables during the period 2007–2008 to 2014–2015.

Correlation Analysis

Having indicated the descriptive statistics, Pearson's correlation coefficients are computed and the results are presented in Table 23.3. More specifically, it shows the correlation coefficients of dependent and independent variables of Nepalese enterprises. Table 23.3 reveals the positive relationship of board size and audit committee with operating performance. This indicates that increase in board size and audit committee

Table 23.2 Descriptive statistics

	Minimum	Maximum	Mean	Std. deviation
ROE	−0.01	46.20	9.46	11.40
MPS	66.00	4351.00	818.40	827.89
BDV	0.00	2.00	0.27	0.58
BSIZE	5.00	11.00	7.32	1.32
AUCOM	1.00	4.00	3.07	0.62
BMET	8.00	106.00	16.83	14.95
BHS	0.00	0.50	0.07	0.14
DUAL	0.00	1.00	0.05	0.22
LEV	11.87	94.49	72.45	24.09
FMZ	−1.32	3.81	1.55	1.50

This table shows the descriptive statistics of dependent and independent variables. Dependent variables are MPS (market price per share defined as average of beginning and ending year market price per share, in rupees), ROE (return on equity defined as net income to shareholder equity, in percentage) and independent variables are BSIZE (board size defined as the absolute number of directors on the board of a company, in number), BMET (board meeting defined as absolute number of meeting held by board of directors, in number), AUCOM (audit committee defined as number of member in audit committee, in number), BDV (board diversity defined as the proportion of women directors to the no of directors on the board of company, in number), BHS (block shareholders defined as the proportion of board members who have at least 5% interest in company's shares to the number of directors on the board, in percentage), DUAL (CEO duality defined as 1 if CEO and chairman are same or 0 if different CEO and chairman), LEV (leverage is defined as the ratio of total debts to total assets, in percentage) and FMZ (firm size defined as the total assets of a company, in rupees). The descriptive statistics are based on panel data of 20 enterprises (10 banks and 10 insurance companies) with 100 observations for the period 2011/12–2015/16 in Nepal

Table 23.3 Pearson's correlation coefficients matrix for Nepalese enterprises

Variables	ROE	MPS	BDV	BSIZE	AUCOM	BMET	BHS	DUAL	FMZ	LEV
ROE	1									
MPS	0.269**	1								
BDV	−0.066	−0.030	1							
BSIZE	0.037	0.101	0.189	1						
AUCOM	0.380**	0.298**	0.059	0.022	1					
BMET	−0.027	0.023	0.094	−0.033	−0.115	1				
BHS	−0.337**	−0.132	−0.134	−0.137	−0.150	0.097	1			
DUAL	−0.191	−0.154	−0.107	−0.231*	−0.396**	0.021	0.158	1		
FMZ	0.604**	0.345**	0.132	0.195	0.283**	−0.155	−0.487**	−0.280**	1	
LEV	0.593**	0.009	0.092	0.245*	0.159	−0.180	−0.301**	0.105	0.639**	1

Note: The asterisk signs (**) and (*) indicate that coefficients are significant at 1 percent and 5 percent levels respectively

This table reveals the bivariate Pearson correlation coefficients of different dependent and independent variables. The coefficients are based on the data from 20 Nepalese enterprises (10 banks and 10 insurance companies) with 100 observations for the period 2011/12–2015/16. Dependent variables are ROE (return on equity defined as net income to shareholder equity, in percentage) and MPS (market per share defined as average of beginning and ending year market price per share, in rupees) and independent variables are BSIZE (board size defined as the absolute number of directors on the board of a company, in number), BMET (board meeting defined as absolute number of meeting held by board of directors, in number), AUCOM (audit committee defined as number of member in audit committee, in number), BDV (board diversity defined as the proportion of women directors to the no of directors on the board of company, in number), BHS (block shareholders defined as the proportion of board members who have at least 5% interest in company's shares to the number of directors on the board, in percentage), DUAL (duality defined as 1 if CEO and chairman are same or 0 if different CEO and chairman), LEV (leverage is defined as the ratio of total debts to total assets, in percentage) and FMZ (firm size defined as the total assets of a company, in rupees) leads to increase in operating performance. Similarly, the result also shows a positive relationship between firm size and leverage, which means that an increase in firm size and leverage leads to an increase in operating performance. However, board diversity and block shareholder have a negative relationship with operating performance. This reveals that an increase in board diversity and block shareholders leads to a decrease in operating performance. Likewise, the result also shows the negative relationship of CEO duality with performance, which denotes that an increase in duality leads to a decrease in operating performance. The result also shows a negative relationship of board meeting with ROE. This reveals that an increase in board meeting leads to a decrease in ROE whereas board meeting has a positive relationship with market price per share.

Regression Analysis

Having indicated the Pearson correlation coefficients, the regression analysis has been carried out and the results are presented in Table 23.4. More specifically, the table shows the regression results of CEO duality, outside directors, board diversity, board size, board meeting, audit committee, block shareholders, firm size and leverage on ROE.

Table 23.4 shows that the beta coefficients are positive for board size. It indicates that the larger the board size, the higher ROE. This finding is similar to the findings of Johl et al. (2015). However, the beta coefficients are negative for audit committee. It denotes that the higher the number of members on an audit committee, the lower the ROE. This finding is similar to the findings of Abbott and Parker (2000). Conversely, beta coefficients are negative for board diversity, which means that the higher the proportion of women directors on a board, the lower the ROE. This finding is not consistent with the findings of Carter et al. (2003). Similarly, beta coefficients are negative for block shareholders. This reveals that the higher the number of block shareholders, the lower the ROE. This finding is not consistent with the findings of Shleifer and Vishny (1997).The beta coefficient for CEO duality is also negative, which indicates that the higher the CEO duality, the lower the ROE. This finding is similar to the findings of Velnampy and Pratheepkanth (2012). Furthermore, the beta coefficients are negative for board meeting, which means that the higher the number of board meetings, the lower the ROE. This finding is not consistent with the findings of Karamanou and Vafeas (2005).

Table 23.4 Estimated regression results of BSIZE, BMET, BDV, BHS, DUAL, LEV, and FMZ on ROE

Model	Intercept	Regression coefficients ROE								Adj R²	S.E.E	F
		BSIZE	BMET	AUCOM	BDV	BHS	DUAL	LEV	FMZ			
1	7.14 (1.1)	0.32 (0.36)								0.001	11.45	0.132
2	9.81 (5.7)**		−0.29 (−0.26)							0.001	11.45	0.07
3	−11.85 (−2.22)*			6.94 (4.06)**						0.14	10.6	16.51
4	9.81 (7.78)**				−1.3 (−0.66)					0.004	11.43	0.43
5	11.33 (9.44)**					−27 (−3.55)**				0.11	10.78	12.6
6	9.96 (8.63)**						−9.92 (−1.92)			0.03	11.25	3.7
7	−10.85 (−3.7)**							0.28 (7.28)**		0.34	9.23	53.03
8	2.35 (1.78)								4.6 (7.5)**	0.35	9.14	56.16
9	10.07 (5.64)**	0.11 (0.13)	−0.02 (−0.2)		−1.26 (−0.63)					0.01	11.49	0.24
10	−8.15 (−1.04)			6.25 (3.78)**	−2.52 (−1.41)	−24.2 (−3.29)**				0.21	10.14	7.53
11	−17.55 (−3.46)**			3.84 (2.62)*	−3.27 (−2.3)*	−5.73 (−0.87)	−4.48 (−0.99)	0.19 (3.95)**	1.91 (2.23)*	0.49	8.14	16.84

(continued)

Table 23.4 (continued)

Note: The asterisk signs (**) and (*) indicate that coefficients are significant at 1 percent and 5 percent levels respectively

The results are based on panel data of 20 enterprises (10 banks and 10 insurance companies) with 100 observations for the period of 2011/12–2015/16 by using linear regression model. The model is $ROE = \beta_0 + \beta_1 BDV_{it} + \beta_2 BSIZE_{it} + \beta_3 AUCOM_{it} + \beta_4 BMET_{it} + \beta_5 BHS_{it} + \beta_6 DUAL_{it} + \beta_7 FMZ_{it} + \beta_8 LEV_{it} + e_{it}$ where, the dependent variable ROE (return on equity defined as net income to shareholder equity, in percentage) and independent variables are BSIZE (board size defined as the absolute number of directors on the board of a company, in number), BMET (board meeting defined as absolute number of meeting held by board of directors, in number), AUCOM (audit committee defined as number of member in audit committee, in number), BDV (board diversity defined as the proportion of women directors to the no of directors on the board of company, in number), BHS (block shareholders defined as the proportion of board members who have at least 5% interest in company's shares to the number of directors on the board, in percentage), DUAL (duality defined as 1 if CEO and chairman are same or 0 if different CEO and chairman), LEV (leverage is defined as the ratio of total debts to total assets, in percentage) and FMZ (firm size defined as the total assets of a company, in rupees

The beta coefficients are positive for leverage. This reveals that the higher the leverage, the higher the ROE. This finding is similar to the findings of Abor (2007). Likewise, the beta coefficients for firm size are positive, which indicates that the larger the firm size, the higher the ROE. This finding is similar to the findings of Ekwe and Duru (2012).

Similarly, the estimated regression of OUD, BSIZE, BMET, AUCOM, BDV, BHS, DUAL, LEV and FMZ on MPS are presented in Table 23.5.

Table 23.5 shows that the beta coefficients are positive for board size. It indicates that the larger the board size, the higher market price per share. This finding is similar to the findings of Johl et al. (2015). The beta coefficients are positive for audit committee. It denotes that the higher the number of members on an audit committee, the higher the ROE. This finding is similar to the findings of Kyereboah-Coleman (2008). Conversely, beta coefficients are negative for board diversity, which means that the higher the proportion of women directors on a board, the lower the market price per share. This finding is not consistent with the findings of Carter et al. (2003). Similarly, beta coefficients are negative for block shareholders. This reveals that the higher the number of block shareholders, the lower the market price per share. This finding is not consistent with the findings of Shleifer and Vishny (1997).The beta coefficient for CEO duality is also negative, which indicates that the higher the CEO duality, the lower the ROE. This finding is similar to the findings of Velnampy and Pratheepkanth (2012). Furthermore, the beta coefficients are positive for board meeting, which means that the higher the number of board meetings, the higher the ROE. This finding is similar to the findings of Karamanou and Vafeas (2005).

Likewise, the beta coefficients are positive for leverage. This reveals that the higher the leverage, the higher the ROE. This finding is similar to the findings of Abor (2007). The beta coefficients for firm size are positive, which indicates that the larger the firm size, the higher the ROE. This finding is similar to the findings of Burson (2007).

SUMMARY AND CONCLUSION

Corporate governance is the mechanisms, processes and relations by which corporations are controlled and directed. Governance structures and principles identify the distribution of rights and responsibilities among different participants in the corporation (such as the board of directors, managers, shareholders, creditors, auditors, regulators and other

Table 23.5 Estimated regression results of OUD, BSIZE, BMET, AUCOM, BDV, BHS, DUAL, LEV and FMZ on MPS of Nepalese enterprises

Model	Intercept	Regression coefficients MPS								Adj R^2	S.E.E	F
		BSIZE	BMET	AUCOM	BDV	BHS	DUAL	LEV	FMZ			
1	353.03 (0.75)	63.58 (1.01)								0.01	827.8	1.01
2	797.1 (6.35)**		1.27 (0.23)							0	831.89	0.05
3	−397.98 (−0.99)			396.21 (3.09)**						0.08	794.17	9.59
4	829.8 (9.05)**				−42.23 (−0.3)					0	831.73	0.09
5	871.37 (9.5)**					−766.06 (−1.32)				0.01	824.84	1.73
6	847.46 (10.05)**						−581.26 (−1.54)			0.01	822.2	2.37
7	796.19 (3.01)**							0.31 (0.09)		0	832.07	0.01
8	523.31 (4.65)**								190.8 (3.64)**	0.11	781.09	13.2
10	−642.04 (−1.07)	27.41 (0.46)	5.25 (1)	301.63 (2.33)*					158.7 (2.86)**			
11	739.96 (2.46)*		2.12 (0.37)		−77.22 (−0.53)		−621.3 (−0.16)	1.31 (0.04)		0.03	833.17	0.69
12	−822.27 (−1.17)	61.8 (0.96)	4.25 (0.77)	387.24 (2.71)**	−122.35 (−0.86)	−533.04 (−0.91)	−45.25 (−0.11)			0.06	803.44	2.02

Note: The asterisk signs (**) and (*) indicate that coefficients are significant at 1 percent and 5 percent levels respectively

The results are based on panel data of 20 enterprises (10 banks and 10 insurance companies) 100 observations for the period of 2011/12–2015/16 by using linear regression model. The model is MPS = $\beta_0 + \beta_1 BDV_{it} + \beta_2 BSIZE_{it} + \beta_3 AUCOM_{it} + \beta_4 BMET_{it} + \beta_5 BHS_{it} + \beta_6 DUAL_{it} + \beta_7 FMZ_{it} + \beta_8 LEV_{it} + e_{it}$, where, the dependent variable MPS (market price per is defined as average of beginning and ending year market price per share, in rupees) and independent variables are BSIZE (board size defined as the absolute number of directors on the board of a company, in number), BMET (board meeting defined as absolute number of meeting held by board of directors, in number), AUCOM (audit committee defined as number of member in audit committee, in number), BDV (board diversity defined as the proportion of women directors to the no of directors on the board of company, in number), BHS (block shareholders defined as the proportion of board members who have at least 5% interest in company's shares to the number of directors on the board, in percentage), DUAL (duality defined as 1 if CEO and chairman are same or 0 if different CEO and chairman), LEV (leverage is defined as the ratio of total debts to total assets, in percentage) and FMZ (firm size defined as the total assets of a company, in rupees)

stakeholders) and include the rules and procedures for making decisions in corporate affairs. Corporate governance includes the processes through which corporations' objectives are set and pursued in the context of the social, regulatory and market environment. A critical factor in good corporate governance appears to be the relationship between board diversity and shareholder value creation. The study attempts to examine the effect of board diversity and corporate governance structure on operating performance of Nepalese enterprises. This study is based on secondary data of 20 enterprises for the period 2011–2012 to 2015–2016. The variables that examine the effect of board diversity and corporate governance structure on impact of operating performance are board size, board meeting, audit committee, board diversity, block shareholders, CEO duality, leverage and firm size.

The study shows that audit committee and firm size have a positive and significant impact on operating performance. It indicates that the higher the number of members on an audit committee and the larger the firm size, the higher the operating performance. The study also reveals that there is positive impact of board size, leverage and board meeting on operating performance. However, board diversity, block shareholders and CEO duality have a negative impact on ROE. It indicates that the higher the board diversity, block shareholder and CEO duality, the lower the operating performance.

References

Abbott, L. J., & Parker, S. (2000). Auditor selection and audit committee characteristics. *A Journal of Practice and Theory, 19*(2), 47–67.

Abdul, R., Haneem, K., & Ali, F. M. (2006). Board, audit committee, culture and earnings management: Malaysian evidence. *Managerial Auditing Journal, 1*(7), 783–804.

Abdullah, S. N. (2004). Board composition, CEO duality and performance among Malaysian listed companies. *Corporate Governance, 4*(4), 47–61.

Abor, J. (2007). Corporate governance and financing decisions of Ghanaian listed firms. *The International Journal of Business in Society, 7*(1), 83–92.

Adams, R. B., & Ferreira, K. (2009). Women in the boardroom and their impact on governance and performance. *Journal of Financial Economics, 9*(1), 291–309.

Adler, R. D. (2001). *Women in the executive suite correlate to high profits*. Working paper, European project on equal pay, Pepperdine University, USA.

Adnan, M. A. (2011). A panel data analysis on the relationship between corporate governance and bank efficiency. *Journal of Accounting Finance and Economics, 1*(1), 1–15.

Agrawal, A., & Mandelker, G. (1990). Large shareholders and the monitoring of managers: The case of anti-takeover charter amendments. *Journal of Financial and Quantitative Analysis, 25*(2), 143–161.

Brickley, J., Coles, L., & Jarrell, G. (1997). Corporate leadership structure: On the separation of the positions of CEO and chairman of the board. *Journal of Corporate Finance, 3*(3), 189–220.

Burke, P. (2000). Concentration and other determinants of bank profitability in Europe, North America and Australia. *Journal of Banking and Finance, 13*(1), 65–79.

Burson, K. (2007). The effect of firm size on profit rates in the financial services. *Journal of Economics Education Research, 8*(1), 67–81.

Cadbury, A. (1992). Report of the committee on the financial aspects of corporate governance. *London Gee Publishing, 7*(4), 24–50.

Carter, D. A., Simkins, J., & Gary, W. (2003). Corporate governance, board diversity, and firm value. *Financial Review, 38*(1), 33–53.

Dalton, D., Daily, C., Ellstrand, A., & Johnson, J. (1998). Meta-analytic review of board composition, leadership structure, and financial performance. *Strategic Management Journal, 1*(9), 269–290.

DrorParnesa, L. (2011). Corporate governance and corporate credit worthiness. *Journal of Risk and Financial Management, 2*(1), 1–42.

Ekwe, M., & Duru, A. (2012). Liquidity management and corporate profitability in Nigeria. *ESUT Journal of Accountancy, 3*(1), 22–28.

Erhardt, P., Niclas, L., Werbel, H., & Shrader, D. (2003). Board of director diversity and firm financial performance. *Corporate Governance: An International Review, 9*(1), 102–111.

Farrell, K. A., & Hersch, P. L. (2005). Additions to corporate boards: The effect of gender. *Journal of Corporate Finance, 11*(3), 85–106.

Ferreira, K. (2010). Women in the boardroom and their impact on governance and performance. *Journal of Financial Economics, 9*(4), 291–309.

Finch, E. M., & Shivdasani, A. (2006). Are busy boards effective monitors. *Journal of Finance, 51*(2), 689–724.

Fondas, N. (2000). Women on boards of directors: Gender bias or power threat? *Issues in Business Ethics, 14*(1), 171–177.

Gill, A., & Mathur, N. (2011). Board size, CEO duality, and the value of Canadian manufacturing firms. *Journal of Applied Finance and Banking, 1*(3), 1–13.

Guli, S., Sajid, M., Razzaq, N., & Afzal, F. (2012). Agency cost, corporate governance and ownership structures. *International Journal of Business and Social Science, 3*(9), 268–277.

Guragain, S., Karki, S., Koirala, S., Upadhaya, S., & Pant, U. (2016). The effect of board size, board composition and ownership structure on bank performance: A case of Nepalese commercial banks. *Nepalese Journal of Finance,* 3(1), 104–116.

Hill, C., & Jones, G. (2001). Corporate governance, board gender diversity and corporate performance: A critical review of literature. *European Scientific Journal,* 12(7), 23–45.

Javid, A. Y., & Robina, I. (2007). Relationship between corporate governance indicators and firm value: A case study of Karachi Stock Exchange. Retrieved from http://mpra.ub.uni-muenchen.de/2225/MPRA. Paper no. 2225, Posted 07. November 2007/02:20, PIDE Working Papers 2007: 14.

Jensen, M. C. (1993). The modern industrial revolution, exit, and the failure of internal control systems. *Journal of Finance,* 48(3), 831–880.

Jensen, M. C. (1994). The modern industrial revolution, exist and the failure of internal control system. *The Journal of Applied Corporate Finance,* 6(4), 1–7.

Jensen, M. C., & Meckling, H. W. (1976). Theory of the firm: Managerial behaviour, agency costs and university structure. *Journal of Financial Economics,* 3(1), 305–360.

Johansen, D. (2008). Corporate governance and board accounts: Exploring a neglected interface between boards of directors and management. *Journal of Management and Governance,* 12(4), 343–380.

Johl, S. K., Kaur, S., & Cooper, B. (2015). Board characteristics and firm performance: Evidence from Malaysian public listed firms. *Journal of Economics, Business and Management,* 3(2), 239–243.

Kang, J. K., & Shivdasani, A. (1995). Firm performance, corporate governance, and top executive turnover in Japan. *Journal of Financial Economies,* 38(1), 29–58.

Kang, H., Cheng, M., & Gray, S. J. (2007). Corporate governance and board composition: Diversity and independence of Australian boards. *Corporate Governance: An International Review,* 15(2), 12–19.

Karamanou, I., & Vafeas, N. (2005). The association between corporate boards, audit committees, and management earnings forecasts: An empirical analysis. *Journal of Accounting Research,* 43(3), 453–486.

Kyereboah-Coleman, A. (2008). Corporate governance and firm performance in Africa: A dynamic panel data analysis. *Journal of Economics and Econometrics,* 32(2), 1–24.

Kyereboah-Coleman, A., & Biekpe, N. (2006). Corporate governance and financing choices of firms: A panel data analysis. *South African Journal of Economics,* 74(4), 670–681.

Lama, M. N., Khadka, P., Acharya, P., Maharjhan, K., & Bhandari, R. (2015). Corporate governance and firm performance: Study in Nepalese firms. *Nepalese Journal of Corporate Governance,* 2(1), 78–92.

Lipton, M., & Lorsch, J. (1992). A modest proposal for improved corporate governance. *The Business Lawyer,* 48(1), 59–77.

Majumdar, S. K. (1997). Foreign ownership and profitability: Property rights, control, and the performance of firms in Indian industry. *The Journal of Law and Economics, 42*(1), 209–238.

Mangena, M., & Tauringana, V. (2008). *Corporate boards, ownership structure and firm performance in an environment of severe political and economic uncertainty.* British Accounting Association Conference, Norton Street, Liverpool, USA.

Ntim, C. G. (2009). *Internal corporate governance and firm financial performance: Evidence from South African listed firms.* Unpublished PhD thesis, University of Glasgow, UK.

Nuryanah, S., & Islam, S. (2011). Corporate governance and performance: Evidence from an emerging market. *Malaysian Accounting Review, 10*(1), 17–42.

Peng, M. W., Zhang, S., & Li, X. (2007). CEO duality and firm performance during china's institutional transitions. *Management and Organization Review, 3*(2), 205–225.

Peni, E., & Vahamaa, S. (2012). Did good corporate governance improve bank performance during the financial crisis? *Journal of Financial Services Research, 41*(2), 19–35.

Pradhan, R. S., & Adhikari, S. N. (2009). Corporate governance and firm performance. *Journal of Management Review, 1*(1), 22–26.

Rhoades, D. L., Rechner, P. L., & Sudramurthy, C. (2001). A meta-analysis of board directorship structure and financial performance: Are two heads better than one? *Corporate Governance-An International Review, 9*(3), 311–319.

Ruin, J. (2001). Essentials of the corporate management. *International Journal of Multidisciplinary Sciences and Engineering, 6*(2), 34–54.

Sami, H., Wang, J., & Zhou, H. (2011). Corporate governance and operating performance of Chinese listed firms. *Journal of International Accounting, Auditing and Taxation, 20*(2), 106–114.

Shah, P., Rai, K., & Shrestha, S. (2013). Impact of corporate governance in financial performance. *Nepalese Journal of Management, 1*(2), 23–45.

Sharma, G., Karki, M., Poudel, M., & Thapa, N. (2014). Role of corporate governance on banks performance: A case of Nepalese bank. *Nepalese Journal of Corporate Governance, 1*(1), 15–26.

Sheikh, N. A., Wang, Z., & Khan, S. (2013). The impact of internal attributes of corporate governance on firm performance evidence from Pakistan. *International Journal of Commerce and Management, 23*(1), 56–74.

Shleifer, A., & Vishny, R. (1997). A survey of corporate governance. *Journal of Finance, 52*(2), 737–783.

Shleifer, A., & Wolfenson, D. (2002). Investor protection and equity markets. *Journal of Financial Economics, 66*(1), 3–27.

Shrader, C. B., Blackburn, V. B., & Iles, P. (1997). Women in management and firm financial performance: An exploratory study. *Journal of Managerial Issues,* 9(3), 355–372.

Silwal, P. P. (2011). Effects of corporate governance on the performance of Nepalese firms. *The International Research Journal of Management Science,* 1(1), 35–47.

Smith, N., Smith, V., & Verner, M. (2006). Do women in top management affect firm performance? A panel study of 2,500 Danish firms. *International Journal of Productivity and Performance Management,* 5(5), 569–593.

Thagunna, K. S., & Poudel, S. (2013). Measuring bank performance of Nepalese banks: A data envelopment analysis (DEA) perspective. *International Journal of Economics and Financial Issues,* 3(1), 54–56.

Thapa, P., Bajagain, R., & Sharma, D. (2013). Corporate governance: Need and significance in Nepalese banking system. *Nepalese Journal of Business,* 3(1), 15–28.

Velnampy, K., & Pratheepkanth, L. (2012). Corporate governance and firm performance: A study of selected listed companies in Sri Lanka. *International Journal of Commerce and Management,* 23(1), 23–49.

Index

A
Accountability, 32, 106, 107, 352
Agent-based model, 303–317
Agriculture production, 17–27

B
Balmer Lawrie, 29, 31, 34–38
Banking, 5, 57, 143–159, 211, 212, 306, 351, 352, 357, 380, 403, 424, 425
Bankruptsy, 143–159, 361, 363, 408
Bayesian approaches, 273
Board diversity, 380, 383, 406, 421–438
Board meetings, 355, 357, 363, 365–367, 369, 370, 372, 401–403, 405, 407, 409–411, 413, 415, 416, 423, 424, 426, 428, 430–432, 434, 435, 437, 438
Bottom of the Pyramid (BOP), v, 2, 55–71
BRICS (Brazil, Russia, India, China and South Africa), 201, 271–279
Business diplomacy, xxvii, 2, 6, 7, 12

Business governance, v–vii, 1, 2, 6, 9
Business opportunities, 6, 36, 316
Business performance, vii, 29–39, 211, 220
Business practices, shifts in, vii

C
Capital structure, 111, 146, 399–416
Collectivism, 70, 71, 81, 98–100
Commercial banking, 156, 351–373, 380, 381, 387, 388, 391, 393, 394, 402, 403, 409, 411, 416, 424, 425
Conflict resolution, 96–98
Consumer activism, 251–264
Consumer behavior, 58, 251–254, 257–264, 281–294, 308
Consumer dissuasion, 251–264
Consumer persuasion, 259
Corporate entrepreneurship, 189–202
Corporate governance, 9, 105–123, 351–373, 377–394, 399–416, 421–438

Cross-border trade, 10
Cultural differences, 98–99, 293
Customer expectations, 55–71
Customer relations management (CRM), 43–51
Customer satisfaction, 38, 43–51

D
Disruptive business, 10, 303
Dividend policy, 377–394

E
Economic growth, 6, 7, 17, 19, 106, 273, 274, 276, 278, 279, 377
Emerging markets, v, vii, 5, 7, 9–11, 56, 57, 59–62, 189–202, 240, 400
Emotional intelligence, 175–186, 202
Employee engagement, 239, 240, 243
Employee mobility, 237–246
Employee rewards, 239, 240, 242
Entrepreneurial behaviour, v, 211, 321–346
Entrepreneurship, 18, 20, 27, 189–202, 209–220
Evidence based analysis, 30, 31
Export relationship, 271–279
Extremism, 161–171

F
Factors of benefit, 207–231
Female employees, 175–186
Financial disclosure, 107, 111, 112, 114–120, 122
Financial loss, 10, 400
Financial performance, 105–123, 394, 422, 423, 428, 429
Financial reporting, 105–123, 359, 410, 411, 413
Firm innovativeness, 189–202

Firm size, 378, 380, 382, 386–389, 391, 393, 394, 402, 403, 408–411, 413, 415, 416, 423, 424, 426, 429–432, 434, 435, 437, 438
Frugal innovation, 304–307

G
Globalization, vi, 2, 4–7, 12, 246
Gross domestic product (GDP), 271–279
Grounded theory, 55–71

H
Human resources (HR), 2, 29–39, 82, 101, 176, 237, 246

I
India, 7, 17–27, 31, 46, 55–71, 75, 108, 127–140, 143, 161–171, 180, 189, 207–231, 273, 303
Innovation
 adoption of, 304, 305, 307, 308, 311, 313
 diffusion of, 303–317
Innovativeness, 189–202
Insolvency, 143–159, 363
Insolvency and Bankruptcy
 Board of India, 157
 Code of India, 143–159
Insolvency professional, 150
Interpersonal relationship, 285–287, 291–292

K
Knowledge dissemination, 239–242
Knowledge intensive companies, 29

L
Leadership, political, 3
 market, 2, 3, 9, 212

Leadership style, 92, 93, 189–202, 245
Liberal trade, 4, 9

M
Market competitiveness, 11
Market price, 25, 27
  per share, 380, 426, 430–432, 435, 437
Mexico, 5, 7, 12, 337
Motivators, 285–287, 292

N
National Company Law Tribunal (NCLT), 144, 146–150, 152–158
Nepal, 208, 223, 354–356, 358, 380, 381, 402, 403, 423–425, 430
Nepalese listed companies, 399–416

O
Organizational change, v, 178
Organizational collaboration, 44, 45, 47, 48, 51
Organizational creativity, 237–246
Organizational performance, 32, 237–246, 377, 429
Ownership structure, 378, 399–416

P
Political aggression, 5
Political ideologies, v, vii, xxvii, 1, 2, 4, 5, 7, 10, 12, 13
Political intervention, 4, 5
Power-play, 6, 12, 13
Price, 4, 12, 13, 18–20, 25, 27, 46, 57, 60, 66, 68–71, 129, 130, 132–136, 138, 139, 208, 221, 226, 228, 273, 275, 285, 286, 290, 291, 293, 303–306, 316, 380, 382, 387, 388, 391, 393
Private lable, 127–140

Productivity, 7, 17–27, 30, 39, 194, 212, 361, 429
Protectionism, v, vi, 4, 7, 12
Public diplomacy, v, 1, 4
Public sector banking, 175–186

R
Relationship lending, 321–346
Resolution professional (RP), 145, 155
Response mechanism, 75–101
  adjustment, 77, 83, 96–99
Retailing, 5, 38, 46, 127–130, 133, 137, 140
Return on equity (ROE), 113, 424, 426, 430–432, 434, 435, 438
Reverse innovation, v, 303–317

S
Shareholder
  management of, 106, 359, 388, 393, 399, 400
  value, 33, 353, 377, 399, 400, 416, 438
Social networking, 241, 242, 251–264, 282, 292, 308–310, 315, 316
Social support, 75–101
Social values, vii, 163
Start-up enterprise, 189–202
Store image, 130, 131, 133–136, 139, 140
Store loyalty, 131, 133–136, 139, 140
Substantive theory, 71

T
Talent analytics, 29–39
Trade agreements, 5, 11
Transparency effects, 92
Trends, v–vii, 2–13, 17–27, 80, 111, 149, 179, 214, 220, 229, 246, 261

Tribal entrepreneurs, 209–211, 217–220, 229
Trust, 9, 36, 66, 89, 91, 92, 101, 131, 138, 154, 162, 163, 192, 287, 345

U
Urban poor, 59–60

V
Violence, 161–171

W
Word-of-mouth (WOM), 251–264, 281, 290
Work environment, 75, 77, 81, 84, 85, 88, 91, 93, 99, 101, 176
Work-family conflict, 75–101
Workplace culture, 245

Y
Youth entrepreneurship, 210, 211, 218–220